OTHER BOOKS BY MARIO GIAMMETTI

Genesis Story
  Gammalibri, Milan, 1988
Genesis Discografia 1968/1993
  Kaos Edizioni, Milan, 1994
Peter Gabriel – Il trasformista
  Arcana, Padua, 1999
Genesis – Il fiume del costante cambiamento
  Editori Riuniti, Rome, 2004
Phil Collins – The Singing Drummer (Genesis Files Vol. 1)
  Edizioni Segno, Tavagnacco, 2005
Steve Hackett – The Defector (Genesis Files Vol. 2)
  Edizioni Segno, Tavagnacco, 2005
Tony Banks – Man Of Spells (Genesis Files Vol. 3)
  Edizioni Segno, Tavagnacco, 2006
Anthony Phillips – The Exile (Genesis Files Vol. 4)
  Edizioni Segno, Tavagnacco, 2008
Musical Box: Le canzoni dei Genesis dalla A alla Z
  Arcana, Rome, 2010
Mike Rutherford – Silent Runner (Genesis Files Vol. 5)
  Edizioni Segno, Tavagnacco, 2011
Genesis – Gli anni Prog
  Giunti, Florence, 2013
Ray Wilson – Gypsy (Genesis Files Vol. 6)
  Edizioni Segno, Tavagnacco, 2014
Genesis – Gli anni Prog (second edition)
  Giunti, Florence, 2015
Peter Gabriel – Not One Of Us (Genesis Files Vol. 7)
  Edizioni Segno, Tavagnacco, 2016
Genesis – 1967 to 1975: The Peter Gabriel Years
  Kingmaker, London, 2020
Genesis – Tutti gli album tutte le canzoni
  Il Castello Editore, Cornaredo, 2020

MARIO GIAMMETTI

GENESIS

1975 to 2021

The Phil Collins Years

KINGMAKER

To my son, Simone

KINGMAKER PUBLISHING
First published in Great Britain by Kingmaker Publishing Limited in 2021
© 2021 Kingmaker Publishing Limited
www.kingmakerpublishing.com

Copyright © Mario Giammetti
Mario Giammetti has asserted his moral right under the
Copyright, Designs and Patents Act, 1988, to be identified
as the author of this work.

The original Italian text was translated into English by J.M. Octavia Brown.
Edited by Gregory Spawton and J.M. Octavia Brown

ISBN 978-1-8384918-0-2

Printed in Great Britain by
Biddles Books Limited, King's Lynn, Norfolk

Contents

- 7 *Foreword by Mike Rutherford*
- 9 *Introduction*

- 12 A Trick of the Tail
- 46 Wind and Wuthering
- 76 …And Then There Were Three
- 102 Duke
- 128 ABACAB
- 150 Three Sides Live (Encore Tour)
- 158 Genesis
- 180 Invisible Touch
- 206 We Can't Dance
- 234 Calling All Stations
- 268 Turn It On Again (Reunion Tour)
- 284 Afterglow

A NOTE ON THE SOURCES

All of the quotes included in this book from members or former members of Genesis are taken from interviews given to Mario Giammetti and Mike Kaufman.

The Mike Kaufman interviews were conducted in October 2007 at The Peninsula Chicago Hotel, Chicago (Banks, Collins and Rutherford) and at Sarm Studios, London (Hackett). Further interviews were conducted in 2007 in Edinburgh (Ray Wilson) and New York (Nir Zidkyahu)

All of the quotes from non-band members involved in the Genesis story are taken from interviews given exclusively to Mario Giammetti.

One record-listening session took place at Chiaja Hotel De Charme, Naples, 12 September 2016 (Steve Hackett with Mario Giammetti – Wind & Wuthering, all quotes previously unpublished)

The following interviews were conducted specifically for this book
- Mario Giammetti's telephone interview with Tony Banks, 26 February 2016, partially published in the article "Senza Gabriel" in Classic Rock, issue n. 44, July 2016
- Mario Giammetti's interview with Tony Banks, London, Tony Smith Personal Management office, 29 November 2016 (previously unpublished)
- Mario Giammetti's telephone interview with Steve Hackett, 8 October 2015, partially published in the article "Senza Gabriel" in Classic Rock, issue n. 44, July 2016
- Mario Giammetti's telephone interview with Mike Rutherford, 25 February 2016, partially published in the article "Senza Gabriel" in Classic Rock, issue n. 44, July 2016
- Mario Giammetti's interview with Mike Rutherford, Munich, Freiheiz, 20 September 2016 (previously unpublished)

The remaining dialogue used in this book from members and associates of the band comes from the following interviews given to Mario Giammetti:

Tony Banks: telephone interviews, 6 March 2001 ("Calling All Genesis - Interviste esclusive a Ray Wilson, Mike Rutherford & Tony Banks", Dusk, Issue n. 35, April 2001); 19 September 2007 ("There Must Be Some Other Way – interviste esclusive a Tony Banks e Ray Wilson", Dusk, Issue n. 57, December 2007); 1 October 2009 ("Nei meandri della memoria" in Dusk, Issue no. 63, November 2009); 8 May 2013 ("Il mistero di Lady Barbara", Dusk, Issue n. 74, July 2013) and 24 July 2015 ("Somebody Else's Mantra", Dusk, Issue n. 81, December 2015)

Bill Bruford: telephone interview 29 March 1995 ("Speciale interviste – Bill Bruford", Dusk, Issue n. 15, June 1995)

Phil Collins: telephone interview 1 December 2016 ("You Know What I Mean", Dusk, Issue n. 85, March 2017)

Nick Davis: Skype interview 10 March 2021 (unpublished)

Nick D'Virgilio: e-mail interview 13 April 2011 ("Come Talk To Me" in Dusk, Issue no. 68, September 2011)

Anthony Drennan: Windsor, Bray Film Studios, 23 January 1998 ("Interviste esclusive Windsor 23.1.98", Dusk, Issue n. 25, April 1998)

Francis Dunnery: e-mail interview 26 February 2021 ("Calling more stations – Francis Dunnery", Dusk, Issue n. 97, May 2021)

Steve Hackett: Twickenham, Kudos Management office, 5 November 1992 ("Intervista esclusiva", Dusk, Issue n. 6, January 1993), telephone interview 20 April 2000 ("Steve & John Hackett – intervista esclusiva", Dusk, Issue n. 32, June 2000), personal e-mail sent by Steve Hackett dated 21 June 2017

David Longdon: e-mail interview November 2010 ("Calling another station" in Dusk, Issue no. 66, December 2010)

Mike Rutherford: telephone interviews 5 September 1997 ("Intervista esclusiva a Mike Rutherford", Dusk, Issue n. 23, October 1997) and 3 March 2001 ("Calling All Genesis - Interviste esclusive a Ray Wilson, Mike Rutherford & Tony Banks", Dusk, Issue n. 35, April 2001)

Daryl Stuermer: Milan, Filaforum, 9 October 1997 ("Daryl Stuermer special – intervista esclusiva", Dusk, Issue n. 24, January 1998), telephone interviews 3 August 2000 ("Intervista esclusiva a Daryl Stuermer", Dusk, Issue n. 33, October 2000), 8 March 2007 ("Daryl Stuermer Special - Go, Daryl go!", Dusk, Issue n. 55, April 2007) and 17 March 2021 ("Sulla strada verso il paradiso", Dusk, Issue n. 97, May 2021)

Chester Thompson: telephone interviews 13 August 1999 ("Speciale interviste – Chester Thompson", Dusk, Issue n. 30, October 1999) and 16 May 2013 ("Nashville Samba Jazz - Chester Thompson intervista esclusiva", Dusk, Issue n. 74, July 2013)

Nick Van Eede: e-mail interview 26 January 2021 ("Calling more stations – Nick Van Eede", Dusk, Issue n. 97, May 2021)

Steven Wilson: telephone interview 21 July 2011 ("Come Talk To Me" in Dusk, Issue no. 68, September 2011)

Ray Wilson: telephone interviews 28 October 1997 ("Intervista esclusiva a Ray Wilson", Dusk, Issue n. 24, January 1998), 18 January 2001 ("Calling All Genesis - Interviste esclusive a Ray Wilson, Mike Rutherford & Tony Banks", Dusk, Issue n. 35, April 2001) and 17 February 1999 ("Intervista esclusiva a Ray Wilson", Dusk, Issue n. 28, April 1999); Orvieto, Sala dei Quattrocento, 22 September 2007 ("There Must Be Some Other Way – interviste esclusive a Tony Banks e Ray Wilson", Dusk, Issue n. 57, December 2007), Erding, Stadthalle, 6 February 2015 ("Arcobaleno in Baviera", Dusk, Issue n. 79, April 2015), personal email sent by Ray Wilson dated 22 December 2020

Foreword by Mike Rutherford

I would like to start this foreword by thanking Mario Giammetti for his amazing support of all things Genesis and for the way he's kept such detailed records of all events. I feel he knows much more than I do!

This book covers a fascinating period in our history beginning with the first album with Phil singing, right through to our re-union tour in 2007 and beyond.

Mario is from Italy which was the first country we had success in and so it was very special for the band that our biggest European show to date took place in Rome at the 'Circus Maximus' – a summer's night I'll never forget.

I know everyone will enjoy reading this book and I look forward to more conversations with Mario.

Mike Rutherford

PHOTOGRAPHIC REFERENCES

Copyright Pete Still p.156
Copyright Alamy pp 174, 176, 273

The author also thanks for the images provided:
Silvio Amenduni pp. 146, 152, 155, 197
Lorenzo D'Accurso pp. 260, 265
Attila Ègerhazi p. 184
Enrico Geretto p. 143
Albert Gouder p. 245
Helmut Janisch pp. 226, 255, 257
Angelo La Duca p. 163
Roberto Paganin pp. 196, 228
Giuseppe Schiavone p. 261
Ina Schneider pp. 256, 258
Roger Salem pp. 111, 112, 122, 123, 124-125
James Stokes pp. 18, 25, 34, 37, 39, 44, 60, 67, 70, 71, 72, 88, 96
Ghislain Tambosso pp. 48, 49, 53, 54, 58, 83, 95
Pier Tintori pp. 20, 22-23, 24, 36, 82, 87, 94
Bruno Zampaglione pp. 275, 277, 278, 281

ACKNOWLEDGEMENTS

The author wishes to thank:
- *Steve Hackett for listening to Wind & Wuthering and sharing his memories with him exclusively for this book;*
- *Tony Banks for the lengthy conversations exclusively for this book and Mike Rutherford for the foreword;*
- *Jo Greenwood at TSPM for collaboration;*
- *Mike Kaufman for full use of his interviews which provide details that would otherwise never have come to light;*
- *George German for his essential contribution to piecing together the list of concerts and memorabilia (concert tickets, posters, flyers);*
- *Mark Kenyon at thegenesisarchive.co.uk for the promotional photos;*
- *Alessandro Borri and Peter Schütz for their hard work helping to throw light onto some of the uncertain live dates;*
- *Riccardo Grotto and Massimo Pola for their advice;*
- *Paul Davis for having transcribed hours of interviews;*
- *Massimo Satta for having translated hours of interviews;*
- *Octavia Brown for her peerless work on translating the original text for this book from Italian into English and for co-editing the English text;*
- *Nick Shilton and Gregory Spawton for helping to make the English publication happen, with additional thanks to Greg for his work as co-editor for the English text;*
- *Dr Geoff Parks for proof-reading the English text;*
- *Jo Hackett for being such a special friend.*

Introduction

The five records released by Genesis between 1970 and 1974 map out a journey which is quite simply perfect in its coherence: the magical, pastoral and twilight landscapes of Anthony Phillips' swan song album (Trespass), the triptych of unrivalled beauty in the field of pure progressive rock (Nursery Cryme, Foxtrot and Selling England By The Pound) and finally the ambitious double concept album (The Lamb Lies Down On Broadway) which illustrated the extent to which the visionary art of Peter Gabriel was already taking account of the changing times, as he embarked upon a metropolitan tale that lay at the opposite end of the spectrum to the fairy tale themes of the prog world, thereby providing the impetus which would induce his bandmates to create fresh and innovative sounds.

In the book *Genesis 1967 to 1975 – The Peter Gabriel Years*, published in 2020, we examined the period in the band's history which is generally considered to be the more typically progressive and artistic.

The term 'progressive' indicates something ongoing, something that evolves into something else, or, as the dictionary defines it, *'happening or developing gradually or in stages'* and, from this point of view, the trajectory of early Genesis, with their incredible output of, on average, one album a year, remains exemplary.

The first two post-Gabriel albums (along with fairly large slices of the band's later albums) still fit perfectly into the 'progressive' category, but it remains undeniable that the Collins era failed to reach the same exalted heights of experimentation. Is this all it takes, therefore, to class the Gabriel era as golden and the Collins era as trash? Not in the slightest.

This over-simplified assessment (often voiced by critics and by fans of early Genesis) couldn't be further from the truth. And, in some respects, the path Genesis took in the post-Gabriel period was a steeper and more difficult one to climb. In the initial years, those five young men in their early twenties had room to experiment and explore, allowing their creativity to flow freely as opposed to being weighed down, as Genesis later were (while still very young), by the musical heritage they had to carry on their shoulders as they attempted to survive in an ever-changing musical scenario.

The two magnificent albums released by the Collins-Banks-Rutherford-Hackett line-up, which even the staunchest Gabriel-era fans have to admit are exceptional, are formally more 'prog' than The Lamb but, objectively speaking, they marked a return to the band's comfort zone, albeit showing a tendency to lean slightly more towards the song formula. When Hackett left the ranks, the three surviving members decided to play the immediacy card, writing shorter, catchier songs and embracing the simpler melodies that would soon

INTRODUCTION

take them into the charts.

This process would continue throughout the following years and, although Duke echoed traces of their glorious past (while ironically taking the band over the threshold into a new decade), Abacab represented a drastic and necessary change in direction, with Genesis to all intents and purposes challenging their very existence: were they to carry on in the style to which they were accustomed and risk relegation to the minor leagues of music or give it their all to reinvent themselves and risk losing even their most ardent fans? The three courageously chose the second path, a decision which would prove to be the key not only to their survival but also to a surge in popularity which would see the band subsequently conquering the charts all over the world and packing stadiums, also boosted, it has to be said, by the gargantuan success of Collins' solo career.

Throughout the Collins era, Genesis continued to bring more and more of their newer material into their live shows while gradually reducing that portion of the setlist set aside for their earlier material. In an ideal world, art should always move in this direction, rather than opting to keep pitifully treading the same ground as some of the band's peers did, constantly churning out the same old setlist that not even the tackiest tribute bands are prepared to do (some of them are still at it!).

The reader will find ample discussion on all these topics within these pages. Meanwhile, I feel the need to explain one or two things, starting with the book's title. At first glance, *'The Phil Collins Years'* could almost be construed as yet another attempt, in keeping with the rather sad example set by Genesis themselves, at brushing the 'Wilson era' under the carpet. Not so. The last studio album released by Genesis and the accompanying tour are discussed fully in this book. That said, the impact Collins has had on the history of Genesis, both artistically and commercially is in a league of its own and, seeing as Collins returned to the fold post-Wilson for a massive reunion tour and (as I write) with another reunion tour on the horizon, we felt it was fitting to identify this volume with a title which makes it immediately recognisable as the sequel to the previous volume published in Italy in 2013 and the UK in 2020.

The major difference between the two volumes, however, lies in the album listen-throughs. Listening to the early albums in the company of Phillips, Hackett and Banks was a key feature of the previous volume. For this book, however, it became immediately apparent that it would be impossible to continue in the same vein (how many albums would poor Tony have had to listen to, given Rutherford's notorious forgetfulness and the inevitable unavailability of Collins?). There is one exception, Wind & Wuthering, which the author listened to in its entirety in the company of Steve Hackett. Otherwise, however, the album descriptions and critiques in this volume were written without the direct input of

INTRODUCTION

band members. That said, a number of interviews were conducted with the main players in the Genesis story specifically for the purpose of increasing the available information about the song-writing and recording of each album.

As is the case with *Genesis 1967 to 1975 - The Peter Gabriel Years,* all the statements contained in the following pages were given directly to myself, the author, (some specifically for this book and others during previous interviews) and to the English journalist, Michael Kaufman, who carried out extensive interviews at the time of the 2008 reissues (only part of which were used in the video content linked to that particular project). Consequently, this book, as with the previous one, consists entirely of material which has never before been published in English. Substantially the book has been 'written' by Genesis themselves, leaving to the author the task of organising the thoughts and memories of the musicians into a logical order, writing a critical synopsis for each album and documenting the live activities which saw the band go from strength to strength, also thanks to the fundamental presence of the other musicians who shared the stage with them, most notably Chester Thompson and Daryl Stuermer.

The first volume, published in English last year, was greeted with much interest in the United Kingdom. I hope this volume will be equally well-received. While nobody can deny that on a creative level it was the first era of Genesis which carved itself such an important niche in the history of rock, the band's entire career is full of wonderful music which has given so much joy and pleasure to fans and will continue to do so for many years to come.

We hope that in bringing together all the pieces of the band's history in our two-volume story of Genesis, we can keep alive an interest in the entire journey (and not just parts of it) of a musical undertaking which is as unique as it is extraordinary.

Mario Giammetti
Benevento, Italy, May 2021

A Trick Of The Tail

(Charisma, 1976)

Dance On A Volcano (Rutherford-Banks-Hackett-Collins) / Entangled (Hackett-Banks) / Squonk (Rutherford-Banks) / Mad Man Moon (Banks) /// Robbery, Assault And Battery (Banks-Collins) / Ripples (Rutherford-Banks) / A Trick Of The Tail (Banks) / Los Endos (Collins-Hackett-Rutherford-Banks)

- Release date: 13 February 1976
- Recorded at Trident Studios, London, October / November 1975
  Engineered by David Hentschel and Nick 'Haddock' Bradford
- Produced by David Hentschel and Genesis
- Sleeve design: Hipgnosis (Colin Elgie)

- Mike Rutherford: 12-string guitar, basses, bass pedals
- Tony Banks: piano, synthesisers, organ, Mellotron, 12-string guitar, backing vocals
- Phil Collins: drums, percussion, lead & backing vocals
- Steve Hackett: electric guitar and 12-string guitars

THE MAKING OF

At the end of May 1975, with the long tour to promote THE LAMB LIES DOWN ON BROADWAY well and truly over, Genesis decided to take a break and think things over. How were they going to deal with Peter Gabriel's departure? Albeit briefly, they did consider calling it a day.

Rutherford: "We weren't stupid. We thought maybe that was it, that we'd had our bit, you know. You don't pretend to know what's coming round the corner. But we had a simple thought (which has happened many times); we just said, 'let's go and write some songs and see what we learn from that'." [1]

Banks: "We thought we'd give it a go, without really having any idea as to how we were going to get it together." [2]

Collins: "It was a gradual thing really because Peter had already left once in the middle of writing THE LAMB, which was a bit of a shock. But because of that, we all knew anything could happen and that he might leave again. Of course, he had very good reasons and I think we were very selfish at the time for expecting him to stay. He was the first one of us to have a child and there'd been problems with the pregnancy and all kinds of stuff, but we didn't understand. Nevertheless, although I loved Pete (and still do, you know), my feeling was one of 'forget the vocals we'll just carry on as an instrumental four-piece'. This was no slight on him, I just thought we could carry on and, by doing so, prove to people that we weren't Pete's band (which by that point is how the press was beginning to perceive us). I've said it before and I'll say it again, we used to do shows in America where the record company people would come backstage and walk straight past us to get to Pete and say 'Fantastic show, Pete! Wow, you were great tonight', you know. And you just started to feel like a spare part. When he did leave, for me, carrying on was just something that we should definitely try. Of course, I never thought it was going to be as successful as it was. And unbeknownst to me, the earlier Genesis had already undergone a similar experience when Anthony Phillips left, which for them was as traumatic as Peter leaving, if not more." [3]

So, with the rest of the world still oblivious to Gabriel having quit the band, the remaining four took the decision to carry on without him, convinced of their ability to continue writing amazing music despite this terrible loss.

Rutherford: "When someone leaves, you don't want it to happen and musically he was incredible. It's a sad thing, obviously, but you respect it. And something new comes along, in every aspect." [1]

Banks: "Well, obviously I missed him. He was a very close friend of mine and we had written a lot of stuff together. But once we started working on this album, I found it really quite exciting; a different combination of people, a different feeling and a lot of ideas around. We'd had a slight problem with THE LAMB in that Peter had wanted to write all the lyrics himself, which is understandable looking back on it now, but at the time it was a bit disappointing as we all saw ourselves as lyric writers; his leaving gave us freedom. I found the whole process of writing and recording THE LAMB a tough time, what with Peter leaving in the middle and everything which made it rather depressing. So, I found the whole process of writing A TRICK OF THE TAIL very light in comparison and a lot of fun. It was probably one of the most enjoyable periods, really." [2]

Steve Hackett took advantage of the Genesis hiatus to record his first solo album between June

GENESIS

> Promotional shot by the American label, Atco Records. Left to right: Mike Rutherford, Phil Collins, Tony Banks and Steve Hackett

and July, featuring both Mike and Phil as guest musicians. Shortly afterwards, Genesis got together to start writing new material while auditions for a new singer were secretly held. History relates that, for the first three days, only Tony, Mike and Phil met up as Steve was still busy with his Voyage Of The Acolyte album (released that autumn to an enthusiastic reception from both critics and the public alike, reaching No. 26 in the UK charts).

Banks: "We came in without anything solid but we had some ideas. We were just playing around and Mike started playing this riff, I put some chords to it, which weren't perhaps the most obvious ones, and we got really excited by it. That was of course the beginning of *Dance On A Volcano*. We elaborated on that and wrote what you might call the more instrumental parts and the chorus on that first day... and we felt very confident after that; we knew we had something." [2]

Rutherford: "The first two or three days were fantastic. I think Steve was doing stuff, promotion on his solo album, so he wasn't there. We went in and got *Dance On A Volcano* and a bit of *Squonk* done. It really felt good. After that, we didn't look back." [1]

The guitarist, however, remembers things slightly differently.

Hackett: "I missed a maximum of one day. In fact I had to miss the mastering of Voyage Of The Acolyte to be there right at the beginning. So, if I missed the first day, forgive me! Peter Gabriel missed a bit more time with The Lamb and I never said I was leaving the group or anything. I tried my damn best, you know. Everyone knew what I was doing and what my schedule was, and everyone was behind it at that point, so if anyone wanted to change the goalposts on me..., again that's that very competitive streak of Genesis. I was always around for Genesis and gave it my all, everything that I was allowed to give it by all the other people." [4]

Friction apart, it became immediately clear that on a musical level, nothing had changed. If anything, the loss of such a strong lead singer boosted further development in the instrumental capabilities of the remaining members. And not for the first time (nor the last), Genesis seemed to come out of difficulties stronger than ever.

Amongst other things, the change in line-up also led to changes in the way songs were credited. From now on, each musician would put his name to the songs he'd brought in or helped to co-write.

Banks: "On previous albums, things like *Firth Of Fifth*, which was my song, or *Harold The Barrel*, which was Pete's, were credited to the whole group because that's what we'd agreed to do. We were happy with that but I think, particularly after The Lamb, that people tended to think that Peter was the major force in the band as a writer, which was not the case really. We all wrote. I just felt quite strongly that on the next album I wanted to give credit where credit was due." [3]

Rutherford: "It didn't change the democratic aspect of the band, but before Peter left it always said 'all songs by Genesis', so the public, our fans, didn't know who'd written what. Had they known, for example, that *Firth Of Fifth* was pretty much Tony's song, and stuff like *The Cinema Show* was myself and Tony, and with Steve still in the band writing songs, they would have felt a bit better about Peter leaving." [1]

Looking at the credits one cannot help but

GENESIS

notice the ubiquity of Tony Banks.

Banks: "When Peter left, there was a possibility that we wouldn't carry on. I had got together three or four pieces for a possible solo album: *Mad Man Moon* and *A Trick Of The Tail*, the bulk of *Robbery, Assault And Battery* and a few other bits and bobs, like the middle bit of *Ripples*. Mike came in with sections, as did Steve, and all the bits we used to finish them off were mine. So, I ended up being credited on every track on this album, which was quite funny." [2]

Hackett: "I suspect that what I used to do was probably throw in a few riffs and licks rather than whole songs, although I put a lot into *Entangled*, *Los Endos* and the intro to *Dance On A Volcano*... I'd just come off the back of having done solo things, so I was fairly dry of ideas. What's more, I very often used to find it intimidating working with people who were so gifted and who were so quick and brilliant. It took a long time for my confidence to get to the point where I felt like an equal. I guess there's a lot to be said for having youth, you know, the confidence and arrogance of youth." [3]

With the band feeling justifiably pleased with their artistic results, in August 1975 Peter Gabriel officially announced he had quit Genesis. Immediately the press was all over the sensational divorce and wasted no time in predicting the demise of the band, believing it couldn't possibly survive without its star member.

Banks: "Well, we expected it really. That's one of the reasons Peter delayed the announcement and it worked better for us as we were underway by then and felt fairly confident. I remember Mike and I went out and talked to a few radio stations, and it was a bit depressing because people had no real feeling that we were going to continue, which I can understand looking back on it, as the image of the

GENESIS

Mick Stickland, the only other singer given serious consideration as a replacement for Peter Gabriel

group was very much built around Peter. Obviously, he was a very important member of the band so we knew we had to redefine ourselves. We all had a lot of self-confidence and knew we were going to do it (without really knowing how we were going to do it). In those days we weren't reliant on singles or anything, which made it a bit easier in a way, as you could get a body of work together instead of having to rely on getting that one hit that wouldn't necessarily make it." [2]

Rutherford: "It was a hard time because the plan was to keep it quiet until we had finished the album. I quite understand the articles in the press as people think he was the lead singer and therefore the main man. Obviously, Peter was incredibly strong, but there were other writers too. The hard thing was, we knew it was sounding good, but you couldn't talk to the press and say, 'no you're all wrong, it sounds great, trust me' because they wouldn't believe you. So, it was an anxious time really, but we felt that what we were doing was different, but strong." [1]

Strong indeed. But it was only when they had finished recording the backing tracks, in November 1975, that they realised they still had a major issue to deal with – one they could no longer ignore: the lead singer. None of the auditions had come up with the goods. The numerous would-be replacements, despite some of them being very able technically speaking, all failed to convince the band. The list of candidates even included some well-known names, such as Mick Rogers (Manfred Mann's Earth Band), Jess Roden and Nick Lowe. At the end of the selection process, the band chose Mick Stickland (*many online sources record Mick's surname as Strickland, which is incorrect – author's note*). Born in 1953 and singer with the little-known band, Witches Brew, Stickland was invited into the studio to start recording.

Rutherford: "In those days we didn't think about singers and we didn't change the key, *that* was the key. He came down to sing *Squonk* in Trident Studios. He had a nice voice but it was in totally the wrong key." [1]

Banks: "We'd recorded the whole album by the time we tried him and the poor guy was screaming his way through the whole thing. I wasn't actually there because I was off sick that day. I came in the next day and thought it was awful, though I felt

A Trick Of The Tail

A long-bearded Collins holds a copy of legendary Italian magazine *Ciao 2001*. This page featured in *Ciao 2001* No. 23, published on 13th June 1976

ples, and he said 'give me a go on *Squonk* and see how it goes' and it sounded good." [2]

Collins: "So I went down to the studio, downstairs into the booth and I started singing. And you know, at the end of the song I looked up and everyone was going 'Yeah, it was all right!'. We tried it again and then we went through the songs one by one, knocking them off really, and we finished the album. I don't know how long it took; a couple of weeks probably." [3]

Hackett: "Phil was absolutely the right choice to replace Pete, but I already knew that because he was already singing on VOYAGE OF THE ACOLYTE and the very first thing I wrote on that first album, NURSERY CRYME, (*For Absent Friends – author's note*) was something Phil sang. I was already very much in Phil's camp there and behind him singing but I know that Tony and Mike didn't want that. I remember being at Phil's first wedding and Jon Anderson was there and he said to me, 'Why don't you make Phil the singer and get in another instrumentalist?'. And I said, 'Yes, that's exactly what I would do. It's a very good idea, Jon, but I don't think the others would go for that'. And I think before the band ran out of options Phil's strength came through, so it was blindingly obvious to me that that was the way we should proceed, but the others fought on this issue and fought Phil on this issue, and it divided the band until we had this whole bloody album done

sorry for the guy, because he had a good voice, but it was so wrong for the way we'd done it." [5]

Collins: "He'd made it through those audition processes and sort of arrived. But we weren't even thinking about keys for singers, such was our 'contempt' for the vocals; we just laid down all the backing tracks and invited this guy in to sing. *Squonk* was the first one and it was plainly in the wrong key for the guy. There was no way he was going to sound good." [3]

At this point, however, an alternative scenario was gaining traction. Rutherford: "We had always felt that Phil could do some of the softer songs but *Squonk* was quite a hard song and Peter's voice used to break, that wonderful crack it used to have, and we needed that." [1]

Banks: "Phil was always going to sing a few of the softer songs, such as *Mad Man Moon* and *Rip-*

17

GENESIS

Phil Collins with Genesis in concert in Berkeley, 29th April 1976

with no vocals. It was a crazy state of affairs." [4]

Collins: "I was quite happy to sit behind the drums or stand up and sing *More Fool Me* and be Peter's stooge. I kind of liked doing the backgrounds. Sometimes Peter let me do it all on my own and sometimes it would be him and I doing it. Nevertheless, I had no intention of ever being anything other than a drummer; there was no secret desire to slowly work my way to the front. In fact, and I've said this before, I didn't like singers; all the singer had to do was just stand there and sing 'ooohh babe', you know. I just didn't take it seriously. So, for me, the real musician's gig was behind the drums. But, as we went through the audition process, we realised that some of the songs weren't as good sung by somebody else or these people came in with their kinda mid-American accents... you know, it didn't really work that well and I always sounded better than they did when I was teaching them the songs at the auditions." [3]

Banks: "I think it took him two or three albums to develop what you might call a really good, hard soulful voice. Of course, the great advantage of Phil already being in the band was that audiences would be more receptive, but it was a question of whether Phil would want to become the singer rather than the drummer. But he was up for it and that made all the difference really." [2]

THE ALBUM

Overcoming Peter Gabriel's departure seemed an insurmountable obstacle, something the press never failed to point out. And yet, careful examination of Genesis' musical history should have made it obvious that the band had never been a mere offshoot of its charismatic lead singer. Genesis' greatest strength had always lain in composition and this is where the four-piece focused its attention when the musicians started writing new material. Whilst Banks had indeed already written some of the songs at an earlier date, it was clear that the band had lost none of its instrumental gloss; if anything it was heightened, if such a thing were possible, due to an ever-greater level of symbiosis between the band members. Of course, on a purely creative level, it is impossible not to acknowledge a return to those atmospheres which had been largely absent on THE LAMB LIES DOWN ON BROADWAY. Take, for example, the triumphant return of the 12-string acoustic guitars and the Mellotron, back providing the romantic sounds the band had seemingly turned its back on during the recording of the last album with Gabriel. What's more, while the songs on THE LAMB had shown a harder, grittier edge with deliberately raw vocals, A TRICK OF THE TAIL reverted to the softer, gentler sounds more akin to the band's earlier work.

An album, therefore which, creatively speaking, did not continue along the path embarked upon with THE LAMB. It was almost as if, in dealing with such a huge crisis, not to mention the expectations of fans and critics alike, the band felt the need to seek refuge in more comfortable and familiar atmospheres. This is definitely the case with *Ripples*. This beautifully melodic track crafted around Rutherford's 12-string guitar includes an instrumental section where the ebb and flow of Hackett's guitar over a piano motif from Banks generates goose bumps in the listener. The other acoustic track on the album, *Entangled*, is made

less linear by its irregular rhythm and ends with a wonderful instrumental finale, this time dominated by Banks on Mellotron and synthesiser.

The title track, *A Trick Of The Tail*, is one of those cheerful little songs that pop up every now and again in Genesis' music, even in the Gabriel era (in fact Banks actually wrote this song several years earlier), while *Squonk* provides a glimpse of a brand new intensity with the whole band at the top of its game.

The most progressive moment on the album is, without doubt, *Mad Man Moon*, a truly complicated symphony woven by Tony, while *Robbery, Assault And Battery* definitely belongs in the 'jaunty prog' category. In this song Phil has fun with Banks' lyrics (in sharp contrast with their rather more dramatic, albeit ironic, content) which give way to a synth solo over drumming in 13/8.

That leaves just the opening and closing tracks, which to some extent are complementary to one another. *Dance On A Volcano* is musically colossal, with the instruments chasing each other over an uneven time signature, while *Los Endos* brings the album to a fitting end. Influenced, as Collins himself admits, by Santana, this instrumental track shows the band at its best and, in order to give a sense of continuity to the album, it briefly reprises two of the previous tracks (*Dance On A Volcano* and *Squonk*).

The four band members are clearly on good form. Collins does a great job on lead vocals and brings in some interesting rhythmic variations, taking Genesis in unexpected directions (somewhere between fusion and world music). Banks is his usual phenomenal self, the architect of complicated symphonies, consummate pianist and an increasingly more confident synth player. Rutherford, leaving behind the distorted bass sound which appeared on the previous album, is back with his trademark acoustic guitar, proving himself yet again to be a formidable 12-string guitarist. Last but not least, Hackett, rather than giving us solos, focuses on fantastic finishing work, contributing to a band that had never before been such a tight outfit.

So, A Trick Of The Tail passed the test with flying

A Trick Of The Tail

Genesis with their acoustic 12-string guitars, in concert in Bern, 26th June, 1976

UK Poster, Charisma Records, 1976

colours in an historical period on the cusp of great change. Other albums released at a similar time to Genesis' first post-Gabriel record include Bob Dylan's DESIRE, Lou Reed's CONEY ISLAND BABY and STATION TO STATION by David Bowie. Meanwhile, a curly-haired guitarist had a quite frankly unexplainable success with FRAMPTON COMES ALIVE! and The Eagles, with THEIR GREATEST HITS, were soon to become the first band in history to be awarded a platinum disc.

In March that year Kiss released DESTROYER and Santana came out with AMIGOS (with the smash hit *Europa*) while April welcomed the arrival of BLACK AND BLUE by The Stones, HIGH VOLTAGE by AC/DC, LIVE BULLET by Bob Seger, STILL LIFE by Van Der Graaf Generator, but, more importantly, the eponymous debut album by The Ramones.

The year is 1976, the year which gave birth to the Sex Pistols, The Clash and The Damned – a revolution is banging on the door. But, for now, no one can hear it.

THE SONGS

DANCE ON A VOLCANO

Genesis' new journey opens with Rutherford playing a riff on his electric 12-string which immediately gets a response from Steve's Gibson. The interaction between the two guitarists in the most rhythmic phases is quite simply fantastic. The sound is less romantic than much of the rest of the album, with mighty drumming from Phil Collins who also gives an impeccable performance as lead vocalist, revealing a hard edge that hadn't emerged while he was Peter Gabriel's sidekick.

Hackett: "It's very, very powerful. You know, great drums from Phil, the odd, natty little sort of lick from myself and Tony, and just sort of a great rhythm section sound. And of course, it's not easy to sing in 7/8; I think Phil's drumming background enabled him to do that." [3]

Rutherford: "That instrumental riff, which is in 7/8, was a great moment, you know, it kind of embodied all of what Genesis did well: majestic, powerful stuff, interesting rhythms, good melodies. The intro had a drama, an excitement about it. I'm not sure the rest of it was always up to scratch, but that intro and the first section, I thought was very strong." [3]

Banks: "Mike wrote the start (probably the best bit of the song actually) and I had this bit hanging around in 7/4 that I hadn't got a home for which ended up being the verse and also the middle of the song." [3]

The final instrumental section features fast solos from Steve and Tony seemingly chasing one

21

another.

Banks: "We stuck this bit on the end which I'm not very sure about. There are a few bits you'd really want to lose from songs and records and that's one of them. I think the final section should have been consigned to the rubbish bin myself." [3]

The lyrics, written by Mike, were inspired by the works of Carlos Castaneda.

Rutherford: "I had just finished reading his most recent book and it just seemed to tie in; that pain and that frustration and madness in a real world and so the song tried to capture that feeling of darkness and chaos." [1]

ENTANGLED

Hackett: "It was largely my baby and then the band sort of picked up the ball and ran with it. Mike kicked in with stuff and Tony did the sort of choral on the Mellotron at the end. We used to write a lot of stuff like that, you know, things that would develop in jams. You'd have set parts and then the play-out might extend and so I think that was particularly effective." [3]

The song is structured around four acoustic and electric guitars played by Steve, Mike and Tony. Phil's vocals have a very soft timbre and he dou-

A Trick Of The Tail

12-strings, Mellotrons and synthesizers, Bern, 26th June, 1976

Pro Soloist synthesiser with the vibrato created using the aftertouch function) intertwining with the guitars and bass pedals.

Hackett: "The ARP Pro Soloist was an early kind of analogue synth, but it used to sound very good. These days you've got keyboards with a thousand patches, but in the old days, if you wanted to make one sound, a keyboard made that sound, which is why people were so interested in Mellotrons. They did a limited amount of things but did them very well. When they deigned to work of course; there was always that worry." [3]

The lyrics are also by Steve.

Hackett: "The lyrics are really about dreams. I was thinking of a kind of dreamscape. It was the idea of a successful businessman who is very troubled by nightmares, in other words, he loses control when he dreams so he was seeing a therapist. I remember Phil saying to me that it had a very Walt Disney feel to it, like Mary Poppins, over the rooftops and houses, and a very kind of floaty feeling to it." [4]

SQUONK

bles it with a second vocal line in the chorus, all the while accompanying himself with a tambourine.

Banks: "Steve had a sort of guitar bit which happened to be in 3/4 and I had this chorus hanging around without a home, also in 3/4. We wondered what they would be like together, so we tried it and it worked well. I'd originally written it on the piano but had transferred it to guitar with the voice then singing what the piano used to play. Where the chords changed it produced quite a nice sort of harmony." [3]

And then there is the fantastic instrumental finale with Tony's instruments (Mellotron and ARP

An unrelenting track driven by a powerful electric guitar riff (both 6- and 12-string) delivered by Mike, not only the instrumental leader on this track (playing rhythm guitar as well as bass pedals and electric bass) but also the song's main composer.

Banks: "*Squonk* was much more Mike's thing than mine really. I wrote what you might call all the bad bits. Mike wrote the main riff and the chorus riff and we had some other bits and pieces that we slotted into it. I had a hand in the melody line. The song is in a minor key and I hit a major note in the chorus and I think that's quite a key thing in the

GENESIS

Mike and Phil, Bern, 26th June 1976

Mike is also the author of the lyrics which talk about a mythical creature reputed to live in northern Pennsylvania (which had already appeared just a couple of years earlier in Steely Dan's *Any Major Dude Will Tell You* on the album Pretzel Logic). Saddened by its ugly appearance, the poor animal's constant weeping makes it easy for hunters to track down as all they have to do is follow the trail of its tears song really but I would say I was definitely a secondary composer on that song." (2)

What makes this track unique is the rhythm section, especially the drumming.

Collins: "It was a musical standout. I mean it was always our Led Zeppelin kind of song, you know, our *Kashmir*, a bit of *When The Levee Breaks*. When you listen to it, it doesn't sound like that but that's what it was meant to be; these heavy guitar chords and me with my John Bonham hat on." (3)

Hackett: "Genesis certainly is a very English sounding band. I mean, the influence of hymns and folk songs, Vaughan Williams and all sorts of things which formed the chords we used, and then there was Phil's ability to make certain slow melodies swing; almost as if he were creating a melody out of lead chords. *Squonk* is an example of that; the bass doesn't move, it's just fixed, and you've got every inversion under the sun going with that." (3)

(when cornered, however, it is able to evade capture by dissolving into a pool of tears).

Rutherford: "I found this old sort of fable, fairy-tale-like little character and that's where the lyric comes from. Our lyrics were always, not so much obscure, but about little subject matters, stories, trying to say things by drawing parallels to them. It took a while to actually get something as direct as 'I love you' into a song, you know. I think Phil was the one who really helped us there, the first one to really start writing slightly more personal and direct lyrics." (3)

Maybe *Squonk* was also an attempt to retain some kind of continuity with the kind of fantasy lyrics Peter used to write.

Rutherford: "I had done fantasy lyrics before really, Tony and I did *Watcher Of The Skies* which is a sort of fantasy. It wasn't hard, it seemed natural to write about quite quirky, quite odd things. But in a

Tony and Phil, Berkeley, 29th April 1976

sense, you couldn't create Peter's off-the-wall way of thinking in the same way he did. We couldn't even try to really. We became something else." [1]

MAD MAN MOON

Banks: "*Mad Man Moon* has always been a big favourite of mine. It was a song I wrote completely on my own. I was very pleased with some of the things. I mean the middle is not played as well as it should have been, but the verse parts and everything there is just nice. At the time I was very pleased with the chord sequences, the chord changes and things like that because they're sort of unusual but without necessarily sounding too unusual. And I think that's a good thing about a song. I don't want it to sound weird. I just want it to be kind of …. you know, it's very romantic." [3]

This absolute gem, written by Tony, is based mainly on his magnificent piano arrangement. An extraordinary instrumental section in the middle part of the song is embellished with grand orchestral sounds fully emphasised by the floor toms played by Phil as he sings lyrics which escape immediate comprehension.

Banks: "It's about yearning and frustration; about being a human being, about not getting what you want when you want it and dreaming of how things could be better. It's a whimsical piece but it's not really fantasy (although the first verse may seem that way). I just kind of let my mind go wherever it would go. I liked a few phrases that came to me and I put it all together." [2]

Collins: "At this point, there were some individual songs, so Tony had his *Mad Man Moon* and, you know, as a singer it was a problem for me sometimes, having to sing other people's lyrics. When you have to sing someone else's lyrics you don't necessarily relate to them, you're singing it because it's a timeshare; you're just going through the motions." [3]

Banks: "It's what comes of being a repressed public schoolboy (in my case anyway). To write about real things, like human relationships, was sort of beyond me. So, I liked to write stories and take ideas from sort of mythological areas or just from other areas where you could write more kinds of philosophical ideas. Which is the case with *Mad Man Moon* really." [3]

ROBBERY, ASSAULT AND BATTERY

This track, with its quirky rhythm, opens with a synth riff which introduces an almost cheerful verse. Written by Tony Banks, with the help of Phil, the synth solo takes flight over a formidable uneven beat. Banks: "Phil wrote the drum pattern the solo is based on. He wrote this rhythm in a fiendish time signature: a bar of 7 followed by a bar of 6, in 13/8 in other words. We liked the feel it had so I wrote this solo on top of that rhythm. It was a nightmare to play as you have to play the first part against the rhythm, then you get bits where I break it up into more bite-sized chunks, so you get 3 bars of 4 or 1 bar of 4 and 1 of 5 to make it a bit easier to do. The bits like 'he's leaving via the roof' are quite fun to do. Obviously, we'd started off with things like *The Cinema Show*, *Apocalypse In 9/8* and later with *Riding The Scree*; Mike would get a riff going, Phil would play something and I'd struggle away on top seeing what I could do. I quite liked writing in a funny time signature as it made you do things you wouldn't otherwise do. So that was Phil's contribution... it's only a small part but, when something is the basis for a part of the song, you have to give them credit for it really. Obviously, people think he wrote the lyrics, but he didn't." [2]

In fact, it was Tony himself who wrote the lyrics. Banks: "English things... I wrote a cops and robbers lyric on that because it had this very fast instrumental in the middle in a very strange time signature which keeps sliding from one place to another. It sounded to me like a sort of wild chase scene, you know, a Keystone Cops thing. So, you know, the idea of it being a chase of cops and robbers seemed quite amusing." [3]

For years it was said that the words were written directly in the recording studio. Banks: "No, I didn't write them in the studio, I wrote them after we had finished the song, after we had done most of the music on it. We were all off at various times writing lyrics and I just brought it into the studio. Then Phil had this idea of doing it in a kind of Artful Dodger accent throughout, which was quite fun and gave it character. He was able to do something with it that Peter wouldn't have done. The lyric is tongue in cheek, it wasn't supposed to be very serious, and he got a little of that humour across with it. I thought he did a really good job with the vocal on it." [2]

Ciao 2001 No. 4, published on 1st February 1976

RIPPLES

An acoustic guitar arrangement, written mainly by Mike whose 12-string chords create a backcloth over which Phil put down a beautiful soft vocal. Before the last chorus there is another classic Genesis instrumental section with interwoven keyboard parts and guitar solos.

Hackett: "I enjoyed doing that kind of semi-backwards guitar solo. It was twinned with a synth, a piece of kit that I had already used on The Lamb, called a Synthi Hi Fli [*made by EMS, a British synthesiser manufacturer famous for the VCS3 used by Pink Floyd – author's note*]. It gave you the ability to do something that made it sound like you were playing backwards, but you could do it in real-time because it lopped off the beginning of the notes. So, I think that that came out particularly melodically, and I think I did the tinkle of 12 strings on that." [3]

Banks: "Well obviously the middle part is entirely mine and the 'face in the water' bit was mine as well. Mike had a verse and a chorus but he didn't have any bridge between them. I had this bit and we put them together and it sounded really good. But it was much more Mike's song than mine really. I managed to get a credit on every track but my contributions were variable; on some I was the major contributor, on others less so. I think the middle bit gave the lyric idea to Mike as it was just called "ripply". The way it builds up to the big chorus is a very strong moment in Genesis' work." [2]

The lyrics are a very touching poem on the subject of getting old, but the lyrics Mike initially wrote were very different; in fact, Mike's working title for the song was *Nipples*.

Rutherford: "With all songs you write there are a couple of times when you're not doing very well and they come out a bit rude, but you know they won't stay that way. When you can't find the right words, you just make up some silly line to fill it in, but it's only temporary." [1]

GENESIS

A TRICK OF THE TAIL

Banks: "I had this piece around from way back in the day… probably even before Trespass, but no one liked it then. Peter was quite good at those bouncy kinds of things, like *Harold The Barrel* and *Willow Farm*, which was his kind of thing. Once he'd left I thought it kind of echoed the sort of things he used to write and it would be good to have it on this record, plus it was a bit more lightweight compared to some of the other tracks." [2]

Characterised by a nice rhythm, with beating piano notes, Phil's vocal harmonies (with the backing vocals in falsetto) and Steve's finishing touches, the lyrics to this song were inspired by the William Golding novel, *The Inheritors*.

Banks: "I like stories. I think what can sometimes be quite simple and seem a bit banal when you write it down becomes something special when it's a song. The emotion can be quite simple but can be very effective in that simple format, like a cartoon really. *A Trick Of The Tail* works quite well on that basis; you do feel for the character, I think." [3]

LOS ENDOS

Collins: "I was always trying to get what I liked to play into Genesis, things that they didn't really go near too much. I was working with Brand X and there was this album by Santana, Borboletta, with a track called *Promise Of A Fisherman*. It was a fantastic track, I mean, optimistic chords and a really soaring rhythm and melody. And I said, 'I want some of that', you know, 'let's do some of that'. And I started playing this rhythm, I dunno quite how it happened, but we already had some of the phrases for a song called *It's Yourself* and *Los Endos* came out of that; it's a bit like free-falling and then the bongos come in. So yeah, it was kinda more my baby than anybody else's, I mean obviously melodically, you know, I'd go 'da, da, da, daa' and Tony would sort of make sense of my humming." [3]

Banks: "It was very much a group composition. Fundamentally it was Phil's idea to have something on the album that was more his kind of thing, more of a jazz-rock thing, using this riff that came from *It's Yourself*; three chords Steve had written which we made into a kind of Big Band thing. It was a very exciting thing to do and then Steve and I exchanged licks in a way that I think worked really well. Then we brought bits of *Dance On A Volcano* and *Squonk* into it and it became a real bookend to the album. The bit of *Squonk* in *Los Endos* sounds much better than it does in the original track. It was a very important track; in fact it could be considered the most important track on the album." [2]

Rutherford: "We always quite enjoyed a theme

that comes back. The 'deh deh deh dehh' was an instrumental bit from one of the earlier songs on the album. It's a great way to finish and it showed Steve and Tony playing so well together." [1]

OTHER SONGS

It's Yourself, the song from which *Los Endos* developed, didn't actually make it onto the album but would eventually appear as the B-side to *Ripples* when this was released as a single in Italy in 1976 (and the rest of the world the following year).

Hackett: "I don't think we thought it was strong enough. We felt that it was more like a B-side. It was something that had been very spontaneous and very kind of Kensington Market sounding, you know, hippyish, almost a kind of successor to *Happy The Man*. It wasn't that focused. It was a spontaneous 'other Genesis' song." [4]

THE ALBUM ARTWORK

Rutherford: "Hipgnosis had done some fabulous stuff. I would say that the cover for A TRICK OF THE TAIL was out of character with what they normally did, what we know them for, you know, Pink Floyd covers and some Led Zeppelin and 10cc. Storm Thorgerson and Aubrey Powell didn't usually do that slightly romantically softer drawing style but I think there was slightly more Powell on this one. They came back with these drawings and the idea felt good straight away, it suited the mood of the album." [3]

Hackett: "Yeah, I think it came out very well, you know, the idea of breaking it down into individual characters worked really well. In those days Hipgnosis were always trying to get us to have a photo on the front but obviously the band was much more about fantasy at that stage." [3]

Banks: "Storm tended to concentrate slightly more on photographic ideas but this other guy [*Colin Elgie – author's note*] thought that making a composite of the characters from the album would be quite a nice thing to do. What he did was really good because he gave it a sort of slightly Dickensian look which worked so nicely, you know, the brown and that kind of parchment-like paper. Album covers can give a very strong identity to an album. I think this is one where that's the case; you get this sort of storybook feel about it and the songs are quite distinct and quite a lot of them do have a kind of story to them." [3]

EPILOGUE

Artistically speaking the band were very enthusiastic about the results. The thing that had worried them most, Phil's voice on lead vocals, was more than up to par and many superficial critics were quick to point to a non-existent similarity between his and Peter's voice.

Rutherford: "Everyone said at the time that Phil sounded like Peter, but he doesn't at all. I think what that says is that when you hear a certain Genesis song – the style and the melody – you imagine the same thing; it's the song that makes you think they are familiar… similar… But their voices are very different really." [1]

Banks: "On previous albums, the music and lyrics, everything had been written by all of us and I think there's something about the way I write a melody or something that tends to make people do it in a certain kind of way. Phil doesn't really sound like Pete but there are moments when you hear them and you think, 'yeah, they do sound similar' plus there had been a number of other quite prominent songs, particularly *I Know What I Like* and *Counting Out Time* where Phil had been singing in unison with Pete throughout the song. Actually, when you hear them now, Phil's voice is slightly more dominant, so that probably confused people a little bit. I think it's the style of singing, the style of music really, that made people think they were similar." [3]

For this album, the band went back to David Hentschel whom they had already worked with back in the days of Nursery Cryme when he was their sound engineer. This time they promoted him to the role of co-producer.

Collins: "We got some great sounds with him. He had an ARP synthesiser. This was back in the early days of synthesisers, and it was a huge thing; we had to rent a truck to get it to Trident Studios and we'd trigger it with one of the drums. The biggest sort of syn-drum ever. Dave was great. I'd known him for a long time, I'd done records with him, moonlighting at Trident Studios, when none of the other guys really did anything else outside Genesis. It kind of became my job, if you like, to find people to bring in to that environment. David was an old friend. He'd just done some things with Elton John, he was a good engineer and he had a great sense of humour. He was great to get on with and he made a big difference to that record." [3]

Rutherford: "I think the new sound came more from the songs. The new Genesis sound, in my opinion, came when we started working with Hugh Padgham. Hearing it now, the sound is a bit tame but the music was so fresh that it kind of worked." [1]

With Gabriel no longer in the band, there was more compositional space for everyone else.

Collins: "We just had no choice but to go on. We all thought that we could because we all knew that only one of our five writers was leaving. It's like Monty Python, you know, when you get to the series when John Cleese isn't there, there's a hole and if you're a big John Cleese fan you notice the hole more than if you're a Terry Jones fan. We just rose to the occasion. From a critical point of view, having written us off because our flagship member had left, that album gave everybody an opportunity to say 'yeah, you underdogs, this is a good album', you know, and put us on a pedestal (from which they were soon to knock us down, of course). But we got some good reviews for that album." [3]

For Phil, it was the beginning of a whole new chapter.

Collins: "You know it was never my intention to put myself in a stronger position than being the drummer; a great drummer in a good band, you know, that's what I wanted to be. It was like falling asleep on a boat: when you wake up and you've been drifting you think, 'How the hell did I get over here? I started off over there' you know. Really, all I wanted to be was the drummer but…" [3]

To highlight their new direction, Genesis also made their first videos.

Collins: "*A Trick Of The Tail*, with me as a leprechaun on the piano, was incredibly embarrassing. *Robbery, Assault And Battery* was filmed on the set of 'Oliver!' at Shepperton Studios in London. That kind of suited me, you know, going back to 'Oliver',

A Trick Of The Tail

Promotional poster to advertise the UK release

dressing up as the Artful Dodger was kind of interesting. Visually it was a big turning point because we had to start making videos and that particular one was a bit of a story video, with everybody in costume on the 'Oliver!' set." [3]

Hackett: "Although we made the odd video, by today's standards they're fairly forgettable. Obviously, you know, video came a long way, but we were hardly a bunch of sex gods. We were a bunch of guys, sort of backroom boys really, who did their stuff and that was that. With Genesis, there wasn't the posturing that perhaps went with other bands." [3]

A TRICK OF THE TAIL was released in February 1976 and was successful both critically and commercially. On home territory it reached No. 3 in the album charts (thus equalling the chart success of SELLING ENGLAND BY THE POUND) and earned the band a gold record. In America, it went ten places higher than THE LAMB, reaching No. 31. More importantly, it put Genesis high up in the European charts reaching No. 7 in Holland and No. 4 in Italy.

Banks: "Mike and I did a little bit of promotion before the album actually came out around Europe. I remember going to places and just no one was the slightest bit interested really. 'No Pete? What's the point?', you know, it was a bit like that. It was quite a funny thing when it came out; there was a certain element of the public who were quite glad not to have Pete there, really, because he sort of made it so strange in some ways. So, for some people who had had a bit of trouble with Pete, it was time to reassess us, put it like that. A lot of the existing fans really liked it and we got some new ones. It just seemed to take off, I suppose." [3]

THE CONCERTS

Having overcome the challenge of writing a new album in spectacular style, Genesis were now faced with an even bigger dilemma: who was going to take Peter's place on stage?

Collins: "So we finished the album, and said, 'Right, that's it. Now, let's find a singer to take it out on the road'. So again we went through an audition process, albeit very half-heartedly, only once we got started we realised that we were just doing what we'd already done. So my first wife suggested, 'Why don't you do it?'. To be honest, the whole idea of coming out from behind the drum kit appalled me really but, as I'd done the album, there didn't seem to be much alternative. So, I suggested it to the guys. They weren't sure if I could do it, from a physical point of view. I mean, they knew I could sing but probably didn't think I could do what singers do." [3]

Rutherford: "Looking back it seems crazy, but at the time I couldn't see Phil leaving the drum kit. He was the drummer. He loved drumming and I couldn't imagine him... I mean you can't drum and sing! OK, Don Henley does, but it's hard with our dramatic songs. I wasn't sure he'd want to do it, I didn't even like to ask." [1]

Banks: "Phil was kind of waiting for us to say, 'give it a go'. In the end we said, 'well, you've done the record... How about it?', and he was really up for it. To share the stage with Phil, you know, looking up and seeing him there and not Peter, was one of the strangest moments of my life, but the audience immediately liked him. And he developed a persona almost from the first show. I knew during that very first show that it was going to work." [2]

Of course, moving Collins to centre stage meant having to find another drummer.

Collins: "I didn't know if I'd find a drummer that I wouldn't be looking around and tutting at. Around that time I was playing in Brand X, with Bill Bruford guesting on percussion. We were rehearsing one day and he said, 'Have you found a drummer yet?'. When I said no, he said 'Well, what about me?'. And I said 'You wouldn't wanna do it. You've been with Yes and King Crimson'. But he said he'd love to do it." [3]

Bruford: "Well, I was playing with Phil Collins in a rehearsal band called Brand X. I was playing percussion and he was playing drums. He told me that Peter Gabriel was leaving the band and that he had auditioned many singers and that none of them were very good. He said he thought he could sing better. So I said to him, 'why don't you sing and I'll play the drums through the next tour until you feel comfortable'. He knew my drumming very well and he knew that I could probably play the parts. That went very well and he got a lot of confidence on the tour and I was surprised at just how well he could do it." [6]

Hackett: "Bill was one of Phil's heroes and I think having Bill, you know, gave us the seal of approval from other like-minded bands." [3]

Banks: "We were lucky that Bill came out on that first tour as he was a bit of a star and a lot of the Genesis audience liked him from his Yes days." [2]

Rehearsals kicked off in March 1976 at the Reunion Centre in Dallas, Texas, where Phil, Tony, Mike, Steve and Bill locked themselves away in order to focus on what promised to be the most challenging tour of their fledgling career. The biggest concern now was how to actually stage the show, after all, by this point, Genesis had become renowned

A Trick Of The Tail

Phil and the live drummer, Bill Bruford, in a promotional shot for Charisma Records, 1976

GENESIS

Robbery, Assault and Battery in Berkeley,
29th April 1976

for their weird and wonderful ideas, mainly the fruit of Peter Gabriel's irrepressible imagination. Of course, Phil was not Peter, so the masks and costumes were the first to go.

Rutherford: "We didn't even consider it, I mean, you progress. Even had Peter stayed, I think we may have gone on a different route and the theatrics would have stopped." [1]

There was, however, one minor exception: for *Robbery, Assault And Battery* Phil would wear the coat of an East End spiv, and throughout the show he would seek to engage and win over the audience, even going so far as to invent a short, sleazy story about Romeo and his girlfriend Juliet to introduce *The Cinema Show*. On a purely musical level, there were clearly no problems at all. Phil sang all the songs impeccably (even those from the Gabriel era) and was accompanied to perfection by his bandmates.

Banks: "In some ways he could probably sing more easily on stage than Peter could; Peter had to work at it a bit whereas Phil had a very natural kind of singing voice. The old tracks we were doing, like *Supper's Ready*, sounded really good and we were playing them probably better than we'd ever done. And we had this great thing of having two drummers on certain tracks, like *The Cinema Show*,

which was very exciting." [2]

Without doubt the music was the most important factor of the show, but the band also focused heavily on lights and slides (some inherited from THE LAMB tour) and the power of sound.

Hackett: "We had Craig Schertz mixing the sound and Alan Owen of Showco doing the lights, both of them sadly no longer with us, and they played a big part in creating the show. I remember later on having this conversation with Brian May of Queen where we were saying, 'I don't know who was winning the competition for having more lights on stage, you guys or us!'. Perhaps, having lost our original frontman, we thought we could be more like Pink Floyd who just stood there and played with a light show going on around them, so we invested more in the lights and I think that helped to sell the music." [3]

Banks: "After Peter's departure, Mike and I became the more visual members of the band. Phil has never really been all that concerned about the visuals, he wanted it to look good but didn't really have that many ideas. Having done such an elaborate thing with THE LAMB we wanted to scale back but still had some ideas of what we wanted to do,

A Trick Of The Tail

> The live line-up, featuring Bill Bruford, in a promotional shot for the American record company, Atco, 1976

GENESIS

Bern, 26th June 1976

so we just thought he might as well do it all. At the beginning of that tour the feeling was that we wanted to make it a bit easier for Phil, so that the whole thing wasn't thrown on him." [2]

Hackett: "I do remember Phil saying, when he was singing and drumming at the same time, 'everyone else gets a chance to recover at the end of each song whereas the singer, being the master of ceremonies, has got to do an announcement'. I think we all felt that Phil was under a lot of pressure at that time and we were starting to come forward as personalities. Mike and I were now standing up for example using a bit more movie stuff, just simple things like the fire on *Dance On A Volcano*. Obvious things in a way, but they gave us a starting point. At that stage we were beginning to think more about lights, but until the later period when we introduced the Vari-Lites, we were just dependent on having lots of them. I can't really remember the whole set on the A Trick Of The Tail tour. We were always very conscious of making it look good; but now we had to make it look good in a way that didn't depend on Peter like The Lamb show had." [2]

Not totally confident in his role as chief communicator for the band, Phil asked his bandmates to help out in engaging the audience, consequently Mike would introduce *White Mountain* and *Supper's Ready*, while it fell upon Steve to introduce *Firth Of Fifth* and *Entangled*.

Rutherford: "Phil is such a natural talker, I'm not sure our intros would have lasted the whole tour. I shared a stage with Peter, who was an amazing talker, and Phil (who became one) but I'm not a natural talker at all, although with the Mechanics I have done some talking on stage." [1]

Banks: "They were OK at it but they weren't great and eventually Phil became as good as Peter

A Trick Of The Tail

The guitarist stands up at Berkeley, 29th April 1976

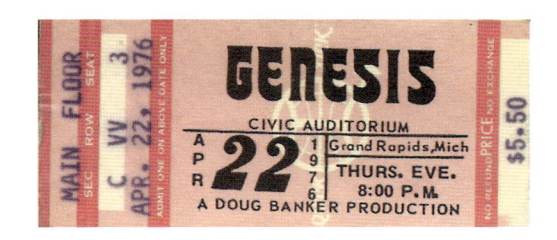

and there was this idea that we should all wear white so we'd be picked up by the lights. So, you know, there was this whole orientation towards changing the band's persona from one where Peter Gabriel was the lead singer and reviewers and journalists only wrote about Pete and not really about the rest of the band. We felt that we had to come forward with more personality so we changed look; I shaved off the beard, dressed up more and stood up (*up to THE LAMB tour, Steve had mainly played sitting down – author's note*). And it was the same with Mike. We looked more like an extrovert band on stage and we helped Phil by sharing out the announcements. I don't know why Tony didn't want to make any announcements, but I think, maybe in terms of the public, he is probably more introverted. I'm sure that if Tony had wanted to do an announcement we would have all said yes." (4)

The setlist for the tour was truly interesting, a fantastic balance between old and new.

Hackett: "When we started with our *Dance on a Volcano*, it was really with a minimum of conferring and we all started playing pretty much the same thing together. Mike had these Taurus bass pedals that sounded enormous and when the band kicked in with 'dun, dun, dun, dun, duddle-a-bah' it was very strong and felt really good. We were hoping the audience would manage to get to the point whereby, you know, they were happy that the star was no longer with us. At that stage I guess the band was getting more slick and more professional." (3)

Five songs off the new album were included in the setlist, with the unexpected omission of *Ripples*.

Banks: "We tended not to do the more acoustic tracks because, when you were playing live, you needed the big tracks. But I think the main reason we didn't do it was because I didn't really have anything on which to play the more piano-based songs. Before the Yamaha CP-70 came out you either had to mic up a grand piano or use an elec-

GENESIS

Charisma poster advertising the concert in Dusseldorf, Germany, 18th June 1976

tric piano and they were both a bit of a nightmare. With songs like *Ripples* or *Mad Man Moon* you needed the piano to be very much part of it. It's the same reason why we never did *Many Too Many*." [2]

Or indeed, the introduction to *Firth Of Fifth*. Banks: "Yes, I stopped doing it after a bit as I didn't think it sounded very good. I used to play the intro on an electric piano and it was pretty nasty to play as it had no touch, you couldn't play with any sensitivity. I had a number of these kinds of introduction bits, like *The Lamb Lies Down On Broadway* and later on things like *Eleventh Earl Of Mar*, so I felt that we didn't need another Tony Banks intro really." [2]

For this tour *Firth Of Fifth*, a Genesis classic, along with *Supper's Ready*, *The Cinema Show* and *I Know What I Like* (with Phil performing his bizarre tarantella dance beating his tambourine all over his body), were brought back into the setlist after being forced to sit out THE LAMB concept tour. THE LAMB album, on the other hand, was represented by a medley of four songs which Phil would rather wittily introduce as *Lamb Stew* (or other such names). It included *The Lamb Lies Down On Broadway*, instrumental versions of *Fly On A Windshield* and *Broadway Melody Of 1974* and rounded off with *The Carpet Crawlers*.

Banks: "We wanted to do some songs from THE LAMB but obviously we didn't want to play the whole album. *The Lamb Lies Down On Broadway* and *Fly On A Windshield* were always band favourites and *Carpet Crawlers* was an audience favourite." [2]

The encore was also taken from THE LAMB; *It* (not particularly well sung by Collins) linked up to an instrumental version of the intro and ending of *Watcher Of The Skies*. But perhaps the biggest surprise was the appearance in the setlist of a song from 1970, *White Mountain*.

Banks: "We did perform it back in the day, at the time of TRESPASS, but we'd never done it with Phil and Steve. I think Phil liked it. I was always keen to get an old song we hadn't done before into the show, which always proved quite difficult to do actually. It just seemed like a nice one to do really,

A Trick Of The Tail

Phil at Berkeley, 29th April 1976

there was no particular reason; it was just to get a bit of variety into the set." (2)

According to some sources (including their old friend, Richard Macphail, once again working with Genesis as their tour manager), *Supper's Ready* was left out of the very first shows in March and was only added to the setlist at the beginning of April. The members of the band, however, can't quite remember.

Rutherford: "I wouldn't have thought we'd have started the tour without it, so I think it was probably there all the time. If we had started playing it later on it, that would have been the first time something like that happened." (1)

Banks: "I thought we did it from the start as it was the strongest song from the days with Peter." (2)

Apart from the doubts as to how and when *Supper's Ready* was included in the setlist (the first documented inclusion provided by a recording is dated 1 April in Toronto), there were no variations over the course of the tour, something almost unique in the history of Genesis. It was as follows: *Dance On A Volcano / The Lamb – Fly On A Windshield – Broadway Melody Of 1974 – The Carpet Crawlers / The Cinema Show / Robbery, Assault And Battery / White Mountain / Firth Of Fifth / Entangled / Squonk / Supper's Ready / I Know What I Like / Los Endos / It – Watcher Of The Skies.*

The tour kicked off in a Canadian city called, of all things, London. The date of this first gig isn't one hundred percent certain, but it was most likely on 26 March. The cause for doubt lies in the fact that tickets have survived showing the date 25 March. No one seems to know with any certainty whether concerts were held on both days or if the first of the two was cancelled and rescheduled for the following day.

The London Arena was packed with over 4,000 spectators, but not all of them were ready to accept the changes. Hackett: "There was this one guy wearing bat wings. He was standing in the front and

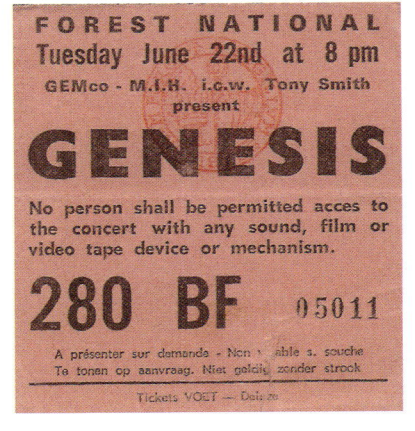

39

GENESIS

Poster advertising a concert in Kingston, Ontario, Canada. This gig, planned for 31st March 1976, was eventually moved to Toronto

refused to sit down until people made him. So I know that was very difficult for Phil. But I have to say that after the very first show the audience was hugely supportive towards him. I realised he was going to be absolutely brilliant from then on. Of course, he was nervous but, you know, Phil is a great singer and a very clever guy; that was the start of great things to come." [4]

Rutherford: "You shouldn't forget his theatre background; his acting days made him a very natural frontman." [1]

To a great extent, the audience's goodwill was definitely down to their love of Genesis and their joy that the band hadn't decided to split up. Collins: "Yeah, the audiences were really behind us but especially behind me and my succeeding in this new role because they still had their band. People didn't want the band to split up, you know, this was their thing, they wanted their annual visits to Toronto, Montreal, Chicago, Sheffield... People liked to see the band and so I think they were willing it to happen, willing it to work." [3]

In fact, on the whole, turnouts were good. For example, the show on 31 March, initially scheduled to take place in the Memorial Centre in Kingston, Ontario (with a spectator capacity of around 3,300) was moved to the larger, 15,000-seater Maple Leaf Gardens.

The tour proceeded really well, despite the odd

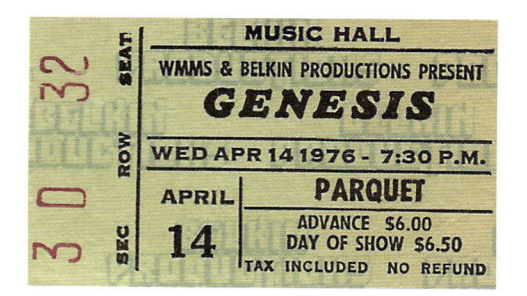

Poster advertising the show in Heidelberg, Germany, 4th July 1976

Poster advertising the show in Stafford, England, 10th July 1976. This was the very last concert of the TRICK OF THE TAIL tour

hiccough along the way. For example, there should have been two shows in Cleveland on 14 April, but a last-minute decision saw the second show moved to the following day. Consequently, the Columbus show, scheduled for 15 April had to be moved to the 19th. The show at the Civic Auditorium in Santa Monica on 27 April, on the other hand, was cancelled and replaced by a show in the bigger Starlight Bowl in Burbank on 1 May.

Hackett: "We were picking up larger sized audiences and Phil was leading the charge. I think it's pretty rare that a band could find someone within the ranks that could just follow on that professionally."[3]

The US tour ended at Fort Worth, cut short after the last show, scheduled for 9 May at the Fox Theatre in Atlanta, was cancelled. The band then took a month off before embarking on the European tour, starting out with 5 shows in London at the Hammersmith Odeon (one of which was attended by Peter Gabriel).

The shows in the British capital were followed by dates in France, Holland, Germany, Belgium, Switzerland and Sweden (however, the show planned for 1 July in Copenhagen was cancelled as it would have meant playing in daylight, totally defeating the whole object of the stage show) before the band returned to home ground for the final concerts.

The last two, in Glasgow on 9 July and Stafford

GENESIS

Australian poster advertising the *Genesis In Concert* film

on the 10th, were captured on film by the director, Tony Maylam. The resulting film, 'Genesis In Concert' (which rarely made it to cinemas but was later published as part of the bonus material on the 2008 CD/DVD edition of A Trick Of The Tail), turned out to be rather controversial not only due to the indiscriminate cuts to the set (only 45 minutes of the filmed concert were actually used: *I Know What I Like / Fly On A Windshield – The Carpet Crawlers / The Cinema Show part 2 / Entangled / Supper's Ready part 2* and *Los Endos*) but also for the use of additional random footage which the band members didn't like at all.

Banks: "The reason they had to add extra film was because it was too dark. They couldn't really do anything about it because, back then, if you wanted to film a live show it had to be very bright and we were unwilling to compromise our show just for the sake of a film. So they had to stick all these different pieces in: atom bombs and girls on beaches and all the rest of it... it's pretty terrible actually. I remember seeing the whole thing and thinking it was pretty bad. Before the advent of video cameras I didn't think recording concerts on film was any good, but when video cameras became more sophisticated you could capture a group as they actually were, as opposed to having to create this artificial environment. But it's quite nice to have something from that period otherwise nothing would exist at all."[2]

Rutherford: "The atomic bomb, the baby being born (which was taken out of the film, thank goodness!)... And the crowd scene was from a Yes concert in Philadelphia with about 100,000 people when we were playing Bingley Hall."[1]

Musically, however, Genesis got top marks. As a lead singer, Collins was flawless, even with him dashing to get back behind the drum kit at every possible opportunity. He turned out to be a great frontman despite still not being overly confident. Banks was the usual cornerstone, the band's flagship member even on stage. Rutherford, a great wingman, was increasingly at ease as he switched between acoustic and electric 12-string guitars, bass guitar and bass pedals.

And Hackett, on his feet at last, was guitar soloist par excellence and fantastic at adding all the finishing touches. The only disappointment was Bill Bruford; despite being an awesome musician, he lacked the humility to put himself at the band's

> Argentinian poster advertising both of Tony Maylam's films, *White Rock* and *Genesis In Concert*

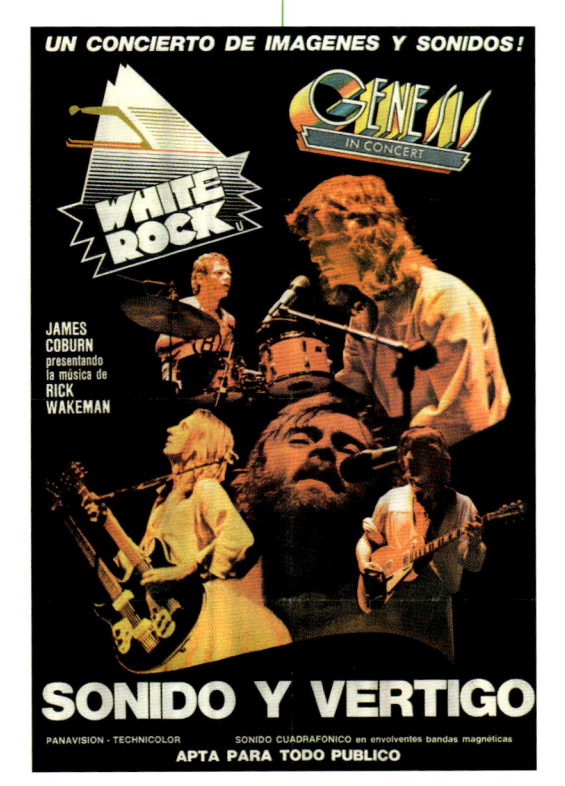

service. His performance, although full of character, left much to be desired as regards taste and sensitivity, with a rather vulgar use of the snare drum in songs such as *Dance On A Volcano* and *Squonk*.

Rutherford: "Bill had a confidence behind the drum kit that gave us a lift. And he was known in America, so that helped a lot. His playing was great but he wasn't a session player. He played like Bill Bruford, which is possibly why we only used him on one tour; he was great but he can't wear hats, he's only him and he can't play the same thing twice the same way. That's a compliment rather than a criticism." [1]

Hackett: "The drumming he did with Yes and on Chris Squire's solo album is absolutely blindingly brilliant. As for his role in Genesis, when he was working with Phil, the idea of trying to make them sound like one drummer was something that was never going to work. Bill was highly individualistic, highly idiosyncratic and he had a very original take on rhythm which was harder to integrate into Genesis." [4]

Banks: "I don't think he was totally right for Genesis; he was a bit too technical, a bit too jazzy. Obviously, Phil was a jazz drummer too, but he could play rock, hard rock very well, but I think Bill found it a little bit difficult. When we were doing *Dance On A Volcano*, which is written in a very natural 7/8 time, I remember him coming out of the riff onto the wrong beat. He liked to think about stuff like that, to construct his parts to a greater degree and was less able to just improvise around a beat the way Phil could. He really had to think about it, whereas when Phil was playing in a funny time signature he seemed to know exactly what to do with it and to come back in as he should." [2]

Bruford: "I know that everybody seems to think that Genesis, Yes and King Crimson are similar groups, but in England we think of them as being very different. In many ways, Genesis seem to me to be very much following in the wake of Yes and King Crimson. The music wasn't too difficult – just a job, you know. My problem was that I was not really emotionally involved in the music, so it wasn't as interesting to me as, perhaps, staying in King Crimson." [6]

Drumming issues aside, the fifty or so dates of the A Trick Of The Tail tour had a great impact on

GENESIS

Mike and Phil at Berkeley, 29th April 1976

audiences and results were extremely positive. And so it was that all the Cassandras who had already been forced to admit that Genesis were still very much alive and kicking as a recording band, now had to come to terms with a second humiliation: Genesis were still a colossal live band, even after losing such a charismatic frontman as Peter Gabriel.

NOTES

(1) Mario Giammetti's telephone interview with Mike Rutherford, 25 February 2016, partially published in the article "Senza Gabriel" in *Classic Rock*, issue n. 44, July 2016

(2) Mario Giammetti's telephone interview with Tony Banks, 26 February 2016, partially published in the article "Senza Gabriel" in *Classic Rock*, issue n. 44, July 2016

(3) Mike Kaufman's Genesis interviews, Chicago / London, October 2007, partially used in the bonus disc accompanying the 2008 remasters

(4) Mario Giammetti's telephone interview with Steve Hackett, 8 October 2015, partially published in the article "Senza Gabriel" in *Classic Rock*, isssue n. 44, July 2016

(5) Mario Giammetti's telephone interview with Tony Banks, 1 October 2009, partially published in the article "Nei meandri della memoria", *Dusk*, Issue no. 63, November 2009

(6) Mario Giammetti's telephone interview with Bill Bruford, 29 march 1995, partially published in the article "Speciale interviste – Bill Bruford", *Dusk*, Issue n. 15, June 1995)

A Trick Of The Tail Tour

1976

MARCH
- 25 **London, ON (CANADA)**, London Arena
  Uncertain show
- 26 **London, ON (CANADA)**, London Arena
- 27 **Waterloo, ON (CANADA)**, Physical Activities Complex - University of Waterloo
- 28 **Buffalo, NY (USA)**, Century Theatre
- 29 **Hamilton, ON (CANADA)**, Great Hall - Hamilton Place
- 31 **Toronto, ON (CANADA)**, Maple Leaf Gardens
  Originally scheduled for Kingston Memorial Centre - Kingston, Ontario

APRIL
- 01 **Toronto, ON (CANADA)**, Maple Leaf Gardens
- 02 **Montréal, QC (CANADA)**, Forum
- 03 **Ottawa, ON (CANADA)**, Ottawa Civic Centre
- 04 **Québec, QC (CANADA)**, Colisée de Québec
  Originally scheduled for Pavillon de la Jeunesse - Québec, Québec
- 07 **Upper Darby, PA (USA)**, Tower Theater
  Two shows
- 08 **New York, NY (USA)**, Beacon Theatre
- 09 **New York, NY (USA)**, Beacon Theatre
  Two shows
- 10 **Boston, MA (USA)**, Orpheum Theatre
- 12 **Baltimore, MD (USA)**, Lyric Theatre
- 13 **Pittsburgh, PA (USA)**, Syria Mosque
- 14 **Cleveland, OH (USA)**, Music Hall
- 15 **Cleveland, OH (USA)**, Music Hall
  Postponed second show from April 14, due to Phil's throat infection
- 16 **Chicago, IL (USA)**, Auditorium Theatre - Roosevelt University
- 17 **Chicago, IL (USA)**, Auditorium Theatre - Roosevelt University
- 19 **Columbus, OH (USA)**, Franklin County Veterans Memorial
  Originally scheduled for April 15 at Ohio Theatre
- 20 **Detroit, MI (USA)**, Ford Auditorium
- 21 **Milwaukee, WI (USA)**, Riverside Theater
- 22 **Grand Rapids, MI (USA)**, Civic Auditorium
- 23 **St. Louis, MO (USA)**, Ambassador Theatre
- 25 **Kansas City, KS (USA)**, Memorial Hall
- 29 **Berkeley, CA (USA)**, Berkeley Community Theater - Berkeley High School
- 30 **Fresno, CA (USA)**, Warnors Theatre

MAY
- 01 **Burbank, CA (USA)**, Starlight Bowl
- 05 **Austin, TX (USA)**, Municipal Auditorium
- 06 **Houston, TX (USA)**, Houston Music Hall
- 07 **Fort Worth, TX (USA)**, Will Rogers Auditorium

JUNE
- 09 **London (ENGLAND)**, Hammersmith Odeon
- 10 **London (ENGLAND)**, Hammersmith Odeon
- 11 **London (ENGLAND)**, Hammersmith Odeon
- 12 **London (ENGLAND)**, Hammersmith Odeon
- 13 **London (ENGLAND)**, Hammersmith Odeon
- 15 **Cambrai (FRANCE)**, Palais des Festivals
- 16 **Den Haag (THE NETHERLANDS)**, Congresgebouw *Two shows*
- 18 **Düsseldorf (WEST GERMANY)**, Philipshalle
- 19 **Berlin (WEST GERMANY)**, Deutschlandhalle
- 21 **Forest (BELGIUM)**, Forest National
- 22 **Forest (BELGIUM)**, Forest National
- 23 **Paris (FRANCE)**, Pavillon de Paris
- 24 **Paris (FRANCE)**, Pavillon de Paris
- 25 **Lyon (FRANCE)**, Palais des Sports
- 26 **Bern (SWITZERLAND)**, Festhalle
- 27 **Munich (WEST GERMANY)**, Olympiahalle
- 29 **Hamburg (WEST GERMANY)**, Hall 1 - Congress Centrum Hamburg
- 30 **Gothenburg (SWEDEN)**, Scandinavium

JULY
- 02 **Düsseldorf (WEST GERMANY)**, Philipshalle
- 03 **St. Goarshausen (WEST GERMANY)**, Freilichtbühne Loreley
- 04 **Heidelberg (WEST GERMANY)**, Rhein-Neckar-Halle
- 08 **Glasgow (SCOTLAND)**, Apollo Theatre
- 09 **Glasgow (SCOTLAND)**, Apollo Theatre
- 10 **Stafford (ENGLAND)**, New Bingley Hall

Wind & Wuthering

(Charisma, 1976)

Eleventh Earl Of Mar (Banks-Hackett-Rutherford) / One For The Vine (Banks) / Your Own Special Way (Rutherford) / Wot Gorilla? (Collins-Banks) /// All In A Mouse's Night (Banks) / Blood On The Rooftops (Hackett-Collins) / 'Unquiet Slumbers For The Sleepers... (Hackett-Rutherford) / ... In That Quiet Earth' (Hackett-Rutherford-Banks-Collins) / Afterglow (Banks)

- Release date: 17 December 1976
- Engineer: David Hentschel
- Assistant Engineer: Pierre Geoffroy Chateau
- Recorded at Relight Studios, Hilvarenbeek, Netherlands, in September 1976
- Remixed at Trident Studios, London, with the help of Assistant Engineer, Nick 'Cod' Bradford
- Co-produced by David Hentschel and Genesis
- Sleeve design: Hipgnosis (Colin Elgie)

- Phil Collins: vocals, drums, cymbals, percussion
- Steve Hackett: electric guitars, nylon classical guitar, 12-string guitar, kalimba, autoharp
- Mike Rutherford: 4-, 6- and 8-string bass guitars, 12-string electric and acoustic guitars, bass pedals
- Tony Banks: Steinway grand piano, synthesisers, Hammond organ, Fender Rhodes electric piano

THE MAKING OF

1976, the year many sceptics believed would bring their career to a close, actually ended up being one of the busiest and most productive in the band's history. In fact, as soon as the A Trick Of The Tail tour came to an end, the band began writing a follow-up to the album which had consolidated and even augmented their standing in the media. Having quickly written a handful of new songs they set off (with a couple of weeks delay due to the birth of Phil Collins' son, Simon, on 14 September) for Relight Studios in Hilvarenbeek, the Netherlands.

Hackett: "It was economically very difficult to make an album in England at that stage. Taxes were punitive for homegrown products, so we did the recording in Holland and that created its own atmosphere. When you go away and make an album in a specific place, it always colours what's going on, you discover certain things, like interesting keyboards stuck in corners." [1]

Collins: "I don't know why we went out of the country; it wasn't for financial reasons. I think it was probably because we liked the idea of being together and not doing anything else apart from the album, like with The Lamb, where we'd had that experience of writing and recording in a kind of live-in situation, whereas A Trick Of The Tail was done in a different environment, popping up to Trident Studios at St. Anne's Court, you know, between the hookers, so we thought we'd com-

bine the two and go to Holland. I don't particularly have any fond memories of Holland. I mean, we just rented this Dutch house in the middle of nowhere. The studio was pretty good though, I really liked it, and we had a good engineer. Actually, more interestingly for me though, this was the time of the illegal, sort of 'fly-on-the-wall' Troggs Tapes, where someone had recorded these conversations between people in the studio. (*Phil is referring to a rather heated and hilarious discussion between The Trogg's lead singer, Reg Presley, and drummer, Ronnie Bond, which was immortalised in a famous bootleg recording called 'The Troggs Tapes' – author's note*). Quite often I'd be out there in the studio singing and I'd see these conversations going on in the control room between the other two guys (Dave Hentschel and the assistant) and I'd be waiting to see whether I could come in. It got to be very frustrating because they might not even have been talking about what I'd just been doing, they may have been talking about the football. So eventually I put my tape recorders on and left them running. The assistant engineer helped me out and changed the tapes every now and again. I recorded all their conversations and it was like:
'No, you tell him, I ain't gonna tell him, you tell him'.
'No, I told him last time, you tell him'.
All this kind of stuff. I've still got the tapes." [1]

Obviously, the success of A Trick Of The Tail brought a new level of unity within the band and greater confidence in their abilities. Still, it defi-

Tony Banks, Brussels.
28th June 1977

nitely wasn't all plain sailing.

Rutherford: "The writing seemed a little flatter to me, I think because writing the second album (in this case the second without Peter) is always a bit harder. I always see it as a feminine album; there are no real kind of ballsy, driving songs on it and I think it probably suffered from that a bit. Tony was very much involved in the sound of this album; it's probably the album where he had the most influence actually, especially on *One For The Vine* and *Afterglow*." [1]

In fact, very little of the writing for this album was done as a group and, in terms of composition, it is dominated by Banks.

Banks: "*Eleventh Earl Of Mar* and obviously the instrumental pieces towards the end of Side Two emerged from working as a group, but I wrote three of the songs on this album totally on my own: *One For The Vine*, *Afterglow* and *All In A Mouse's Night*." [1]

Rutherford: "Each album has certain songs that are more in someone else's camp. To me, this album feels to be what Tony likes best of all. If you listen to one of Tony's solo albums, the similarities are evident. Which is probably why for me it's a good album but it's not my favourite." [1]

Collins: "Although Pete and Tony were best friends, they were also very different. And possibly, with Peter long gone by this point, Tony realised that he was able to spread out a little bit and get much more of his work out. And of course, with me not writing and Steve writing but maybe not everybody liking what he was bringing in, there was only Tony and Mike. Apart from when we wrote together as a group, out of nothing; that was always one of the strong things about Genesis." [1]

And Hackett was beginning to show increasing signs of disaffection.

Collins: "Sometimes, at group dinners, when everyone started getting past the nicely drunk stage, Steve started to get to the let-me-tell-you-something stage. He started saying things like, 'there are four of us in this band, why can't I have 25% of the material'. I get the impression he felt that he was there and therefore his material should be heard, but, you know, we'd never really worked like that; we've always worked on material that we liked. I mean, I kept bringing things in, you know, and if they weren't liked then I wouldn't have expected them to be heard just because I was in the band." [1]

Rutherford: "It was always a strange scenario when it came to what went on an album; it was a mixture of 'may the best stuff win', so to speak, and who shouted the loudest. There was a certain amount of jockeying to get the stuff you liked most on the album, not so much your song, because they were group written, but each song

Steve Hackett, Brussels, 28th June 1977

had one or two people who were very much in control of it and driving it. So I think Steve had gained confidence and wanted to do more of that. To be honest, there's more of his stuff on this album than on any of the others."[1]

Banks: "You have to appreciate that when we started off, both Phil and Steve were very much junior members, particularly in relation to the composition. At this stage, Mike and I were perhaps more dominant. But Steve definitely had more moments when he came to the fore. This is particularly true on *Blood On The Rooftops* which is a lovely track and one of my favourites from all the ones we ever did."[1]

In the meantime, however, musically speaking, things were changing radically.

Collins: "At the same time we were doing this album, punk was just starting. And there was I thinking 'they can't be talking about us, they're talking about all those other bands that I don't like either. Good, let's get rid of the other lot'. But, yeah, of course, they were talking about us. And I actually agreed, you know. I loved all that stuff, all that 'let's shake the tree and get rid of the rotten stuff', you know, I was all behind that. And it's funny because not long after that, I'd bumped into Topper Headon (*drummer of The Clash – author's note*) or various other people from different bands who would be working at the same studios as me, and they would come up and say, 'I

GENESIS

Italian magazine *Ciao 2001* n. 41, 16th October 1977

just wanna say I'm a big fan of yours'. They would've been fired if anybody had heard them. I know there were a few musicians in those bands who were fans of me as a drummer and probably fans of some of the stuff Genesis did, but maybe not a lot of it."[1]

Rutherford: "Genesis were always slightly outside the loop in terms of the firing line, which is not a bad thing actually, it works both ways; you get less press but it also means that when the press is bad, you get less bad press. I thought it was quite fun and I think it was a good time for music because a lot of bands had got to the stage where they couldn't actually make an album without spending a fortune and having all the big mixers and gear, you know, and then punk came along with just a couple of amps, which I think was very healthy. It was like shaking the apple tree; the good ones stayed and the bad ones came down.

We managed to fool them all, obviously."[1]

The album owes its title to the English novelist, Emily Brontë.

Banks: "It was the working title for what ended up being called *Unquiet Slumbers For The Sleepers*.... The first bit was called *Wind* and the next bit was just called *Wuthering* because it reminded us of an old-fashioned movie score. We were searching for a title for the instrumentals and I just looked at *Wuthering Heights* and saw the last line and thought it could be broken up quite nicely into titles."[1]

THE ALBUM

In the few weeks between completing the A TRICK OF THE TAIL tour and entering the recording studio, the four-piece appeared more together than ever and quickly developed over an hour's worth of music (in fact, three songs had to be left off the album). Whereas the album released in February 1976 had shown a Genesis more focused on vocal tracks, albeit long and complicated ones, the new album saw a decisive shift towards instrumentals. It was almost as if, having now proved to the world that the band's existence did not depend on Peter Gabriel, the four musicians realised they could dedicate their time to what they had always done best: complicated and structured instrumentals, both as song sections and as individual tracks. In fact, three of the new tracks are pure instrumentals. And if *Wot Gorilla?* is basically a (not entirely successful) follow-up to *Los Endos*, the linked tracks, *Unquiet Slumbers For The Sleepers...* and *...In That Quiet Earth*, with their distinct Hackett flavour, highlight a more melancholy musical quality (the former) and a return to fusion (the latter, with solos equally balanced between Steve and Tony). Another track full of instrumental sections is the monumental *One For The Vine*, written by an inspired Tony Banks.

However, a couple of the more direct tracks are not to be ignored. Mike Rutherford's solo writing debut, *Your Own Special Way*, is without a doubt an indicator of the writing style the bass player would pursue in the band's not too distant future, while Banks' anthemic *Afterglow* is definitely a highlight.

Tony also wrote *All In A Mouse's Night*, a quirky song with humorous lyrics which alternates some rather flat moments with others that are extraordinary (above all the final guitar solo which is apt to bring the listener out in goosebumps), whereas *Blood On The Rooftops*, with its classical guitar intro and lovely chorus, is the result of a rare Hackett-Collins compositional joint-venture.

And finally, the opening track, *Eleventh Earl Of Mar*; written as a group effort, it represents the perfect synthesis of the sophisticated entity which is WIND & WUTHERING.

As an album, it comes across as a return to that fantastic balance achieved back in the days of SELLING ENGLAND BY THE POUND. Once again, each member of the band appears to have equal space in terms of both composition and execution. If any one member is slightly more prominent than the others, it has to be Hackett; his unusually high contribution puts his signature on almost half of the songs while his guitar definitely stands out more in the mix than on previous albums. The star player, however, is still Tony Banks, with his multiple keyboards and the complex arrangement of *One For The Vine*, while Rutherford provides his usual solid guitar and exemplary bass (the bass playing on *Eleventh Earl Of Mar* is superlative). As for Collins, his voice gives the necessary softness when required (sometimes even climbing into the realms of falsetto), all the while showing greater prowess. And it goes without saying that his contribution on drums and percussion is, as always, extraordinary.

So, another great record that delights their stalwart fans but which, objectively speaking, on a musical level represents yet another, albeit small, step backwards in musical development after the unrepeatable levels of innovation seen on THE LAMB. This slight regression was exacerbated because of extraordinary developments in the music scene; in the few months separating the release of WIND & WUTHERING from A TRICK OF THE TAIL the world of rock and pop music had been changing at a rate of knots. While Collins, with Brand X, had created the UK's response to the jazz-rock of Weather Report and Joni Mitchell was moving towards jazz with her album HEJIRA, the West Coast was still holding its own with WHISTLING DOWN THE WIRE by Crosby & Nash and LONG MAY YOU RUN by The Stills-Young Band, followed in December by the Eagles' colossal HOTEL CALIFORNIA. Other important, yet very disparate, albums that came out the same year include Al Stewart's YEAR OF THE CAT, Boston's eponymous debut album and Stevie Wonder's SONGS IN THE KEY OF LIFE, not to mention ZOOT ALLURES by Frank Zappa. In the meantime, former band members, Peter Gabriel and Anthony Phillips were busy recording their solo debuts, PETER GABRIEL and the masterpiece

GENESIS

Mike and Steve Brussels, 28th June 1977

The Geese & The Ghost respectively. But more importantly, at the end of November 1976, the Sex Pistols released their single *Anarchy In The UK*. Nothing would ever be the same again.

THE SONGS

ELEVENTH EARL OF MAR

Banks: "This was more of a group song really; it combined bits that I'd written and bits Steve had written and then Mike wrote a lyric for it. It's a little bitty but I'm really pleased with the opening, it's just very distinctive with strange chords. I mean, if you can arrest people with an opening, here's one. I was very pleased with that at the time." [1]

Hackett: "It was mainly put together by Tony, Mike and myself. I also wrote the lyrics to part of the song [from 4'40"], Mike wrote the rest, but musically it's mine." [2]

Hackett's main contribution lies in the bridge, which comes from one of his acoustic pieces, *The House Of The Four Winds*.

Hackett: "I was writing much more material and presenting a lot of ideas to the band. For instance using the kalimba [4'25"] in one part, which was like another song within a song. There's that da da-dar riff [6'08"] with those lead chords where the chord changes actually create the melody... That was something which became part of the band's style and it was an idea I would explore later in my solo work with things like *Spectral Mornings* and the beginning of *Every Day*: a fixed bass note with the chords changing, something that's very easy to write on guitar. It's a style of writing and a style of synthesiser and guitar playing together; a combined melody from the two. It was typical of Genesis to have two instruments making up one sound and I think that predates quite a few of the fusion people who used synth and guitar." [2]

Rutherford: "It was an exciting song and when we wrote it, I thought it could be really powerful but in the end it never quite lived up to its potential. Looking back on it now, it has a rather dodgy lyric (by me), although I'm not sure you can judge lyrics by how you see them today. I suppose it's sort of a period piece." [1]

Hackett: "The story was about a failed Scottish uprising. Funnily enough, in recent years my wife, Jo, and I visited the actual castle where the *Eleventh Earl Of Mar* was based. We looked around at everything and it was funny to visit the scene of the song." [2]

ONE FOR THE VINE

Banks: "When I played this to the guys, I just played the whole thing through, with me sort of warbling on top (I don't know what they thought of that). I think they thought that if we didn't do it I'd get irritable and start throwing things, so they'd just have to give it a go. We put the whole thing down in the studio, just with a piano and drums really and then we sort of overdubbed everything else on top of it. It was just a matter of faith really. In the end, they stuck with me and I think it turned out well actually, and the contribution of all the others is really good. So, I was quite pleased with that also because I had been working on that song since A Trick of the Tail, honing it and trying to get it right." [1]

The track starts with a guitar and keyboard playing in unison.

Hackett: "This is guitar and piano. If I remember correctly, there was also a monophonic synthesiser. So, if you wanted another track, you had to track it again." (2)

Based mainly on piano and, from the second verse, a light rhythm and arpeggio electric guitar, the track develops throughout its 10-minute running time. It alternates between slower and more rhythm-driven moments before coming back to the piano sequence. The piano also dominates the large instrumental section as it chases Collins' relentless drumming.

Hackett: "This track fits the kind of epic mould, with many sections. I think in many ways it's closer in spirit to orchestral music or owes something to opera. That's merely an opinion as I didn't write the song, but you have this central motif [4'40"] that sounds as though it could have come from somewhere between Rimsky-Korsakov and Borodin. It sounds like the influence of the Russians looking towards the Eastern hemisphere. Essentially we were borrowing from other areas. For example, I played the kalimba on this, as I did on the previous track, and later I played the autoharp, but I didn't want to be credited with those otherwise my credits would have gone on and on, leaving other people's looking quite short. I was still quite deferential at this time... Just in case it upset anybody." (2) (*The two instruments do, however, appear alongside Steve's name in the album credits – author's note.*)

The length of the song gives Genesis room for almost limitless development.

Hackett: "I think that, harmonically, Genesis were the most developed group working in progressive music. I think the template was set very early on, by writers such as Jimmy Webb, stuff like *MacArthur Park*, a song that was perhaps 7 minutes long. Many Genesis songs borrowed from that. In other words, you'd have a verse-chorus song structure, but many times with no chorus, just the idea of repeated verses and then it would move away like a concerto or a symphony; it didn't have to remain fixed but was flexible in terms of form and in tempo. It was like having an invisible conductor and we change tempo completely [at 8'37"]. I think

GENESIS

Mike Rutherford, Brussels, 28th June 1977

this is the last of the albums written without the click track. As soon as you have that, you start to tie things down more and there is a tendency to want to maintain the tempo." [2]

Banks: "There were bits that sort of came and went a few times. It's about trying to think how something works and what you're trying to get out of it. I spent a lot of time thinking about it and getting it (hopefully) to my level. Some people will think differently, obviously, but I was pleased with it and I think it works the way it is; I think it moves. When I write, I'm hoping to build people up to a certain point and then, if it works, it sends a shiver down their spine at the right moment. That's what you're trying to do really, so I judge a lot of music by this criterion. I think this song does it two or three times and that's pretty good for me. And while *Eleventh Earl Of Mar* seems a little bitty, particularly the middle section, I think this song works as a totality; although it goes through more sections, each one leads onto the next and to some extent each bit is justified by the lyric as well, which is important to me." [1]

Hackett: "It tells a story; the idea of a leader and peoples and war and so you've immediately got two songs on the subject of leadership. It's not the stuff of regular pop music which is mostly concerned with the idea of love." [2]

YOUR OWN SPECIAL WAY

Rutherford: "I very rarely remember where I wrote something, but I remember writing the riff for this song in a hotel in Brazil. We were there doing some kind of promotion." [1]

Definitely one of the lesser tracks on the album, this song represents the solo writing debut of the band's bass player who plays acoustic guitar while Steve adds the finishing touches, arpeggios and the chorus riff.

Hackett: "I played the autoharp with the tremolo arm. It made those bubbly noises on the chorus which gave it Genesis colour. The band was all about textures and orchestrating. Even if you are only playing one nylon guitar, you can still orchestrate very brightly or very muted like Segovia. It's a very hooky chorus. Mike showed he could write a very accessible song and Phil sounded absolutely right singing that sort of song; he brought in falsetto harmonies, almost like the ones you get on Tamla Motown." [2]

There is also an instrumental passage performed with lightly played electric piano.

Hackett: "This is a beautiful section. If I remember rightly it was something of Tony's that was just inserted inside Mike's song… probably so he could have a credit on it." [2]

The truth, however, is that this section was also composed by Mike. Banks isn't credited at all for this song which carries only Rutherford's signature.

Hackett: "It depends what you consider to be writing. When I joined Genesis, Peter said, 'as soon as you write a guitar part you are a fully-fledged writer and we write as a group', but for these two albums there was this insistence that there should be individual credits. I think Tony wanted to write the majority of the songs but in the name of keeping the band together there was concession and all of a sudden everyone was a writer again." [2]

Rutherford: "It's a song I have a good feeling for and no, not because I wrote it. In those days I was still playing a lot of 12-string with funny, weird tunings, sometimes tuning the double strings in harmony which is quite unusual. This song was done with a funny tuning; I haven't got a clue what it is, I would never be able to find it again now. It came out as a single in America; it didn't do anything but it got some airplay. And suddenly, for the first time ever, the record label thought maybe the band could do something, that we could actually get played on the radio (other than the long songs that got played on late-night radio). It was sort of the start of an uptick in America." [1]

Hackett: "We were able to get on 'The Mike Douglas Show', which was a coast-to-coast TV show. The fact that we appeared doing this song made us accessible to a wider audience and then we were able to play to larger crowds. It's amazing what one TV show can do for you in America; it can do more than 1000 clubs or concert halls. It put us into arenas and consolidated our position in America." [2]

WOT GORILLA?

Collins: "This was actually one of my favourite songs on the whole record because it was a bit like *Los Endos*. It was the fusion, Weather Report side of me, you know, and suddenly I was able to make Tony Banks play this stuff! And they seemed to like it, so it ended up on the album." [1]

The long digressions from Tony on the synthesiser are superbly counterpointed by the powerful drum rolls from Phil in an instrumental track which develops a theme from *One For The Vine* and which was originally intended to have been connected to a piece written by Hackett.

Hackett: "*Wot Gorilla?* used the same Baião rhythm (*a Brazilian rhythm which can be interpreted in different time signatures – author's note*) that is on *Please Don't Touch*. In fact, originally the two songs were joined. It keeps the *One For The Vine* melody, making it more thematic, and therefore the band didn't do *Please Don't Touch*, which is one of the reasons I left the band. I felt that my song had the stronger melody. To me, *Wot Gorilla?* is just a jam and the weakest moment on the album. It's rhythmically very good but insubstantial musically, it's just a bit of atmosphere and a bit of a jam." [2]

For years it was said that *Please Don't Touch* didn't make it onto the album because Collins found it difficult to get behind, but Hackett sets the record straight on that point.

Hackett: "I don't remember saying that and I don't think Phil had trouble drumming on it; in fact, he's the one who suggested the rhythm. *Please Don't Touch* is a variation of *Unquiet Slumbers For The Sleepers…*, which comes up later. For me, if something was very strong, then we should have done it, which is why I really went to town when I did *Please Don't Touch* with Chester Thompson. The whole team that worked on that did a great job and I gave it everything. I was very proud of the way that sounded." [2]

Another song Steve brought into the Wind & Wuthering sessions is *Hoping Love Will Last*. This too was rejected by his bandmates and later appeared in 1978 on Hackett's second solo album Please Don't Touch (along with the title track) beautifully sung by the American singer, Randy Crawford.

ALL IN A MOUSE'S NIGHT

After a spectacular keyboard intro with a mathematical construction (going backwards and forwards on the two-chord descending thirds sequence), the song then completely changes atmosphere and launches into multiple variations over a great rhythm.

Hackett: "As on *Wot Gorilla?*, I played a Fender Stratocaster through a Fender Jazz Chorus amp which gave it a very jangly quality which mixed with the keyboards very well and made it slightly Beatles-y." [2]

The guitar solo in the closing section of the song is one of the finest musical moments in the entire history of Genesis.

Hackett: "I wrote my own phrases for the solo. At times Tony and I played the same thing but I wanted to play controversially, harmonically against what he was doing… what I was doing changed the nature of the chord. My favourite bit [5'27"] is particularly me. I used the same type of thing on *The Steppes* (*from his 1980 album* Defector *– author's note*). Then there's this technique of holding a string and tapping it so you get a sound that's a bit like a siren. And it goes out on a bolero rhythm. The bolero rhythm and rock & roll belong together very much in progressive music. You have that at the end of *Supper's Ready*, so there are certain things that we come back to." [2]

The lyrics narrate the nocturnal escapades of a house mouse including near capture, feline encounters and lucky escapes. At the end of the adventure, the rodent hero is saved by a pot falling on the cat's head (although the cat's side of the story is that rather than being knocked out by a pot, he was confronted by a monster mouse who is 'ten feet tall').

Hackett: "I think that stylistically it's what we were doing around the time of Nursery Cryme. It's clearly a comedic song, quite childlike in that mould heavily influenced by early Gabriel. My wife, Jo, likes a lot of Genesis. She said this song was like visiting other worlds. I think she was about 15 when she heard it and at that age you are just starting to carve out a world of your own, a world of the imagination as at that point in life most of us are still living with our parents. And I think Genesis represented a passport to other worlds, to other times and places. I find myself in a Tom and Jerry cartoon here (nothing wrong with that), the influence of Disney, threads of The Beatles' *I Am The Walrus* and all of that." [2]

Banks: "Peter had gone and he had been good at the humorous lyric, I mean *Harold The Barrel* is a marvellous lyric, and so I was consciously thinking about that even when I did *Robbery Assault And Battery*. With *All In A Mouse's Night*, I was trying to keep it quite light. I'm not sure that the song didn't deserve a better lyric, but anyhow there you go." [1]

BLOOD ON THE ROOFTOPS

Rutherford: "It's a lovely, rather forgotten song and Steve had a big part in it. On the writing side, I think it's one of Steve's best moments." [1]

Opened by a magnificent nylon-string guitar intro performed by Hackett, the song develops with voice and bass joining the classical guitar before the entry of Banks' rich tapestry of keyboard sounds.

Hackett: "I wrote this introduction and I was trying to write something that was complex harmonically and a song based on Phil's suggestion of the title. So, you've got this kind of baroque introduction to something that was intended to be a very unobvious melody, with very unobvious chords. Whenever I play it live (*as a solo artist – author's note*) I have to relearn all the chords as there's not a straight chord in there really, it's always on the move. It's not the kind of thing you can play when you first pick up a guitar. I would expect these changes more from keyboard players than I would from guitarists. I owe it to the fact that I started out listening to Bach and he was the supreme chordsmith. And Jimmy Webb, of course, with his unlikely changes with romantic melodies; he remains a huge influence on Genesis." [2]

The chorus (although Hackett prefers not to call it that) is rich in pathos and enhanced by the drums.

Hackett: "The music here [2'12"] is Phil's. If we'd been writing this years later, this would have been a chorus but actually there is no chorus; it's the same music but the lyrics are changing all the time. That's the product of a young mind at work. I would have straightened it up now so people could sing along with it, but we didn't have radio play then, so we weren't catering to the idea of 'let's hit them with a chorus', we were writing for another kind of audience, one that had the time to deal with all of these variations. There were many changes throughout all the songs, like this harmony [3'14] which is complex and not straightforward. Tony is being the string orchestra with the Mellotron and he's also doing the melody with the ARP Pro Soloist on the oboe setting and then again it goes into the faux chorus. You don't get the song title until a reprise of what would normally have been a chorus. In a way, it's part of the song's strength." [2]

Collins: "My strength in Genesis, even though I was the singer, up until and including Wind & Wuthering was as an arranger. I could see how other people's material could work or could be arranged, you know, 'why don't you play that and I could play this'. An interpreter if you like. I had yet to really write, I just wrote bits (one of my bits ended up on The Lamb). By this point, Steve was starting to get a bit frustrated about his lack of ability to contribute to the band. He had the material he was doing on his own albums and so we may have sided together in as much he had this bit and said, 'have you got anything that you could put with this?' and I brought in something I had. Blood On The Rooftops is the favourite song of comedian, David Baddiel. I heard that he became a Genesis fan as soon as he heard that song. That was one of my earliest things apart from the instrumental stuff of course, like Los Endos and Wot Gorilla?." [1]

Banks: "A couple of times in our career Steve wrote some beautiful songs but without a chorus to hold them together. You needed these focus points for the rest to make sense. So, I wrote the chorus for Entangled and Phil wrote it for Blood On The Rooftops. And Steve proved to be a surprisingly good lyric writer for both of them." [3]

Hackett: "All the levels of action happen on the TV so it's sort of about couch-potatoes in a way, but the younger generation is differing slightly from what the older generation is saying. The older man in the song, the father, wants to turn the TV off as soon as it comes to the news because he knows it's going to be all about bombings and killings, and the implication is that he's seen all of that with the Second World War." [1]

The lyrics start out with the idea of jumping from one TV channel to another.

Hackett: "Channel surfing on the TV is much easier to do these days. Back then you had to get up

Steve and Mike, Brussels, 28th June 1977

and go to the damn thing and push the buttons. It's also about apathy and war and I think it's very relevant at the moment when we have this tremendous time of political apathy. I think the most provocative line, possibly, is 'for when we got bored, we'd have a world war' which is a bit insulting in some ways for those who were just stuck in it… And yet at the same time it's apathy that creates wars and suddenly we are back in that time where the finger is being pointed at the refugees, where everything is their fault and Europe is adopting a fortress mentality. But I'm proud of the song and I think it means more now than it did then. It's complex lyrically and harmonically and ultimately it's a song about peace." [2]

UNQUIET SLUMBERS FOR THE SLEEPERS… … IN THAT QUIET EARTH

Unquiet Slumbers For The Sleepers… is very reminiscent of Steve's solo work: classical pizzicato guitar with a restless softness and an ephemeral and dark synth over which only the tympanic bass provides some sense of rhythm.

Hackett: "Yeah, this is very floaty and diaphanous. I wrote this melody [0'11"] which is wistful and dreamlike. I still think it's a pretty little melody, more akin to classical music really and a bit of Spanish music. It's very difficult to do it live. I have played it live but it's not easy… all songs that are based on arpeggios are hard to play live as the whole band has to be able to hear it but you have the arpeggios creating a kind of wash, so it's hard to keep tempo with it. I would say that from *Blood On The Rooftops* to the end of the album is where my heart is. It's not the strongest but it's what I believed in the most. At 1'30" you have Mike's melody and at this point you have piano carrying on the idea of the rippling guitar and I'm playing the guitar in a way that's almost like the music to accompany a silent film, again very wistful, I think of this as being very WIND & WUTHERING. It's like playing the piano to a black and white film." [2]

But then, anticipated by a long snare drum roll, the song segues into … *In That Quiet Earth*. Collins' opening drum pattern is in 9/8 and drives the track forward at a high tempo and with hints of fusion. This first section of … *In That Quiet Earth* is led by Hackett's solo electric guitar, accompanied by Rutherford's 12-string arpeggios. The second section (starting at 2'48" and introduced by a reprise of a theme from *Eleventh Earl Of Mar*) is led by Banks' synthesiser and Rutherford's heavy rhythm guitar.

Hackett: "At this stage I think what was more important to Phil was arranging, taking melodies and transforming them, as with these two tracks. In particular you have … *In That Quiet Earth,* which was originally written in a different tempo, and Phil suggested changing that to facilitate a fast rhythm, as he'd done with *Los Endos*. It's a very interesting rhythm; it might be 3/4 but what you have is a very unlikely melody over the top of it. I worked on this with Mike; he played chords and I played lead. The next change [2'23"] is Mike's… it's like fusion where you have synth and guitar playing together. If I'm right, this predates all the work that Jeff Beck did with Jan Hammer etc. I may be wrong, but I like to think that we were doing all that stuff as Genesis many years ago… Part of the calling card of Genesis, you know, 'what instrument is it?' 'what is he doing with that?'. Some people thought it was

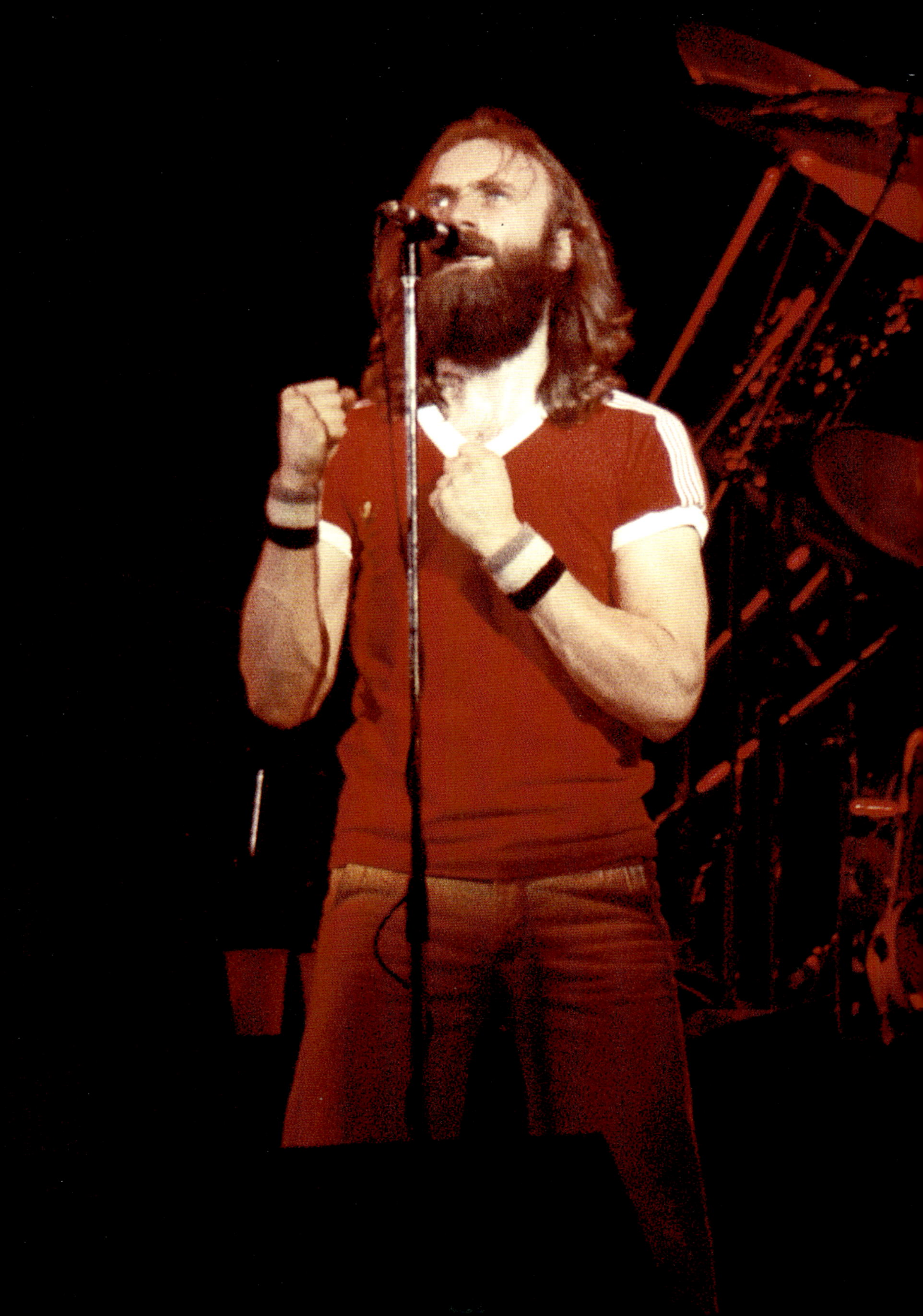

Phil Collins, San Francisco,
25th March 1977

synth playing at first but it was guitar. I was using the Strat, recording it three times with lots of tremolo, and then the synth takes another lead from that. Great drumming from Phil, I have to say, great breaks; the influence of Buddy Rich... And then the synth [2'43"] and Mike's bit [2'48"] where the band sounds wonderful, and then there's a bit where Tony comes in over the top with the most unlikely but truly creative thing and then stops [3'08"] to then continue in a way that's a bit like *Dance On A Volcano* [3'23"]." [2]

At the end [4'34"] there is another reprise of the melody from *Eleventh Earl Of Mar*.

Collins: "The whole instrumental thing in ... *In That Quiet Earth* and *Unquiet Slumbers For The Sleepers*... also stands up pretty well. We've actually been playing whole sections of that in recent years because sometimes the instrumental stuff stands up better than some of the vocal songs." [1]

AFTERGLOW

A glorious finale for the album, with a song based on delicate arpeggios on electric guitar and featuring one of Collins' best ever vocal performances. Banks: "I wrote it in just about the time it took to play it. I just sort of sat down and thought I just fancied using that chord sequence and then started singing on it. I was really excited by that because I don't normally do things like that. But then a couple of days later, I suddenly thought, 'shit! what I've done is rewrite *Have Yourself A Merry Little Christmas*!'. A terrible thought! So, I went and listened to that particular song (*written in 1943 by Hugh Martin and Ralph Blane, originally sung by Judy Garland and later by Frank Sinatra – author's note*) and realised that it wasn't the same and I could get away with it. *Afterglow* went on to become a big stage favourite. It's a very strong anthemic kind of piece and I think it closed the album really well." [1]

Hackett: "Something else which is used on this album is an idea I had about using voice loops. So often, a lot of the big "ahhhs" is Phil's voice tracked up a lot of times. You hear it on *Eleventh Earl Of Mar* but most fully on this track. That was my idea but we were using the 24 tracks on the console, so to make chords you had to use faders as there wasn't any sampling like you have now. We tracked Phil's voice three times on each loop with a slight distortion so when you get 3 together it sounds quite brassy. You can tell when they come in as you get a kind of Panavision feeling across the stereo as though you are travelling. Again, it's a lovely song but with no real chorus as you don't get the repeated refrain. Even now I find it very emotional even if I didn't write it. I tried to play it like George Harrison, you know, a jangly sound. I didn't want to play a solo on it. I could have pushed for it but it would have ruined it; it's a perfect song, it didn't need embellishing. I just doubled up on some parts [2'18"]." [2]

Banks' lyrics seem to be the story of lost love, but it's open to being interpreted in different ways,

Banks: "It's more about putting yourself in an imaginary situation, you know, like death and destruction and how you'd respond to it. So, I was actually visualising a relationship within it but not one that related totally to me but to how I might be in a certain situation. That slightly personal thing does help it a bit, I think; it pulls it slightly back." [1]

Hackett: "It's essentially about losing someone...

I won't comment further on the source of that story. It's a beautiful song and probably served as a healing, I should think. It's the last song on the last album and a good one to go out on… leave it there… leave it on a perfect sunset…" [2]

OTHER SONGS

During the Wind & Wuthering sessions the band also recorded another three tracks which would later be released as the EP Spot The Pigeon.

Match Of The Day is a light-hearted song based on a bass loop and rhythm guitar riff (by Mike and Steve). In his lyrics, Phil talks about the English people's veneration for football (the drummer would later be so embarrassed about the lyrics as to veto the song's inclusion in the Genesis Archive #2 box set released in 2000).

The rather short *Pigeons* is a sort of repetitive march with Hackett playing one single constantly repeated note the whole way through it. The lyrics by Mike, incredible as it may seem, talk about the damage caused by pigeons and their droppings.

Inside And Out is on a different level entirely; introduced by acoustic 12-string guitars, it has a lovely chorus with Collins' voice doubled two octaves higher, singing words he himself had written that narrate why the main character is in prison. The second part, entirely instrumental, is led by a fine electric guitar solo performed by Hackett.

Hackett: "Spot The Pigeon marks the moment when the band started to move away from rock and edge towards pop. Whereas *Inside And Out* develops and picks up energy, the two shorter songs never really lent themselves to further development. To some extent they were attempts at London comedy, but neither of them was musically developed enough to be included on Wind & Wuthering: they simply weren't good enough, they were just a couple of fillers." [4]

THE ALBUM ARTWORK

The beautiful cover art is again by Colin Elgie at Hipgnosis. Elgie painted an image of autumn: a tree shrouded in mist with leaves that have already turned, twirling away in the wind. The artwork was influenced by a scene from a film (set in the Medieval period) called *The War Lord*, where birds take flight from a tree.

Hackett: "I like it. I think it reflects the album title very well. You really feel the strong wind implied there. Wuthering means a strong wind and a sense of the wild. It is a Yorkshire word. Emily Brontë, who wrote *Wuthering Heights*, lived on the windy moors of Yorkshire. It also picks up on the words "dark and grey" on the song *Blood on the Rooftops*." [5]

EPILOGUE

Banks: "We were more confident with this album, in the sense that we didn't feel we had to prove we could survive without Peter. We had quite a lot of music written beforehand for this album and when we finished recording it, the only thing that worried me a little was that it was really quite a heavy album (particularly when we left out those three quite simple tracks). It's quite a difficult album, but I like that. I always like an album to be a challenge. This wasn't an album that was going to

US promotional poster, Atco Records

be liked first time; apart from *Your Own Special Way*, virtually every other track requires quite a bit of listening to get into it. I remember the reviews were sort of 'oh, a bit disappointing after A TRICK OF THE TAIL' type thing, but I think for the fans it's a better album and it's one of my two favourite Genesis albums. I think it's got so many good moments on it and it's also the most extreme in terms of the harmonic area and probably the most complex album we did in musical terms." (1)

Hackett: "This was the last album, I think, where Genesis did things on a wider scale, with romantic music. I think as the band got smaller there was a different atmosphere, they wanted to change and have less emphasis on instrumental work. But at this time you can tell there is still a tremendous amount of instrumental stuff which gives the album colour and richness and it still fits into the progressive music mould." (2)

Banks: "ON A TRICK OF THE TAIL, two or three things were quite instant. The transition over to Phil went very smoothly and we had a couple of really great live songs such as *Los Endos* and *Squonk*. WIND & WUTHERING was a little trickier, a little more thought-out. It was great really because Steve's contribution on that album was probably a bit more than it had been on previous ones." (6)

Genesis proceeded on the commercial wave of their new direction, even though the record dropped four places in the UK charts (reaching only No. 7), while in the US it made it to No. 26. The single, *Your Own Special Way*, entered the charts at No. 46 back home and No. 87 in the States (the EP SPOT THE PIGEON fared somewhat better, reaching No. 14 in the UK).

Banks: "I think it's a romantic album. That's probably why I like it as much as I do. That area of music excites me more. The chords are much more expansive and the way they totally change is more sort of yearning. It's about as far away as you can get from straight-ahead, three-chord rock." (1)

Hackett: "I know Tony's fond of this album and so am I. I think it's an album that was probably still uncompromised by the need to have hit singles. Looking back, I think perhaps *Afterglow* could have made a hit single. I doubt my strongest song, *Blood On The Rooftops*, would have made a single. But, you know, when we were making the album there wasn't the pressure of having to do three-minute songs that were going to be acceptable for a video, etc. I do think it's the band at its best, doing perhaps what it did best, at least with my inclusion in it. So, yeh, I am very fond of it." (1)

However, Mike Rutherford's views on the album are more critical: "I don't think Genesis has ever really pandered to the styles of fashion. We've always been in our own little sort of world really. With this album I was starting to find that we were becoming a slight caricature of ourselves, you know, one long song of a certain style and one short one... A little pattern was emerging which is probably not a good thing. And no one really wrote very direct lyrics; that came more with the next album." (1)

THE CONCERTS

With the unexpected success of the A Trick Of The Tail tour now behind them, Genesis again found themselves in the uncomfortable position of having to sort out their live line-up, seeing as Bill Bruford, who had not, in any case, been a perfect musical fit, was never intended to be more than a temporary solution. The band chose Chester Thompson (born 1948, Baltimore, US) whose impressive CV included Weather Report and Frank Zappa's The Mothers Of Invention.

Thompson: "I was playing in San Francisco when Alphonso Johnson, who'd met Phil, told me Genesis were looking for a drummer. Phil had heard Zappa's live album, Roxy & Elsewhere, and he'd seen me play live with Weather Report in London. He got the number of where I was staying off Alphonso, called me up and asked if I was interested in playing with Genesis. Of course I was. I'd only ever heard one album of theirs, A Trick Of The Tail, but I loved it." [7]

Thompson arrived in the UK at the end of November. This left very little time for him to rehearse Genesis' repertoire as the tour was due to start on New Year's Day 1977 to mark a special occasion: the reopening of the legendary Rainbow Theatre following four years of closure. The first leg of the tour envisaged eighteen UK dates, sometimes with two shows on the same day. After the three consecutive nights at the Rainbow, the tour moved on to Birmingham, Liverpool, Manchester, Dundee, Edinburgh, Newcastle, Southampton, Leicester and Bristol.

On 1 January, Genesis performed the following setlist: *Eleventh Earl Of Mar / The Carpet Crawlers / Firth Of Fifth / Your Own Special Way / Robbery Assault And Battery /... In That Quiet Earth – Afterglow / Lilywhite Lilith – Wot Gorilla? / One For The Vine / Squonk / All In A Mouse's Night / Supper's Ready / I Know What I Like / Dance On A Volcano – Los Endos / The Lamb Lies Down On Broadway – The Musical Box*. Despite getting an ecstatic response from the audience, things were not all perfect: Chester, understandably, still wasn't quite up to speed and, of the new songs, *Your Own Special Way* really didn't work well live, especially the central part steered by Tony's keyboards. Hackett: "Even though it's a fairly long song it doesn't have the drama of other songs. I felt that it was a good love song but it was compromised by the need to have too many sections." [2]

The next day the band decided to alter the setlist. The rather odd medley made up of *Lilywhite Lilith* and *Wot Gorilla?* (including a few fragments of *The Waiting Room*) was dropped and some minor changes were made to the running order: *Robbery, Assault And Battery* was brought forward to become the third song on the setlist, while *Firth Of Fifth* was moved to be placed after *One For The Vine*. More changes were seen at the Liverpool show on 9 January as the band played: *Squonk / One For The Vine / Robbery Assault And Battery / Your Own Special Way / ... In That Quiet Earth – Afterglow / I Know What I Like / Eleventh Earl Of Mar / The Carpet Crawlers / All In A Mouse's Night* (afternoon concert only) */ Firth Of Fifth / Supper's Ready / Dance On A Volcano – Los Endos / The Lamb Lies Down On Broadway – The Musical Box*. This setlist remained in place for the rest of the UK tour except for one slight change; starting on the 14th in Edinburgh *Firth Of Fifth* was, appropriately enough, moved up to fifth place on the setlist coming straight after *Your Own Special Way*.

Poster from the Brazilian magazine *Hitpop*, 1977

It was a superb setlist which afforded ample space to both albums recorded as a four-piece (four tracks off A TRICK OF THE TAIL and six off WIND & WUTHERING) while at the same time continuing to delve into their fantastic past, confirming most of the classic tracks included on the previous tour.

Hackett: "We were doing *Squonk* as an opener and I remember going on stage and the whole audience standing up as we kicked in with the first strains of that; it was a really powerful live number." [1]

Dance On A Volcano, now without its instrumental ending, was linked up to *Los Endos*.

Banks: "I have to be honest, I was never very keen on the last part of *Dance On A Volcano*; it was a bit too tricksy and, for me, it didn't really work. It was one of Steve's bits and it was an area of his work that I was less keen on and I know that Mike and Phil felt much the same way about it. Later on, when we did medleys, we'd always try to get rid of the bits we were less keen on, and this was one of those." [3]

Particularly interesting is the bridge between two songs, a short drumming duet which in later tours would become an increasingly more important part of the set.

Thompson: "We changed it with each tour and it got bigger and better, for me and Phil it was always great fun. The problem was we'd often put it towards the end of the show, and by then, after playing a whole concert, we were already pretty exhausted. It would probably have been better if we'd done it earlier on." [7]

Rutherford: "It was a great sound; there's nothing like Phil and Chester. Two drummers is a very powerful machine, especially when they are sympathetic." [8]

The other surprise came with the encore which put together an unabridged version of *The Lamb Lies Down On Broadway* and the end of *The Musical Box* (from the guitar arpeggio leading into 'She's a lady....' through to the end, with Phil running to get back behind the second drum kit for the closing notes).

Not only did the band put on an elaborate light show, especially the double row of overhead lights and laser beams, but, having already brilliantly overcome the shocking loss of Gabriel on the pre-

GENESIS

Promotional photo, Atlantic Records 1977

Poster taken from the German magazine *Pop*, October 1977

Tony Banks • Chester Thompson • Mike Rutherford • Phil Collins • Steve Hackett

GENESIS

vious tour, they seemed much more at ease on stage. Phil continued to talk about the erotic feats of Romeo and Juliet, only now before *Supper's Ready* and not *The Cinema Show* (which was no longer in the setlist) and Mike and Steve were still introducing a few of the songs (Mike introducing *Your Own Special Way* and *Eleventh Earl Of Mar*, and Steve *Firth Of Fifth*).

After just a week's break, the tour moved across the Atlantic. Starting out in Boulder, Colorado, it then made its way through the states of Oklahoma, Missouri, Minnesota, Wisconsin, Michigan, Illinois, New York, Massachusetts, Pennsylvania, Maryland, Tennessee, Georgia, Louisiana, Texas, California, Arizona and Washington whilst squeezing in half a dozen or so shows in Canada along the way.

The setlist was switched around again slightly for the concerts in North America (*The Carpet Crawlers* was moved forward a couple of places and *All In A Mouse's Night* was dropped). So, throughout the North American leg of the tour the set-

Wind & Wuthering

The new Jerusalem - San Francisco 25th March 1977

Hall in Arlington on 18 March and at the Paramount Theatre in Portland on 1 April), the tour was a resounding success.

The previous A TRICK OF THE TAIL tour in Northern America had included over thirty shows, this time round that number had almost doubled and one cannot help but notice three consecutive dates in Chicago and shows held in venerable venues such as Madison Square Garden in the Big Apple.

This success was almost definitely boosted by the band's first appearance on a popular US television show; filmed in Philadelphia just a few days

list was: *Squonk / One For The Vine / Robbery Assault And Battery / Your Own Special Way / Firth Of Fifth / The Carpet Crawlers / ... In That Quiet Earth – Afterglow / I Know What I Like / Eleventh Earl Of Mar / Supper's Ready / Dance On A Volcano / Los Endos / The Lamb Lies Down On Broadway – The Musical Box.*

Despite two dates being cancelled (at the Texas

Poster advertising the concert in Seattle, 3rd April 1977, promoted by the John Bauer Concert Company

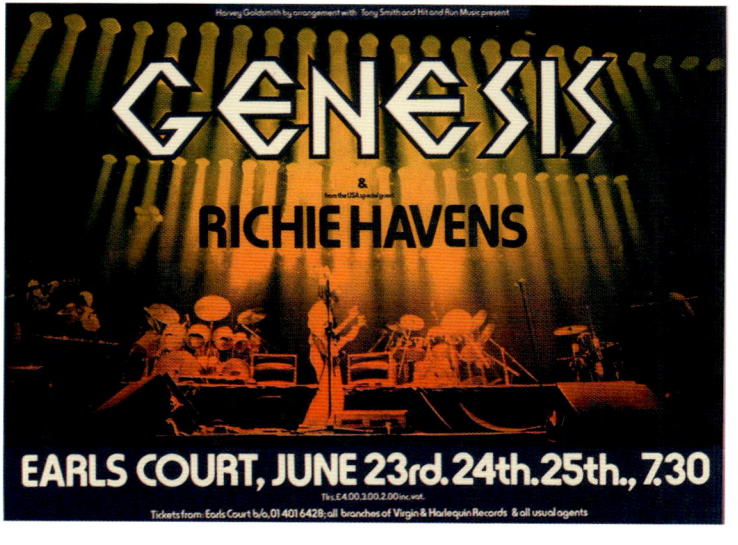

Poster advertising the three concerts at London's Earls Court in June 1977, with Richie Havens supporting. Concerts promoted by Harvey Goldsmith

/ *Musical Box*. This is a fantastic piece of footage which for some mysterious reason would be almost the only omission in the bonus video material included in the 2008 remastered reissue.

After a month off, the band departed for their first ever visit to South America with a dozen shows between 10 and 22 May. Some cities (such as Rio De Janeiro and San Paolo) benefitted from two shows on the same day, one in the afternoon and one in the evening. The setlist was the same as for the North American leg with just one, but important, change: *Your Own Special Way* was finally dropped, making way for *Inside And Out*.

The Brazilian tour was also a huge success, with the band playing in large venues to around half a million fans over a dozen or so shows. The only setback occurred during the second of the two shows in Porto Alegre (11

before being aired on 29 March, 'The Mike Douglas Show' featured Genesis miming to the two catchiest songs on the album: *Your Own Special Way* (in an abridged version) and *Afterglow*. In terms of archive film footage, of even greater importance on an artistic level is the 25-minute excerpt from the concert given 10 days earlier in Dallas (19 March) capturing *Firth Of Fifth*, *Dance On A Volcano* / *Los Endos* and *The Lamb*

Wind & Wuthering

Poster advertising the Festival in Cologne, Germany, on 17th June 1977. Promoted by Mama Concerts

May) when a rather unwell Rutherford had to dash backstage halfway through the performance bringing it to an abrupt end. A statement released by management the following day said that bacteria in the city's water supply had caused the musician's indisposition.

In June, Genesis were back in Europe. They started out in Stockholm on the 4th before moving on to Berlin. The band then played four shows in Paris (recordings of these concerts in the French capital were released a few months later as the extraordinary live album Seconds Out) followed by dates in Cologne, Offenbach am Main and Bremen in Germany before three shows at London's Earls Court opened by Richie Havens. Genesis gave their home fans an additional encore, an abridged version of *The Knife* (without the long instrumental interlude).

The last shows in the tour, between the end of June and the beginning of July, took place in Brussels, Rotterdam, Colmar and Zurich with the tour ending in Munich on 3 July (this show had originally been scheduled for 26 June).

This tour succeeded in consolidating Genesis' standing; at long last they were stars in the UK, popular throughout Europe and had a growing following in America, added to which they gained their first and fantastic foothold in the South American market. The five musicians were, quite simply, in magnificent form. Chester Thompson was the perfect drummer for Genesis; with his great technique placed at the band's service, he thankfully lacked Bruford's wilfulness. Now, more confident than ever in his role as frontman and having acquired a certain amount of rapport with the audience, Phil sang perfectly, ironing out the few imperfections of the previous tour, and his contribution on drums was spectacular, not only in the instrumentals … *In That Quiet Earth* and *Los Endos*, but also in sections of *One For The Vine*, *Robbery, Assault And Battery*, *Firth Of Fifth*, *Supper's Ready* and doubling up on drums for the final sections of *Afterglow* and *The Musical Box*. Mike was at the top of his game as an instrumentalist, playing on his new Shergold double-neck guitar with a 12-string at the top and bass at the bottom, not forgetting his essential contributions on bass pedals.

GENESIS

Mike Rutherford, San Francisco, 25th March 1977

Wind & Wuthering

Phil Collins, San Francisco, 25th March 1977

Tony was phenomenal as always on his array of keyboards, while Steve (who had already stopped playing sitting down on the previous tour) appeared at perfect ease, with his guitar solos enjoying greater space than usual. With major success finally knocking on their door, what more could Genesis have wanted? However, for one band member, success did not appear to be enough.

Hackett: "I was starting to write more and more material and it was harder and harder to incorporate that into a band format. Plus, I wanted to work with other people. Brilliant though the members of Genesis were, I felt I had to take the risk in order to find out just how good I was on my own. There's a voice that tells you that you've got to see whether you're up to scratch or not. Doing the first solo record (VOYAGE OF THE ACOLYTE, 1975) was a bit like turning on a tap."[1]

Steve Hackett, San Francisco, 25th March 1977

Banks: "I think Steve probably felt that he couldn't get enough of his own writing into the band. He felt that Genesis was always going to be dominated a little bit by what Mike and I decided and that he wouldn't be able to get his stuff through. I have to say, there were various things that he wrote that we didn't do, you know, that maybe we didn't particularly go for. You know the important thing was that we all had to like it, unless you shouted very loud, in which case you ended up doing it anyhow, like I did with *One for the Vine*. I think he felt frustrated by that and I'm sure that was one of the reasons why he left. Beyond that, I've no idea. Perhaps he thought it was time to try and go solo and you know, take his chances." [1]

Hackett: "Wind & Wuthering is a great album and the stuff I had left stood me in good stead for future albums. Some of the ideas I had presented to the band and were turned down went onto Please Don't Touch and Spectral Mornings (part of *Tigermoth*). Forty years ago I had something to prove, and I still do. I don't think group's members should be competitive with each other, you should try to bring out the best in everyone. If I work on a solo album for someone else, whoever they are, I do what they want. If Tchaikovsky asks me to do a guitar solo, well, he's the boss... But in a group it shouldn't be like that, but one person always wants to be the Fuhrer. The Beatles, the Stones all managed to produce good stuff, but I sympathise with Bill Wyman who wrote the riff *Jumpin' Jack Flash* is based on but got no writing credit at all for. I can't complain with Genesis because I am credited with a number of things that I didn't really write, as we used to put it all as being done by everyone." [2]

Banks: "I always suspected that Steve was going to leave at some point but I thought, with Wind & Wuthering, things would be OK as he was getting rather more across on that album. But I think, having done a solo album, he had psychologically moved on. But we certainly missed his presence on the next album." [6]

NOTES

(1) Mike Kaufman's Genesis interviews, Chicago / London, October 2007, partially used in the bonus disc accompanying the 2008 remasters

(2) Mario Giammetti listening to 'Wind & Wuthering' with Steve Hackett, Naples, Chiaja Hotel De Charme, 12 September 2016

(3) Mario Giammetti's telephone interview with Tony Banks, 26 February 2016 - partially published in the article "Senza Gabriel" in *Classic Rock*, issue n. 44, July 2016

(4) Mario Giammetti's telephone interview with Steve Hackett, 20 April 2000, partially published in the article "Steve & John Hackett – intervista esclusiva", *Dusk*, Issue n. 32, June 2000

(5) Personal e-mail sent to Mario Giammetti by Steve Hackett, dated 21 June 2017

(6) Mario Giammetti's interview with Tony Banks, London, Tony Smith Personal Management office, 29 November 2016

(7) Mario Giammetti's telephone interview with Chester Thompson, 13 August 1999, partially published in the article "Speciale interviste – Chester Thompson", *Dusk*, Issue n. 30, October 1999

(8) Mario Giammetti's telephone interview with Mike Rutherford, 25 February 2016 - partially published in the article "Senza Gabriel" in *Classic Rock*, issue n. 44, July 2016

Wind & Wuthering Tour

1977

JANUARY

- **01** **London (ENGLAND)**, Rainbow Theatre
- **02** **London (ENGLAND)**, Rainbow Theatre
- **03** **London (ENGLAND)**, Rainbow Theatre
- **07** **Birmingham (ENGLAND)**, Odeon Theatre
- **08** **Birmingham (ENGLAND)**, Odeon Theatre
- **09** **Liverpool (ENGLAND)**, Empire Theatre
  Two shows
- **10** **Manchester (ENGLAND)**, Free Trade Hall
- **11** **Manchester (ENGLAND)**, Free Trade Hall
- **13** **Dundee (SCOTLAND)**, Caird Hall
- **14** **Edinburgh (SCOTLAND)**, Playhouse Theatre
  Two shows
- **15** **Edinburgh (SCOTLAND)**, Playhouse Theatre
- **16** **Newcastle (ENGLAND)**, City Hall
- **17** **Newcastle (ENGLAND)**, City Hall
- **19** **Southampton (ENGLAND)**, Gaumont Theatre
- **20** **Southampton (ENGLAND)**, Gaumont Theatre
- **21** **Leicester (ENGLAND)**, De Montfort Hall
  Two shows
- **22** **Leicester (ENGLAND)**, De Montfort Hall
- **23** **Bristol (ENGLAND)**, Hippodrome
  Two shows

FEBRUARY

- **02** **Boulder, CO (USA)**, Macky Auditorium - University of Colorado at Boulder
- **04** **Tulsa, OK (USA)**, Municipal Theater
- **05** **Kansas City, MO (USA)**, Municipal Auditorium
- **06** **St. Louis, MO (USA)**, Kiel Auditorium
- **08** **Minneapolis, MN (USA)**, Orpheum Theatre
- **09** **Madison, WI (USA)**, Dane County Memorial Coliseum
- **10** **Milwaukee, WI (USA)**, Milwaukee Auditorium
- **12** **Detroit, MI (USA)**, Masonic Auditorium
- **13** **Kalamazoo, MI (USA)**, Wings Stadium
- **15** **Chicago, IL (USA)**, Auditorium Theatre - Roosevelt University
- **16** **Chicago, IL (USA)**, Auditorium Theatre - Roosevelt University
- **17** **Chicago, IL (USA)**, Auditorium Theatre - Roosevelt University
- **19** **Winnipeg, MB (CANADA)**, Winnipeg Arena
- **21** **Kitchener, ON (CANADA)**, Kitchener Memorial Auditorium
- **23** **New York, NY (USA)**, Madison Square Garden
- **24** **Boston, MA (USA)**, Music Hall
- **25** **Hartford, CT (USA)**, Bushnell Center
- **26** **Syracuse, NY (USA)**, Onondaga County War Memorial
- **27** **Richfield, OH (USA)**, Richfield Coliseum
- **28** **Buffalo, NY (USA)**, Buffalo Memorial Auditorium

MARCH

- **02** **Montréal, QC (CANADA)**, Forum
- **03** **Québec, QC (CANADA)**, Colisée de Québec
- **04** **Toronto, ON (CANADA)**, Maple Leaf Gardens
- **05** **Ottawa, ON (CANADA)**, Ottawa Civic Centre
- **06** **Toronto, ON (CANADA)**, Maple Leaf Gardens
- **08** **Philadelphia, PA (USA)**, The Spectrum
- **09** **Baltimore, MD (USA)**, Baltimore Civic Center
- **10** **Pittsburgh, PA (USA)**, Civic Arena
- **12** **Nashville, TN (USA)**, Memorial Gymnasium - Vanderbilt University
- **13** **Atlanta, GA (USA)**, Fox Theatre
- **16** **New Orleans, LA (USA)**, Municipal Auditorium
- **17** **Houston, TX (USA)**, Sam Houston Coliseum
- **19** **Dallas, TX (USA)**, Moody Coliseum - Southern Methodist University
- **21** **Austin, TX (USA)**, Municipal Auditorium
- **24** **Inglewood, CA (USA)**, The Forum
- **25** **San Francisco, CA (USA)**, Winterland Arena
- **26** **San Francisco, CA (USA)**, Winterland Arena
- **27** **San Diego, CA (USA)**, San Diego Sports Arena
- **29** **Phoenix, AZ (USA)**, Civic Center

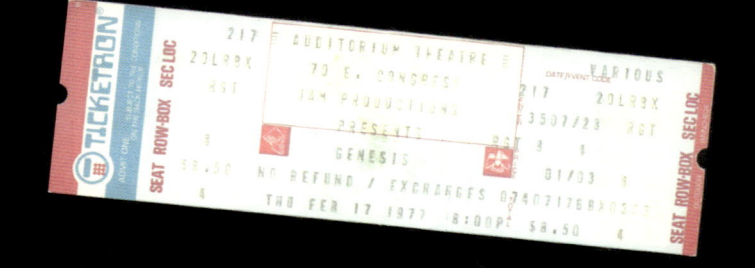

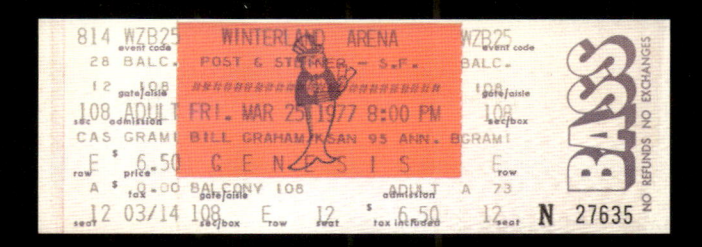

APRIL
02 **Vancouver, BC (CANADA)**, Pacific Coliseum
03 **Seattle, WA (USA)**, Paramount Northwest

MAY
10 **Pôrto Alegre (BRAZIL)**, Ginásio Gigantinho
11 **Pôrto Alegre (BRAZIL)**, Ginásio Gigantinho
14 **Rio de Janeiro (BRAZIL)**, Maracanãzinho
   Two shows
15 **Rio de Janeiro (BRAZIL)**, Maracanãzinho
   Two shows
18 **São Paulo (BRAZIL)**, Estádio Anhembi
19 **São Paulo (BRAZIL)**, Estádio Anhembi
20 **São Paulo (BRAZIL)**, Ginásio do Ibirapuera
   Two shows
21 **São Paulo (BRAZIL)**, Ginásio do Ibirapuera
   Two shows
22 **São Paulo (BRAZIL)**, Ginásio do Ibirapuera
   Two shows

JUNE
04 **Stockholm (SWEDEN)**, Johanneshovs Isstadion
06 **Berlin (WEST GERMANY)**, Deutschlandhalle
11 **Paris (FRANCE)**, Palais des Sports
12 **Paris (FRANCE)**, Palais des Sports
13 **Paris (FRANCE)**, Palais des Sports
14 **Paris (FRANCE)**, Palais des Sports
17 **Cologne (WEST GERMANY)**, Müngersdorfer Stadion
19 **Offenbach (WEST GERMANY)**, Stadion am Bieberer Berg
20 **Bremen (WEST GERMANY)**, Stadthalle
23 **London (ENGLAND)**, Earls Court
24 **London (ENGLAND)**, Earls Court
25 **London (ENGLAND)**, Earls Court
28 **Forest (BELGIUM)**, Forest National
   Two shows
29 **Rotterdam (THE NETHERLANDS)**, Ahoy Sportpaleis

JULY
01 **Colmar (FRANCE)**, Parc des Expositions
02 **Zürich (SWITZERLAND)**, Hallenstadion
03 **Munich (WEST GERMANY)**, Olympiahalle
   Re-scheduled from June 26

...And Then There Were Three...
(Charisma, 1978)

Down And Out (Collins-Banks-Rutherford) / Undertow (Banks) / Ballad Of Big (Collins-Banks-Rutherford) / Snowbound (Rutherford) / Burning Rope (Banks) /// Deep In The Motherlode (Rutherford) / Many Too Many (Banks) / Scenes From A Night's Dream (Collins-Banks) / Say It's Alright Joe (Rutherford) / The Lady Lies (Banks) / Follow You Follow Me (Rutherford-Banks-Collins)

- Release date: 24 March 1978
- Engineer: David Hentschel
- Assistant Engineer: Pierre Geoffroy Chateau
- Recorded at Relight Studios, Hilvarenbeek, Netherlands, in September 1977
- Mixed at Trident Studios, London, with the help of Assistant Engineer, Steve Short
- Produced by David Hentschel and Genesis
- Sleeve design and photographs: Hipgnosis

- **Tony Banks: keyboards**
- **Philip Collins: drums, percussion, vocals**
- **Mike Rutherford: basses, guitar**

THE MAKING OF

Genesis had never been so popular. As soon as the Wind & Wuthering tour was over, they began work on mixing a live album, mainly from recordings of the Paris show held on 14 June 1977 (just one track, *The Cinema Show*, with Bill Bruford on drums, was taken from the previous tour). It was right in the middle of all this that Steve Hackett left the band.

Hackett: "When we were doing the A Trick Of The Tail tour, one of the guys from Chrysalis Records asked if he could film one of the soundchecks and the band agreed. But because it was Chrysalis (*the label that had just released Hackett's solo album in America – author's note*) the camera was on me. Mike Rutherford got very annoyed, threw down his guitar and walked off. Then he wanted to have a meeting with Tony and myself. He had obviously spoken to Tony and wound him up and this is where it all came out. They started saying 'we don't think you're giving everything to the band blah blah'. So I said, 'well, give me space within the band', but that wasn't on offer. Clearly Tony felt that they could be a huge success without me… and who was I to doubt them? So, I stuck with it for one more album (Wind & Wuthering) in case there might be a change in the amount of ideas that I might give. But, as you can see, it's got Tony's credits everywhere." [1]

Rutherford: "I'm not quite sure to this day what happened really. We were mixing the live album and Phil bumped into Steve in the street. He'd said hello but then he didn't come into the studio. It was sort of weird really, I'm not sure we knew what was going on. He didn't come and talk to us; he just sort of left. But, in a way, maybe I sensed it coming. His solo album had been very important to him and I think he wanted to do more work in that area. And probably he felt that with Genesis he couldn't be as free." (2)

Collins: "We were mixing SECONDS OUT and I passed him on Ladbroke Grove waiting for a cab. So, I stopped and said 'hey, hop in, I'll take you there'. He said 'No, no. It's okay, I'll call you later'. I didn't think anything of it. When I got to the studio, I said I'd seen Steve, and Tony and Mike said, 'did he tell you?'. 'Tell me what?' And they said he'd left. He has since said, apparently, that had he got in the car with me that day, he wouldn't have left the band. He said I was the one person who would've talked him out of it. It's probably true. I'd have worked out some way of being the diplomat. I can be that sometimes, when there's a difficult situation between people. I'm a confrontationist to be honest; I'd rather say, 'listen, if you've got a problem with him, sort it out now'." (2)

Hackett: "I was providing a lot of material for the band at this point, but in terms of writing credits I wasn't really getting what I thought I should. I had already managed to get a hit album on my own, so I needed to be respected as a writer and I don't think I was getting that from Mike and Tony. I think their agenda was always to run the band. Pete, who had been an enormously important part of the band, had always wanted a democracy, as had Anthony Phillips. Democracy in bands is a great ideal, but rarely works in practice because to achieve it you need to recognise everyone as being equally talented as yourself and I think that's difficult for certain people to take on board. It's usually one talented person who ends up getting their way more than the others, but it doesn't keep bands together forever as everyone needs to develop. I think to get a band like Genesis to all flow in formation, to make an album like WIND &

GENESIS

Promotional picture shot at Knebworth on 24th June 1978

Poster advertising the live album Seconds Out, Atlantic Records 1977

Wuthering, was quite an achievement. I gave it everything I had and I gave it as much as I was allowed. By the time I was doing A Trick Of The Tail I felt I was a fully-fledged writer rather than someone who was learning from the others who had been writing more fully in the early days (although I was already writing some stuff with Phil way back on Nursery Cryme: *For Absent Friends* and parts of *The Return Of The Giant Hogweed*, *The Musical Box*, *Fountain Of Salmacis*). If I'd been more of a politician, I may have ridden it out, but I wasn't given the chance to continue doing solo albums whilst I was a member of the band, even though Phil was allowed to work with Brand X (*the first album by Brand X, Unorthodox Behaviour, came out in 1976 – author's note*). Maybe if I'd had another band, I'd have been allowed to do that, but not under my own name. Tony said I couldn't do more solo albums and be a member of Genesis. Tony was assuming leadership at that point and Mike was backing him up, so there was no guarantee of a proportion of the song-writing being divided up equally. Tony said, 'if you don't like it, you know what you can do'." [1]

Hackett's departure left the remaining members of Genesis faced with a major decision: get a new musician or carry on as a three-piece. Banks: "I don't think we really thought twice about it; we knew we could do this. Not only because we'd already been through it with Pete, but while the lead guitar and everything that came with that was Steve, the rhythm guitar, which had been so prevalent in things like *The Cinema Show* or *The Musical Box*, had always been Mike. The only thing was whether or not he would also be able to cope with lead. He definitely had to work a bit to get the right mindset for that." [2]

Rutherford: "I don't think any of us really thought about getting in another guitar player. Having replaced Peter with Phil, we knew we'd get a good feeling from the audience with someone who was already in the band. Guitar-wise, I'd done an awful lot of stuff but I hadn't really played lead, that was Steve's job and he was a great lead player. But I think we felt we could sort this out in-house." [2]

Collins: "Mike had a big mountain to climb because being a guitar player is one thing, being a fluent lead guitar player is something totally different. He struggled with that for a little while." [2]

Rutherford: "Yeah, but I was quite excited too, you know. When a change happens, you're forced to do something else which is often not a bad thing." [2]

And so it was that in August 1977 the trio were already in the rehearsal room writing new material. In terms of writing, Steve's absence didn't create any real issues, if anything, it made things easier; the guitarist was growing significantly as a composer by that point and Tony and Mike, traditionally the main song-writing forces in the band, were reluctant to give him more space. His leaving therefore resolved disagreements that had built up over the last couple of albums: without Peter and Steve, and with Phil largely continuing with the role of arranger rather than composer, Tony and Mike finally had the chance to control almost the entire song-writing process. Which, in reality, is essentially what they had been doing ever since the departure of Anthony Phillips.

Banks: "One great advantage of there being fewer people in the band was that we had even more writing space. We were doing one album a year at that point as we hadn't done any solo albums, so we did tend to fight a little bit to get our stuff on the album." [2]

After about six weeks of rehearsing in Shepperton Studios, the trio had managed to sketch out about fifteen songs, thirteen of which would be recorded between September and October, again in Hilvarenbeek under the guidance of co-producer, David Hentschel. A new direction was immediately evident with the band focusing more on the song format and showing a marked loss of interest in extended instrumental passages. Banks: "When we were writing for four and I wanted to write a solo, it meant that Steve, for example, would just busk along and then have his moment elsewhere. Mike and I had written various instrumentals over the years, it just didn't happen this time round." [3]

One of the consequences is the distinct lack of

solos on this album. Banks: "There are keyboard solos, like on *Down And Out* or *Follow You Follow Me*, but they are short, concise things which just really fit with the chords. They're not separate solos in the way they were with previous albums. There's not much lead guitar on this album, just two or three parts, but what there is, Mike plays them well. So that was a loss I think, and from my own point of view in losing Steve I had lost an ally; you know we both liked to do weird things and we could sometimes drag it along that way for a bit longer." [2]

As soon as the album was recorded, however, Tony and Mike got side-tracked when they were asked to write a film score. Banks: "They needed the music very quickly, so we adapted some pre-existing material. Mike and I worked on it together, but it's fair to say that I wrote more than Mike, as he didn't have a theme or anything; he came up with some of the incidental music. We created the rest of the soundtrack, such as it is, out of those bits." [3]

Directed by Jerzy Skolimowski, *The Shout* is a psychological horror movie, released in June 1978. Beautiful yet disturbing, the recurring musical theme in the film is in typical Banks style (in fact, it would later be expanded on the keyboard player's first solo album, A Curious Feeling). Unfortunately it was subsequently modified with the addition of a series of electronic effects. Banks: "Mike was very dissatisfied with how the music was used and we fell out with the director. They needed a bit more music after the first showing and Rupert Hine stepped in. Perhaps they wanted something we couldn't provide for them." [3]

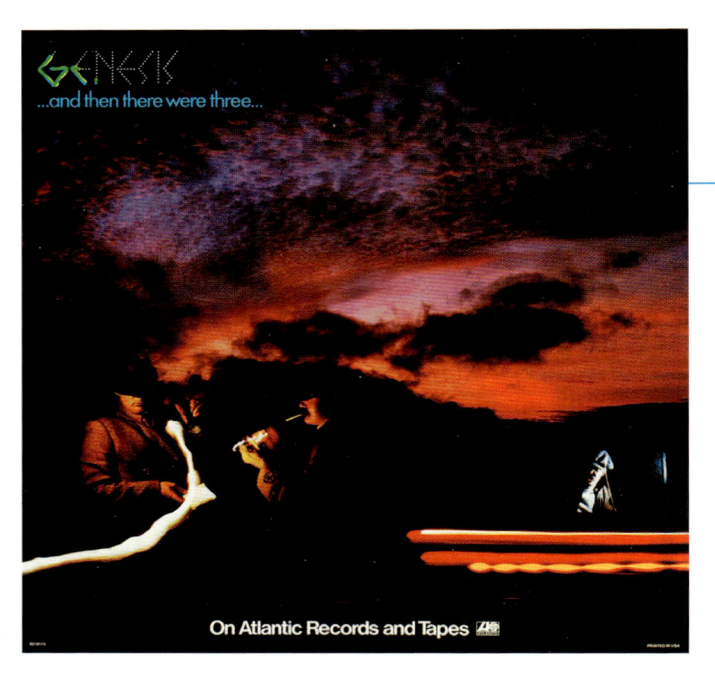

In September 1977, continuing at the band's usual unstoppable pace of that period, Genesis had a new album ready, but it was decided to delay its release for a few months while they planned a new tour. Yet again, fans were oblivious to the change in line-up.

Hackett: "When Pete left, he agreed not to release the news officially for some months and I honoured the same agreement, so news of my departure was released when it was most beneficial to them rather than to me. I deferred so that I could help the group as much as possible. I'm not a competitive guy and neither is Pete." [4]

The announcement came in October 1977, coinciding with the release of Seconds Out, a stunning live album which did very well in the charts (No. 4 in the UK and No. 47 in the States). Shortly after came the announcement that a new studio album was to be released, with a title (…And Then There Were Three…) derived either from the traditional counting rhyme or from the similarly titled Agatha Christie novel.

…And Then There Were Three… turned out to be a

Poster for the new album, Atlantic Records 1978

totally different album to anything Genesis had previously released. Banks: "The idea of trying to keep the songs a little more concise and to get more ideas on the album was quite appealing. The other thing about this album is that it was written when Phil was probably most distant from the group in many ways, so Mike and I ended up writing just about all the tracks individually, apart from *Follow You Follow Me*, which emerged more in the studio as a group track along with a couple of others like *Ballad Of Big* and *Down And Out*. But the rest of it was almost like a dual solo album. I did *Undertow* pretty much as I would have done as a solo project and the same thing goes for Mike with songs like *Snowbound* or *Say It's Alright Joe*. Which produced a certain kind of result." [2]

Collins: "This is probably my least favourite record, but maybe that's just because it wasn't a particularly happy period in my life. I contributed little bits but the songs were kind of short, a little inconsequential (apart from *Follow You Follow Me* which I thought was great). I remember writing some lyrics for different things, but certainly not the kind of lyrics I would go on to write a couple of years later, which were much more personal. I suppose there are a couple of lyrics in there that I might have written based on personal experiences, but I was still writing some fantasy things, based on what the Genesis history was, as opposed to what I would become. I was always more direct while Genesis were always more 'round the houses' storytellers." [2]

Rutherford: "We were starting once again to find slightly simpler styles of playing and writing and, lyrically speaking, Tony was simpler, more immediate. In a way there was less desire to always prove that we could do complicated stuff and do long songs to make it work. We were getting better at writing short songs. We were always very intense young men, trying to prove that we were the best and the greatest at everything, and suddenly we were getting a bit older, we had kids... maybe you just reach a moment in life when you feel you don't have to try so hard. Songs like *Follow You Follow Me* and *Many Too Many* for example, I don't feel like anyone was in any way trying and I think that's why they work well." [2]

THE ALBUM

The album finally came out in March 1978 and starting with the title, ...AND THEN THERE WERE THREE..., it immediately revealed a different side to a band that was in continual evolution. Having made the decision to leave longer tracks behind them, the album holds eleven songs, on average lasting around four minutes, making it without doubt the most accessible album the band had published since their naive debut back in 1969.

Gone are the long instrumentals, replaced by short and structurally more linear compositions. Mostly absent are the sudden changes in rhythm and syncopated time signatures. And the acoustic 12-string guitar sections, while present in *Snowbound, Undertow* and *Say It's Alright Joe*, were much less of a feature. The aim, in other words, was to create an album of seemingly simple songs. However, whilst the songs were more straightforward, a feeling of sadness surfaces more than once in both the musical atmospheres and in the lyrics. Obviously the fruit of an understandable state of internal upheaval, the album also highlights a division in roles that had never before been so marked: Phil is the singer-drummer, Mike the bassist-guitarist, Tony the keyboard player. No backing vocals for Mike and Tony and no guitar for Tony.

And the spotlight is obviously on Rutherford. The musician does his best on lead guitar, giving just a few, simple solos which are often overdubbed with harmonies added on a second guitar (for example on *Many Too Many*), but he is still in magnificent form with his rhythmic riffs and on acoustic guitar, while his bass playing remains extraordinary (and worthy of particular acclaim on *The Lady Lies*). Without Hackett, Banks can finally take centre stage as the unchallenged soloist of the band; that said, there are very few solos on this album and, apart from the one on *Down And Out*, they are all of very simple execution. Collins plays and sings well, but it is easy to discern his detachment from the band and his lack of involvement at a time when he was going through both personal and artistic issues.

The end result is therefore a somewhat individualistic effort, with only three of the songs being written by the group as a whole. That said, it would be desperately unfair to hastily dismiss an album which still holds some moments of dazzling beauty: the irregular opening of *Down And Out*, the poetry of *Undertow*, the complexity of *Burning Rope*, the disturbing tenderness of *Snowbound*. As albums go, it is a product of its time which, if nothing else, has the indisputable merit of disproving all those who had committed the unforgivable off-handedness of tarring Genesis with the same brush as their peers, bands such as Yes and Emerson, Lake & Palmer who, with their GOING FOR THE ONE and WORKS VOLUME 1 respectively, showed that they really hadn't grasped the fact that times were changing. Other bands, however, were faring better; Jethro Tull with their pastoral SONGS FROM THE WOOD and Pink Floyd with their claustrophobic ANIMALS.

In the meantime, a more immediate pop-rock genre was growing in popularity, led by bands such as Fleetwood Mac (who had hit the jackpot with RUMOURS) and the Electric Light Orchestra (OUT OF THE BLUE achieved significant success). But, more importantly, The Damned, Television, The Clash, The Stranglers, The Jam and Talking Heads all released their debut albums, while Peter Gabriel brought out his first solo album, Bob Marley

...And Then There Were Three...

Mike in Zurich, 4th June 1978

Tony in Brussels, 21st May 1978

released EXODUS and even David Bowie was exploring new shores with HEROES.

Genesis, however, still had many strings to their bow and couldn't wait to prove it. Consequently, ...AND THEN THERE WERE THREE... constitutes a transition that was absolutely essential if the band were to continue into the 1980s which were just around the corner.

THE SONGS

DOWN AND OUT

Banks: "This song developed in the studio. We got a riff going that we liked, in a strange time signature, and Mike and I just wrote something over it. So that was very much a group track actually." [5]

With a subtle synthesiser intro, this song boasts a good performance by Rutherford on guitar and bass pedals as well as a masterful synth solo by Banks.

Banks: "On the previous albums there had been some quite extended pieces but here we tried to keep it down slightly. Here there was a chance for a solo, so I just went for it." [5]

The lyrics are actually a dig at the music industry, written by Collins, who is also responsible for the 5/4 time signature.

Collins: "Rhythmically this was an incredibly complicated sort of song, which was probably my fault, I suppose." [2]

UNDERTOW

Based on the piano played by its composer, Banks, this touching ballad is embellished with

GENESIS

> French magazine *Rock & Folk* Number 137, June 1978

12-string guitar and a lovely fretless bass line played by Rutherford, while the chorus, sung by Collins partly in a falsetto voice, is accompanied by bass pedals and layers of keyboards.

Banks: "It was a slightly different way for me to write really. Slightly less chord-dependent and a bit more dependent on the melody. The piano part is very much the melody with the chords all enveloped in it. I think it was the first time I used the Yamaha CP70 on a record with the chorus sound which gives it quite a distinctive effect (*the piano was processed through the Boss CE-1 chorus effect – author's note*). And then Mike was playing a fretless bass on it. I think it turned out really well; it's probably my favourite track on the album." [2]

Originally there was an instrumental introduction to the song which ended up being cut.

Banks: "It was quite long, so I wasn't too concerned when the others said they didn't want it, also because we already had a long introduction for *Burning Rope*. Had they been enthusiastic about it we would have kept the intro; as it was, it meant I had this piece of music left over which had just been a little link in the middle. After changing it, it became the main part of a new song which sort of set the atmosphere for the rest of my album." [3]

Here Banks is referring to his first solo album, A Curious Feeling, released in 1979, and in particular to the first track on that record called, for obvious reasons, *From The Undertow*.

BALLAD OF BIG

Banks: "I'd written the verse part but didn't know what to do with it. Mike had this big chorus so we joined them together and Phil wrote the lyric. It's OK. It's not our best track but it's quite fun." [5]

Definitely one of the lesser tracks on the album, it stands out for its guitar riff over quick drumming, while the chorus is a succession of organ chords followed by a short guitar solo.

Even the lyrics are a bit corny; set in the Wild West, they narrate the inglorious end of a cowboy.

Banks: "Phil was always keen on the Wild West, as you know from his Alamo stuff. He got that in there now and then, but it wasn't his strongest area of writing. He hadn't really found his writing voice by then, but that all changed after Face Value. I mean, he could write lyrics, but I don't think he really had his heart in it yet." [5]

Collins: "I think I wrote the words to this song. Things I'd probably rather forget. Yeh, let's forget about it." [2]

SNOWBOUND

An acoustic ballad built up around Rutherford's 12-string arpeggios and a chorus highlighted by the dramatic riff of the synthesiser and drums. Written by Mike, the song's lyrics are open to interpretation.

Rutherford: "Just the word 'snowbound' creates a certain kind of atmosphere. But it isn't just about snow. It's about life, when you can't find your feet on the ground, but also mentally, when you're a bit lost. It's more to do about how you feel when you are removed from the world a bit, locked away." [6]

BURNING ROPE

At just over seven minutes long, this is the track that comes closest to the classic Genesis sound: a complex composition by Banks, it is based mainly around keyboards with an array of rhythm changes and melody variations.

Banks: "It was going to be like *One for the Vine*; in fact, originally there were other sections in the song but then I decided to kind of abbreviate it and make it a bit shorter, partly because I didn't want comparisons being made to that and secondly because I thought, 'well, I've done that already'." [2]

In the middle of the song there is a powerful guitar solo by Rutherford, although, if truth be known, Rutherford is merely playing Tony's guide part.

Banks: "Mike was still very much developing as a lead guitarist. When I'd written guitar parts on other albums or suggested them, Steve was able to run with them. Mike, on the other hand, just played the notes as I'd written them, as is the case with this track. If Steve had been there, we would have developed it more." [5]

DEEP IN THE MOTHERLODE

Banks: "This was mainly Mike's idea but had arrangement ideas from the rest of us. I love the middle bit of the song; it's very strong. It was used in a rather bad documentary a couple of years ago where they used an old bit of footage from a 1970s 'Nationwide' TV programme and that bit of music. I thought it sounded really good." [5]

A more rhythmic song, with a synth solo theme and a guitar riff by the song's writer, Rutherford.

Rutherford: "Sometimes, if the music is written first, it dictates the kind of song you write. You couldn't write a love song to that music; you have to write something a bit more earthy. And so the lyrics are about the gold rush." [6]

MANY TOO MANY

A song mainly for voice and piano accompanied by layers of string sounds and featuring a guitar solo by Rutherford as well as his counterpoint finish to the vocal line.

Banks: "Mike worked quite hard on the little solo at the end of this song, which I think works really nicely." [2]

For the first time ever, Tony had written a love song. Banks: "I was obviously coming out of my

GENESIS

Many Too Many was the second single released from the AND THEN THERE WERE THREE album. It featured two unreleased tracks on the b side

ised the words were terrible and the others didn't argue with me when I said, 'let's scrap this lyric, I've run out of ideas'. Phil said, 'let me write it, I love these old Nemo cartoons'." (5)

The comic strip Tony is referring to is 'Little Nemo In Slumberland', created by the American cartoonist, Winsor McCay, in the early 1900s.

shell here. It's still a bit weird. It's not totally straightforward. One of the things I remember was trying to convince Phil that it was all right to sing 'mama'; he was so against it. I said, 'Stevie Wonder uses 'mama' in his lyrics all the time, so you can do it'. Then of course, a couple years later, there was the song, *Mama*, where it's the main lyric throughout the song, but at the time perhaps he felt a bit self-conscious, you know, trying to be something we weren't." (2)

SCENES FROM A NIGHT'S DREAM

A rhythm-driven song which includes a great performance from Mike on both bass and various guitars, one of which he uses to give a pleasant closing solo. The music, hardly his best work, is by Tony.

Banks: "I'd written the whole thing, including the lyric. But when we were recording the lyric I real-

SAY IT'S ALRIGHT JOE

A song constructed around an arrangement for piano and 12-string guitar, with impressive finishing touches on bass. There are wistful vocals from Collins as he sings about an old alcoholic. The chorus features an explosive synth line.

Rutherford: "It was a very different song to anything I had done before or after really. Quite a period song, it was great the way Phil used to sing it on stage in a mac and hat, giving it that image of a guy in a nightclub at the piano." (6)

THE LADY LIES

Banks: "Musically it's a good song but lyrically it's a bit iffy, a bit self-conscious. I think it's interesting musically. I had to change the key of the verse in relation to the chorus which was slightly awkward. It sounds OK now, as I'm used to it, but when

...And Then There Were Three...

Phil performing *Say It's Alright Joe* in Zurich on 4th June 1978

The thing that truly stands out, however, is Mike's splendid bass playing.

Banks: "Yes, well I wrote most of it. It was so good for Mike." [5]

FOLLOW YOU FOLLOW ME

The song which brings the first album by the trio to a close, kicks off with a captivating backcloth created by Mike's guitar and goes on to feature an exceptional groove from Collins and, unusually for Genesis at that time, an extremely catchy chorus.

Banks: "Mike had a riff, I had a chord sequence and the skeleton of a melody and then Phil just sort of warbled on it and added the drums obviously, which are quite an important feature on that song." [2]

Rutherford: "That riff wasn't for a song; we were going to try and make it into a solo, I think, but I can't remember. I played the guitar, Tony started playing some chords underneath it and Phil just started singing along in a way that just captured a certain mood." [2]

Collins: "It was based on a guitar riff Mike had, you know, going through his flanger and with a sort of repeat echo, Tony plays a few chords and I come in and sing a few lyrics. I remember when Chester Thompson joined the live band he said that they always used to play that song on the Weather Report bus. And I thought, if Wayne

I wrote it, it wasn't right for the voice." [5]

The keyboards are very dominant. Banks: "I like the solo. It was influenced very much by a Beach Boys track, *Leaving This Town*, one that's not actually written by the Wilsons. It's got a solo in it that's very kind of trundling. And I like the piano on the end, that kind of jazzy ending." [5]

Shorter and Joe Zawinul can listen to this and say, 'this English stuff's cool, man' then we must have done something right. (*Collins is probably mistaken here as Thompson worked with Weather Report some years before this song came out – author's note*). I used to say 'Why can't we do something that's kind of edgy? Something that's kind of cool and hip?', you know. And it looked like we'd manage to do something like that, only it then became a pop single, which kind of took the edge off the cool, hip thing. But it's still played on the radio today and it's a lot of people's favourite song from that period." [2]

Banks: "We kept it very simple because it just sounded really good and, even when we were writing it, I thought 'well, this has gotta be a hit surely'. I don't know much about hit records because I don't particularly listen to top 40 stuff, but when we played the album to Charisma, they picked it as a single. When we were recording it, our engineer and producer at that time, Dave Hentschel didn't rate it at all, so he was a bit dismissive about it and we did a mix of it which wasn't

Mike in Oakland, 14th April 1978

terribly good. After the record company had heard it and said it was a hit, we went back and remixed it and got it a bit better. I felt it was the first time we'd ever written a hit; it just had this sort of slightly yearning quality about it thanks to just a couple of little chord changes." [2]

Rutherford: "Lyrically it was the easiest song to write that I have ever written in my life; it took about ten minutes. I sat down and it just came out very easily. They're not astounding words but I think being simple and not being embarrassing is often quite hard. We'd come from a much more complicated background of lyric writing and I thought 'I can't just do that, can I?'. But it's an interesting song because it's very simple. I remember Pete Townsend in an article saying that *Follow You Follow Me* was a great little song on the radio, just classy without being trite. It's a timeless piece really." [2]

Banks: "As I said, *Your Own Special Way* had a love lyric. I think Mike had just got engaged at this point, so the idea of the lyric obviously reflects how he was feeling at that time." [2]

Rutherford: "It was a funny album because we decided not to do such long songs this time, you know, the ten-minute long song which had become a bit of a caricature and try instead to get more variety in it. I think the album suffered for it, because the balance of long and short songs always was (and still is) good." [2]

OTHER SONGS

The B-side of the second single, *Many Too Many* featured two songs recorded at the same time as the album, which are short but very interesting.

The Day The Light Went Out is a rhythmic electronic pop / rock song written by Banks with sci-fi influenced lyrics, while *Vancouver* is characterised by the melancholy mood created by Rutherford's music (acoustic guitars, piano and light percussion) with lyrics written by Collins which tell the story of a young girl's brief experience of running away from home.

THE ALBUM ARTWORK

The cover features a photograph with time-lapse light trails, a spectacular sunset skyscape and three half-lit figures in the foreground.

Banks: "We felt it didn't really do much; it was a bit nebulous. We were a bit stuck for ideas and I don't think Hipgnosis came up with their best idea really. I mean, it sort of has a character to it because you relate it to the album now, but when you think that the album was probably a bit more straightforward and quite fresh, it's got a very gloomy, dark cover. It could have had something a little bit more upbeat, but that was our fault as much as anything." [2]

Rutherford: "I felt that the album cover was a bit weak. I think I'm right in saying that there was a tour coming up and the cover had to be done otherwise the album couldn't come out. If we'd had more time, I would have looked harder." [2]

EPILOGUE

The first album without Gabriel sold more than previous releases and the same happened with the first album after Hackett's departure. In fact, ...And Then There Were Three… consolidated the band's suc-

Poster advertising the concert in Saarbrucken, Germany, on 3rd September 1978. Promoted by Lipp + Rau

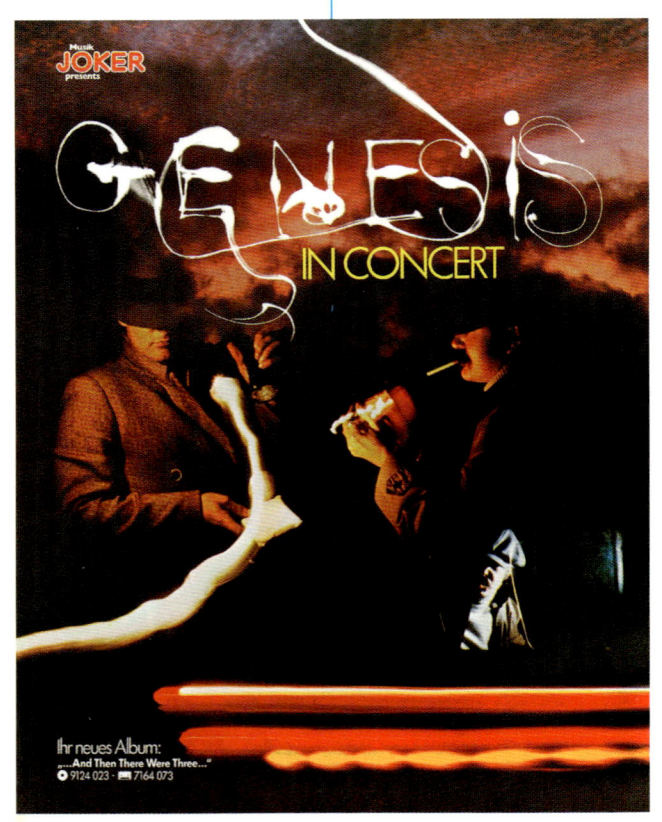

esis, *Follow You Follow Me*, which made it to No. 7 in the UK charts and No. 23 in America (a second single, *Many Too Many*, only managed to make it to No. 43 in the UK).

Banks: "The album came out just after punk. It was kind of strange, we were still surviving even though I couldn't quite work out why. Everyone else seemed to have gone. Emerson, Lake & Palmer had died. Yes had died. And we were still going along. I think we just thought we were lucky, suddenly in the middle of all this we had a hit single and we were OK because it meant we were on the radio, so people couldn't ignore us. And I don't think it was such a clear-cut thing with audiences anyhow, this whole sort of punk rock thing. I remember a guy searching for something for me to sign. We were walking down Wardour Street and the only thing he could come up with was the single *Pretty Vacant* by The Sex Pistols, so I signed that. I think people had pretty wide taste. They could appreciate lots of music." [2]

cess on home territory, where not only did it reach No. 3 in the charts (as high as A TRICK OF THE TAIL and four places higher than WIND & WUTHERING), it also managed to stay in the Top 100 for a year. In America, it got as high as No. 14 (a leap up the charts of 12 places) and earned the band a Gold Record.

These impressive chart placings were surely assisted by the first hit single in the history of Gen-

While the record label and management had reason to be pleased, the same could not be said of the band's long-standing fans. The more immediate nature of the album created what can only be described as a watershed moment between old and new fans. Many of those fans who had already had difficulty digesting Gabriel's departure, now lost all interest in Genesis. But, in absolute terms, the band had never had it so good.

THE CONCERTS

As soon as the recording of ...And Then There Were Three... had been completed Genesis found themselves, for the third time in just two years, having to introduce a new member into the live line-up. After bringing in Bill Bruford in 1976 and Chester Thompson in 1977, they now had to find a replacement for Steve Hackett. Collins: "By this time we were getting used to it. I wasn't worried about it and I don't think any of us were. By the time someone leaves, it's a bit like having gangrene. You just want the pain dealt with. Because, you know, when a person's not happy and it shows, it spreads, so it's better that this stuff happens. I always make this Monty Python analogy: when they were all a lot younger, they all bounced off each other, hung out with each other, were best friends with each other. As you get older you get families, your interests change slightly, you want to be more in control of what you do. As a mothership, Python couldn't possibly contain all those people. In much the same way, everybody in the band was getting older and discovering what they wanted to do and hadn't done yet and realising how they could do what they wanted to do better, so it didn't really surprise me that people kept falling off. But they'd already weathered Anthony Phillips leaving and together we'd all weathered Peter leaving, so I thought Steve leaving would just be something else we could get over." [2]

To fill Hackett's role, the band auditioned a handful of guitarists and, it has to be said, they displayed a certain degree of broad-mindedness in taking into consideration mainly American musicians who, generally speaking, had different musical sensibilities to their English counterparts. In fact, great musicians such as Pat Thrall and Elliott Randall were contacted and auditioned and, at one point, Phil was leaning towards Weather Report's Alphonso Johnson, an amazing bass player but not such a great guitarist. Obviously, Genesis needed someone who could play both instruments (in particular lead guitar for the older material and bass for the new songs) and it was actually Johnson who pointed them in the direction of Daryl Stuermer who had already collaborated with important jazz fusion artists such as Jean Luc Ponty and George Duke.

Stuermer: "I was in my house in Milwaukee, I got a call from the band's tour manager and he asked if I would be interested in auditioning and, since I wasn't working with Jean Luc Ponty at the time, of course I was. I didn't know anything about these guys. Jean Luc had played me A Trick Of The Tail and Wind & Wuthering; he was a big fan of those two albums but I'd never had a Genesis album. Anyway, I turned up in New York for an audition. To be honest, only Mike Rutherford was there. I played maybe four songs. I can remember *Squonk, Dance On A Volcano, Down And Out* and I can't remember the other one. I only played one minute of each song and Mike said, 'I think you'll be the one'." [7]

The new Genesis line-up got together for a week in Las Colinas, near Dallas, in March 1978 where they also tried out Showco's sound system. Here they set about putting together a setlist which would achieve the right balance between old and new. A tape recording made on the last day of rehearsals (26 March) was smuggled out of the band's archives and found its way into the hands of collectors; it provides evidence of the following partial setlist: *Eleventh Earl Of Mar / In The Cage / Burning Rope / Ripples / Deep In The Motherlode /*

GENESIS

Atlantic promo shot, 1978

Poster advertising the concert in Toronto, Canada, on 10th July 1978, promoted by Concert Productions International

Chester Thompson   Michael Rutherford   Phil Collins   Daryl Stuermer   Tony Banks

GENESIS

welcome the new Genesis line-up, initially with a rehearsal gig on 27 March followed by the official tour opening show the following day. The first setlist included: *Eleventh Earl Of Mar / In The Cage / Burning Rope / Ripples / Deep In The Motherlode / The Fountain Of Salmacis / Down And Out / One For The Vine / Squonk / Say It's Alright Joe / The Lady Lies / The Cinema Show – Afterglow / Follow You Follow Me / Dance On A Volcano – Los Endos / I Know What I Like*. So, six songs from the new album were alternated with substantial parts of 'old' Genesis, which emerged as the highlights of the show. Songs such as *The Fountain Of Salmacis* (back on the setlist for the first time since 1974), *Ripples* (which, despite being on the A TRICK OF THE TAIL album, oddly enough had never been played live while Hackett was still in the band) and *In The Cage*, extracted from THE LAMB for the first time ever and brought to a close with the cascading notes of Stuermer's guitar. Banks: "*In The Cage* was always a very strong song live; it didn't sound as good on the album as it should have done. Of course, it became a real stage classic over the years. It could always be done as a good rock number and it worked really

The Fountain Of Salmacis / Down And Out / One For The Vine / Squonk / Follow You Follow Me / Apocalypse In 9/8 – As Sure As Eggs Is Eggs.

At last, the new Genesis machine was ready to be set in motion. While the WIND & WUTHERING tour had lasted six months, the …AND THEN THERE WERE THREE… tour was scheduled to last for almost nine, with the declared objective of cracking the US. To achieve this, management made the rather crazy decision to organise three different trips to North America (in April, July and October) which were to be followed by a Japanese tour.

Binghamton, in Broome County in the state of New York, had the privilege of being the first to

well in the later days; with Chester and Daryl it really came alive." [8]

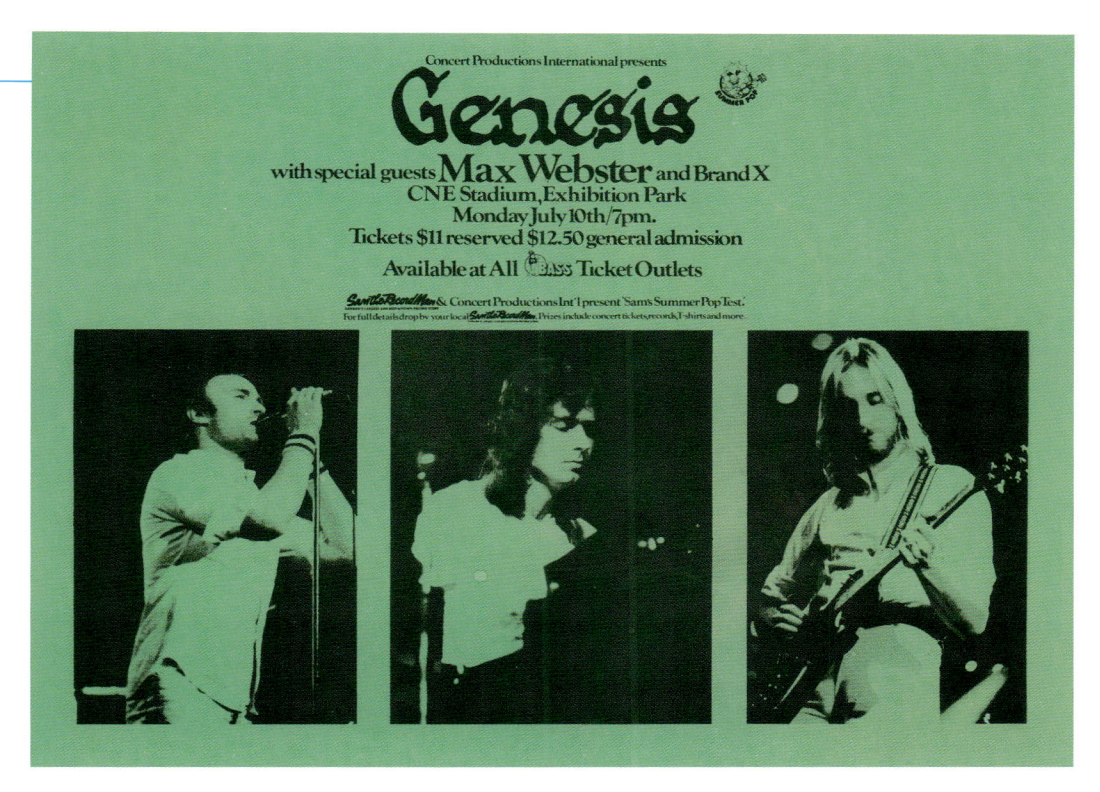

After being left out of the previous tour, *The Cinema Show* was back in the setlist but with some interesting variations; in fact, in the middle of the long keyboard solo, Tony added a riff from *Raven* (a fragment of *The Colony Of Slippermen*) before coming back to the theme of *The Cinema Show*, the ending of which was cut short so it could be linked up to the last section of ... *In That Quiet Earth* which then flowed straight into *Afterglow*.

Now, increasingly more intent on impressing their audiences with an amazing stage show, Genesis proceeded to make their concerts even more spectacular. Alongside the laser and spotlights, the defining feature of this tour was the mirrors, an idea put forward by roadie, Jeffrey Shaw, who had already worked on the screens used in THE LAMB tour together with Theo Botschuijver. Initially the plan was to have the entire lighting system installed on the floor with it projecting up onto the mirrors, but the band thought this solution was too risky and came up with an alternative: six enormous octagonal mirrors installed above the stage rotated by a computer and reflecting intermittent rays of light onto the musicians. The tour carried exorbitant production costs (estimated to be somewhere in the region of £150,000 a day) and required seven trucks to transport all the gear and a 30-man crew of roadies and technicians.

And when it came to the band, despite the recent line-up changes, it certainly did not disappoint: Daryl Stuermer immediately proved to be a very technical guitarist. His playing style was, without doubt, very different to Steve Hackett's, but it fitted in perfectly.

Stuermer: "The hardest part for me was knowing that was a guitar playing. Sometimes it sounded like a synthesiser. I was a very straight player and Mike put all these pedals in front of me and said, 'do you want to play this one?'. The music itself wasn't as difficult to play as the concept. I had never played that kind of music." [7]

GENESIS

Tony in Zurich on 4th June 1978

Zurich, 4th June 1978

...And Then There Were Three...

Daryl in Brussels, 21st May 1978

Mike in Brussels, 21st May 1978

During this period, Daryl almost always played guitar (in particular excelling in the execution of *The Fountain Of Salmacis*), switching over to bass only for the more recent songs and not even all of them (he played electric guitar for *The Lady Lies*, with Rutherford on bass, and for *Say It's Alright Joe*, with Mike on acoustic guitar). This song also included Phil Collins' only theatrical touch; playing the part of an alcoholic, lit up by a table lamp he would lean on Tony's piano and keep pouring himself a drink. Collins also went back to telling the story of Romeo and Juliet before *The Cinema Show* and gave an impeccable performance both on vocals and, of course, in the drumming duets with Chester Thompson (who was quite simply perfect).

As reliable as always on bass, when put to the test on lead guitar, Mike did his best, happily relying on the assistance of the Roland GS500 guitar synth, for example on *Burning Rope*, where he executes both the initial melody line and his only real solo of the entire concert.

Banks maintained his role as leading instrumentalist, supported by an impressive array of keyboards which now included, alongside his piano, organ, Mellotron 400, Polymoog and ARP 2600, an instrument with duophonic capabilities which he used when playing, for example, the main riff of *Deep In The Motherlode*.

The first North American leg of the tour, which conceded very few days off, was a huge success. Genesis stopped off in Pennsylvania, Michigan, Illinois (it was in Chicago, due to the huge demand for tickets, that they played their first ever stadium show), Ohio, Indiana and Missouri, ending the tour triumphantly with three arena concerts in California (the last was on 17 April at the Inglewood Forum near Los Angeles).

After about one month off, Genesis were back on the road, this time for the first European leg of the tour which started on 14 May with a series of dates in Germany. Here, on the 17th in Mannheim, *Down And Out* was dropped from the setlist. A few shows in Holland and Belgium were followed by nine concerts in France, including four consecutive nights at the Paris Sports Stadium (from 26th to 29th). The first new entry in the setlist, which had remained unaltered up to this point, came about in Lyon on 1 June: *Ballad Of Big* replaced *Down And Out*. The two songs were then often alternated over the following dates which saw the band travel through Switzerland, Sweden and Norway. In particular, *Ballad Of Big* was played in Dijon, Zurich, Oslo and in Berlin on 11 June, before a further handful of gigs in Germany which came to a climax on the final date on 14 June in Dortmund, where not only *Down And Out* found its way back into the setlist (this time at the expense of *Say It's Alright Joe*), but the audience were given an unexpected treat: a second encore after *I Know What I Like* – the shortened version of *Supper's Ready* (*Apocalypse In 9/8* and *As Sure As Eggs Is Eggs*) which the band had rehearsed but until then had never played.

In all of this, the UK was astonishingly neglected, possibly because the band felt they had already consolidated their success on home turf and wanted to focus on other markets, but maybe also because of the explosion of the punk scene, following which Genesis, along with other contemporary groups, suddenly found themselves in the firing line of the British music press.

The only English concert was at Knebworth Festival on 24 June, where Genesis headlined after performances by Roy Harper, Atlanta Rhythm Section, Tom Petty & The Heartbreakers, Devo, Brand X and Jefferson Starship. Due to the number of bands on the line-up, Genesis were obliged to significantly reduce their setlist to: *Eleventh Earl Of Mar / In The Cage / Burning Rope / Ripples / The Fountain Of Salmacis / Deep In The Motherlode / One For The Vine / Squonk / The Lady Lies / The Cinema Show – Afterglow / Follow You Follow Me / Dance On A Volcano – Los Endos / I Know What I Like*.

Knebworth was an absolute triumph, with the band playing to 100,000 worshipping fans. It was also documented by the then still very austere BBC which aired the documentary "Three Dates With Genesis" including a fantastic unabridged version

...And Then There Were Three...

Oakland on 14th April 1978

Poster advertising the Summertime Open Air Festival, planned for August 26th in Ulm and September 3rd in Saarbrucken, both in Germany. Genesis headlined both shows

of *The Lady Lies*. Never before had Genesis played to such a huge crowd, a record, however, which was destined to be very short-lived.

After a two-week break, the band flew out for the second leg of the North American tour, this time starting out in Canada with a concert in Toronto (10 July, with *Ballad Of Big*) and two in the Montreal Forum (the second date, on 13 July, included the last ever live performance of *Down And Out*). The group then travelled down to the States, playing in Michigan, Ohio, Missouri and Rhode Island. In some of these concerts (such as Milwaukee on the 19th and Columbia on the 25th), *Ballad Of Big* was dropped from the setlist.

The date in Madison Square Garden, New York, on 29 July would make history due to the guest appearance of Peter Gabriel, who during the encore sang *I Know What I Like* with Collins, while in the final show of the second leg, on 31 July at Saratoga Springs, as well as *Ballad Of Big*, *The Cinema Show* was strangely left out and *Afterglow* was played as an individual song.

After four weeks off, at the end of August, Genesis were back in Europe. They started out on the 26th headlining the 'Summertime Open Air Festival' near Ulm. Again, the number of artists in the line-up (John McLaughlin, Alvin Lee, Scorpions, Brand X and Joan Baez) meant that they had to shorten the setlist which consequently became: *Eleventh Earl Of Mar / In The Cage / Burning Rope / Ripples / The Fountain Of Salmacis / Deep In The Motherlode / One For The Vine / Squonk / The Lady*

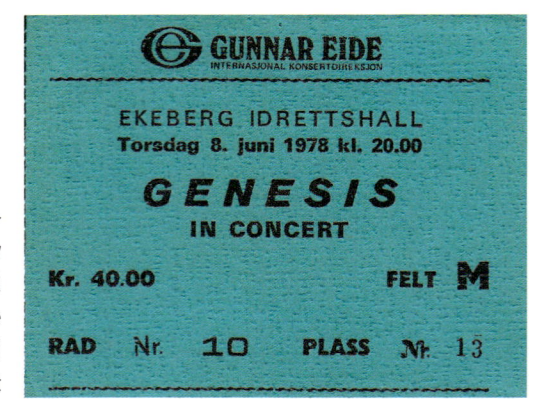

Lies / The Cinema Show – Afterglow / Follow You Follow Me / Dance On A Volcano – Los Endos. The set was back to full length on 28 August at the Wiener Stadthalle. As well as the return of *Ballad Of Big*, for the second encore *I Know What I Like* made way for the old *The Lamb Lies Down On Broadway – The Musical Box* medley.

The tour continued with three concerts in Germany (the last one, in Saarbrücken on 3 September, was considerably shorter due to *Ballad Of Big*, *The Fountain Of Salmacis* and *Say It's Alright Joe* being left out) and a further three in Holland, before the band played at another festival, the 'Féte de L'Humanité' in Paris on 9 September. This event smashed the attendance record set at Knebworth just the previous month with numbers reaching 120,000 (one should bear in mind, however, that festival ticket holders automatically had access to the concert). The shortened setlist seen at Saarbrücken was also played here with *Ballad Of Big* and *The Fountain Of Salmacis* at this point being dropped for good.

With the triumphant month of September drawing to a close, Genesis were getting ready for the third (and last) leg of their North American tour. This time the aim was to win over those states where they still had only a small following whilst consolidating their fan bases in those states where they had already achieved a certain degree of success. They started out in Florida on the 29th and 30th, to then move on to Georgia, Missouri, Louisiana, Tennessee, Ohio, Michigan, Illinois, Oklahoma and Texas in October. Things didn't all go to plan, however, with the concerts in Birmingham, Alabama, scheduled for 5 October and in Norman, Illinois, on the 18th both being cancelled. That said, the two dates in Chicago, on the 13th and 14th, are worthy of particular note. The first of the two included a fantastic new element in the setlist: the addition, after *Burning Rope*, of a medley made up of the first part of *Dancing With The Moonlit Knight* and the second half of *The Musical Box*. Only this time it wasn't just a case of putting together two very short sections of songs as had previously been the case: the classic track from Selling England By The Pound was continued into the more rhythm-driven section (with Collins notably struggling with the higher notes), whereas *The Musical Box* didn't start from "She's a lady…" but from halfway through the guitar solo, now of course assigned to the capable hands of Daryl Stuermer. In other words, a totally unique version, which fortunately was saved for posterity (and in rather good quality) by a radio programme recording.

And with this, it could finally be said that Genesis had conquered America.

Collins: *"Follow You Follow Me* was a huge hit, not only in Europe but also in America and that made a big difference to us. It was another step on that ladder that made us a bigger band; we were playing to more people, there was more interest, more play on the radio and suddenly there were even a few girls in the audience."[2]

After the last show in the US (Houston on 22

November) the band returned to the UK for a few days, where Phil was greeted with a bitter surprise: tired of a husband who was always on the road, his wife, Andrea, had run off with the painter and decorator who was doing up their apartment, taking the two children with her. It came as a huge shock, but Collins had no time to dwell on it as Genesis were scheduled to make their first trip to Japan to exploit the success of ...AND THEN THERE WERE THREE..., their first album ever to enter the Japanese charts.

Initially Genesis were booked to play the Budokan Theatre, with a seating capacity of 10,000, but the band opted to play in smaller venues holding around 3,000 spectators. As a result, the band added another two dates to the ones originally planned which meant they played a total of six concerts between 27 November and 3 December: five in Tokyo (albeit in two different venues) and one in Osaka. The shows gave audiences the consolidated setlist of *Eleventh Earl Of Mar / In The Cage / Burning Rope / Ripples / Deep In The Motherlode / One For The Vine / Squonk / Say It's Alright Joe / The Lady Lies / The Cinema Show – Afterglow / Follow You Follow Me / Dance On A Volcano – Los Endos / I Know What I Like*.

Genesis ended the tour secure in the knowledge that they had taken a giant leap forward towards worldwide popularity. And they had: the strategy of attacking the American market on more than one front brought with it the much-desired fruits. Phil Collins, however, was quite understandably at rock bottom.

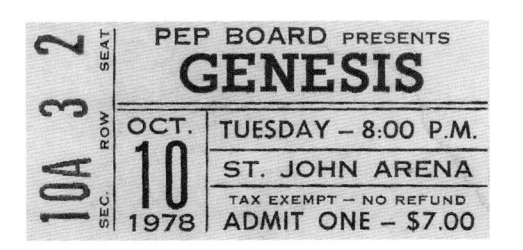

NOTES

(1) Mario Giammetti listening to 'WIND & WUTHERING' with Steve Hackett, Naples, Chiaja Hotel De Charme, 12 September 2016

(2) Mike Kaufman's Genesis interviews, Chicago / London, October 2007, partially used in the bonus disc accompanying the 2008 remasters

(3) Mario Giammetti's telephone interview with Tony Banks, 1 October 2009, partially published in the article "Nei meandri della memoria" in *Dusk*, Issue no. 63, November 2009

(4) Mario Giammetti's telephone interview with Steve Hackett, 8 October 2015, partially published in the article "Senza Gabriel" in *Classic Rock*, issue n. 44, July 2016

(5) Mario Giammetti's interview with Tony Banks, London, Tony Smith Personal Management office, 29 November 2016

(6) Mario Giammetti's interview with Mike Rutherford, Munich, Freiheiz, 20 September 2016

(7) Mario Giammetti's interview with Daryl Stuermer, Milan, Filaforum, 9 October 1997, partially published in the article "Daryl Stuermer special – intervista esclusiva", *Dusk*, Issue n. 24, January 1998

(8) Mario Giammetti's telephone interview with Tony Banks, 26 February 2016, partially published in the article "Senza Gabriel" in *Classic Rock*, issue n. 44, July 2016

...AND THEN THERE WERE THREE... TOUR

1978

MARCH

- 27 **Binghamton, NY (USA)**, Broome County Veterans Memorial Arena
  Rehearsal concert
- 28 **Binghamton, NY (USA)**, Broome County Veterans Memorial Arena
- 29 **Buffalo, NY (USA)**, Buffalo Memorial Auditorium
- 30 **Rochester, NY (USA)**, Rochester Community War Memorial
- 31 **Philadelphia, PA (USA)**, The Spectrum

APRIL

- 01 **Suffern, NY (USA)**, Rockland Fieldhouse - Rockland Community College
- 02 **State College, PA (USA)**, Recreation Building - Pennsylvania State University
- 04 **Kalamazoo, MI (USA)**, Wings Stadium
- 05 **Normal, IL (USA)**, Horton Fieldhouse - Illinois State University
- 06 **Chicago, IL (USA)**, Chicago Stadium
- 07 **Richfield, OH (USA)**, Richfield Coliseum
- 08 **Dayton, OH (USA)**, Hara Arena
- 09 **Bloomington, IN (USA)**, Assembly Hall - Indiana University
- 10 **St. Louis, MO (USA)**, Kiel Auditorium
- 14 **Oakland, CA (USA)**, Oakland-Alameda County Coliseum Arena
- 15 **San Diego, CA (USA)**, San Diego Sports Arena
- 17 **Inglewood, CA (USA)**, The Forum

MAY

- 14 **Cologne (WEST GERMANY)**, Sporthalle
  Originally scheduled for May 18
- 15 **Frankfurt (WEST GERMANY)**, Festhalle
- 16 **Munich (WEST GERMANY)**, Olympiahalle
- 18 **Mannheim (WEST GERMANY)**, Eisstadion
  Originally scheduled for May 17
- 20 **Leiden (THE NETHERLANDS)**, Groenoordhal
- 21 **Forest (BELGIUM)**, Forest National
- 22 **Forest (BELGIUM)**, Forest National
- 24 **Nantes (FRANCE)**, Grand Palais - Parc des Expositions de la Beaujoire
- 26 **Paris (FRANCE)**, Palais des Sports
- 27 **Paris (FRANCE)**, Palais des Sports
- 28 **Paris (FRANCE)**, Palais des Sports
- 29 **Paris (FRANCE)**, Palais des Sports
- 30 **Poitiers (FRANCE)**, Arènes de Poitiers

JUNE

- 01 **Lyon (FRANCE)**, Palais des Sports
- 02 **Clermont-Ferrand (FRANCE)**, Palais des Sports
- 03 **Dijon (FRANCE)**, Parc des Expositions
- 04 **Zürich (SWITZERLAND)**, Hallenstadion
- 06 **Malmö (SWEDEN)**, Isstadion
- 07 **Gothenburg (SWEDEN)**, Scandinavium
- 08 **Oslo (NORWAY)**, Ekeberg Idrettshall
- 11 **Berlin (WEST GERMANY)**, Deutschlandhalle
- 12 **Bremen (WEST GERMANY)**, Stadthalle
- 13 **Hamburg (WEST GERMANY)**, Ernst-Merck-Halle
- 14 **Dortmund (WEST GERMANY)**, Halle 1 - Westfalenhallen
- 24 **Stevenage (ENGLAND)**, Knebworth Park

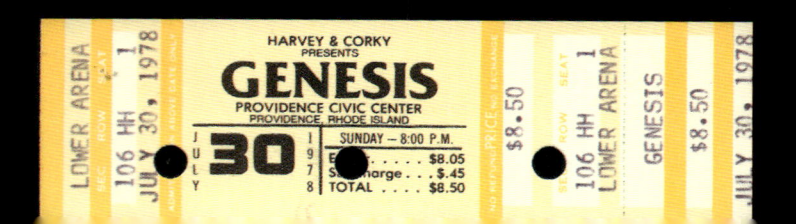

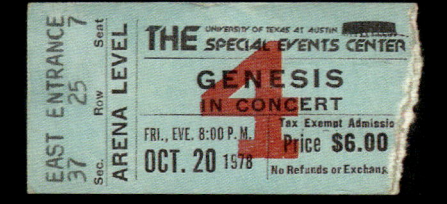

JULY
- **10** Toronto, ON (CANADA), Canadian National Exhibition Grandstand
- **12** Montréal, QC (CANADA), Forum
- **13** Montréal, QC (CANADA), Forum
- **15** Clarkston, MI (USA), Pine Knob Music Theatre
- **16** Clarkston, MI (USA), Pine Knob Music Theatre
- **19** Milwaukee, WI (USA), Main Stage - Henry Maier Festival Park (Summerfest)
- **21** Cincinnati, OH (USA), Riverfront Coliseum
- **22** Pittsburgh, PA (USA), Civic Arena
- **23** Syracuse, NY (USA), Onondaga County War Memorial
- **25** Columbia, MD (USA), Merriweather Post Pavilion
- **26** Columbia, MD (USA), Merriweather Post Pavilion
- **27** Hampton, VA (USA), Hampton Coliseum
- **29** New York, NY (USA), Madison Square Garden *Peter Gabriel guest vocals on I Know What I Like*
- **30** Providence, RI (USA), Providence Civic Center
- **31** Saratoga Springs, NY (USA), Saratoga Performing Arts Center

AUGUST
- **26** Ulm (WEST GERMANY), Friedrichsau-Festplatz
- **28** Vienna (AUSTRIA), Halle D - Wiener Stadthalle
- **30** Hannover (WEST GERMANY), Messegelände Halle 20

SEPTEMBER
- **01** Cologne (WEST GERMANY), Radstadion Müngersdorf
- **03** Saarbrücken (WEST GERMANY), Ludwigspark-Stadion
- **04** Maastricht (THE NETHERLANDS), Eurohal
- **05** Arnhem (THE NETHERLANDS), Rijnhal
- **06** Rotterdam (THE NETHERLANDS), Ahoy Sportpaleis
- **09** La Courneuve (FRANCE), Parc Paysager de La Courneuve *Fête de L'Humanité*
- **29** Hollywood, FL (USA), Hollywood Sportatorium
- **30** Lakeland, FL (USA), Lakeland Civic Center

OCTOBER
- **04** Atlanta, GA (USA), The Omni
- **06** Baton Rouge, LA (USA), Riverside Centroplex
- **08** Nashville, TN (USA), Nashville Municipal Auditorium
- **10** Columbus, OH (USA), St. John Arena - Ohio State University
- **11** East Lansing, MI (USA), Jenison Fieldhouse - Michigan State University
- **12** Champaign, IL (USA), Assembly Hall - University of Illinois
- **13** Chicago, IL (USA), Uptown Theatre
- **14** Chicago, IL (USA), Uptown Theatre
- **16** Springfield, MO (USA), John Q. Hammons Student Center - Southwest Missouri State University
- **17** Kansas City, MO (USA), Municipal Auditorium
- **20** Austin, TX (USA), Special Events Center - University of Texas at Austin
- **21** Dallas, TX (USA), Dallas Convention Center Arena
- **22** Houston, TX (USA), The Summit

NOVEMBER
- **27** Tokyo (JAPAN), Kōsei Nenkin Kaikan
- **28** Tokyo (JAPAN), Nakano Sunplaza Hall
- **29** Tokyo (JAPAN), Nakano Sunplaza Hall
- **30** Osaka (JAPAN), Kōsei Nenkin Kaikan

DECEMBER
- **02** Tokyo (JAPAN), Nakano Sunplaza Hall
- **03** Tokyo (JAPAN), Kōsei Nenkin Kaikan

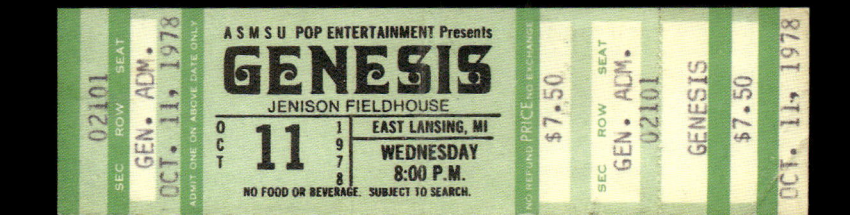

Duke

(Charisma, 1980)

Behind The Lines (Banks-Collins-Rutherford) / Duchess (Banks-Collins-Rutherford) / Guide Vocal (Banks) / Man Of Our Times (Rutherford) / Misunderstanding (Collins) / Heathaze (Banks) /// Turn It On Again (Banks-Collins-Rutherford) / Alone Tonight (Rutherford) / Cul-De-Sac (Banks) / Please Don't Ask (Collins) / Duke's Travels (Banks-Collins-Rutherford) / Duke's End (Banks-Collins-Rutherford)

- **Release date: 21 March 1980**
- **Recorded at Polar Studios, Sweden, November and December 1979**
- **Engineer: David Hentschel**
- **Mixed at Maison Rouge, London**
- **Mastered by Ray Staff at Trident Studios, London**
- **Assistant Engineer: Dave Bascombe**
  Production: David Hentschel and Genesis
- **Sleeve design: Lionel Koechlin**

- **Tony Banks: keyboards, backing vocals, 12-string guitar, duck**
- **Mike Rutherford: basses, guitars, backing vocals**
- **Phil Collins: drums, vocals, drum machine, duck**

- **Dave Hentschel: backing vocals**

THE MAKING OF

With the short Japanese tour in December 1978 concluding an absolute marathon enterprise, one that had kept Genesis on the road for the best part of the year, management had good reason to feel satisfied; the band had finally cracked America, consolidated its standing in Europe and got a foothold in a new continent.

The schedule now envisaged a well-earned holiday so band members could spend a quiet Christmas with their families. And while Banks and Rutherford did just that, for the Collins family, the 1978 tour had been as devastating as an earthquake. After a brief fling with a painter and decorator, Phil's wife, Andrea, headed off to Canada with the couple's children, Joely and Simon, to live with her mother. Distraught, Phil called a meeting with Tony and Mike. Collins: "I left the band and went to Vancouver to try and save my marriage. They went off and did their solo records while I tried to sort myself out." [1]

Alas, Collins' attempts to save his marriage were short-lived and once he realised that the break with his wife was irreparable, he had no choice other than to return to England where he found Tony and Mike immersed in their solo projects. Unable to work with Genesis, in April Collins went back to his second group, Brand X, with whom he recorded PRODUCT, probably their most mainstream record, at Ringo Starr's Startling Studios.

But more importantly, in Collins, a whole new need was beginning to stir. Collins: "When I got back, they were in the middle of doing their solo albums, so they kind of had to finish them. I didn't have anything to do so I started writing." [1]

Moving back into his house in Surrey, Phil opted to sleep in the guest room, setting up a small 4-track recorder in one of the bedrooms. It was there, while trying to come to terms with the heartache caused by the newly imposed distance from his family, that he developed a previously unknown talent for composing songs. Written almost entirely about his marriage break-up, Phil's torch songs are decidedly different from Genesis' usual style. He had Tony and Mike listen to some of his new songs and they chose two of them.

Banks: "I know some people would say we should have chosen a few more. And yes, he did also play us *If Leaving Me Is Easy* and *I Missed Again*, but they didn't appeal to me as much as *Misunderstanding* and *Please Don't Ask*. I think we sort of thought that two were more than enough. He didn't play us *In The Air Tonight* because at that stage it hadn't been completed or maybe even started."[1]

Eternal discord between the two abounds on this point, however. Collins: "Tony insists that I never played him *In The Air Tonight*; he says that if he *had* heard it, he would have wanted to do it with Genesis, but I know I did because I was very proud of it."[1]

Whatever the case may be, when the three actually got back together in October 1979, the starting point was very different to that of the previous album, because in terms of writers, ...*now* there were three.

Banks: "This album is still more dominated by what Mike and I wrote but Phil was coming up to be an equal kind of writer, which I think is a strength because it gave us more variety. Phil's the most direct, I'm the least direct and Mike's somewhere in the middle. It was a combination which

GENESIS

Poster printed by Premier, the famous American brand of drums

Press photo shot during writing sessions for DUKE, 1979

worked quite well. Phil and I would pull each other in different directions; I'd make him expand a bit and he'd make me contract, which was no bad thing otherwise every song would have been 25 minutes long." [1]

Rutherford: "Phil's writing stuff on his own helped change the balance. He's always been very good at writing songs that work in sort of four minutes, which was never our forte and that helped balance the album." [1]

Banks: "Mike and I had both done solo albums at this point which kind of took the independently written stuff more out of the equation really. Even Phil had started to work on what would later become FACE VALUE, so I think we came in a little bit barren of ideas. So, we sat down and did a lot more improvising, working on some of the ideas that we hadn't really developed." [1]

Rutherford: "I think it's a very important album, because if it hadn't happened, in my mind we wouldn't have carried on. We sort of re-found ourselves a little bit. By this point, we had done some solo albums so we were less pushy about getting our individual stuff on our albums. Phil was living alone in his house in Guildford and we wrote the album there, in one of the bedrooms." [1]

Collins: "At Old Croft (my house in Surrey) I already had the second bedroom as my little studio but we ended up moving all the furniture out of the master bedroom and setting up all the gear in there. By this point, we'd decided that what we did best and what we preferred, now that we had our solo outlets, was writing together, you know, doing things that we couldn't do anywhere else."[1]

Rutherford: "After this album, because we did more solo albums, we started writing together more. I think the solo stuff made it possible. I mean, if you've got three guys bringing in lots of songs it's hard to actually find enough room. But with solo albums being done, you had less stuff to bring in, you no longer came in saying 'here are my ten songs'. You actually arrived with only a few bits of material."[1]

Many of the new songs showed evident signs of being linked by common themes, so much so that the band even considered creating a new suite. Banks: "It would have gone *Behind The Lines / Duchess / Guide Vocal / Turn It On Again / Duke's Travels / Duke's End*, which is how we went on to perform them live. But in the studio we decided not to link them up for two reasons. One reason was that we didn't want the comparison with *Supper's Ready*. Secondly, we felt that maybe it wasn't the moment to do a totally combined thing like that. As it is, there is quite a lot of linkage between those tracks anyhow, being as the first three are already connected."[1]

Collins: "At one point we did think about revisiting the idea of doing a long track on one side, but in the end we started and finished with *Behind The Lines* as there are some reprises of *Behind The Lines* in *Duke's End*. It's kind of bookended in musical form, from the beginning of Side One to the end of Side Two. Maybe we simply felt that the idea of a long track was just a little too thought-out. *Supper's Ready* was something that kind of developed by itself, whereas to go into it saying 'let's write this big thing' probably isn't the way to go about it."[1]

Rutherford: "On the Duke album we returned to recalling themes, like the intro reprised in *Duke's End*, so it's not a concept as such, but it does have a thread running through it. I never saw it as being

105

like *Supper's Ready*, it was more of a loose thread. You have the beginning and then stuff going on before rounding it off with the reprise. It was more like topping and tailing it; trying to keep a little bit of similarity and feel throughout the album."[1]

Phil's greater involvement in the writing process also gave him greater confidence as a singer.

Banks: "He sang well on the previous albums, but somehow on this one, as opposed to just being a singer of a band, he'd become a great singer. Probably, his having written his own songs for FACE VALUE and singing in a certain kind of way had taught him to use his voice more."[1]

Collins: "By that point, I'd done more singing out on the road, so I was beginning to find my feet as a singer. Although, if the truth be known, it still meant more to me to play the drums on tracks than sing on them. I was still singing other people's words, even on songs that were group written, but some of the songs were mine, like *Misunderstanding* and *Please Don't Ask*, of course. Ironically that was one of the most personal songs I'd ever written and yet the Genesis guys wanted to do it because they liked the sound of it. By the time we wrote DUKE I'd written all the stuff for FACE VALUE and done all the demos. It wasn't finished but I had been through the writing process, so I'd changed, I'd become a songwriter. And that meant I'd become more of a singer because I was singing songs that I'd written, emoting if you like, putting things out there. So yeah, it's probably true that this was the first album where I felt more comfortable as a singer."[1]

The album was recorded in Stockholm, yet again with Dave Hentschel as co-producer.

Collins: "Nearly everything on the album has a live feel about it and actually sounds almost the way we wrote it because once we'd written the songs we went to Polar Studios and recorded it live. Abba had just opened this wonderful studio which had a lovely, great big drum room. I think Led Zeppelin had recorded there actually. I worked there a few times afterwards."[1]

Banks: "But we mixed it back here, at a studio called Maison Rouge, and although it was a very nice studio, I don't think it had a totally faithful monitoring system; it wasn't really up to the standard we would have liked."[1]

Poster printed in Scotland, 1980.
Edited by Pace Minerva

Promotional poster for the album DUKE, Charisma Records, UK 1980

THE ALBUM

The end of the '70s represented a massive turning point in the development of rock music. The toppling of the idols of progressive rock ushered in a plethora of new styles and genres, with punk to all intents and purposes already consigned to the history books. The only band still flying the iconoclastic flag in 1979 was The Clash with LONDON CALLING, while what is usually referred to as New Wave was already in full swing. The Police had sent their ground-breaking album REGGATTA DE BLANC to press, artists like Talking Heads, Elvis Costello, Devo, XTC, The Stranglers and Blondie already had at least two albums under their belts, while debut releases included LIFE IN A DAY by Simple Minds, THREE IMAGINARY BOYS by The Cure, The B-52's eponymous album and U2's EP, THREE. In the meantime, other newcomers were also sending ripples through the music scene: Joy Division, with UNKNOWN PLEASURES, created an exemplary dark, existentialist album, while Madness took ska into the charts with ONE STEP BEYOND.

Of course, not everything on offer was so innovative, take for example Toto who, with their album HYDRA, clearly didn't want to stray outside their comfort zone, and the one-hit wonders, The Knack, with their single *My Sharona*. On the other hand, this was the period when disco music was enjoying its last wave of popularity (the Bee Gees, still cashing in on the success of SATURDAY NIGHT FEVER, released SPIRITS HAVING FLOWN, Donna Summer brought out BAD GIRLS, the best-selling album of her career, and Michael Jackson proved he was in a class of his own with OFF THE WALL). Hard rock, in the meantime, was going through a transitional phase: while members of Deep Purple went their separate ways (some would go on to pursue their musical careers in other bands: Gillan, Rainbow and Whitesnake), Led Zeppelin released their last studio album (IN THROUGH THE OUT DOOR) and rock veterans Status Quo released their classic WHATEVER YOU WANT. However, in May 1979 Geoff Barton, writing for Sounds music magazine, coined the term 'New Wave of British Heavy Metal' to describe all those bands who, tired of punk, were going back to explore hard rock in depth. Alongside established bands UFO, Thin Lizzy, Judas Priest and Motörhead, new arrivals included Saxon, Def Leppard,

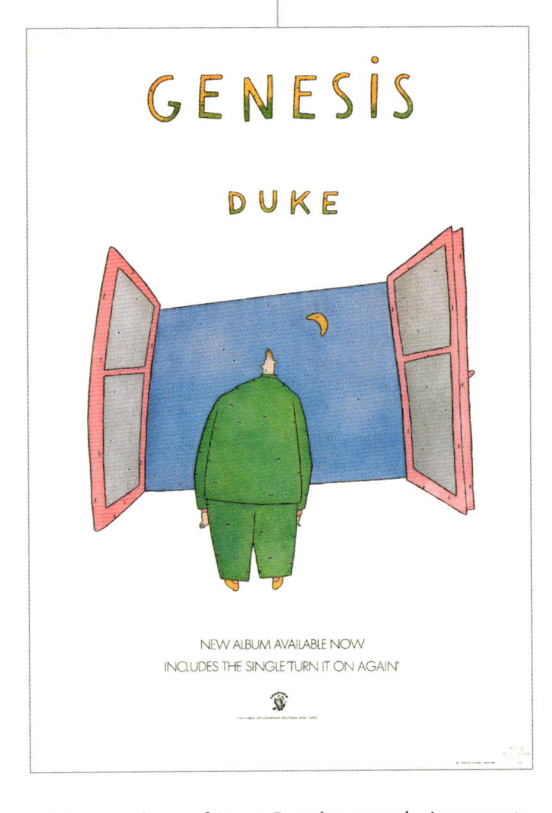

GENESIS

Promotional poster for the album DUKE, Atlantic Records, USA 1980

Tygers Of Pan Tang, as well as the legendary Iron Maiden.

In the meantime music's biggest names were still churning them out: Frank Zappa released no less than three albums in 1979, Bob Dylan brought out SLOW TRAIN COMING (his first album after converting to Christianity), Bob Marley confirmed his rise in popularity with SURVIVAL, Joni Mitchell went over to jazz with MINGUS, Neil Young was back on form with RUST NEVER SLEEPS and David Bowie completed his Berlin trilogy with LODGER. On the other hand, the standard-bearers of progressive rock were in a complete daze, the obvious exception of course being Pink Floyd, who created one of their masterpieces, THE WALL. This album by Waters & Co. is probably the most representative record of 1979, but the extraordinary hits, BREAKFAST IN AMERICA by Supertramp and THE LONG RUN by the Eagles, are certainly not to be ignored.

And in the midst of this whirlwind of styles which kept coming and going, Genesis' new album represents a state of balance between their musical past and their evolution. From the very opening of *Behind The Lines*, the band appears to be much more relaxed and dynamic on an instrumental level and much more receptive to non-European sounds, while at the same time marking a return to those wider-ranging compositions they had deliberately eschewed in the previous album. This doesn't just refer to the journey that is *Duke's Travels / Duke's End*, but also in a number of ambitious harmonic and instrumental ideas flowing from the pen of Tony Banks (who else?): the orchestral pomp of *Cul-De-Sac* and the romanticism of *Heathaze* and the outtake *Evidence Of Autumn*. On the other hand, Rutherford (as fantastic as ever on bass but still finding his feet in the role of lead guitarist) wrote the gem, *Open Door*, which alas didn't make it to the album, and two lesser songs, the pared-down *Man Of Our Times* and *Alone Tonight*, which stands out as the prototype of the ballads he would go on to develop with Mike + The Mechanics. DUKE also includes Collins' debut as a solo writer: *Misunderstanding* is as incomprehensible (and a cause for shock at the time of its release) on a Genesis album as it was unexpectedly well-received on the American market,

Italian magazine *Popster* n. 35, May 1980

while *Please Don't Ask*, in its wonderful simplicity, cannot fail to arouse emotion in the listener thanks to the lyrics which go straight to the heart. Moreover, these two tracks gave a clear indication as to where Collins' solo career was about to take him.

So, the three musicians were back to happily writing together as a compact unit for this album. What was initially the so-called '*The Duke Suite*' is the perfect melting pot between old and new Genesis and is representative of the album as a whole, an album which succeeded in assuaging the sensibilities of the band's progressive era fans while at the same time attracting legions of new followers.

Duke is the album which would take Genesis into the 1980s, both literally and musically. Aware of the changes in the music world, instead of covering their ears, the trio took note and acted accordingly. And would do so even more in the not-too-distant future.

THE SONGS

BEHIND THE LINES

The opening track exemplifies to perfection the transformation of Genesis: the instrumental intro driven by the keyboards running over an effective bass and drum rhythm is both beautiful and powerful, as well as being almost devoid of solos seeing as Tony's keyboard brass sounds deliver the chords and Mike's finishing touches on electric guitar are limited to a few flourishes.

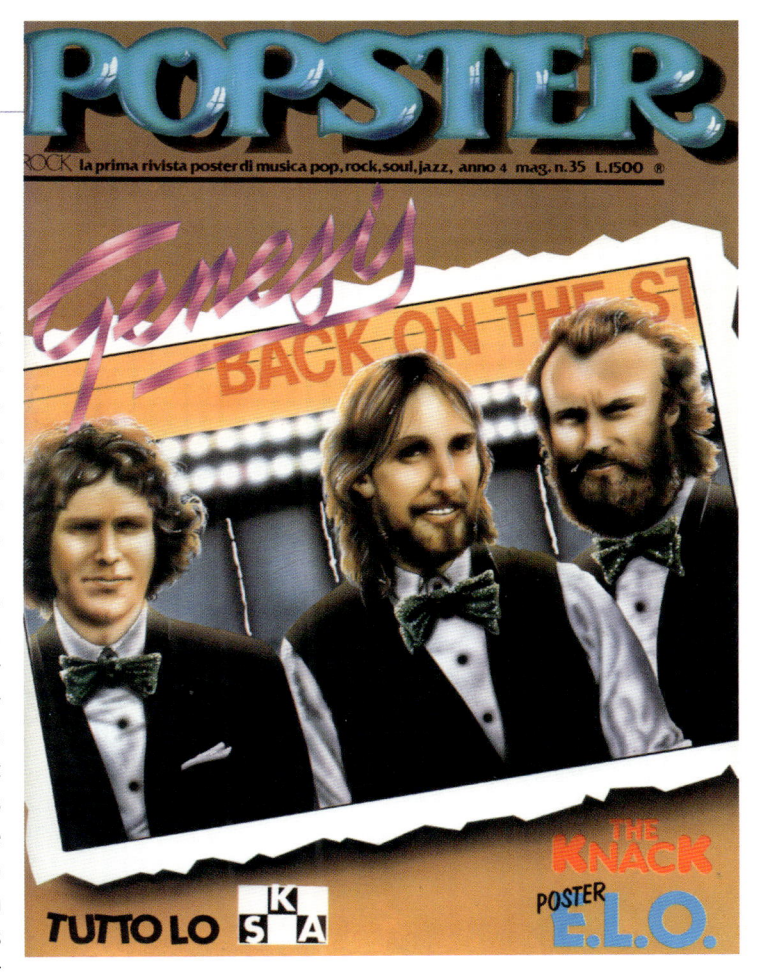

The beginning of the track came about at the very start of the writing sessions for the new album.

Banks: "I had this one, this riff, which was just a rotational sort of riff that I hadn't really developed. So we sat down, started playing it and immediately began to develop little ideas. The whole song was actually just a development of that first part, it wasn't something written beforehand, it emerged in the studio from that one idea. We were playing as an ensemble." [1]

GENESIS

Tony in New York, 29th June 1980

Collins: "The horn things (on this and on *Turn It On Again*) were actually played on Dave Hentschel's ARP synthesiser. I had a duck call, which meant I could play it like a horn player. It wouldn't be in tune of course but then it went into a microphone and Dave would play the tune. So when you next hear it, think of ducks!"[1]

An unusual set of casual circumstances would give Phil the idea of later recording a cover of the track. Collins: "Polar Studios had one of the very first, state-of-the-art digital machines. When you wanted to erase tracks you did it at double speed. We'd recorded the *Behind The Lines* backing track and we put it at double speed to erase the tracks we wanted to free up. And listening to it, we all said, 'It's the Jackson Five for God's sake'. I said, 'We should do it; it'd be great to do it like this!'. But they said, 'No, no, no, no... You do it like that if you want it like that'. So I did, on FACE VALUE."[1]

In the preliminary draft, Phil's lyrics were very cynical, along the same lines as *Down And Out*, only this time inspired by the negative attitude of certain critics towards Genesis. However, Tony and Mike managed to convince their bandmate to moderate his tone.

DUCHESS

This is the first Genesis song to feature a drum machine. Collins: "In '78 we went to Japan for the first time. We were there for a couple of weeks and they treated us like royalty. Roland, a Japanese company (at least it was then, I don't know now) gave us each one of these drum machines that were fresh off the production line (*the CR-78, now much sought after as a vintage model – author's note*). It was slightly programmable and not quite all cha cha cha and waltz (a little bit of that, but still original). Anyway, when I got back home, I had this marriage stuff going on and so I finished my studio and started to write what was to become FACE VALUE, and, of course, *In The Air Tonight* uses that drum machine (it's all over the place on that record)."[1]

Banks: "Mike and I were very keen on it because this replaced the drummer as far as we were concerned. Phil didn't want to know about drum machines; well, he is a drummer after all! Anyhow, later on he suddenly got to thinking it was quite interesting and so he started playing with it and got totally hooked on it. The song *Duchess* sort of emerged as the drum machine was going. Mike was doing the little twiddly things and I started doing little tinkles on the piano and then this whole idea came out of it. Very simple. Because it was a drum machine and it was repeating in 4/4, you got stuck into certain time signatures. The first time we ever used one was really exciting: it would carry on without you having to do anything. That's what was nice about it, you could try something, and then if it didn't work, try again. Whereas a drummer always wants to do something fiddly, a drum machine just keeps on relentlessly doing the same thing."[1]

Collins: "But the drums still played a big part of it, because you thought you had the sound and then suddenly the drums come in and it goes 'cinemascope'. And Dave Hentschel was great, he'd worked at Trident Studios with ex-Beatle engineers and so he got this great, sort of very compressed Ringo-type sound. That track is one of our best. It's one of those things where you've just captured it at that moment. If we'd done another half dozen takes, it wouldn't have had the same freshness."[1]

Banks: "*Duchess* is probably one of my favourite tracks we've ever done. Very simple. And a lyric that is very easy to relate to; the rise and fall of a female rock star called Duchess. Could have called it Madonna if we'd thought about it because Madonna hadn't been created by that point. There hadn't been many female pop stars but there were more of them by 1980 when we were doing this, so it seemed quite an interesting thing to write about." [1]

Collins provides a strong vocal performance on the track.

Banks: "I think the singing on this is really tremendous. I wrote the lyric and the melody on what we'd done as an improvisation, then I sang it and taped it. All the elements were already there but when he sang it... it's not just that he's got a better voice than me, it was all the little embellishments and tales and things that happened on it which just transformed it completely from being something a session guy might do to something that a singer does. His own character is sort of right across it and the resultant effect is very, very strong." [1]

GUIDE VOCAL

A very short song written by Tony for piano and voice with a sprinkle of bass and synth strings.

Banks: "I had this little melody line that I really liked, but I couldn't make anything bigger of it, so I decided to write a lyric for it. It was one of those days when you feel like the whole world is going up the spout, so many bad things were happening. I'm not a believer in God but what if God existed; why wouldn't he abandon us at this point and say, 'Screw you! Why should I save you? You've screwed up the whole of creation'. So that's what that was all about, the guide vocal was God, but it was just a dismissive kind of thing. And then we reprised it at the end of *Duke's Travels*." [2]

MAN OF OUR TIMES

Rutherford: "I saw this as a Gary Numan vocal and it never, never worked. Looking back and knowing what I know now I should have said, 'let's just dump this song'. But at the time I was younger

GENESIS

Mike in New York, 29th June 1980

and a bit more defensive about it, I suppose, but it's not a great moment. I haven't heard it since we did it, and let's keep it that way please." [1]

The track is based on guitar synth parts written by Mike over drum beats with an arpeggioed 12-string guitar chorus. What's more, David Hentschel sang backing vocals on it.

Banks: "I love the way the chorus comes in with the guitar sounds. It's a great song but I didn't like the way the vocals were done." [2]

The lyrics (a summary description of a man in modern times) are disappointing, as even the author is happy to admit. Rutherford: "It was not a good lyric. I think if we'd done that song two albums later it would have been better lyrically." [3]

MISUNDERSTANDING

Collins: "This is a song I'd written based on a certain kind of rhythm; it was a little bit between Toto's *Hold The Line* and *Sail On Sailor* by the Beach Boys. I love that kind of rock thing, like *Rocky Mountain Way* by Joe Walsh, although I don't say it ended up being as good as that. I was going to have it on FACE VALUE but then I played it to the guys and Tony and Mike really liked it for the same reasons; they like the Beach Boys rock thing. So they took that song and we recorded it." [1]

Phil's debut as the sole writer of a song is hardly outstanding: a joint guitar and bass riff over a thumping piano, the '60s style backing vocals and some pretty obvious lyrics on the subject of unfaithfulness. That said, when it was released as a single in the States, it was a hit.

Collins: "It had *single* written all over it. And now we had more girls in the audience and more radio stations played it. I was pleased that something I'd written was doing so well. I was growing as a writer at that time, I was kind of surfacing from some personal stuff and I'd written what were to become great songs, like *Against All Odds* and *In The Air Tonight*." [1]

HEATHAZE

A touching ballad led by the piano which becomes heart-wrenching when the vocals start along with an arpeggioed guitar. Rutherford's bass is splendid, interacting wonderfully with the synth in the bridge to create a suspended atmosphere.

Banks: "It's almost like a follow up to *Undertow* on the previous album. It's a little bit overlooked because there are a lot of other good songs on this album. I was rather pleased with it. It's sort of romantic, more philosophical musings really. It's probably the last song I wrote in this kind of slightly pianistic and romantic manner for Genesis (although I've done it lots of times since on my solo albums)." [1]

TURN IT ON AGAIN

Side Two opens with a very catchy, rhythmic song that was to become the first single off the album.

Banks: "The bit that became *Turn it On Again* was originally just a link. We went once round the whole sequence and then into *Duke's Travels*, but then I thought, 'that's much too strong to do it just the once'. So we did it twice and then looped out on the choruses at the end. After doing our solo albums, Mike and I had lots of bits left over. Mike had this one riff (and I have no idea why he didn't use it on his solo album because it's such a great riff) and I had this other bit that sort of became the rest of the song. And so we just put the two together. And then we doubled it and Mike wrote a lyric for it." [1]

The guitar riff was originally at a slower tempo. Banks: "My bit was slower too. But Phil, you know, he was in a certain kind of mood in those days and wanted to speed it up. The drums are what make it, they're the key element. That's why it's so much a group song even though musically it was written by me and Mike. Phil gave it an energy and something that we hadn't contemplated at all originally." [1]

Rutherford: "Phil wanted to pick it up a lot. At one point I was going with a sort of Queen harmony on guitars. This just shows how a band works, how someone can just take an idea and develop it. If he hadn't wanted to speed it up, it wouldn't have had that driving feel to it. He said to me, 'you do realise it's not in 4/4', which I thought it was, 'but in 13/8, don't you?'." [1]

Collins: "It's in 13/8, which always stops people from dancing, but they tend to dance right through it. It's got a good drum part that makes it sound simple rather than as complicated as it really is. I think if we'd told the record company it was in 13/8, they'd have said it couldn't be a single." [1]

Rutherford: "People have said that it would have

been our greatest single if the chorus had come in earlier and not after four minutes. They're right. There is a chorus, but I didn't do it until the end. It's a great chorus though."[1]

Banks: "I often wonder whether *Turn It On Again* would have ever been played on the radio if we hadn't already had *Follow You Follow Me* because it's a more complex piece of music and it's deceptively simple; it has that extra beat every third bar. And it goes through a lot of chords and things and there is no particular chorus line until the end of the song."[1]

ALONE TONIGHT

A vocal line over 12-string guitar is the basis of this love song which includes rich, rhythmic keyboards in the chorus.

Rutherford: "It's a nice romantic ballad. DUKE was the first time we'd written together as a band for a while since Peter left, so it was an important time. Because with my *Alone Tonight* and *Snowbound* and Tony's *The Lady Lies*, we were starting to get into a habit; there would be a Tony Banks song, different compositionally, and then an acoustic

Press photo, 1980

ballad from me... a pattern emerging. That's why the next album, ABACAB, was all band-written." [3]

Banks: "Personally, I think it's one of Mike's weakest tracks. We were so disappointed, you know, when we played the album to Charisma Records and they said this was the single. We said it had to be *Turn It On Again*, as we were really proud of that, it has a subtlety about it, it's deceptive as it's a great rock song. *Alone Tonight* isn't a great song. The other song Mike wrote, which we left off the album, *Open Door*, is a better track." [2]

CUL-DE-SAC

Banks: "It came out of the same writing period as A CURIOUS FEELING, along with *Evidence Of Autumn* and *Heathaze*. Musically I think it's really interesting but I'm not sure about the lyrics." [2]

Magnificent and intricate, the track is based on Banks' piano with some amazing bass work from Rutherford and an impressive vocal performance from Collins.

Banks: "It was the first time Phil got that sort of crackling voice. He was working on FACE VALUE by now and I think he'd started to get that voice on his home demos and developed it. We'd done a few songs where his singing was still quite sweet, but this was the first where he sang differently. We thought it was great because when you put loads of compression on the song, it gave it real grit; he was able to hit an almost shouty type of vocal which he developed to great effect on things like *In The Air Tonight*. This was the first time we heard it on a Genesis track and it was very exciting really because, although he had managed to get through things like *Squonk*, he wasn't really quite there, whereas suddenly he was sounding like a rock singer, which was interesting as it opened up a whole new world. And yet it was a curious song for it to happen on as *Cul-De-Sac* is a typical airy-fairy progressive Genesis track (but a good one)." [2]

PLEASE DON'T ASK

A piano and vocal ballad. The most notable feature lies in Collins' lyrics which talk about the end of his marriage and missing his kids; as direct and to the point as pages torn from a diary.

Rutherford: "We were all going in that direction a bit, but I think Phil writes better lyrics for this sort of direct song than either myself or Tony. And I think the time felt right, we'd already done a lot (too much) of the romantic storytelling, you know, the fables and stuff." [1]

Banks: "It's a simple sentiment, but just really well done (which is what Phil does very well on his own). He went the other way from us; we were writing about, you know, Greek gods and things and he was just writing about himself. And he worked out a way of doing it really well. When he tried to write a bit more like we did, like on some of the earlier songs, I don't think he was such a good lyric writer. But once he got into writing about reality, he was able to contribute far more to the band." [1]

DUKE'S TRAVELS / DUKE'S END

The album closes with a lengthy instrumental piece dominated by Phil's rolling drums and Tony's various synthesisers while Mike, besides having provided the impetus for the song, ensures the necessary cohesion.

Banks: "It started off as one of Mike's ideas. He was using a guitar synth and came up with this riff 'de-da-de-da, de-da-de-da' [1'56"], and I played in triplets over the top of it. In 6/8 time you can play very fast, a much easier way to play triplets, and of course this was before the days of sequencers. So it started as this idea of Mike's and developed from there into all the other bits. There's a very strong moment when the song changes to the more driving beat. It's a very difficult part to play on the drums." [2]

Whilst these tracks are instrumentals, there is a brief reprise of the sung melody from *Guide Vocal* in the closing section of *Duke's Travels*. Banks: "I was doing quite a few of the solos and I thought it was a good idea to come back to the chords in *Guide Vocal* because I thought they were really strong and I wanted to do more with them than we had done originally (in the track on Side One) as I hadn't managed to develop them into a full song. I thought we could put them in there and do it differently and that was quite exciting for me. The chords done at that really fast rhythm sounded good and I was so glad that we could do it on tour." [2]

OTHER SONGS

Written by Mike Rutherford, *Open Door* is an acoustic ballad with no drums. Mike steers it along with his acoustic guitar while Tony limits himself to giving a little support with a layer of keyboards. Phil's voice reaches in and touches the listener's heart as he sings about someone being forced to make a painful farewell.

Rutherford: "There are moments in life when you get to see a snapshot of what's going on around you, what's going on in life, and you go away with that image." [3]

Evidence Of Autumn is a typical Banks composition, centred on a piano arrangement of almost dissonant chords and with a grandiose atmosphere highlighted by the jazzy mood of the cymbals while Rutherford plays a great bass line and a melancholy guitar riff.

Promotional photo, Charisma / ATCO Records 1980

Banks: "This is one of my favourite songs from that era but, like *Cul-De-Sac*, it was a leftover from A Curious Feeling. I wanted to have two different choruses with one verse and then the middle eight which has a yearning quality about it in a way. That was many years ago but that idea always sends a shiver down my spine. I thought it was a really good song and it's a pity it didn't end up on one of the albums as it deserved to be really." [2]

THE ALBUM ARTWORK

A fat man with a small head looking out of a window all in very delicate lines and pastel shades. Taken from Lionel Koechlin's book, *L'Alphabet d'Albert*, the cover of Genesis' tenth album is, in its simplicity, one of the most beautiful.

Banks: "We wanted something different, so we looked in a different area for a designer. He gave us various suggestions and possibilities, including this 'ABC' done by this French guy which had this character in it. We looked through it, really liked the style and chose the picture for Q. It had a question mark above it which we took out. He's called Albert and is always thought of as Duke. I like that it's nice, concise and clear. It was nice to have something quite straightforward because I think this is a very positive album." [1]

Collins: "I love the cover. When we saw this picture we all gravitated towards it. I think there was a little bit of 'Tin Tin' in it, you know, a bit of a cartoony, caricature kind of imagery that we all liked. This fat guy, I mean, he wasn't Duke but he could have been." [1]

Rutherford: "It's like buying books in the airport shop: you go into the shop and if you don't know about the books and just want an easy thriller to read, sometimes you just choose the cover or the title, you haven't got time to even read what it's about. I think, in Genesis, we've always been very keen on quite simple images, graphic ones rather than on a mishmash of lots of ideas and Duke kind of embodies that; it's a really simple, strong and quirky style image." [1]

EPILOGUE

Released at the end of March 1980, Duke was Genesis' first album to reach the top of the UK charts, while also improving the band's positioning in the US, where it reached No. 11.

Banks: "Throughout our career, every album outsold its predecessor. I think we tended to accumulate people. People would buy the album and then another lot would come in for the next one and most of the fans you had for the previous album would still be there. So we were very lucky in that really. To be honest this is my favourite Genesis album really. I love the way it starts, I love *Duchess* (it works fantastically) and I love all the instrumental towards the end too. There's a strong emotional moment when it gets to the repeat of *Guide Vocal* within *Duke's Travels* which is a very intense piece of singing and everything; that to me is one of the strongest moments in Genesis' music." [1]

Collins: "We were starting to get a bit harder and edgier than on …And Then There Were Three… As you know, Mike had this guitar riff for *Turn It On Again* in 13/8. He started playing it and I played along and because we were rehearsing in a bedroom it kind of sounded really rock'n'roll, you know, it was a lot more vibrant than the things we'd done

GENESIS

> Poster advertising all the Genesis discography, including solo albums on Charisma Records. This unique item was included in the original Italian release of DUKE in Italy by Polygram Records

before. *Duke's Travels*, *Duke's End*, *Behind The Lines*, all that stuff is very, very strong. There's a lot of energy and a live sound. To me, that was the first time we started to sound good on record." [1]

The first single to come out in the UK was *Turn It On Again*, which reached No. 8 in the charts, while the two following singles weren't quite as successful: *Duchess* only managed to get as high as No. 46 and *Misunderstanding* No. 42. The latter, however, was a hit in the States where it climbed to No. 14, the highest place in the US singles charts the band had ever reached.

Rutherford: "I never liked being defined as a progressive rock band, but I don't think we were a hit-making machine either. I don't really care; I mean you have to do what you want to do and never worry about it. It happens to any band that has a big cult following and gets mass appeal." [1]

Notwithstanding the threat posed by punk, Genesis band members, past and present, seemingly couldn't put a foot wrong, with all their releases being met with rave reviews. Tony's and Mike's solo albums did well: Banks' A CURIOUS FEELING, released in October 1979, had reached No. 21 in the charts, while Rutherford's SMALLCREEP'S DAY, which came out in February 1980, made it all the way up to No. 13.

And just a few months after DUKE, two former band members, Gabriel and Hackett, consolidated the success of their solo careers: Peter's third solo album, released on 31 May, reached No. 1 in the UK album charts, while Steve's DEFECTOR would reach No. 9 just a few weeks later.

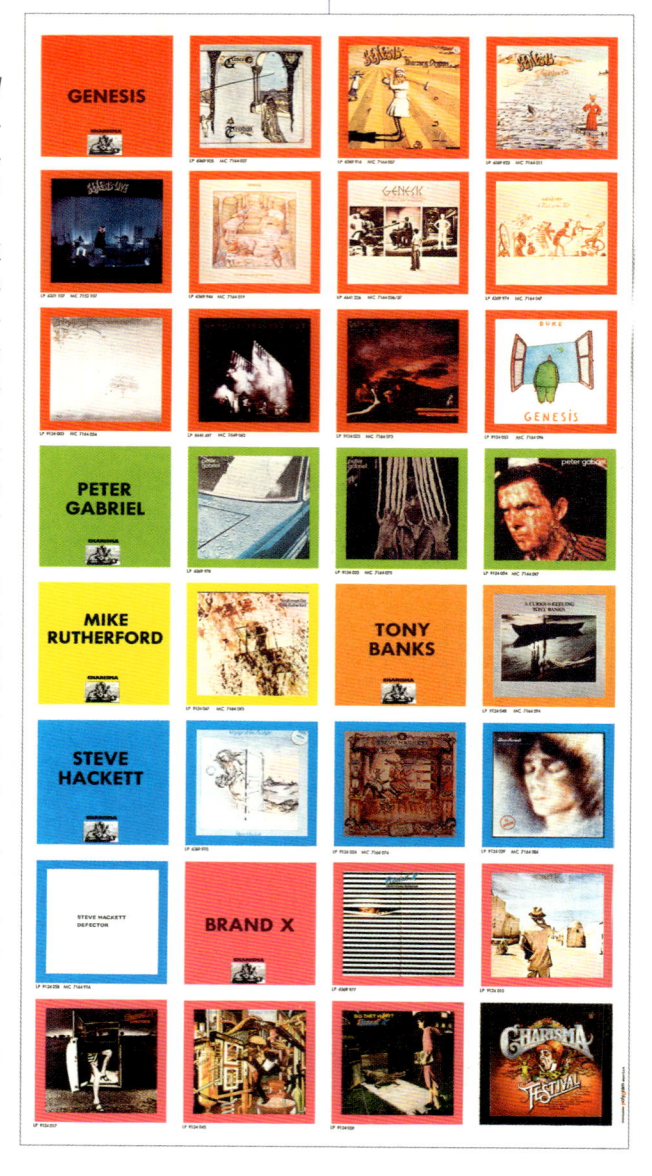

THE CONCERTS

Tony, Mike, Phil, Chester and Daryl met up at Shepperton Studios, London, in the early weeks of 1980 to start putting together a live repertoire for the forthcoming tour. To make amends with their home-country fans (who in the previous exceptionally long world tour had been forced to make do with just a single show at Knebworth) the band changed tack completely, opting to cut out all dates in mainland Europe while scheduling a UK theatre tour with almost 40 dates; something they hadn't done for five years.

The announcement of the tour was met with sensational fervour, with fans sometimes queuing through the night and sleeping in the street just to be sure of getting tickets. This was hardly surprising when demand reached 500,000 for an overall maximum of 80,000 seats, being as the biggest concert hall selected, the Hammersmith Odeon in London, had a capacity of just 3,000.

Genesis kicked off with a few warm-up gigs, the first of which was in Paignton on 17 March 1980. The hypnotic pulsing of the bass led into the unexpected resurrection of *Back In N.Y.C.*, followed by *Dancing With The Moonlit Knight – The Carpet Crawlers / Squonk / One For The Vine / The Duke Suite: Behind The Lines – Duchess – Guide Vocal – Turn It On Again – Duke's Travels – Duke's End / Say It's Alright Joe / The Lady Lies / Ripples / In The Cage – Raven – Afterglow / Follow You Follow Me / Dance On A Volcano – Los Endos / I Know What I Like*.

From a purely musical point of view, the DUKE tour went one notch higher than the previous one with the band entering that state of executional grace they would hold onto for years.

Thompson: "I think when I joined, the feeling changed a lot. Before, Genesis were very British and direct, but then they loosened up a bit. It's funny, as kids, me and Phil listened to the same stuff, we liked the same jazz and Motown drummers." [4]

For his part, Stuermer appeared much more at ease, playing guitar for all the old songs along with (as on the previous tour) *The Lady Lies* and *Say It's Alright Joe*, but also on the new tracks, such as *Behind The Lines*, *Duchess*, *Guide Vocal* and *Misunderstanding*.

To accommodate over half of the DUKE album, namely 'The Duke Suite' (six unabridged songs played in sequence without a break), a significant reshuffle of the setlist was needed which led to some painful omissions, not only of tracks such as *Down And Out* and *Ballad Of Big* which were never permanent fixtures, but also of *Burning Rope* (which only made it to the setlist in '78) and classics from the past such as *Eleventh Earl Of Mar, The Fountain Of Salmacis, The Cinema Show* and the encore *The Lamb Lies Down On Broadway / The Musical Box*. Consequently, the contents of the setlist began to lean decidedly towards the new era, much to the disappointment of the old fans who saw their beloved classics gradually being usurped by new tracks in the live shows.

But there were some exceptions. Alongside *Back In N.Y.C.*, which hadn't been played live since 1975, the setlist featured a newly restyled version of *In The Cage*. On the 1978 tour the song had been played along the same lines as the original track, apart from the end crescendo driven by Daryl's guitar, but in 1980 Genesis decided to join the instrumental sections that had been added to *The Cinema Show* in the previous tour (the reprise of the synth solo from *Raven* and a speeded-up sec-

GENESIS

Promotional photo by Retna Pictures Ltd

Jo Chester & Tony Smith poster advertising the sold out UK tour, 1980

tion of *Riding The Scree*) onto the end of *In The Cage* with this additional fragment steering the band straight into the beautiful *Afterglow*.

Another feature of the tour was the medley made up of the first two verses of *Dancing With The Moonlit Knight* (at a much slower tempo) and *The Carpet Crawlers*, back on the setlist after being left out of the previous tour.

However, the first setlist variations were seen as early on as the third show: on 19 March in Exeter, *Ripples* was dropped and *Squonk* was to meet a similar fate the following day in Guildford, with *The Lady Lies* being brought forward to take its place in the running order.

Of these warm-up gigs, special mention should be made of the Aylesbury show on 22 March at the legendary Friars Club where the band, thanks to promoter, David Stopps, had taken its first steps a decade earlier. During this show, before the second encore (exceptionally reserved for the abridged version of *The Knife*), Stopps stood up on stage and read out all the names of the fans who had queued up to buy tickets.

Once the warm-ups were over the actual tour was due to begin, but things got off to the worst possible start when the first two official dates on 24 and 26 March (respectively at the Guildhall in Portsmouth and the Winter Gardens in Bournemouth) had to be cancelled when Phil came down with laryngitis. The tour finally got under way with the three consecutive concerts at the Hammersmith Odeon starting on the 27th. Here Genesis reshuffled the setlist slightly, selecting *Deep In The Motherlode* as the opening track (a song which oddly enough uses the same rhythmic beat as *Back In N.Y.C.*). The 1974 track did, however, manage to hang on for

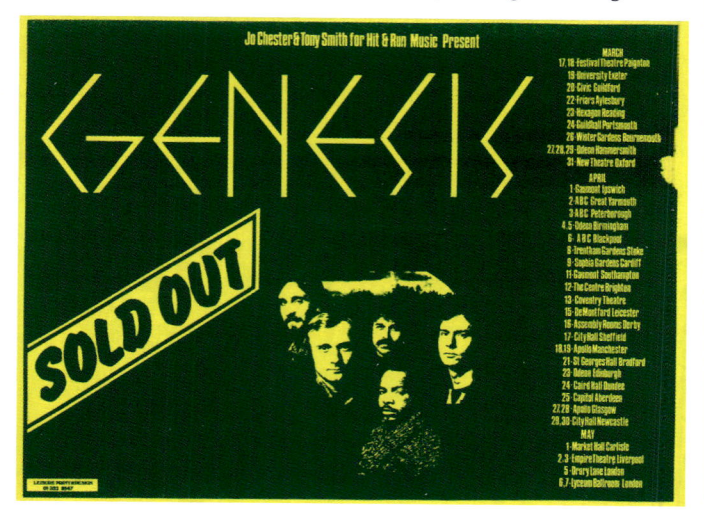

Japanese poster with Daryl Stuermer advertising Ibanez guitars

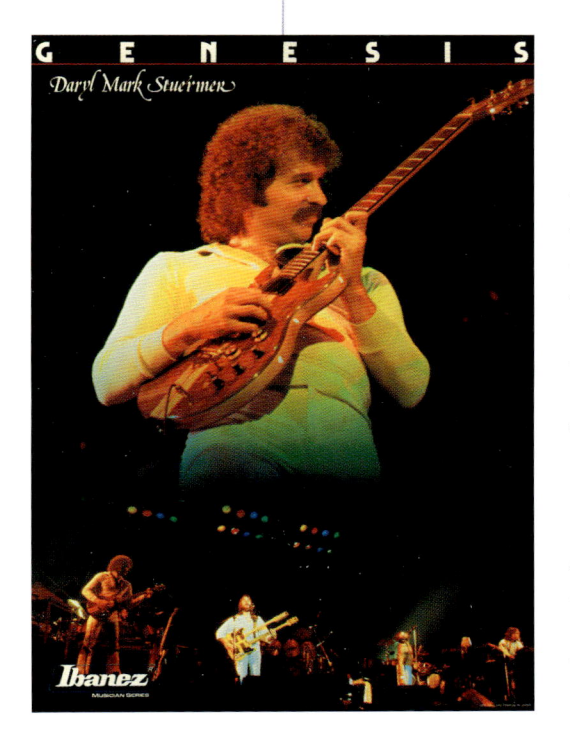

the very first Hammersmith concert (played before *One For The Vine*) before being crossed off the setlist (almost) definitively. The new running order thereafter was *Deep In The Motherlode / Dancing With The Moonlit Knight – The Carpet Crawlers / One For The Vine / The Duke Suite / Say It's Alright Joe / The Lady Lies / Ripples / In The Cage – Raven – Afterglow / Follow You Follow Me / Dance On A Volcano – Los Endos / I Know What I Like* and stayed the same throughout the UK tour with the only addition of *The Knife* as a second encore. Fans were lucky enough to hear this added bonus on several occasions: the third evening in London, in Oxford and Cardiff, at both shows in Manchester, in Glasgow, Liverpool on 2 and 3 May, in London on the 5th and 7th and finally in Portsmouth (when the cancelled March date was rescheduled).

After the interest shown by the BBC with its documentary 'Three Dates With Genesis', Britain's third television broadcasting channel, ITV, decided to air their own programme dedicated to the band called 'Live In Liverpool', including interviews with the band and members of the audience and long sections of the concert filmed at the Empire Theatre on 3 May.

Re-scheduled Portsmouth concert aside, the UK tour ended with a series of shows in London at the Drury Lane Theatre and the Lyceum Ballroom. Here, the BBC once again showed interest in the band, filming both evenings at the Lyceum. A 40-minute extract from the second of those two evenings was aired as part of BBC Two's 'The Old Grey Whistle Test' while the full concert filmed on the 6th was never shown on television but years later found its way into the hands of collectors (unfortunately, film footage of *Ripples* is incomplete).

At the end of the UK tour, the band took just one week off before heading to North America. Here they found themselves obliged to add *Misunderstanding* to the setlist, being as it had climbed its way up the Billboard Hot 100. Oddly enough on stage, it ran straight into the *In The Cage* medley.

Rutherford: "*Misunderstanding* was our first real hit in America. You could sort of sense the record label manager going, 'goodness, we've got a song that we can actually get on the radio'. Obviously, things really changed for the live shows; it wasn't just long songs now but also the shorter ones."[1]

The other variation in the North American tour was the exclusion of *The Carpet Crawlers*, while the more aggressive *Squonk* was joined up to the beginning of *Dancing With The Moonlit Knight*.

The setlist thus became: *Deep In The Motherlode*

GENESIS

Phil introducing the *Duke Suite* in Oakland on 23rd May 1980

/ Dancing With The Moonlit Knight – Squonk / One For The Vine / The Duke Suite / Say It's Alright Joe / The Lady Lies / Ripples / Misunderstanding / In The Cage – Raven – Afterglow / Follow You Follow Me / Dance On A Volcano – Los Endos / I Know What I Like.

As of 26 May (San Diego), *Say It's Alright Joe* was also dropped from the setlist, after which it would only be played one more time, at Pittsburgh on 13 June.

While the UK tour had focused on smaller venues, in North America (where the band's popularity was growing at a rate of knots) this simply wasn't possible. Over the 34 dates which saw the band play in California, Texas, Louisiana, Georgia, Illinois, Missouri, Wisconsin, Ohio, Pennsylvania, Massachusetts, New York, New Jersey and Canada, Genesis performed in relatively large venues with average seating capacities ranging from 15,000 to 20,000, including Madison Square Garden in New York and Maple Leaf Gardens in Toronto.

However, after the tribute paid to Aylesbury in England, the band wanted to pull off a similar feat in the States, organising a surprise concert at the Roxy Club in Los Angeles, where the band had enjoyed their first stateside success in December 1973. The only problem, however, was that the Roxy could only hold 500 people and even though the concert on 25 May was only advertised in the local press, news got out and spread like wildfire leading to ardent fans camping out in the street all night waiting for the box office to open. The following morning, the long wait was amply rewarded when the fans found the box office manned not by the Roxy Club staff but by Tony, Phil and Mike themselves, who sold and autographed tickets before handing them over to incredulous fans. The concert at the Roxy, the only one in America which included *The Carpet Crawlers* linked up to the beginning of *Dancing With The Moonlit Knight* followed by *Squonk*, also gave fans *The Knife* as a second encore, a privilege which would only be replicated at Rosemont on 6 June.

But there were evidently some real diehard early Genesis fans in America, so much so that on a few occasions (for example in Cleveland on 11 June and Boston on the 18th) Phil was practically forced

122

Mike and Chester in Oakland on 23rd May 1980

to sing a quick burst of *Supper's Ready* to the absolute delight of the audience. Maybe this is why, on 16 June in Philadelphia and again on the 24th in Toronto, Genesis added the closing section of *The Musical Box* as another special encore, whereas *Back In N.Y.C.* was resurrected for the first encore at Madison Square Garden in New York.

The North American tour went exceptionally well, but, even this time round, there was no shortage of hitches. The Vancouver show scheduled for 20 May was cancelled, while in Milwaukee on 7 June, Phil accidentally sang the third verse of *Squonk* twice, taking the song's overall length up to 8 minutes.

But this was nothing compared to what happened on 9 June when Daryl Stuermer was forced to go into hospital due to a dental infection.

Stuermer: "We played Milwaukee a couple of nights before and I had problems with my wisdom teeth. They got so bad that I went to a dentist and he said, 'we have to pull these out – today!', they were so infected. I phoned Mike and asked him if I could do that. He said if I had to, I had to. So, they worked out the set because they couldn't do all the songs but they could use bass pedals. Even my roadie played my bass pedals." (5)

In fact, Daryl's absence at Clarkston, near Detroit, meant that the setlist had to be pared back and *One For The Vine*, *Ripples* and *Follow You Follow Me* were dropped. A recording of the show, despite being of poor audio quality, is of interest as the listener gets to hears some quite different versions of songs with no guitar (the lack of which is most noticeable on *Behind The Lines*, *Dance On A Volcano* and *Afterglow*, played without the arpeggio) and with Mike only a couple of times attempting to play additional parts on *Duchess* (a guitar solo on the last bars of the song) and on *I Know What I Like* (the electric guitar riff, but only in certain points).

The stage show for the Duke tour was deliberately understated. Gone were the mirrors and the lasers, as Genesis focused the audience's attention more on the music. Tony, Mike and Daryl were dressed in white, while Phil wore multi-coloured Hawaiian shirts and appeared much more jovial than on the previous troubled tour, especially after meeting the woman who would become his second wife during the North American tour.

Philadelphia 16th June 1980

alongside a life-size cardboard cut-out of a naked woman.

Overall, the tour was another resounding success. While all their peers, with the exception of Pink Floyd, were reeling from the shock waves of the new young music, Genesis were able to count on a fan base which instead of dwindling was actually going from strength to strength.

Rutherford: "In America the audience wasn't really related to radio and records, you know; we were a much bigger live band than we were a recording band. Sometimes we were selling out two or three nights in arenas; bands who were doing the same thing would have albums in the Top Ten, something we hadn't had until DUKE."[1]

NOTES

(1)   Mike Kaufman's Genesis interviews, Chicago / London, October 2007, partially used in the bonus disc accompanying the 2008 remasters

(2)   Mario Giammetti's interview with Tony Banks, London, Tony Smith Personal Management office, 29 November 2016

(3)   Mario Giammetti's interview with Mike Rutherford, Munich, Freiheiz, 20 September 2016

(4)   Mario Giammetti's telephone interview with Chester Thompson, 13 August 1999, partially published in the article "Speciale interviste – Chester Thompson", *Dusk*, Issue n. 30, October 1999

(5)   Mario Giammetti's interview with Daryl Stuermer, Milan, Filaforum, 9 October 1997, partially published in the article "Daryl Stuermer speciale – intervista esclusiva", *Dusk*, Issue n. 24, January 1998

As well as playing out the role of the drunk in *Say Its Alright Joe*, Collins would really play to the audience when introducing his bandmates (Daryl, Chester and even Frank, the drum machine) and above all, the songs. Particularly long and entertaining was the introduction to *The Duke Suite*, during which Phil would tell the bizarre story of Albert (the character depicted on the album cover of DUKE), a sort of loser who keeps falling in love with the wrong people (and things), even citing a number of books supposedly written by Albert, such as 'Albert Through The Looking Glass', 'Albert In Wonderland', 'Albert Lies Down On Broadway')

DUKE TOUR

1980

MARCH

- 17 **Paignton (ENGLAND)**, Festival Theatre
- 18 **Paignton (ENGLAND)**, Festival Theatre
- 19 **Exeter (ENGLAND)**, Great Hall - Exeter University
- 20 **Guildford (ENGLAND)**, Guildford Civic Hall
- 22 **Aylesbury (ENGLAND)**, Maxwell Hall - Civic Centre
- 23 **Reading (ENGLAND)**, The Hexagon
- 27 **London (ENGLAND)**, Hammersmith Odeon
- 28 **London (ENGLAND)**, Hammersmith Odeon
- 29 **London (ENGLAND)**, Hammersmith Odeon
- 31 **Oxford (ENGLAND)**, New Theatre

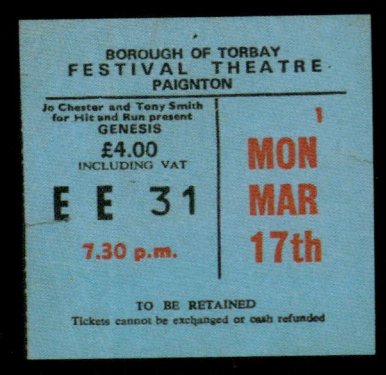

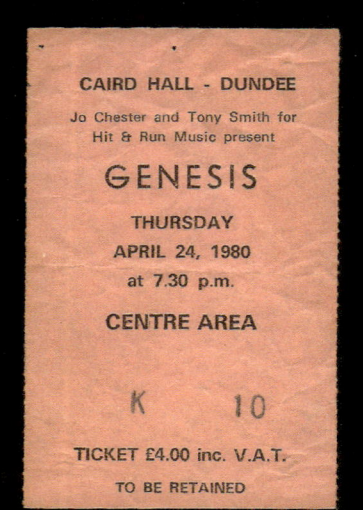

APRIL

- 01 **Ipswich (ENGLAND)**, Gaumont Theatre
- 02 **Great Yarmouth (ENGLAND)**, ABC Theatre
- 03 **Peterborough (ENGLAND)**, ABC Theatre
- 04 **Birmingham (ENGLAND)**, Odeon Theatre
- 05 **Birmingham (ENGLAND)**, Odeon Theatre
- 06 **Blackpool (ENGLAND)**, ABC Theatre
- 08 **Stoke-on-Trent (ENGLAND)**, Trentham Gardens
- 09 **Cardiff (WALES)**, Sophia Gardens
- 10 **Southampton (ENGLAND)**, Gaumont Theatre
- 11 **Southampton (ENGLAND)**, Gaumont Theatre
- 12 **Brighton (ENGLAND)**, The Brighton Centre
- 13 **Coventry (ENGLAND)**, Coventry Theatre
- 14 **Leicester (ENGLAND)**, De Montfort Hall
- 15 **Leicester (ENGLAND)**, De Montfort Hall
- 16 **Derby (ENGLAND)**, Great Hall - Assembly Rooms
- 17 **Sheffield (ENGLAND)**, Oval Hall - Sheffield City Hall
- 18 **Manchester (ENGLAND)**, Apollo Theatre
- 19 **Manchester (ENGLAND)**, Apollo Theatre
- 21 **Bradford (ENGLAND)**, St. George's Hall
- 23 **Edinburgh (SCOTLAND)**, Odeon Theatre
- 24 **Dundee (SCOTLAND)**, Caird Hall
- 25 **Aberdeen (SCOTLAND)**, Capitol Theatre
- 27 **Glasgow (SCOTLAND)**, Apollo Theatre
- 28 **Glasgow (SCOTLAND)**, Apollo Theatre
- 29 **Newcastle (ENGLAND)**, City Hall
- 30 **Newcastle (ENGLAND)**, City Hall

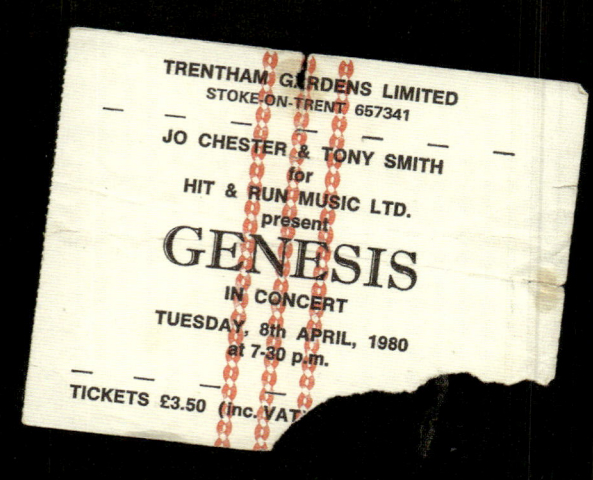

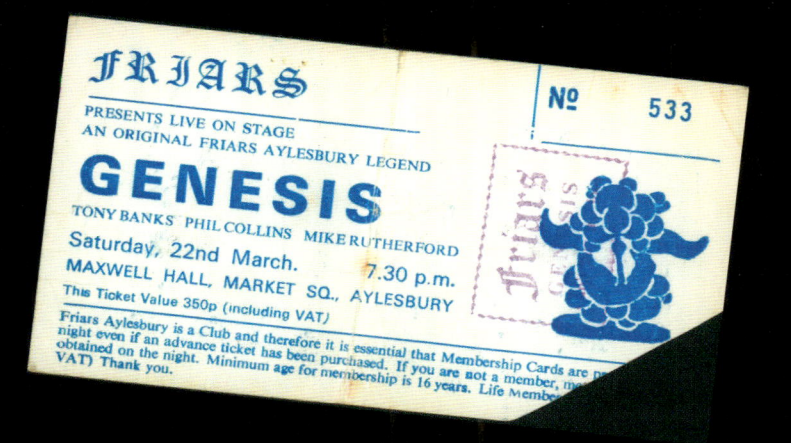

MAY

- 01 **Carlisle (ENGLAND)**, Market Hall
- 02 **Liverpool (ENGLAND)**, Empire Theatre
- 03 **Liverpool (ENGLAND)**, Empire Theatre
- 04 **London (ENGLAND)**, Theatre Royal Drury Lane
  Uncertain show
- 05 **London (ENGLAND)**, Theatre Royal Drury Lane
- 06 **London (ENGLAND)**, Lyceum Ballroom
- 07 **London (ENGLAND)**, Lyceum Ballroom
- 09 **Portsmouth (ENGLAND)**, The Guildhall
  Rescheduled from March 24 due to Phil's laryngitis
- 17 **Edmonton, AB (CANADA)**, Northlands Coliseum
- 18 **Calgary, AB (CANADA)**, Max Bell Centre
- 23 **Oakland, CA (USA)**, Oakland-Alameda County Coliseum Arena
- 24 **Long Beach, CA (USA)**, Long Beach Arena
- 25 **Los Angeles, CA (USA)**, The Roxy
- 26 **San Diego, CA (USA)**, San Diego Sports Arena
- 27 **Los Angeles, CA (USA)**, Greek Theatre
- 30 **Houston, TX (USA)**, The Summit
- 31 **New Orleans, LA (USA)**, Saenger Theatre

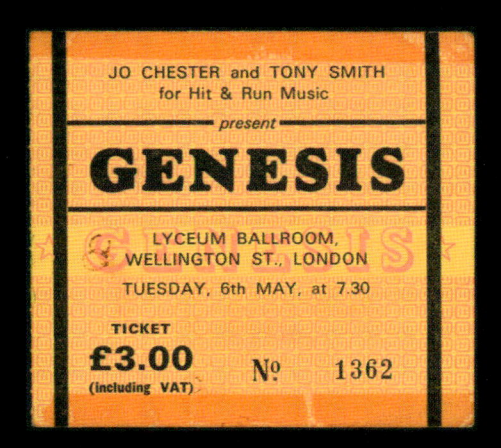

JUNE

- 01 **Atlanta, GA (USA)**, Fox Theatre
- 03 **Chicago, IL (USA)**, Park West
- 04 **Kansas City, MO (USA)**, Municipal Auditorium
- 05 **St. Louis, MO (USA)**, Kiel Opera House
- 06 **Rosemont, IL (USA)**, Rosemont Horizon
- 07 **Milwaukee, WI (USA)**, Milwaukee Arena
- 09 **Clarkston, MI (USA)**, Pine Knob Music Theatre
  4-piece line-up, due to Daryl Stuermer's absence
- 10 **Clarkston, MI (USA)**, Pine Knob Music Theatre
- 11 **Richfield, OH (USA)**, Richfield Coliseum
- 12 **Cincinnati, OH (USA)**, Riverfront Coliseum
- 13 **Pittsburgh, PA (USA)**, Stanley Theatre
- 14 **Columbia, MD (USA)**, Merriweather Post Pavilion
- 16 **Philadelphia, PA (USA)**, The Spectrum
- 17 **Philadelphia, PA (USA)**, The Spectrum
- 18 **Boston, MA (USA)**, Orpheum Theatre
- 19 **Montréal, QC (CANADA)**, Forum
- 20 **Montréal, QC (CANADA)**, Forum
- 22 **Ottawa, ON (CANADA)**, Ottawa Civic Centre
- 23 **Toronto, ON (CANADA)**, Maple Leaf Gardens
- 24 **Toronto, ON (CANADA)**, Maple Leaf Gardens
- 25 **Rochester, NY (USA)**, Rochester Community War Memorial
- 26 **Buffalo, NY (USA)**, Buffalo Memorial Auditorium
- 28 **Passaic, NJ (USA)**, Capitol Theatre
- 29 **New York, NY (USA)**, Madison Square Garden
- 30 **Saratoga Springs, NY (USA)**, Saratoga Performing Arts Center

ABACAB

(Charisma, 1981)

Abacab (Banks-Collins-Rutherford) / No Reply At All (Banks-Collins-Rutherford) / Me And Sarah Jane (Banks) / Keep It Dark (Banks-Collins-Rutherford) /// Dodo (Banks-Collins-Rutherford) / Lurker (Banks-Collins-Rutherford) / Who Dunnit? (Banks-Collins-Rutherford) / Man On The Corner (Collins) / Like It Or Not (Rutherford) / Another Record (Banks-Collins-Rutherford)

- **Release date: 18 September 1981**
- **Engineer: Hugh Padgham**
- **Recorded and mixed at The Farm, Surrey, March to June 1981**
- **Produced by Genesis**
- **Sleeve design: Bill Smith**

- **Tony Banks: keyboards**
- **Phil Collins: drums, vocals**
- **Mike Rutherford: basses, guitars**

- **Earth, Wind & Fire Horns on No Reply At All (arranged by Tom Tom 84)**

THE MAKING OF

At the outset, the 1980s didn't look too promising for Genesis, what with the rise in new musical trends and Phil's marriage issues, but as it turned out the decade could hardly have gone better. Notwithstanding the open hostility now shown by the press towards the band (in sharp contrast with the adulation reserved for them in the first half of the 1970s), their fans remained unwaveringly loyal. Proof of this was clearly seen in the 1980 end of year Melody Maker Readers' Poll published at the beginning of 1981; Genesis were voted Band Of The Year and Best Live Act along with reaching second place in the Album and Writers categories (DUKE) and third in the singles poll (*Turn It On Again*), while David Hentschel won Best Producer. Things look even better if you take the individual musicians; Tony, Phil and Mike topped the polls respectively in the Best Keyboards, Drums and Bass categories and plenty of glory also went to former band members, Peter Gabriel (Best Male Singer) and Steve Hackett (second in the Best Guitar category). Even Collins' second band, Brand X, did well winning the Jazz category. Having weathered punk and with new rock and New Wave heroes pushing their way to the fore, this string of accolades only served to confirm yet again the intrinsic quality of a band like Genesis.

The time separating DUKE from its successor seemed much longer than just eighteen months, mainly because in the meantime something not just big, but immense had happened: the huge success of Phil Collins' solo career. Having become a solo artist by chance rather than by design, above all to find an outlet for the songs he'd written during his isolation following the separation from his wife, Phil released his album FACE VALUE in

February 1981. This was preceded by the single *In The Air Tonight*; a hit all over the world, it only failed to reach No. 1 in the UK singles charts due to the emotional outpouring caused by the murder of John Lennon (Phil had to make do with the No. 2 spot behind the former Beatle's posthumous hit, *Woman*).

Banks: "That was during the making of this album and I have to say it was kind of a shock for me and Mike. *In The Air Tonight* came into the charts at sort of No. 30-something or other and we thought, 'it'll do well – good stuff, Phil!' and then the next week it was at No. 2! Because we'd already started the album, I don't think it really changed, you know, the dynamics in the group too much (which it might have done had it happened at a different time)." [1]

Anyone who may have been under the impression that Collins' solo success would jeopardise the future of the band need never have worried. Without doubt, many other musicians in his shoes would have opted to pursue a purely solo career, but the great friendship between the three and possibly even a certain lack of confidence in his skills as a writer (up until a couple of years earlier, Collins had hardly written anything at all) led the drummer to stay in the band to pursue a dual career that would last for many years to come.

Another element, which may to some extent have influenced Collins' decision to stay, was possibly the joint investment undertaken in 1980, when Tony, Phil, Mike and manager, Tony Smith, (by this time sitting on a rather fine nest egg) bought a farm in Surrey with the idea of converting the cowshed into a recording studio. It would have been simpler to knock everything down and build a brand new studio but, being as the band wanted to start recording as soon as possible, the new songs were written in the farmhouse while the cowshed was being converted.

Collins: "We needed somewhere where we could feel comfortable, a bit like home, where we could have our equipment all the time, you know, and just set it up there for months. And, you know, cook there and sleep there if necessary. So we bought this place in Surrey. The people were trying to show us around the house and we were looking at the garage saying, 'that garage'll do all right'. So, eventually we bought a five- or six-car garage with a house attached and started to convert it into a studio and we thought the roadies could live in the house. We actually started off writing the album in the house because the studio wasn't ready, of course. I remember very well that the song, *Abacab*, was written in the living room with Tudor beams."[1]

Banks: "The studio wasn't finished when we started writing so we wrote in the sitting room of the house it was attached to. I think having our own studio really came into its own slightly more on the next album, but even on this album it just freed us up so much. You can sort of spend the time on it, you can try things out and, you know, see what happens because you're not clock watching. In a normal studio you're always looking at the clock and every minute that goes by you're thinking 'that's another tenner' or something and then they start piddling about with some bit of tape and you're thinking, 'oh Gawd', you know. You can have a different attitude when you're doing things in your own studio. It was a great freedom, a great luxury, I mean we're obviously talking about the days a long time before things like Pro-Tools existed, so if you wanted to record an album you had to have some sort of studio, you couldn't just do it in your living room."[1]

Press photo 1981

Atlantic Records promotional picture, 1981

Rutherford: "It had been a dream since we first started out, you know, to actually have our own place to write and record in rather than writing songs and then going off to record them at a £1,000/day studio, you know, to actually be in an environment where you could write something and if it sounded good record it. At that time our studio wasn't actually good enough to record in but we thought, 'what the hell, we've got a small room – we can put a mixer in there' and then Hugh Padgham came on board to produce it."[1]

Tony Banks   Mike Rutherford   Phil Collins

GENESIS

Banks: "In the early days, basically you'd have maybe two or five days to do an album, it was longer each time. You had to set yourself a time and if you hadn't really finished in that time, then it was just tough really. You had to just take what you got. I remember THE LAMB LIES DOWN ON BROADWAY particularly well; by the time we got to the end of that we were just rushing through everything, trying to get it all finished and mixed."[1]

Consequently, having their own studio and being able to work without all the pressure usually generated in an expensive hired studio proved to be a key factor in the transformation of Genesis; a transformation which was undeniably already on the cards but which now finally had the chance to develop. The decision to produce their own music was clearly in keeping with this new scenario and so, after many years of working together, the David Hentschel chapter in the Genesis story came to a close. The role of sound engineer was handed over to Hugh Padgham who had already worked with The Police and XTC, not to mention Peter Gabriel and Phil Collins on their solo projects. This change made an enormous difference in terms of sound.

Collins: "By this point we thought it was time to change the people we worked with a bit, so we brought in the engineer I'd been working with on FACE VALUE, Hugh Padgham. I mean, he had this sort of drum sound from Mars, you know, that occupied a lot of space. Everybody seemed to want to embrace that as well. I wasn't pushing for it, you know, saying 'I want more room', it was just that the guys were up for changing and sort of, you know, putting little tripwires in front of ourselves. We started to scale down a little bit on the keyboard arrangements, you know, 'do we really need that overdub? Do we really need the sound to be that thick?'."[1]

Rutherford: "Hugh has a much simpler sound dynamic and for the first time the drums sounded

GENESIS

Poster advertising ABACAB with all the different coloured covers, Vertigo Records

really great; they really took a huge leap. Not wishing to take anything away from David, but in the past the sound I'd hear when the band was playing songs was great, but then we'd go and record them and it would be a struggle to get the sound back up to where it was when we'd first played, you know, it was always a bit of an uphill job. The sound Hugh got was the sound we actually made, which was wonderful." [1]

For the new album the band also adopted a different approach towards the writing process and, as it progressed, a growing need to give the new music a different feel began to emerge. This essentially meant deliberately setting aside anything and everything that people had come to associate with the classic Genesis sound.

Rutherford: "It really was time to cut with the past a bit and drop the traditional pattern of a long song from Tony and a short acoustic one from me and so forth. It was just time to be a bit braver and that coincided with us moving into The Farm Studios. I think ABACAB was a cut with the past in terms of the way we wrote but probably even more so in terms of the sound." [1]

Banks: "It was a definite, very conscious decision to try and break some of the Genesis traditions, to get rid of the reprises, the extended solos, the big choruses and tambourines and everything and just do something with a different approach. Because Phil had recently had this experience of working on Peter Gabriel's album, particularly on this drum sound effect [*on the track 'Intruder' – author's note*] and because we used the same engineer who'd worked on that, the size of the tracks are created by the drums rather than by keyboards. We'd always done it with keyboards; the big keyboard pad came in on the chorus and so it was wide and everything. But this time it was the drums themselves; just by bringing out the ambient sound of the kit gave it such a big size. It was very exciting, I really liked it. It meant you could write in a slightly different way and have a different approach." [1]

Phil's greater symbiosis with the band, something already evident on DUKE, became even stronger with the new album. Collins was a new man, on both a personal level (the scars of his failed marriage were beginning to heal thanks to his new relationship with Jill Tavelman, whom he had met on the 1980 US tour) and on a professional one, having finally unleashed his artistic potential.

THE ALBUM

Pigeon-holing ABACAB from an artistic standpoint is far from easy. It goes without saying that at first listen one cannot help being dazzled by the modern sounds (albeit somewhat passé for today's listener) and it is difficult to fall in love with an album of such unexpected (and possibly inadmissible) harshness released under the name of Genesis. For many of the band's earliest fans, ABACAB was quite simply the last straw. Even those who had managed to come to terms with the more direct song formula that had emerged in the first two post-Hackett albums were disconcerted when they found themselves listening to an album in which rhythm and electronics prevailed, leaving very little trace of the glorious Genesis trademark sound.

However, it has to be said that this change was in keeping with a well-defined design: while WIND & WUTHERING was a magnificent album musically speaking, it was still tied down heavily to the past, if anything it was a step backwards compared to its predecessor, A TRICK OF THE TAIL. Deprived of their genius lead guitarist, Genesis had undertaken a process of irreversible metamorphosis starting with the shorter tracks on …AND THEN THERE WERE THREE… and continuing with the modern sounds found on DUKE (including the first use of an electronic drum machine). ABACAB is nothing more than the sublimation of this very deliberate decision to move in a new direction. If, up until DUKE, Genesis had always featured on albums whatever their creativity conjured up, on ABACAB they self-imposed certain restrictions. Mike Rutherford decided against using acoustic guitar, especially the 12-string, and the three musicians, by mutual agreement, set one rule: any tracks reminiscent of the past were to go straight in the bin. As previously stated, ABACAB comes across as a relatively harsh-sounding album with both synths and Phil's voice adopting a much harder edge allied to the overpowering volume of the drums, Tony's keyboards favouring brass sounds over strings and Rutherford's guitar mainly featuring riffs, with very few solos.

In hindsight, ABACAB should be recognised for what it really is: a watershed album. It was a deliberate break with the sound and image they had created for themselves in the past and which, in that particular period of musical turmoil, would never have allowed Genesis to survive for much longer. Punk was virtually dead and New Wave was pulling out all the stops; worthy of note are JUJU by Siouxsie And The Banshees and the self-titled PRETENDERS II. New Order had risen from the ashes of Joy Division and Ultravox, now fronted by Midge Ure, released the hit album, VIENNA.

In terms of rock legends, John Lennon and Yoko Ono had released the album which was to become Lennon's epitaph, DOUBLE FANTASY, while The Rolling Stones were keeping themselves exceptionally busy, releasing not one but two new albums: EMOTIONAL RESCUE (1980) and TATTOO YOU (in 1981). David Bowie had released the impressive SCARY MONSTERS and The Who, with their FACE DANCES, were trying their best to overcome the death of Keith Moon.

Bruce Springsteen, in the meantime, had consolidated his fan base with the double album THE RIVER, while other hits were PRIVATE EYES by Hall & Oates and MAKING MOVIES had turned Dire Straits into superstars.

In terms of prog rock, on the other hand, Gentle

GENESIS

Atlantic Records poster, 1981

Giant, Van De Graaf Generator and Emerson, Lake & Palmer had all broken up and Jethro Tull jumped on the electronic bandwagon with A (initially conceived as an Ian Anderson solo album). Meanwhile, with DRAMA, Yes attempted to reinvent themselves by recruiting help from The Buggles to replace the recently resigned Wakeman and Anderson, while the latter had begun working with Vangelis.

The most courageous band, however, proved to be King Crimson who had reformed after a long hiatus and, with their new album DISCIPLINE, sounded like a completely new band, always open to experimentation and receptive to innovative sounds.

On the topic of experimentation, MY LIFE IN THE BUSH OF GHOSTS by Brian Eno and David Byrne (who just a few months earlier had released the masterpiece REMAIN IN THE LIGHT with Talking Heads) and Peter Gabriel's third solo album, a revolutionary mix of tribal rhythms and electronics, can both be considered musical milestones. Meanwhile, Steve Hackett with DEFECTOR was staying true to his progressive-rock roots.

But this was the beginning of the '80s and the forerunners of the New Romantic movement were beginning to appear, with debut albums from Spandau Ballet and Duran Duran, while bands like Depeche Mode and the Eurythmics were formed along with the passable all-female rock band The Go-Go's.

So, with this totally unexpected album, Genesis took a different path. This is therefore the moment which marks the band's transformation from epitome of prog to a modern group blessed with radio airplay and a growing all-round media presence (they were even getting played in discotheques).

A pill which for many of their old-school fans was to prove simply too bitter to swallow, it was, however, a necessary step in the direction which would steer Genesis into a new era with the authority of a band that still had something new to say and not a group of musicians who at just thirty years of age were irremediably slaves to their own past.

THE SONGS

ABACAB

The opening of the new album comes as a shock: a regular rhythm which gives room to a back-and-forth exchange between guitar and keyboards.

Banks: "We wanted to start with a much more rocky kind of track because we were trying to get across that this was a different album, a different approach. And it worked. Back in the days of vinyl, you were very conscious that the track order of an album was crucial. You know, every song had its place really, and you tried very hard to make certain it was right. You thought very hard about the beginning of Side One and the beginning of Side Two. It's something you don't have to think about anymore really, but back then you had to have a strong opening track and I think *Abacab* was definitely the right approach." [1]

Rutherford: "It was a different feel for us to start an album with; it was a bit rocky, a bit more aggressive, with a simple guitar feel but quite high energy for us." [1]

Collins: "By this point we were being played an awful lot on American radio and the compression they always used always made things sound really great. This song starts well." [1]

A highly electronic song, sung with a very harsh lead vocal (supported by Phil doing his own backing vocals) it has an instrumental section which is miles away from the usual Genesis clichés, with heavy percussion and edgy synth riffs.

Collins: "We were stretching out a lot more. The end of *Abacab* on the record was all improvised. We were writing all that stuff sitting in a room with nothing but thin air." [1]

Collins explains how the track got its title.

Collins: "Originally, ABACAB was a way of remembering the sequence of the song. A was the verse, B was the chorus and C was the bridge, so you went verse, chorus, verse, bridge, verse, chorus. We didn't do the song like that in the end but the way we did eventually do it was unpronounceable. But the name stuck." [1]

Rutherford: "I wrote the lyrics. They're okay but not great, but the title is quite fun." [1]

NO REPLY AT ALL

A funky track which would have been inconceivable for Genesis just a year earlier, this song is bolstered by an outstanding performance from Rutherford on bass and above all by a rare external collaboration on a Genesis album: Earth, Wind & Fire's horn section with Don Myrick on sax, Louis Satterfield on trombone and Rahmlee Michael Davis and Michael Harris on trumpet.

Rutherford: "The sound feel was very much brought in by Phil, who was full of excitement from having done his own album. I didn't really know the Phenix Horns (the guys from Earth, Wind & Fire, a band I didn't know), so I went to Los Angeles with Phil and Hugh. They got the charts out and these lovely guys came in. I thought they'd go one, two, three, four and get it right, but the first time they played it, it was absolute chaos, you know, all over the shop. And I thought, 'god, and these are supposedly the hottest guys around?'. But then I realised that they are quite characters, quite funky guys. After a while they lock in and they don't play the right notes; they have a sound, that's what I didn't realise. When the sound works and they tighten together there's a definite sound that only those four guys can do. It was fun to do and different." [1]

Collins: "I thought, 'If we're going to reinvent ourselves, why not have some horns on there? I mean this song we've written sounds kind of funky, you know, an R&B thing, why not have horns on it? It's our fucking record, you know!'. So we did

GENESIS

Italian magazine *Tutto – Musica & Spettacolo*, November 1981

it and people hated it."[1]

Rutherford: "Why not? I mean, you always want to do something new and I'm sure this is one of the reasons why Genesis has lasted so long. One or two changes over the years help you find something a bit fresh. It's quite hard being all the same people."[1]

Banks: "Phil had used them on FACE VALUE and he was quite keen on the idea. I didn't feel that strongly about it either way actually. The only thing I thought about was whether or not people would say, 'oh Phil's doing it and so you're doing it now', and all that. But we had a couple of songs that lent themselves to it. I didn't actually do it; Phil and Mike went out to LA to record the horns and came back with it. I particularly like what happens on *Paperlate*, I really like the horns on that, it makes the song. On *No Reply At All* it's fine but really they just play what the drums play and that's OK, it works, but it's not my favourite song. It was fun doing the video though, pretending to play the stuff." (*Tony 'playing' trumpet, Mike on trombone and Phil on sax – author's note*)[1]

ME AND SARAH JANE

This track sounds a little more like a traditional Genesis song, almost a continuation of *Cul-De-Sac*. The overall sound is mainly determined by the song's writer, Banks, on piano, with the addition of long electric guitar notes and some great bass. However, the song as a whole is a lot less elaborate, revealing a rather curious ska influence as well as sounds that are far from retro, like the use of the vocoder together with sumptuous keyboards.

Banks: "This is the last track I wrote for Genesis that I got credited for as an individual. I really had to hold myself in, you know, in terms of not letting it get too long. I mean, there were whole other sections on this, some of which ended up in *You Might Recall*. It's a favourite of mine, I have to say. It's a very simple idea of just using a two-note piano riff which kind of just slightly changes and then adding chords to it all the way through the song. Then I tried to write a lyric that has a sort of abstract quality about it. It's not really about anything, but this idea of this relationship with this fictitious female, Sarah Jane, sort of emerges throughout and takes over the whole song."[1]

KEEP IT DARK

A decidedly electronic track (born in the recording studio from one of Mike's ideas while instruments were being tuned). Phil sings falsetto in the vocal crescendos where you can clearly hear Mike's finishing work on guitar. But the main feature is Tony's synth which sticks to monophonic counterpoints made up of single notes up to the chorus when he plays the first chord.

Rutherford: "Phil played this straight beat pattern and it was so good that we actually looped it. Then we got a bit of tape and hung a weight on it and it actually looped it down. It always had a great, sort of heavy sound and I think the song always kind of worked that way."[1]

Banks: "We wanted to try to keep that kind of inhuman aspect: that's what we liked about it, you know, it becomes something inhuman and relentless. When a thing repeats absolutely like that it becomes almost subliminal so you don't pay too

DODO / LURKER

Banks: "We joined a couple of bits together for this: mine, which was all the verse parts, and the disco type part was Mike's bit. I think it would have made a good disco record, but we joined it all together into what was quite a difficult track. The way I played along to it wasn't necessarily right, but it's a really great riff. We could have made a really great song out of just the riff but we didn't think of it at the time. But it's a good song, it works well as an opening. It has all the silly chords at the beginning, but it's arresting." [2]

Rutherford: "I think this couple of songs was, in a funny way, a more modern version of the longer, more complicated songs we used to do, only done in

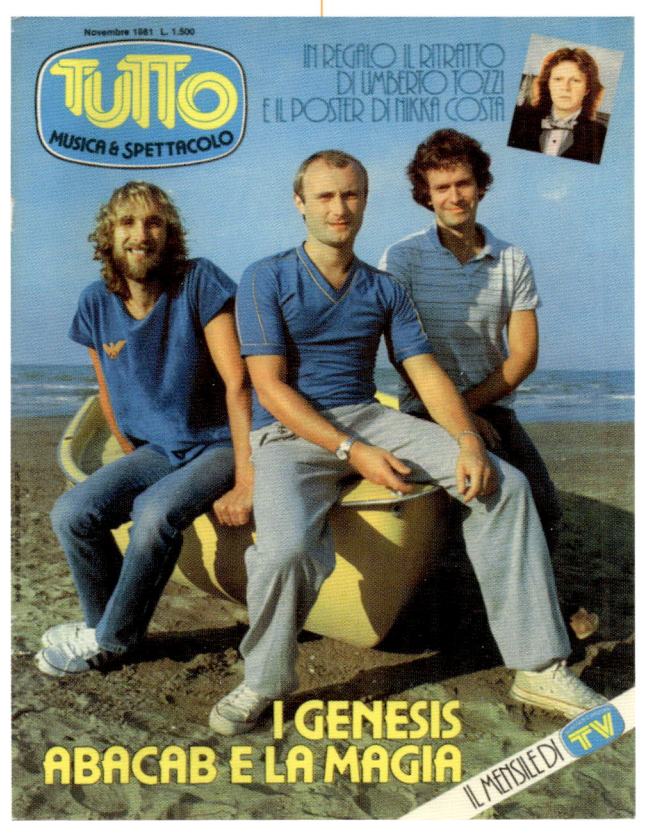

much attention to it. And then Mike was playing this riff which kind of goes very much against the rhythm. The two things are quite strangely positioned and, when you listen to it, sometimes you think it's all out of time. Then the chorus comes in and all the chords are sort of anticipated and the resultant effect is kind of strange. I think the song works really well. It's got very stark verses and very romantic choruses. The lyric is about this character who had to pretend he'd just been kidnapped and that's why he disappeared for a few weeks, when in fact he'd actually been taken up in a spaceship and gone to some fantastic world where everything was wonderful and beautiful and everything, but he couldn't tell anybody about it because no one would have believed him." [1]

a slightly more contemporary way, you know more aggressive, a little less wodgy in sound, a kind of newer version." [1]

Opened by a powerful keyboard intro enriched by long notes from Mike's guitar, the song is built around a nice chord sequence and stands out for Phil's excellent performances on both drums and vocals. Although it was given its own title, *Lurker* is in fact quite simply the second part of *Dodo*, the part which opens with a bizarre section characterised by a weird synth riff over a very electronic and percussive base.

Banks: "In the disco bit I wanted Phil to put on a strange sort of voice. I told him to think of Frank Zappa. I'm not sure he ended up sounding much like Zappa but it did sound a bit like that. The chorus had a very different feel to the verses which was just Phil singing in his standard voice. Originally *Lurker* was just a silly solo. I like the synthesiser part but not the vocal part." [2]

The dodo might well have been a large flightless bird which became extinct in the mid-1600s, but Banks' lyrics have very little to do with nature.

Banks: "For *Dodo* I wanted to write a lyric that wasn't really about anything but that had some quite good phrases in it. I suppose it was about killing things really. I don't know what *Lurker* was about. It was supposed to be a riddle. I was hoping someone would ask me what the answer was so I could reply that, of course, there is no answer. But no one ever did, no one ever seemed to bother to read it as a riddle. I wrote it after reading a lot of those middle-ranking science fiction books that have those kinds of riddles in them, written in a form that you don't really know what they're talking about." [2]

At one point the band considered putting *Dodo* as the album's opening track.

Banks: "There was a vague idea of having some kind of longer piece on this album. It would have started with *Dodo/Lurker* and then gone into what ended up being called *Submarine* and finished up as the B-side of another song. It has quite an arresting beginning but it's much more traditional Genesis and I think that's why we didn't go with it." [1]

In fact, the so-called *Dodo Suite,* had it made it onto the album, would have been a 16-minute piece of music, incorporating not only *Submarine* but also *Naminanu*, which, like *Submarine*, also ended up as a B-side. There are various fan-edited versions of the *Dodo Suite* on the internet, with some suggesting that the suite would most likely have begun with *Naminanu*.

WHO DUNNIT?

A deafening drum beat with an incredibly strong and electronic sound and a smattering of synthesisers provide the prelude to the most shocking song in the entire history of Genesis. A relentless piece completely devoid of chords (Tony's synth plays only monophonic notes) in which the bass doubles the main riff together with the synth while a number of overdubbed vocals insist on singing, with mindless word repetition, some sort of childish nursery rhyme with totally meaningless lyrics.

Collins: "Our punk track. It was fantastic! Tony had this keyboard and he was just fiddling around with it. He was trying to get these different sounds and it was all in rhythm for some reason, so I started playing along. It was the most horrible sound but we really liked it and so it made it onto the record. And I wrote the lyrics, you know, 'Was it you or was it me? Or was it he or she?'." [1]

Banks: "For many people it's, you know, the worst track we ever did! I really like it but perhaps I'm just perverse. I had this thing of abusing a Prophet-5 synthesiser and I'd sit there doing this all the time [*playing the same musical phrase while quickly going from one pre-set to another – author's note*]. Mike and Phil thought that the only way they were going to shut me up was to record it, so we did. Then Phil put this sort of very simple but very slappy drum on it and then he wrote a lyric for it which was as irritating as the song itself. And the result is great, I think. I love it. We used to play it on stage and get booed, and if you mention it around here [*i.e. amongst the crew – author's note*] some of the roadies will say 'oh no, not *Who Dunnit?*', you know. There was a possibility of not using *Who Dunnit?* because we had two or three other songs we could have put on the album. One, a very nice romantic song called *You Might Recall*, was a strong contender. But I remember saying, 'you've got to put that track on', because it had such a character to it. So, in the end we decided to go for the ugly rather than the beautiful. By having an ugly song, everything else sounds more beautiful." [1]

MAN ON THE CORNER

Based on an electronic drum pattern and chords on the electric piano doubled by the brass of the Prophet-5, this song by Phil, who also gives a tremendous vocal performance, is without doubt the best of the three individually written tracks on the album.

Rutherford: "This was Phil and the drum machine and it had this rather lovely beat, but you haven't got a clue where *one* is. But then you find it and it's great. Many a night when we did it on stage I'd see Tony kind of going, 'where the fuck is one?'. And if you miss that moment, you can't get it. It's a great song but it's difficult to play live, well, not for me because I don't start; the drum machine comes in first and then Tony, so if he doesn't get it right, it's his fault." [1]

LIKE IT OR NOT

Dry drum beats precede the lead guitar riff which then dilutes down into guitar arpeggios, including 12-string (a real rarity on this album). The chorus, with the addition of keyboard, exploits an unusual accent on the seventh chords.

Banks: "This was a song we had rehearsed for Duke but it hadn't quite come together at that stage so we left it out. But we were quite dry of ideas on Abacab and it was there and it sounded quite good. When Mike first played it to us he had his guitar and he was playing his bass pedals and he may have had a tambourine. So the song's working title was always *Don* as in Don Partridge, a street busker in England who had this one hit called *Rosie*. He appeared on 'Top Of The Pops' with this thing around his neck and playing the bass drum and guitar." [2]

ANOTHER RECORD

The intro (a melancholy piano, a crescendo of keyboards and a distant and heart-wrenching lead guitar) leaves the listener expecting something completely different before the spell is broken by the entrance of the drums and the harmonica effect of the synth.

Banks: "This is a rock type song. It's not great but I like the feel of it. I got this quite good synthesised harmonica sound which I went on to use again on *And The Wheels Keep Turning* on The Fugitive [*Banks' second solo album released in 1983 – author's note*]. It sounded quite convincing." [2]

Phil's voice (counterpointed an octave lower) sings the tale of a rather sad old rock'n'roller. Both the lyrics and the melody were written by Mike.

OTHER SONGS

The two songs which were originally intended to be part of the *Dodo Suite* are *Submarine* (an instru-

Print of three of the four different options for the ABACAB cover, signed by the designer Bill Smith

mental delicacy driven by aquatic synthesisers, with drum-beats that get increasingly more powerful) and *Naminanu* (a fusion track with alternating solos from Rutherford on guitar and Banks on piano with Collins using his voice only to nonsensically repeat the song title). They would become the B-sides of *Keep It Dark* and *Man On The Corner*.

A further three tracks would be released a year later on the EP 3×3: the theatrical and grandiose *Me And Virgil*, with an interesting rhythmic doubling and a guitar solo halfway through, *Paperlate*, again featuring the Phenix Horns (which would become a successful single) and finally *You Might Recall*, a pleasant track with unusual percussion alternating with the main keyboard riff and some 12-string arpeggios in the bridge, a song which Tony would quite happily have put on the album instead of *Like It Or Not*.

Banks: "I thought *You Might Recall* should have ended up on an album. I mean you look back on these things now, but at the time there was a certain amount of making sure that everyone got represented." [2]

THE ALBUM ARTWORK

The transformation in Genesis is immediately apparent in the album cover. A random arrangement of four blocks of colours which, to the joy/despair of collectors everywhere, came out in four different combinations (not to mention the various subsequent pressings on CD and those released in other countries).

Banks: "A lot of the album tracks were very stark and had a much more straightforward approach and we wanted to get that across with the cover. So we went for a design on the cover that wasn't definable; just nice shapes and colours and a title which means nothing at all. I saw it as being like an abstract painting; it didn't really give anything away about the album at all before you listened to it, you just knew that it wasn't going to be about goblins and fairies. Which is right, it wasn't." [1]

Collins: "With DUKE and this cover, we did think that they weren't quite as ornate and, you know, maybe as feminine as some of the other covers, particularly WIND & WUTHERING. This was our punk album, if you like. It was meant to make people go 'Wow! This is a Genesis cover? Well, if this is the cover, maybe the music's different'. It was trying to get people to feel that they could re-assess us without, you know, feeling that they still had to go and hide. I don't know if it did that or not, I mean, some people feel that this album was the beginning of the end, you know, because they preferred what we were leaving behind. It depends on who you talk to and when." [1]

What's more, for the first time ever, the lyrics to the songs weren't printed on the sleeve and the record came out under a different label – at least in part. In fact Charisma, on an irreversible road to economic demise, was undergoing acquisition by Virgin Records, ceding in the meantime, the rights to European publications. Consequently, starting with this album, Genesis records were released on the European market by Vertigo, while the Charisma label continued to survive only in the UK. In 1983 the distribution of Charisma records was handed over to Richard Branson's Virgin Records which went on to definitively absorb the Stratton-Smith label in the early 1980s. Branson later sold Virgin to EMI in 1992.

EPILOGUE

Analysis of the first five post-Gabriel albums clearly highlights a metamorphosis.

Rutherford: "The funny thing is, at the same time Peter was also changing. This change was coming. Often the hardcore fans don't see it, but the transition from THE LAMB was the start of the end of an era and I think it was actually inevitable if we were to survive. I can't imagine us playing the same kind of stuff and music and sound that we did back in the early '70s and not change. To be honest, the journey as a writer and as a recorder of music has been interesting. I think if we'd stayed in the same place, I'd have been bored stiff years ago. You've got to move all the time. This album also coincided with the fact that we were doing more work with outside musicians for our solo stuff, so you'd bring a bit of that back with you; you'd say, 'well, I tried it like this with these guys, why don't we give it a go?' and no one ever said no. You learnt things working out in solo projects." [1]

However, it would appear that the dizzying changes in musical direction were no great cause of concern for Genesis; ABACAB was released on 18 September 1981, went to No. 1 in the UK and improved on its US rankings by reaching No. 7 and was certified double platinum (in 1988). All the singles did pretty well too: *Abacab* reached No. 9 in the UK, *Keep It Dark* got to No. 33 and *Man On The Corner* No. 41, whereas the Americans preferred *No Reply At All* (No. 29) and, a few months later, *Paperlate*, which reached No. 32 (No. 10 on home turf, where it was released as part of the EP 3x3).

Banks: "ABACAB was an important move really, because suddenly we went quite a long way in a different direction and from then on we brought a bit of that with us. This album was also the last album where we credited anything to individuals. We each put one track of our own on there and everything else was very much group-written. It emerged out of just jamming and improvising, letting ideas evolve." [1]

THE CONCERTS

At the time of going on tour, as always Genesis were faced with the dilemma of how to structure the setlist. Without doubt the intention was to give ample space to the new album, but at the same time they didn't want to totally disappoint their old fans, already upset by the new artistic direction the band had taken.

After two weeks of rehearsals at Shepperton Studios, the European tour kicked off in Spain on 25 September 1981. The songs played in Barcelona were: *Behind The Lines / Duchess / The Lamb Lies Down On Broadway / Dodo / Abacab / Me And Virgil / Firth Of Fifth / Man On The Corner / Who Dunnit? / Misunderstanding / Me And Sarah Jane / No Reply At All / In The Cage – The Cinema Show – Raven – Afterglow / Turn It On Again / Dance On A Volcano – Los Endos / I Know What I Like.*

Six songs from the new album, ABACAB, plus a seventh, *Me And Virgil*, from the same recording sessions (as fans would discover a year later). Playing a previously unheard song (this hadn't happened for almost a decade) was a treat reserved solely for their Spanish fans, as the band played *Me And Virgil* one more time at San Sebastian on the 27th before dropping it from the setlist.

And while a goodly portion of the setlist was also given over to DUKE (four songs), the rest was dedicated to their more recent (A TRICK OF THE TAIL and WIND & WUTHERING) and distant past, with the full execution of *The Lamb Lies Down On Broadway* and *Firth Of Fifth* (the first time Daryl Stuermer had had to take on such a long and impressive solo) plus *In The Cage,* which, taking as its starting point the version on the previous tour, was extended to include large segments of *The Cinema Show* and *Raven* before flowing into *Afterglow.*

Between one Spanish concert and the next, on 26 September 1981 to be precise, Genesis made a flying visit to Italy, but not for a show. The embargo banning foreign artists from playing in the country following the political unrest of the mid-70s was almost over but wasn't lifted in time for the band to schedule an Italian date for the tour, so instead the band spent time in Venice (where they picked up an award for the number of sales achieved by ABACAB) and appeared in a number of TV shows. The band appeared at the 'Mostra Internazionale Della Musica Leggera' (*The International Pop Music Exhibition*, also known as the 'Gondola d'Oro' – the Golden Gondola Awards)

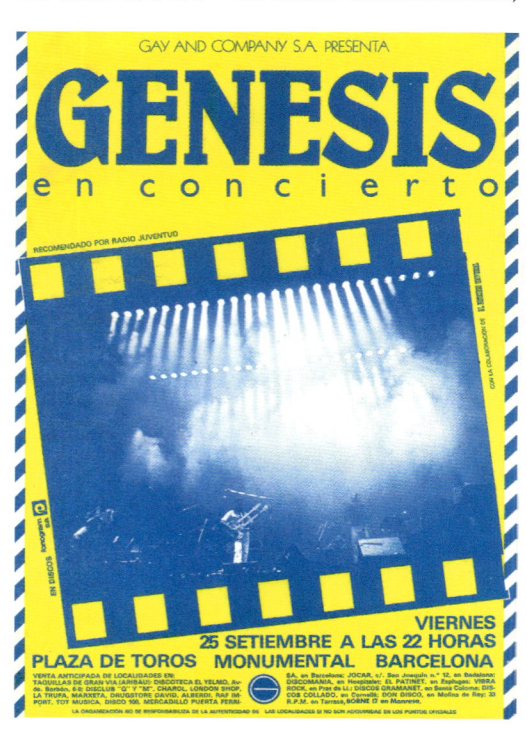

142

ABACAB

Left: Poster advertising the very first show of the ABACAB tour, performed in Barcelona, Spain, on 25th September 1981. Promoted by Gay And Company

Phil in Zurich, 24th October 1981

and recorded the TV special 'Incontri Musicali' for RAI television (the Italian equivalent of the BBC). Bizarrely, the show was only aired 15 years later. This is fun and interesting footage to watch, because, although the band was limited to miming, after performing *Turn It On Again* and *Man On The Corner* some of the musicians switched instruments: for *No Reply At All* Mike 'plays' sax and Phil picks up a trumpet, whereas for *Keep It Dark* Mike dashes behind the drum kit and Chester takes it away on bass (both returned to their respective instruments for the last song of the programme, *Abacab*).

Starting with the first show in France (Fréjus on 29 September), the band made a few minor changes to the setlist which became: *Behind The Lines / Duchess / The Lamb Lies Down On Broadway / Dodo / Abacab / Misunderstanding / Man On The*

GENESIS

Atlantic promotional photo, 1978

Pic. Gered Mankowitz.

from Cologne on the 17th onwards, with the return of *No Reply At All*, that a certain amount of stability was established in the setlist with *Behind The Lines / Duchess / The Lamb Lies Down On Broadway / Dodo / Abacab / The Carpet Crawlers / Me And Sarah Jane / Misunderstanding / No Reply At All / Firth Of Fifth / Man On The Corner / Who Dunnit? / In The Cage – The Cinema Show – Raven – Afterglow / Turn It On Again / Dance On A Volcano – Los Endos / I Know What I Like*. In fact, it would remain the same for the rest of the European tour with only one exception, in the aforementioned Cologne show on the 17th, *The Carpet Crawlers* was left out.

The European tour took the band through France, Holland, Germany (15 dates!), France (again, this time with three consecutive nights in Paris), Belgium and Switzerland, finally coming to a close in Berlin on 2 November.

After a ten-day break, Genesis were off to the States, starting out in Madison on 12 November. The setlist for the North American tour basically replicated the one from the European tour, with a few minor adjustments, including the removal of

Corner / Who Dunnit? / No Reply At All / Firth Of Fifth / Me And Sarah Jane / In The Cage – The Cinema Show – Raven – Afterglow / Turn It On Again / Dance On A Volcano – Los Endos / I Know What I Like.

From 6 October (Essen, in Germany) *The Carpet Crawlers* was inserted after *Abacab* and in the following days some changes were made to the running order: on the 14th, in Kiel, *Who Dunnit?* and *Me And Sarah Jane* were brought forward in the set, while the next day, in Hamburg, *Who Dunnit?* was moved to after *Man On The Corner*. It was only

ABACAB

German promoter Mike Scheller Concerts advertising for the West Germany tour (Phonogram / Charisma 1981)

The Carpet Crawlers in Cincinnati on the 21st.

The biggest change came on 26 November in Philadelphia when *Me And Sarah Jane* was sacrificed to make way for *Like It Or Not* (which came after *Who Dunnit?*); the same would also happen on the 30th in Landover. *Like It Or Not* was played for another handful of shows, always to replace *Me And Sarah Jane*, but didn't have a set position in the running order. On 2 December in Hartford (where the band also switched over the positions of *Misunderstanding* and *No Reply At All*) it was played after *The Carpet Crawlers*, whereas on the last occasion it was played, 4 December, it followed *Firth Of Fifth*.

The North American tour was another huge success, with a number of cities benefiting from two shows (Chicago, Philadelphia, New York, Montreal, Toronto). The band's energy on stage was captured by a film crew hired to film the concerts in New York and Long Island (28 and 29 November) for the subsequent release of a live VHS.

After the last show in North America, in Syracuse (NY) on 11 December, Genesis had a couple of days off before tackling the final leg of the Abacab tour in England, with three concerts in London and four in Birmingham (the ones on the 22 and 23 December were recorded to add to the material available for a live album and video cassette release).

THE CONCERT TOUR '81
GENESIS
presented by Mike Scheller Concerts

5.10. Bremen — Stadthalle	11.10. Kassel — Eissporthalle	27.10. Dortmund — Westfalenhalle
6.10. Essen — Grugahalle	13.10. Hannover — Eilenriedehalle	28.10. Ludwigshafen — Eberthalle
8.10. München — Olympiahalle	14.10. Kiel — Ostseehalle	29.10. Böblingen — Sporthalle
9.10. Nürnberg — Messehalle	15.10. Hamburg — Congress Centrum	30.10. Frankfurt — Festhalle
10.10. Würzburg — Carl-Diem-Halle	16.10. Köln — Sporthalle	2.11. Berlin — Deutschlandhalle

Der Vorverkauf hat begonnen!
Kartenbestellungen: Mike Scheller Concerts Kartenservice; Mousonstr. 14 6 Frankfurt 1; ✆ 0611/43 99 88 Zustellung per Nachnahme

aus dem Hause phonogram

GENESIS

Mike and Chester at Frejus on 29th September 1981

Back home the setlist reverted back to the consolidated European version with the return of *Me And Sarah Jane*, but special mention must go to the last pre-Christmas show on 23 December in Birmingham where a couple of things occurred. While the first can be considered mere trivia (after *Who Dunnit?*, while the audience were crying out for some of the old songs, Phil began to play, although not entirely in tune, a bit of *Silent Night* on trumpet), the second is far more interesting: the inclusion in the setlist (as a first encore) of an exceptional rendition of *The Knife*, again in the abridged version already played in some of the shows during the D*uke* tour, before the finale which, as always, was *I Know What I Like*.

On this tour Genesis were the first band in the world to try out the revolutionary computerised Vari-Lite system which allowed the lights to change shape and colour but above all move as operated by the lighting team sat next to the mix-

UK poster advertising the Genesis merchandise

ing desk (production designer, Alan Owen, assisted by programmer, Tom Littrell, and lighting engineers, Tom Walsh and Jim Bornhorst). The effect was particularly breathtaking during the finale of *Afterglow* when a myriad of soft coloured lights shone behind Phil's and Chester's drum kits.

Musically the band was in spectacular form, with Daryl now totally integrated into the fabric of the group, alternating with Mike on bass and guitar. The American musician played guitar not only on the songs from the Hackett period but also on a number of more recent compositions (*Behind The Lines, Duchess, Misunderstanding, Me And Sarah Jane*) whereas for *Turn It On Again* both he and Mike played guitar using pedals for the bass line. The way *No Reply At All* was played is of interest, with Stuermer's guitar trying to make up for the absence on stage of the Phenix Horns.

On the other hand, something really bizarre occurred for *Who Dunnit?*: Rutherford, seated at Phil's drum kit, duetted with Chester on drums and Phil sang on a raised platform behind them while Daryl played bass and Tony the keyboards.

Collins: "Punk had left its mark, you know, and we didn't really want to be thought of as being stuck in a certain genre. I remember when we played this album live in Holland, in this place called Leiden, we were booed. Every time we played an ABACAB track they booed us. They didn't like the scaled-down thing at all. When we did *Who Dunnit?* live it was fantastic. People used to put goggles on with snorkels and stuff; it was kind of a surreal moment but at that point we were really trying to reinvent ourselves a bit." [1]

Despite the booing episode in Leiden, the tour can only be considered a triumph. Genesis then went on to take a break which would turn out to be much shorter than anyone could have possibly expected.

NOTES

(1)   Mike Kaufman's Genesis interviews, Chicago / London, October 2007, partially used in the bonus disc accompanying the 2008 remasters

(2)   Mario Giammetti's interview with Tony Banks, London, Tony Smith Personal Management office, 29 November 2016

1981

SEPTEMBER
- 25 **Barcelona (SPAIN)**, Plaza de Toros Monumental de Barcelona
- 27 **San Sebastian (SPAIN)**, Velódromo de Anoeta
- 29 **Fréjus (FRANCE)**, Arènes de Fréjus
- 30 **Avignon (FRANCE)**, Parc des Expositions de Châteaublanc

OCTOBER
- 01 **Lyon (FRANCE)**, Palais des Sports
- 03 **Leiden (THE NETHERLANDS)**, Groenoordhal
- 04 **Leiden (THE NETHERLANDS)**, Groenoordhal
- 05 **Bremen (WEST GERMANY)**, Stadthalle 1
- 06 **Essen (WEST GERMANY)**, Grugahalle
- 08 **Munich (WEST GERMANY)**, Olympiahalle
- 09 **Nürnberg (WEST GERMANY)**, Messehalle
- 10 **Würzburg (WEST GERMANY)**, Carl-Diem-Halle
- 11 **Kassel (WEST GERMANY)**, Eissporthalle
- 13 **Hannover (WEST GERMANY)**, Eilenriedehalle
- 14 **Kiel (WEST GERMANY)**, Ostseehalle
- 15 **Hamburg (WEST GERMANY)**, Hall 1 - Congress Centrum Hamburg
- 16 **Cologne (WEST GERMANY)**, Sporthalle
- 17 **Cologne (WEST GERMANY)**, Sporthalle
- 19 **Paris (FRANCE)**, Hippodrome de Paris
- 20 **Paris (FRANCE)**, Hippodrome de Paris
- 21 **Paris (FRANCE)**, Hippodrome de Paris
- 22 **Forest (BELGIUM)**, Forest National
- 23 **Metz (FRANCE)**, Parc des Expositions
- 24 **Zürich (SWITZERLAND)**, Hallenstadion
- 25 **Zürich (SWITZERLAND)**, Hallenstadion
- 27 **Dortmund (WEST GERMANY)**, Halle 1 - Westfalenhallen
- 28 **Strasbourg (FRANCE)**, Hall Rhénus
- 29 **Böblingen (WEST GERMANY)**, Sporthalle
- 30 **Frankfurt (WEST GERMANY)**, Festhalle
- 31 **Frankfurt (WEST GERMANY)**, Festhalle

NOVEMBER
- 02 **Berlin (WEST GERMANY)**, Deutschlandhalle
- 12 **Madison, WI (USA)**, Dane County Memorial Coliseum
- 13 **Rosemont, IL (USA)**, Rosemont Horizon
- 14 **Rosemont, IL (USA)**, Rosemont Horizon
- 15 **Chicago, IL (USA)**, Park West
- 16 **Milwaukee, WI (USA)**, Milwaukee Arena
- 17 **South Bend, IN (USA)**, Athletic and Convocation Center - University of Notre Dame
- 18 **Detroit, MI (USA)**, Cobo Arena
- 19 **Pittsburgh, PA (USA)**, Civic Arena
- 21 **Cincinnati, OH (USA)**, Riverfront Coliseum
- 22 **Richfield, OH (USA)**, Richfield Coliseum
- 23 **Kalamazoo, MI (USA)**, Wings Stadium
- 25 **Philadelphia, PA (USA)**, The Spectrum
- 26 **Philadelphia, PA (USA)**, The Spectrum
- 27 **Philadelphia, PA (USA)**, The Spectrum
- 28 **New York, NY (USA)**, The Savoy
- 29 **Uniondale, NY (USA)**, Nassau Veterans Memorial Coliseum
- 30 **Landover, MD (USA)**, Capital Centre

DECEMBER

- 02 **Hartford, CT (USA)**, Hartford Civic Center
- 03 **Montréal, QC (CANADA)**, Forum
- 04 **Montréal, QC (CANADA)**, Forum
- 05 **Ottawa, ON (CANADA)**, Ottawa Civic Centre
- 06 **Toronto, ON (CANADA)**, Maple Leaf Gardens
- 07 **Toronto, ON (CANADA)**, Maple Leaf Gardens
- 08 **Buffalo, NY (USA)**, Buffalo Memorial Auditorium
- 10 **East Rutherford, NJ (USA)**, Brendan Byrne Arena
- 11 **Syracuse, NY (USA)**, Carrier Dome - Syracuse University
- 17 **London (ENGLAND)**, Wembley Arena
- 18 **London (ENGLAND)**, Wembley Arena
- 19 **London (ENGLAND)**, Wembley Arena
- 20 **Birmingham (ENGLAND)**, Birmingham International Arena - National Exhibition Centre
- 21 **Birmingham (ENGLAND)**, Birmingham International Arena - National Exhibition Centre
- 22 **Birmingham (ENGLAND)**, Birmingham International Arena - National Exhibition Centre
- 23 **Birmingham (ENGLAND)**, Birmingham International Arena - National Exhibition Centre

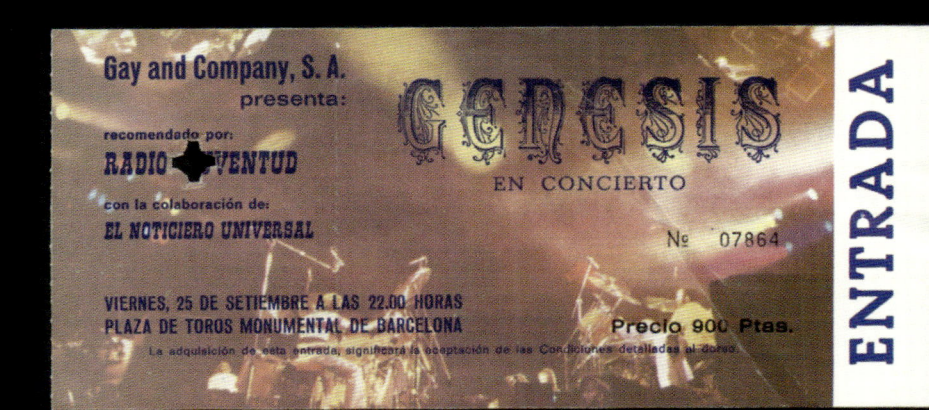

Three Sides Live
Encore Tour

At the beginning of 1982, Tony, Phil and Mike turned down the opportunity of taking the Abacab tour to the faraway lands of Australia, South America and Japan because they wanted to get back to pursuing their solo careers. First, however, in June 1982 they released Three Sides Live. The title reflects the fact that three sides of this double album contained live recordings made mainly during their Abacab tour, while the remaining side contained studio recordings: five out-takes from the Duke and Abacab recording sessions. Except, that is, in the UK. Here, despite having the same title, all four sides of the album (which would reach No. 2 in the album charts) featured live recordings. The three Abacab out-takes, *Paperlate, You Might Recall* and *Me And Virgil*, would later be released on the EP 3x3 (the Duke out-takes had already been released in 1980 as B-sides).

Three Sides Live is also the title of Genesis' first home video release, consisting mainly of lengthy sections of the concerts filmed in New York and Long Island at the end of November 1981, along with interviews and other documentary content.

Following Three Sides Live, the first solo artist to reveal his hand was Mike, who in September 1982 brought out his album Acting Very Strange, followed in November by Phil's release, Hello, I Must Be Going!. The Fugitive by Tony Banks, on the other hand, would only be released in June 1983 (preceded two months earlier by the release of his film score The Wicked Lady).

With so much going on in their solo careers, the announcement of another Genesis tour came as a real surprise, especially as it wasn't linked to any needs imposed by the record label seeing as the band had already officially completed the Abacab tour. Essentially, the band planned to tour for one month in North America (August) and one month in Europe (September). Being as the tour wasn't aimed at promoting any particular album, the three musicians decided to treat their fans to a different setlist to the one played in the Abacab shows just a few months earlier, taking the opportunity to bring back some classic Genesis tracks that hadn't been played live for years. The setlist for the opening concert (in Peoria, Illinois, on 1 August 1982) was as follows: *Dance On A Volcano / Behind The Lines / Follow You Follow Me / Dodo / Abacab / Supper's Ready / Misunderstanding / Man On The Corner / Who Dunnit? / In The Cage – The Cinema Show – Raven – Afterglow / Turn It On Again / Los Endos / The Lamb Lies Down On Broadway – Watcher Of The Skies*.

This was a decidedly original way to open a concert, with three linked songs: *Dance On A Volcano*, *Behind The Lines* (without *Duchess*) and *Follow You Follow Me*, which had not been played on the Abacab tour.

Dance On A Volcano and *Los Endos* remained on the setlist but no longer as an integral and inseparable part of the encore (as on the previous tour). Instead, they acted as opener and closer (the drumming duet between Collins and Thompson, that had previously served as a bridge, was now directly before *Los Endos*). The new encores included a version of *The Lamb Lies Down On*

Charisma Records advertising the live album and the Birmingham shows

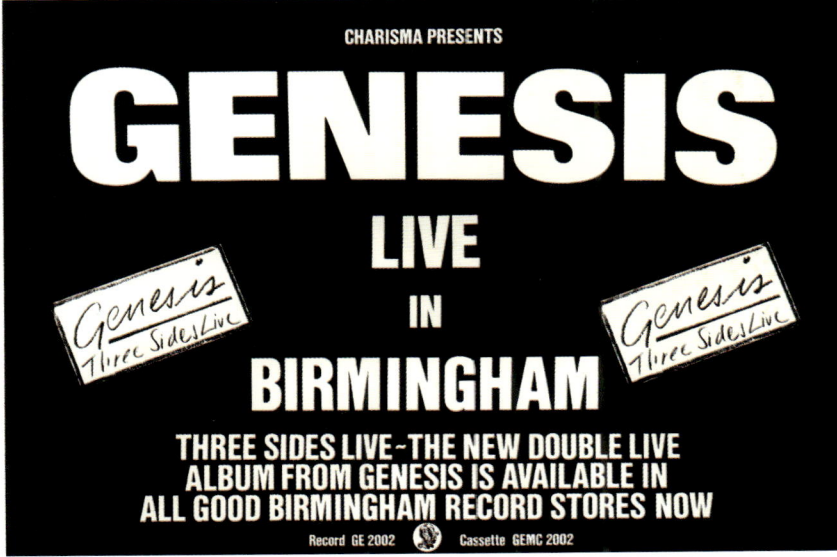

Broadway without intro and with a slower ending which merged into an instrumental version of *Watcher Of The Skies* (introduction and ending only).

But by far and away the best and most popular surprise, requiring Mike, Tony and Daryl to dust off their 12-string guitars, was the inclusion of *Supper's Ready* in all its entirety for the first time since 1974; a song, as Phil would remind the ecstatic audiences every night, was 'almost ten years old'. To make way for all these classic tracks, as well as the already mentioned *Duchess*, the axe also fell on *No Reply At All*, *Me And Sarah Jane* and *Firth Of Fifth*.

The stage show remained basically the same as on the previous tour: the Vari-Lites were still very much a big part of the set which now also included the use of dry ice which produced a wonderful effect for certain songs. Mike used his Shergold double-neck for the last time on this tour and left ample space for Stuermer to play guitar. Sometimes both he and Rutherford would play guitar and use bass pedals to cover the vacant role of bass player. Thompson: "This was an important part of their sound, particularly on songs like *Supper's Ready* and *Turn It On Again*. It sounded very different even though personally, as a drummer, I think I would have preferred it if one of them had played bass!" [1]

All five musicians were on great form and the sound was starting to incorporate different nuances. Thompson: "Both Daryl and I obviously influenced things a bit, but the different sound was mainly due to the fact that Mike Rutherford was playing more of the guitar parts. Mike has a great ear for guitar, even if, to begin with, the sound hadn't been quite so solid." [1]

GENESIS

This tour was one of the most stable in terms of the setlist which remained pretty much unchanged apart from the *I Know What I Like* encore which was added as early on as the second date (Hoffman Estates, Illinois, on 2 August) but was left out numerous times both in America in August (Berkeley, Dallas, St. Louis, Columbia, New Haven) and Europe in September (Tirrenia, Hamburg, Copenhagen, Gothenburg, Birmingham on the 21st and London on the 28th).

The most interesting variations occurred in the States when the availability of the Phenix Horns who had recorded *No Reply At All* and *Paperlate* with Genesis, paved the way to their exceptional guest appearance. This happened for the first time in Inglewood, near Los Angeles, on 9 and 10 August. The two songs were squeezed in before and after *Supper's Ready*, consequently *No Reply At All* followed *Abacab* and *Paperlate* came before *Misunderstanding*.

But in the first of those two concerts, the one on the 9th, the audience were in for yet another big surprise. Bill Bruford joined the rhythm section to play percussion on *The Lamb Lies Down On Broadway / Watcher Of The Skies* and *I Know What I Like*.

Being as *Paperlate* was the single promoting the THREE SIDES LIVE album, Genesis decided to play it again at the next concert in Dallas, only this time, alas, without the horns. It worked reasonably well, but it was to remain an isolated experiment.

But the Phenix Horns did join Genesis on stage again, at the Forest Hills Stadium in Queens (NY), on the 22nd and 23rd. This time, to simplify matters, the two songs were both inserted between *Abacab* and *Supper's Ready* and played directly after each other (first *No Reply At All* and then *Paperlate*).

With the North American leg of the tour over, the band took a couple of days off before starting out on the European leg in Switzerland (Geneva) before moving onto France (Fréjus). However, before setting foot in Germany, Sweden, Denmark and Belgium, after an absence of seven and a half years, Genesis finally returned to Italy.

Unfortunately, the venue for this great return, scheduled for 6 September, was somewhat disappointing: the Cosmopolitan Film Studios (formerly known as Pisorno Studios because of its location between Pisa and Livorno) in Tirrenia. Bought in the 1960s by Carlo Ponti and Sophia Loren, this

152

Mike and Daryl back on their 12-strings at Tirrenia on 6th September 1982

Poster advertising the triumphant return of Genesis to Italy after an absence of seven years. Concerts promoted by David Zard

array of buildings was the largest film studio in Italy after Cinecittà (Rome) and was used to film outdoor scenes for a number of cinema productions. Added to the bizarre choice of location was the even more bizarre decision to schedule the show as part of the Festa de l'Unità organised by the Italian communist party. This may be why the long-awaited return of Genesis was not met with the anticipated enthusiasm: many members of the audience were probably totally unfamiliar with the band and its music and were merely curious bystanders. On the other hand, members of the audience who were actually there to see the band did nothing to hide their disapproval for the perceived blasphemous proximity of *Supper's Ready* to songs like *Who Dunnit?* and began throwing things at the stage. This marked the beginning of a uniquely Italian attitude towards the latest iteration of Genesis, one that some distinctly did not wish to embrace.

Things were to go very differently at the two shows held at the packed PalaEUR sports arena in Rome on 7 and 8 September, although on the second night the band decided to drop *Man On The Corner* and *Who Dunnit?*, a decision that would be repeated in Hamburg on the 10th.

Who Dunnit? would also be dropped in two other important shows in the incredibly successful 12-date tour of the UK (over 500,000 tickets were sold within days of the tour being announced). The first of the two was in Shepton Mallet on 19 September, where former bandmate Peter Gabriel was in the audience (leaving immediately after *Supper's Ready*), while the second date without *Who Dunnit?* was at the band's return to the legendary Marquee Club on the 27th. At the start of his career, Mike Rutherford said that his biggest ambition was to play at the Marquee Club, where some of rock's biggest stars had played on their way to the top. Ten years down the line and Genesis were so big that, in order to meet their wishes to tread the boards of the Marquee stage once again, they had to advertise the concert under a different name (Garden Wall, the name of Gabriel and Banks' very first high school band) to avoid an onslaught of fans, being as the venue's capacity was a mere 500 people.

Despite this still being in the pre-internet days, the news got out and quickly spread, leading to many fans being only too happy to spend the night sleeping in the street outside the club just to be sure of getting hold of one of those precious tickets. By 10.30 in the morning, tickets had sold out and the lucky holders were treated to a magnificent performance.

The three shows at London's Hammersmith Odeon (28, 29 and 30 September), on the other hand, not only represented another important step in the band's history, but these were also the dates of the rehearsals for another very imminent event: the reunion with Peter Gabriel. In fact, it was in the afternoon of these three days in London that Genesis met up with Peter to get ready for the benefit gig which would keep the bailiffs away from the singer's door. In July of the same year, Gabriel and his associates had organised the WOMAD Festival to promote ethnic music with participating artists from all over the world. It was a total flop and financial disaster due to the excessive costs, lack of funding, poor ticket sales and, adding insult to injury, a rail strike which hampered attendance.

The Festival registered losses in the region of £190,000 and Gabriel, as the only celebrity member of the organising committee, became the financial scapegoat. Facing financial ruin, his former bandmates led by manager, Tony Smith, stepped in to help. And so it was that on 2 October (incidentally also Mike Rutherford's thirty-second birthday) the last Act of Genesis with Peter Gabriel was performed at a concert organised in Milton Keynes where 50,000 fans were moved to tears as they stood knee-deep in mud beneath the incessant rain.

After the support bands (Talk Talk, The Blues Band and John Martyn) had completed their sets, the honour of introducing the band went to their first producer and Charterhouse alumnus, Johnathan King. For the occasion the 'Six Of The Best' (the name under which Gabriel, Banks, Collins, Rutherford, Thompson and Stuermer played that day) had put together a setlist which would soften even the hardest heart, as was plainly evident from those first beating pulses on Mike's bass which open *Back In N.Y.C.* And it was at this point that Gabriel made his entrance inside a white coffin with roadies acting as pallbearers. With Thompson and Collins on drums the band went on to play *Dancing With The Moonlit Knight / The Carpet Crawlers* (performed in the most recent arrangement), *Firth Of Fifth* and *The Musical Box* (played in its entirety for the first time since THE LAMB tour and consequently representing an all-time first for Stuermer and Thompson).

To remind the audience that Genesis and Gabriel were by this time two very distinct entities, Peter's *Solsbury Hill* came next followed by Genesis '80s hit *Turn It On Again* with Phil moving to centre stage while Gabriel played drums.

A large slice of THE LAMB (*The Lamb Lies Down On Broadway, Fly On A Windshield, Broadway Melody Of 1974* and *In The Cage*) gave way to the inevitable *Supper's Ready*. After having worn an old man mask for *The Musical Box*, Gabriel once more donned a flower costume for *Willow Farm* (neither of which were the original ones as those had rotted away beyond repair).

However, the real icing on the cake came with the two encores (*I Know What I Like* and *The Knife*) when Peter invited another old friend to come up on stage to join them: Steve Hackett.

Hackett: "I was in Brazil when I found out about

Three Sides Live

Tirrenia, 6th September 1982

the concert. I phoned and asked if they wanted me to join them, because it was a great idea and a great way to help Peter. I arrived the day before and could only do two songs as there wasn't enough time to rehearse. I did everything I could; I was 3,000 miles away and got a plane just to be there. I desperately wanted to be there, and I think I put much more effort into it than the others did even if it probably looked like I was the one who did the least." [2]

Stuermer: "I remember it was very muddy and it rained. I enjoyed that show very much because I had never played with Peter Gabriel and I felt like there was a little bit of history being made. This was almost the old band! This was Phil Collins on drums and this was Peter Gabriel singing! I just enjoyed that whole dynamic between Peter and Phil and then Steve Hackett came up and played

An angel standing in the rain: Peter Gabriel returns to Genesis, 2nd October 1982

and I think it was a very emotional time for all of them as it was the first time Steve had played with Mike, Tony and Phil since their break-up. And I think that mended any fence, you know, any problem that they had before that was gone." [3]

NOTES

(1) Mario Giammetti's telephone interview with Chester Thompson, 13 August 1999, partially published in the article "Speciale interviste – Chester Thompson", *Dusk*, Issue n. 30, October 1999

(2) Mario Giammetti's interview with Steve Hackett, Twickenham, Kudos Management office, 5 November 1992, partially published in the article "Intervista esclusiva", *Dusk*, Issue n. 6, January 1993

(3) Mario Giammetti's telephone interview with Daryl Stuermer, 3 August 2000, partially published in the article "Intervista esclusiva a Daryl Stuermer", *Dusk*, Issue n. 33, October 2000

Three Sides Live Encore Tour

1982

AUGUST

- 01 **Peoria, IL (USA)**, Peoria Civic Center
- 02 **Hoffman Estates, IL (USA)**, Poplar Creek Music Theater
- 03 **Hoffman Estates, IL (USA)**, Poplar Creek Music Theater
- 06 **Berkeley, CA (USA)**, Greek Theatre - University of California, Berkeley
- 07 **Berkeley, CA (USA)**, Greek Theatre - University of California, Berkeley
- 08 **Berkeley, CA (USA)**, Greek Theatre - University of California, Berkeley
- 09 **Inglewood, CA (USA)**, The Forum
  Special guests: the Phenix Horns on No Reply At All and Paperlate; Bill Bruford on The Lamb Lies Down On Broadway / Watcher Of The Skies and I Know What I Like
- 10 **Inglewood, CA (USA)**, The Forum
  Special guests: the Phenix Horns on No Reply At All and Paperlate
- 11 **Phoenix, AZ (USA)**, Veterans Memorial Coliseum
- 13 **Dallas, TX (USA)**, Reunion Arena
- 14 **Houston, TX (USA)**, The Summit
- 15 **Oklahoma City, OK (USA)**, Myriad Convention Center
- 16 **St. Louis, MO (USA)**, Checkerdome
- 18 **Clarkston, MI (USA)**, Pine Knob Music Theatre
- 19 **Columbia, MD (USA)**, Merriweather Post Pavilion
- 21 **Philadelphia, PA (USA)**, John F. Kennedy Stadium
- 22 **Flushing Meadows, NY (USA)**, Forest Hills Stadium
  Special guests: the Phenix Horns on No Reply At All and Paperlate
- 23 **Flushing Meadows, NY (USA)**, Forest Hills Stadium
  Special guests: the Phenix Horns on No Reply At All and Paperlate
- 25 **New Haven, CT (USA)**, New Haven Veterans Memorial Coliseum
- 26 **Saratoga Springs, NY (USA)**, Saratoga Performing Arts Center
- 27 **Rochester, NY (USA)**, Rochester Community War Memorial
- 28 **Toronto, ON (CANADA)**, Canadian National Exhibition Grandstand
- 29 **Montréal, QC (CANADA)**, Stade Jarry

SEPTEMBER

- 03 **Geneva (SWITZERLAND)**, Stade des Charmilles
- 04 **Fréjus (FRANCE)**, Arènes de Fréjus
- 06 **Tirrenia (PISA) (ITALY)**, Studi Cosmopolitan Film *Festa Nazionale de L'Unità*
- 07 **Rome (ITALY)**, PalaEUR
- 08 **Rome (ITALY)**, PalaEUR
- 10 **Hamburg (WEST GERMANY)**, Wilhelm-Koch-Stadion
- 12 **Stockholm (SWEDEN)**, Johanneshovs Isstadion
- 13 **Brøndby (DENMARK)**, Brøndby-Hallen
- 14 **Gothenburg (SWEDEN)**, Scandinavium
- 16 **Forest (BELGIUM)**, Forest National
- 18 **St. Austell (ENGLAND)**, Cornwall Coliseum
- 19 **Shepton Mallet (ENGLAND)**, Showering Pavilion
- 20 **Birmingham (ENGLAND)**, Birmingham International Arena - National Exhibition Centre
- 21 **Birmingham (ENGLAND)**, Birmingham International Arena - National Exhibition Centre
- 22 **Deeside (WALES)**, Deeside Leisure Centre
- 23 **Leeds (ENGLAND)**, Queens Hall
- 24 **Ingliston (SCOTLAND)**, Royal Highland Exhibition Hall
- 25 **Ingliston (SCOTLAND)**, Royal Highland Exhibition Hall
- 27 **London (ENGLAND)**, Marquee Club
- 28 **London (ENGLAND)**, Hammersmith Odeon
- 29 **London (ENGLAND)**, Hammersmith Odeon
- 30 **London (ENGLAND)**, Hammersmith Odeon

OCTOBER

- 02 **Milton Keynes (ENGLAND)**, Milton Keynes Bowl
  'Six of the Best' reunion concert with Peter Gabriel. Special guest: Steve Hackett on I Know What I Like and The Knife

Genesis

(Charisma / Virgin, 1983)

Mama / That's All / Home By The Sea / Second Home By The Sea /// Illegal Alien / Taking It All Too Hard / Just A Job To Do / Silver Rainbow / It's Gonna Get Better

- All songs written by Banks/Collins/Rutherford
- Release date: 03 October 1983
- Engineer: Hugh Padgham
  Technical Assistance: Geoff Callingham
  Recorded and mixed at The Farm, Surrey, 1983
- Produced by Genesis [with Hugh Padgham]
- Sleeve design: Bill Smith

- **Tony Banks: keyboards, backing vocals**
- **Mike Rutherford: guitars, bass, backing vocals**
- **Phil Collins: drums, percussion, lead vocals**

THE MAKING OF

With the long ABACAB tour and the additional string of live shows (which later became known as the THREE SIDES LIVE tour) now over, the band continued along its path of metamorphosis. In a certain sense, it could be said that the reunion concert with Peter Gabriel, on 2 October 1982 in Milton Keynes, represented a sort of unplanned final farewell to the old way of doing things.

To reinforce the impression that 1982 was a turning point, alongside the increasingly more successful Phil Collins (who in November set out on his first solo tour, taking both Thompson and Stuermer with him), the parallel careers of Mike and Tony also developed further. Their two new solo albums showed that they too had moved away from the old sound. Turning their backs on the sumptuous and romantic atmospheres of their debut solo albums released just a couple of years earlier, Tony and Mike were now focusing on short, catchy songs and (with rather debatable results) both had opted to take on the role of lead singer. Fans were hardly fazed, but Tony and Mike were steering towards more immediate musical expression, giving the lie to all those who by this point saw Genesis as nothing more than a projection of Phil Collins.

Rutherford: "The writing careers of myself and Tony developed over many years, while Phil's career as a writer suddenly just took off. His speed of improvement was, you know, tenfold to ours. Confidence, with anything you do, always helps and I'm sure Phil's solo success helped him gain that confidence and it seemed to come out very naturally with him."[1]

The band scheduled a get-together at The Farm in March 1983 with the studio now fully operational. Or almost.

Collins: "Abacab was written in the house while the cowshed was being converted, so this was the first album we actually wrote, recorded and mixed in that environment. But we had some terrible storms! I mean, we seemed to have bought the place in an area where the Godalming Electrical Company was still in existence; it was the first electrical system in England or something and it was still above ground. Every time the wind blew, the cables came down and we had a lot of power problems, so we ended up getting a generator because it always seemed to happen while we were mixing. We actually mixed a few tracks by candlelight with the generator running the tape machines. Occasionally watching dirty movies while we were mixing, things like that. Ahh, those were the days."[1]

There was, however, an important change on the writing level: for the first time since Gabriel's departure, Genesis decided that no songs written individually would be taken into consideration for the new album.

Banks: "Every piece on this album was written with all three of us writing together and improvising in the room. I don't think there was anything on this album that came from before, apart from the odd riff. I remember just about everything I contributed to this album was written on the spot. That obviously means that things end up being a little simpler and slightly less developed, which is not necessarily to everybody's taste but it means you do capture a moment, you know, someone starts playing a riff and you play along with it and things happen. Of course, a lot of pieces go by the board. Sometimes you're playing something really good but if no one else gets off on it, it doesn't happen."[1]

GENESIS

Promotional photo, Charisma Records 1983

However, the sessions do seem to have been a lot less fruitful than usual.

Banks: "We didn't have any excess material on this album; everything we had we used. We didn't have the over-abundance we had on some of the other albums. We went short of ideas."[1]

Rutherford: "I think we went into every album feeling a bit nervous actually because you never presume it's going work. We arrived with no bits and sort of just turned on the gear and played. There was always a little edge there, worry that maybe nothing would come out. It's an important album for us in many ways because it was the first time we'd had our own studio from the word go."[1]

Banks: "When you start a project or a new album, you're never confident about what you're going to come up with. I think with ABACAB we felt, you know, that in many ways we'd cleared out all the furniture, and so with this album it was a question of re-decorating a little bit. You know, we had some areas we hadn't been in before and then the song *That's All* which is a bit more straightforward. I think we always liked the idea of writing concise things as well as long things. It was always something we'd tried to do but only occasionally in the past had we had the courage to really stick with this sort of thing and develop it. We'd just had one or two hit singles, so we'd got more confident in that."[1]

Rutherford: "You just go into the studio and dick around, crossing your fingers that something good will come out of it. I think *Mama* is a great example of how this album worked. As you can hear, the version that was recorded very early on had a slightly longer section [*Rutherford is referring to the version included in* GENESIS ARCHIVE #2 *released in 2000 – author's note*]. So you captured spontaneity, for the first time actually, by writing things and playing them very early on and then recording them, rather than finishing a song and going in to record it somewhere else later."[1]

On this album, with sound engineer Hugh Padgham promoted to the role of co-producer, there is a significant increase in the amount of technology used.

Collins: "I don't remember thinking that we were always wanting to be on the cutting edge of technology, but someone was always saying, 'hey, have you seen that new keyboard' and Tony would try it and fool around with it. Of course, these were the days of the Fairlight synthesisers and, you know, all these new breeds of sampler/sequencers. We still had a few of the original, kind of White Elephant drum machines. I had a Movement Drum System which was a huge orange plastic box (like the Eurythmics had used) but this was the first time we used the LinnDrum machine. If something was easy to manage we'd use it, you know, if we could just turn it on and muck around with it before reading the manual (I don't think any of us are very big manual readers)."[1]

Japanese poster, Vertigo 1983

Banks: "I used a sampling synthesiser for a lot of the sounds on the album, I mean things like the koto used in the middle of *Mama*. The other thing, I think, was the digital synthesisers and the Synclavier, which was not a sampling instrument but had very complex and distinctive sounds, like the one at the beginning of *Mama* which everyone immediately recognises. The lead solo sound used on *Home By The Sea* came from the same instrument; it just has a presence and power about it that the earlier synthesisers weren't able to get." [1]

Collins: "The Simmons was this new drum system that had come out. It was like playing on hexagonal Formica tops. They eventually started to make them feel more like drum skins, you know, real drums, but it never really worked. I actually didn't mind playing the Formica tops; everyone used to have wrist problems but I quite liked it. Around that same time I played with Robert Plant and when I went on tour with him we actually used them a lot on stage. *Home By The Sea*, *That's All* and *Silver Rainbow* were all based on this sound, this instrument." [1]

With the recording of the album complete, for the first time in their history, the band decided to call it, quite simply, GENESIS. Collins: "We all knew that *Mama* was a key track, but I think we felt that if we called the album by the name of any one song it would draw attention to that one song. Of course, with ABACAB it was a song, but it was an abstract word which didn't really mean anything so we kind of didn't really feel threatened by that. It could well be that we simply couldn't actually agree on anything." [1]

Banks: "We did think of various different possibilities and obviously all the song titles came up. It's always referred to as the *Mama* album now, so perhaps we should have just called it that. But at the time it didn't seem that obvious and we thought, 'well we've never called an album GENESIS, let's call it that'." [1]

And let's face it, many other artists have done this way more often than Genesis have.

Collins: "Led Zeppelin have done four – no reason for it." [1]

Banks: "PETER GABRIEL 1, PETER GABRIEL 2, PETER GABRIEL 3… I'm not quite sure which album of ours it was. Anyhow, it is the only one called GENESIS and if we ever do another album it won't be called GENESIS again." [1]

GENESIS

Promotional banner, 1983

Rome, 6th September 1982

THE ALBUM

The idea of entering the recording studio without anything already composed (apart from the odd riff) was a new approach which in some ways was reminiscent of early Genesis, only in a more extreme way (back then, band members had often come in with at least some previously written ideas). The overall result is obviously excellent in terms of capturing spontaneity, but it is also blatantly obvious that the limited amount of time available (especially with Collins' busy schedule) didn't do the band any favours in terms of quality. Not in the absolute sense, after all, Side One of the album is full of remarkable things, but it is still difficult to shake off the feeling that it was all a rather rushed job.

To this we should add the innovations on a sound level which are all rather of their time. In addition to the already extensive use of the drum machine and the by now usual sound of the drums filtered by Hugh Padgham, the Simmons electronic drum kit made an appearance, an instrument that was very popular in the '80s. Having used it while playing live on tour with Robert Plant, Collins would play around on it also during the writing sessions for the new album and this is inevitably reflected in the overall sound. The same applies to the Synclavier used by Banks.

In terms of writing, *Mama* is without doubt one of the top moments in the band's entire catalogue and *Home By The Sea*, with its instrumental appendix, is a musical ride almost reminiscent of the old Genesis atmospheres. Another enjoyable track, albeit of a completely different mould, is *That's All*. But Side Two seems to fall short with a few tracks (*Illegal Alien* above all) that seem lacking in inspiration. Probably, with a little more time at their disposal, the band would have been able to create more material and make a more careful selection.

It also has to be said that, after so much extraordinary music, the overall impression at this time is of a marked drop in the level of creativity. These were hedonistic years in which the quest for novelty for novelty's sake led the way and it was all too easy to hit the accelerator pedal on easy-going pop with frequent digressions into dance music. The New Romantic genre was at its height, as exemplified by the hugely successful Rio by Duran Duran, while new bands and singers were appearing such as Culture Club (Kissing To Be Clever), Wham! (Fantastic), Paul Young (No Parlez), and ABC (The Lexicon Of Love). More importantly, 1982 was the year when an American singer of Italian descent, Madonna, released her debut single, Michael Jackson released Thriller (which would prove to be the biggest selling album of all time) and Prince brought out the ground-breaking album, 1999.

Of course, not all pop was easy listening; Donald

Fagen and Joe Jackson, for example, had respectively released their classy THE NIGHTFLY and NIGHT AND DAY, while Talk Talk had brought out THE PARTY'S OVER, and Simple Minds had released the ambitious NEW GOLD DREAM.

Among the historical names, Robert Plant released his debut album (PICTURES AT ELEVEN), Paul McCartney brought out TUG OF WAR and Mike Oldfield finally recaptured something of his previous success with CRISES. In the meantime, The Clash were still flying high on the back of COMBAT ROCK and Roger Waters called it a day with Pink Floyd after releasing THE FINAL CUT. The Police drew what then seemed to be a last (but exhilarating) breath with SYNCHRONICITY and Yes caused a sensation with 90125, an album in a completely new and lighter style (above all thanks to the arrival of guitarist, Trevor Rabin) from which they would reap ample rewards in terms of sales and a return to popularity, an evolution which, in all probability, was more than just a little influenced by the transformation seen in Genesis.

If certain debut albums appear interesting for the new and different areas explored (R.E.M. with the EP CHRONIC TOWN, Big Country with THE CROSSING, Metallica, KILL 'EM ALL), two albums in this period swam against the tide, rekindling the hopes of all those feeling bereft of progressive rock. In March 1982, Asia, the supergroup made up of members of King Crimson, Yes and ELP, released its self-titled debut album, which climbed the charts with its romantic and catchy pop. A year later, an Aylesbury-formed band made up of four great musicians and a charismatic lead singer released SCRIPT FOR A JESTER'S TEAR; Marillion represented a lifeboat for all those early Genesis fans (of which there were many) who no longer related to Collins & Co. The reaction of the latter, however, very much like Sun Tzu, was to stand quietly at the river's edge and wait for the bodies of their enemies to float by.

THE SONGS

MAMA

Rutherford: "I had one of those old LinnDrum machines and I put it into a Boogie amplifier and turned it up incredibly loud so it was distorted. I got this great sound and it sort of set the mood for the song." [1]

GENESIS

Promotional photo, Charisma Records 1983

Banks: "I remember when Mike first played us the drum machine part. He put it through an echo machine and then through an amplifier. The poor little amplifier was jumping around but it was just a fantastic sound, and just from hearing that we felt we'd got a song. I like the sort of chance element you get with technology, like playing a chord with a sample and getting a totally different effect to what I was originally intending. Every time you get serendipity, something occurs and you take advantage of it, and we've never been frightened to do that. It doesn't always lead somewhere, but when it does it can be something quite special." [1]

Over the electronic drum pattern, Banks brings in an eerie sounding keyboard melody which in the verse is followed by protracted guitar notes. This high level of emotive tension explodes with the thunderous entrance of the drums, with many critics quick to point out how this replicates the idea used by Collins in his hit single *In The Air Tonight*.

Banks: "Well, obviously we knew there was going to be a slight comparison with that, so we avoided having a distinctive drum riff to introduce it. But slow moody chords like that have been quite a Genesis thing over the years and Phil had a certain way of singing and he'd brought a certain kind of drum sound with him. So, the final effect echoed it but I think it was a completely different song. What I really wanted to do with it was keep the chords very sparse throughout the first part of the song and then bring in this massive chord in the middle. And that is actually the peak of the song in many ways, so it's something totally different to *In The Air Tonight*." [1]

Rutherford: "That big drum sound was already out there; it started with Phil playing on Peter's album and then on *In The Air Tonight*. So it was reminiscent of that, yeah, but you can't stop a good sound being the right thing for a song. I think what's more important than the drum pattern is what we did with this song." [1]

Collins: "I think we were using the drums as a kind of secret weapon at that moment, you know, something we'd save until we really needed it. In a song like *Mama*, the drum machine took up so much space and it had so much atmosphere you kind of didn't feel the need for anything else until

164

that moment where you sort of had to unleash the artillery. It's one of those songs that still sounds good on the radio today. It certainly captured an atmosphere and I think it's a great example of what we always wanted to do: record things at the right time before we'd worn them out. It was quite interesting actually. It was Mike's drum machine and it was in the early days when you had to take a midi-cable out of the back of the drum machine and plug it into a keyboard. So, if you had a cowbell going, Tony would put his hand on the keyboard and it wouldn't just play the rhythm, it would play the notes."[1]

The other outstanding feature of the song is Collins' vocal performance, quite simply stunning on a technical and expressive level.

Rutherford: "Phil just came in and sang the middle bit. I hadn't heard the lyrics and it sounded incredibly strong. A bit like Peter in *Supper's Ready*; that '666' bit. Those two moments: when you hear something for the first time and go, 'shit! That's fantastic!'."[1]

Collins: "I was into this sort of John Lennon *Be-Bop-A-Lula* echo thing, so in the 'I can't see you' bit, it was kind of me pretending to be John Lennon. And Hugh Padgham had brought in this record that had just come out, *The Message* by Grandmaster Flash. It was the really early days of rap, so no one had really heard this stuff before, you know, *'It's like a jungle sometimes / It makes me wonder how I keep from going under / Ha ha ha'*. We all thought that laugh was great, you know, with such character, so we kept playing it. We just happened to be going back into the studio after having listened to it to do *Mama* and so, you know, we were just sort of improvising our way round it and every now and again I'd go 'ha ha ha' and the guys would laugh. Anyway, it kind of became the hook of the song. And it's all because of Grandmaster Flash! If you were to ask most Genesis fans, that would be a million miles away, but that's how it happened."[1]

The lyrics definitely provide a stark contrast with their earlier works. Banks: "Phil had got to that stage where in some cases it was more important how the lyrics sounded rather than what they meant, and I think *Mama*'s an example of that. It's loosely about a sort of prostitute or something really, but you don't quite know what she is. It has this dark, steamy sort of feel, you know, and we sort of encouraged that kind of attitude in the video."[1]

Collins: "It's kind of about this teenage or adolescent fascination with a prostitute. Mama is this elderly, voluptuous hooker and this teenager's got this thing about her, you know, and he just dreams about her. She kind of takes him under her wing, not in a sexual way, but, of course, he's just turned on because she's, you know, a sexy, sexy woman. We tried to get that across in the video as well (but probably not as successfully). It was meant to sound very steamy and sweaty, a bit like Charles Laughton, you know, in a white suit constantly wiping the back on his neck; you know, the sweat and steam and mosquitoes kind of thing."[1]

Rutherford: "Because of the nature of the chords Tony used to play, it was easier for Phil to write slightly darker lyrics and *Mama* is a great example of that. It's one of our best moments in terms of recording and it's got all those elements that we do well vocally, lyrically and in terms of chords. Genesis has this ability to create this dark atmos-

GENESIS

UK poster advertising the second single taken off the album (Charisma / Virgin)

phere and *Mama* is a great example of that. It's probably one of my favourite songs of all time actually." [1]

THAT'S ALL

Driven by piano over Phil initially playing only the bass drum and hi-hat that develops into a rhythm similar in many ways to country music, this song also has a fine bass line, a simple keyboard solo from Tony and clean guitar lines from Mike over a double-time rhythm.

Banks: "It was a kind of slightly quirky little thing, something different for us really. I always think it's reminiscent of The Beatles' *Rocky Raccoon*, which is a song I've always liked a lot, and so it had a great feel really. I just started playing that piano riff and then Phil started doing this drum fill and I purposely kept all the chords very simple." [1]

Rutherford: "Our little happy beat song, you know, with that sort of Beatles sound. I was kind of surprised it turned out to be a big hit in America; it was just a catchy little phrase that Phil had. I think it was just that our time was right in America. Things just started working on the radio. We'd been playing the States for years and years and suddenly... We got better at writing shorter songs and they seemed to work." [1]

HOME BY THE SEA / SECOND HOME BY THE SEA

Divided into two parts with two titles, this track is in fact one single song lasting over 11 minutes. The second half of the song is almost entirely instrumental with a short reprise of the vocal part at the end.

The drum sound was created using a Simmons electronic kit. Collins: "I played the drum pattern with pre-sets. It had such a lot of atmosphere and everyone started playing along. It was almost comparable to what happened on Peter's *Intruder*, where you just sort of get a sound and you play around with it and suddenly you have a musical part that everybody jams along with. I don't know why, but I just started singing the words 'Home by the sea' with that melody. Tony took that line, went away and came back with this ghost story. It's kind of strange, I mean, you have a little idea floating about, someone grabs it, takes it and makes it into something totally different. That's what it's like being in a band like that: it's great! This was the interesting way Genesis used to work and, you know, we could work in the same way if we were ever to do something again." [1]

Banks: "When we were writing the song, Phil had this one phrase he kept singing: 'Home by the sea'. I was writing the lyrics to it and I asked myself what that phrase conjured up. I thought, 'well, let's have a spooky home by the sea', you know, and the idea of a burglar going in there and actually getting enveloped and suddenly having all these ghosts surrounding him. Also, some of the melodic little keyboard things felt a bit ghostly and so it quite appealed to me and I thought it would be quite a nice thing to do. And then the line in the 3rd verse, 'as we relive our lives in what we tell you', really represents this idea that we're telling you our life story through our songs, which I think is quite a strong thing, it's sort of what you do in a group." [1]

Rutherford: "The long instrumental section was written how we usually did those things: we'd start with a beat and a jam and off we'd go. Phil had that boom sound on the Simmons and Tony and I, we would sort of dick around, try things out, finding little bits that worked and then kind of put it all together." [1]

ILLEGAL ALIEN

The sound of traffic introduces this song based on a fast rhythm with a repetitive chorus broken up by continual guitar riffs. A mediocre song played just for fun.

Rutherford: "It's one of our sort of humorous moments which I think balances out the longer songs on the album nicely. I think a bit of humour always helps." [1]

Mike's lyrics deal with the issue of illegal immigration into the States. If one considers Phil's singing in a mock Mexican accent and the accompanying video, hardly politically correct by any standards, it's easy to understand why the band was criticised and accused of being racist. Their actual intent, however clumsily expressed, was to highlight the plight of people seeking a better life in a different country and the difficulties encountered.

TAKING IT ALL TOO HARD

A melodic song rather unusually characterised by percussion and acoustic guitar with Phil excelling on vocal harmonies over Tony's piano arrangement.

Banks: "I had this little piano piece and we just played around with it and it came out well in the end. Mike wanted to do the lyrics and I was happy with that as I didn't have any ideas for it. It was a nice track but for me the lesser track on the album." [2]

JUST A JOB TO DO

A fast funky / R&B track similar to Collins' solo work, with the horns replaced by Tony's synthesiser brass.

Banks: "Mike started playing this riff and I echoed it, as we did on *Abacab*. At the time both Mike and Phil were into Michael Jackson and they wanted that kind of rhythm. But me being who I am, I dragged it more back towards Genesis territory by putting in a couple of funny chords. It's one of those songs that after we'd done the album, I wasn't too sure about, but I heard it just recently and I thought it worked well. In some ways it was a bit of a one-off for us really. There's nothing else we've done that is quite like it; perhaps it's more in the realm of something like *No Reply At All*, a bit funkier than some of the things we did at the time. Mike wrote the lyric." [2]

GENESIS

US poster advertising three nights at the Inglewood Forum in January 1984, promoted by Avalon Attractions

SILVER RAINBOW

After an interesting intro, this track soon descends into the banal with a backing track of piano, drums, a moderately inspired rhythm guitar and a chorus with romantic nuances highlighted by the backing vocals and strings.

But Banks disagrees: "This is a real favourite of mine. Phil started playing this kind of Adam And The Ants drum thing with the Simmons, you know, just banging his way through it, and I started playing this piano riff on top. I thought it was a really strong song and I hoped it would go a little further than it did, but it wasn't recognised or independent from the album at all." [1]

IT'S GONNA GET BETTER

Featuring synthesiser bass over a keyboard sequence, this track transmits hope and optimism.

Banks: "What I always liked to do (it's done a lot nowadays) was sample little bits of music and then see what you could do with them. An example of that is in the introduction to this track where I just recorded the beginning of this classical music album, just 4/4 cello notes, originally recorded to try and get a good string sample. When I pressed it, it sounded awful but then, for some reason, I pressed 4 notes at the same time and this incredible inter-weaving harmony suddenly came up. It was brilliant, you know, fantastic; I was doing nothing and it sounded wonderful. So that sort of made me think and this idea became quite a big feature within Genesis from then on." [1]

THE ALBUM ARTWORK

An image of Shape-O toy pieces scattered over a dark surface: for their self-titled album, Genesis certainly didn't choose the most interesting sleeve design.

Banks: "Yeah, there are some pieces of a Tupperware child's toy arrayed on it. I think it was just a Polaroid picture or something. The idea seemed better than the result, let me put it like that. It's a better CD cover than it is an LP cover and I don't know why that should be. Perhaps because everything looks better in miniature, doesn't it?" [1]

Collins: "Children's little shapes, you know, star, square, circle... It's very distinctive. It's nice. I can't even remember who did the cover, was it Hipgnosis?" [1]

Banks: "We used Bill Smith, the same guy who'd done the previous ABACAB album cover which we thought was great, but, for this one, we were a bit stuck for ideas. He'd got this photo which we looked at and thought was quite interesting, but then, when we actually put it on the album, we didn't think it was very good and we almost tried to do a last-minute change." [1]

Rutherford: "I think this was probably our worst cover. I remember it was one of those moments where we had the album coming out and there was a tour coming up, so it was a case of 'here are the choices, which one do you dislike the least?'. The guys who did album covers used to come along and they'd show us these books and ideas and we wouldn't like any of them. I feel there was a sort of creative gap at that stage, but not in the music, thank God!" [1]

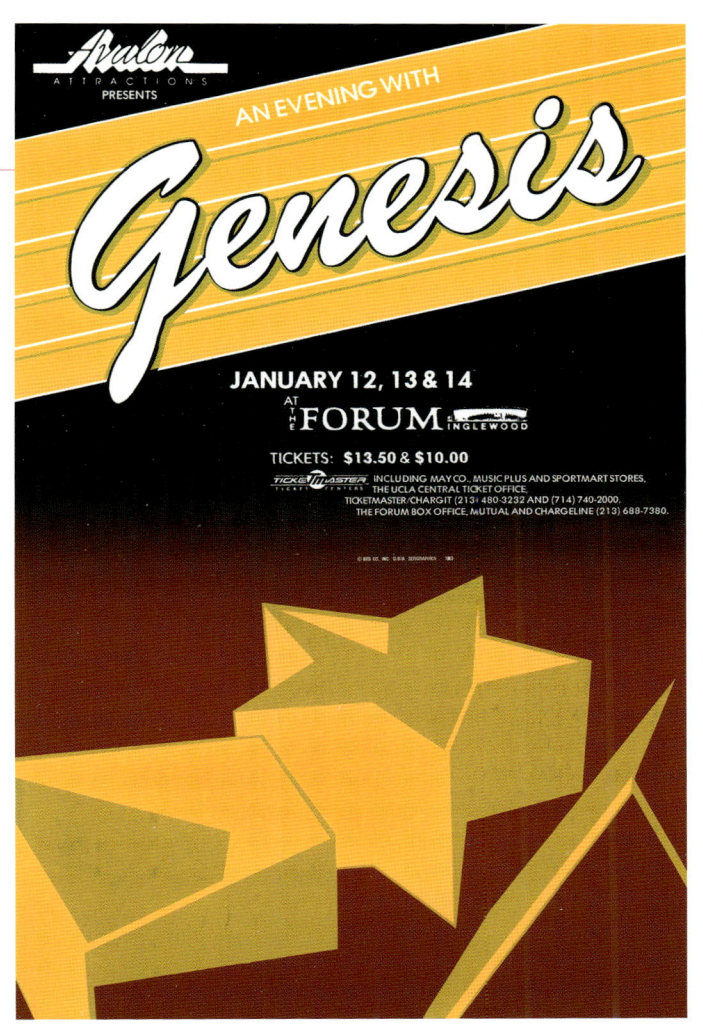

EPILOGUE

Rutherford: "I would put Genesis down as one of my favourite albums because it's got a nice balance of long songs and short songs. I think one of the main things about this album is that it was the first time we actually went in to record having slightly changed our sound with Hugh Padgham. With Hugh, it wasn't so much about the technology but the fact that for the first time we actually sounded on record like we sounded when we rehearsed. In the past we had a good sound live in the rehearsal room but then in the studio it was a battle to get anywhere near as good as we normally just naturally sounded. Hugh just went in and plugged in, we played and sounded just like we were. That was a real pleasure for me." [1]

Banks: "All the tracks on Side Two of the album are quite strong as they all have their own character, but none of them are as bold as the tracks on Side One. The three major tracks are on Side One, but my favourite is from Side Two, *Silver Rainbow*, that didn't quite get the attention it should have done." [2]

Genesis wasn't exactly received with open arms by either their old fans or the critics. But the general public simply shrugged their shoulders and went out to buy the album regardless, making it the band's third consecutive No. 1 in the UK charts and dropping only two places in the US where it reached No. 9, achieving 4 x Platinum sales.

Some of the singles taken off the album were almost as successful. *Mama* reached No. 4 in the UK but made little impact in the US where, on the other hand, *That's All* was a hit. Reaching only No. 16 back home, this was the first song to take Genesis into the Top Ten of the US Billboard Hot 100 singles charts, climbing all the way to No. 6 (*Illegal Alien* only reached No. 44 and *Taking It All Too Hard* climbed no higher than No. 50).

Collins: "At the time, *That's All* was obviously much more radio-friendly than *Mama*, which was a

GENESIS

Genesis celebrate their tenth anniversary with Atlantic Records. The band is here pictured with the manager Tony Smith, Atlantic boss Ahmet Ertegun and vice president Dave Glew. Photo taken in Hollywood on 17th January 1984

little bit of a dark horse for AM radio in America."[1]

Record sales were without doubt boosted by the publicity afforded by videos. Banks: "The idea of acting was fun and, I mean, we were obviously aware right from the word go that Phil was pretty good at doing this kind of thing. So videos became more and more prominent and we used to do them for every album in the hope that they might get shown on 'Top of the Pops' rather than us having to go on there and sort of look stupid which was what we normally did. The video for *Mama* was pretty strong and for *Illegal Alien* we had a lot of fun dressing up and, you know, putting a moustache on and slicking back our hair and stuff. We got a taste for it and thought, 'well, why not?'. It became the easiest way of promoting an album. You'd do two or three videos, take time over them and, if the song lent itself to it, you could end up with something pretty good and the whole thing got a lot of publicity which was great."[1]

Collins: "My solo career was running parallel to this and, although the *Mama* and *Illegal Alien* videos were produced and directed by Ruth and Stuart Orme, we kind of changed horses a little bit and also started using Jim Yukich and Paul Flattery. Probably the first video they directed for us was *That's All*. It has nothing to do with the album; we filmed it in this disused derelict house in Dallas dressed up like James Cagney, you know, with blacked eyes, flat caps and long coats. It just seemed more tailor-made for the American market."[1]

At this point in time, the US television channel MTV, launched in August 1981, had become an exceptionally important media outlet which heavily influenced record sales.

Collins: "I remember being in the Mandalay Four Seasons in Dallas, almost the day when MTV started. I've since become great friends again with Mark Goodman, you know, one of the early VJ's; it's funny how the world goes like that, it ends up bringing you back together again, doing stuff. Videos became a very important part of what we were doing; it was as important as radio promotion."[1]

Rutherford: "The thing about making videos and the MTV era is that it coincided very much with Phil's acting background and his natural ability to sort of portray a character on stage with the band and especially on video. I think video also gave us a chance to show a bit of humour. You know, Genesis is always perceived as quite a serious band, by nature of the music, but video-wise we tried to show another side."[1]

THE CONCERTS

With the band's success in the UK by this time undeniable, Genesis wanted to try and consolidate their position in America in the wake of their hit *That's All*, the band's first single to make it into the US Top Ten. Consequently, to promote Genesis, the band organised a tour which focused almost exclusively on North America, scheduling around 70 dates between November 1983 and February 1984. European fans, on the other hand, had to make do with just five shows in Birmingham, also in February '84.

For this tour the stage show was totally revolutionised, starting with the phenomenal lighting system, the likes of which had never been seen before. Costing over $4 million at the time, the futuristic lighting rig was so big that it had to be transported from city to city in five trucks. As with the previous tour, the presentation was based on the use of Vari-Lites, special stage lights offering infinite possibilities thanks to adjustable beam intensities, diameters and colours which could be changed in a mere fraction of a second. Furthermore, every light could revolve 360° around each axis. Under the direction of lighting engineer, Alan Owen, who had already been working with Genesis for a number of years, 200 Vari-Lites were hung above the stage in an enormous hexagon-shaped rig creating a further spectacular effect.

Band member positions on stage were also switched around. On this score, Genesis had always been very conservative, in fact; aside from the early years (when Hackett sat alongside Gabriel while Mike was on the far left of the stage), the band had always had the same stage positions, from left to right: Steve (later Daryl), Mike, the singer, Phil's drum kit, Banks on keyboards and (as of 1976) a second drum kit was set up behind Mike. For the *Mama* tour, the band had a reshuffle: Banks was now centre stage, raised up on a platform, almost as if to highlight his essential role in constructing the atmospheres of every Genesis era. On either side of him, two more platforms housed the drum kits (Chester Thompson's on the left and Phil's on the right), while at the front of the stage Mike stood to the left, Daryl on the right with Phil in the middle.

And if that wasn't enough, there was no lack of surprises on the musical front either, starting with the setlist. From the new album the band played Side One in its entirety together with *Illegal Alien* and *It's Gonna Get Better*, the latter linked up to the end of *Keep It Dark*, from Abacab, which for some reason had never been played live in either the album tour or the 1982 encore tour. Alongside some questionable repeat setlist choices (*Man On The Corner* and above all *Who Dunnit?*), Genesis slotted in other recent hits such as *Follow You Follow Me* (omitted in the previous tour), *Abacab*, *Misunderstanding* and *Turn It On Again*, while, in accordance with tradition, they selected a track from the previous studio album as an opener, in this case, *Dodo*.

The band's early history was essentially reduced to *The Carpet Crawlers, Los Endos* (preceded by the drum duet) and two medleys, both of which were rather unusual. In the so-called *In The Cage* medley, unlike in the 1981 and 1982 tours, the second part of *…In That Quiet Earth* (with the long synth solo) was added to the other already established excerpts from the history of Genesis (*The Cinema Show* and a touch of *Raven*) before flowing into *Afterglow*.

Poster advertising the concert in Norfolk, Virginia, on 10th December 1983, promoted by Whisper Concerts

November 1983, the tour was scheduled to start in Normal, Illinois on 7 November (following a warm-up gig on the previous day) with the following setlist: *Dodo / The Carpet Crawlers / That's All / Mama / Illegal Alien / Medley: Eleventh Earl Of Mar – Ripples – Squonk – Firth Of Fifth / Man On The Corner / Who Dunnit? / Home By The Sea* (as always, including *Second Home By The Sea*) */ Keep It Dark – It's Gonna Get Better / Follow You Follow Me / In The Cage – The Cinema Show – …In That Quiet Earth – Raven – Afterglow / Abacab / Drum Duet – Los Endos*. The encores were *Misunderstanding* and *Turn It On Again*.

The first thing to change, almost immediately, was the medley: the first sung verse of *Eleventh Earl Of Mar* was only featured in the very first show, while *Ripples* had already been crossed off the setlist by Milwaukee on 10 November, the date on which the medley only included *Eleventh Earl Of Mar, Squonk* (with Phil singing about two thirds of the song but in a different order to the original studio recording) and *Firth Of Fifth* (from the synth solo to the end).

The running order of the setlist was mixed around as of Rosemont, near Chicago, on the 11th: *Abacab* was played as the second song, while *Illegal Alien* and the *Eleventh Earl Of Mar* medley were swapped over and *The Carpet Crawlers* was moved to halfway through the show.

The new setlist (*Dodo / Abacab / That's All / Mama / Medley: Eleventh Earl Of Mar – Squonk – Firth Of Fifth / Illegal Alien / Man On The Corner / Who Dunnit? / Home By The Sea / The Carpet Crawlers / Keep It Dark – It's Gonna Get Better / Follow You Follow Me / In The Cage – The Cinema Show – …In That Quiet Earth – Raven – Afterglow / Drum Duet – Los*

The biggest surprises, however, were to be found in the second medley which started with the instrumental intro of *Eleventh Earl Of Mar* and went on to string together three or four old Genesis songs in different combinations, taking the overall length of the show up to two and a half hours.

Banks: "Genesis have always been a very dynamic group live which I think is a good thing. A lot of groups go on stage and play pretty much every song at the same level, you know, you don't get much variety. With Genesis you're never quite sure what you're going to get; one moment the speakers are shaking and the next you're off with acoustic guitars. I think we've always been quite a difficult group to pin down, we have so much variety and when people say they don't like us, there probably is a bit they like somewhere, they've just forgotten about it." [1]

After a couple of weeks rehearsing in a hangar in Las Colinas (near Dallas) from 22 October to 3

Poster advertising the concert in Normal, Illinois, on November 7th 1983, promoted by Jam Productions

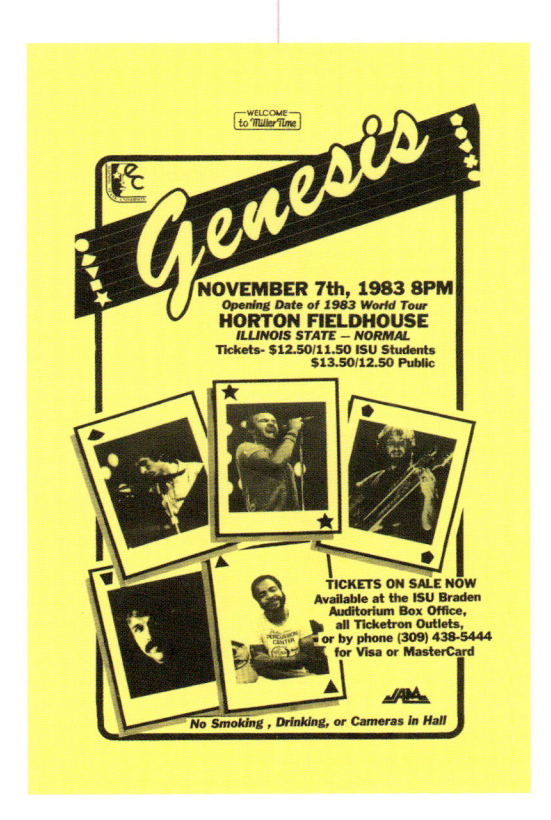

The Corner.

The song pair made up of *Man On The Corner* and *Who Dunnit?* was regularly played but only up until 21 January before it disappeared definitively from the setlist (although *Man On The Corner* did make a one-off reappearance on 3 February in Omaha, following *Home By The Sea*).

As for the *Eleventh Earl Of Mar* medley, this would remain the same for the whole of 1983, changing only with the new year. In fact, as of the show in Tempe, Arizona on 15 January, it was as follows: *Eleventh Earl Of Mar – Behind The Lines – Firth Of Fifth – The Musical Box*. Of *Behind The Lines*, as well as the initial instrumental, Phil also sang the first verse, first chorus and second verse, at the end of which a couple of new chords formed a bridge into *Firth Of Fifth*. After the guitar solo, the medley linked up with the closing section of *The Musical Box*, starting from the arpeggio preceding "She's a lady..." as heard on SECONDS OUT. This sequence was destined to last for only a dozen or so concerts, because on 29 January, in Kansas City, at the end of the North American tour, *Behind The Lines* was replaced by *The Lamb Lies Down On Broadway*, making the sequence: *Eleventh Earl Of Mar – The Lamb – Firth Of Fifth – The Musical Box*.

The end of the North American tour registered a handful of dates which omitted *Misunderstanding* (Dallas, New Orleans, Madison, St. Paul and Winnipeg, while in Kansas City it seems it was played between *Illegal Alien* and *Home By The Sea*). The song would, however, reappear as a fixed part of the setlist as of 16 February in Reno, Nevada.

The encore was therefore often just a version of *Turn It On Again*, also due to its progressive growth in length. In fact, the song taken off DUKE, the audi-

Endos / Misunderstanding / Turn It On Again) remained identical for about a month (with the only possible exception occurring on 16 November in Landover because there is no trace of *Mama* on the amateur recording which later came to light). From the 13 December in Atlanta, right up to the end of the North American tour, *The Carpet Crawlers* was dropped.

From 13 January, in Los Angeles the medley of old Genesis songs was brought up the running order to number five, swapping places with *Illegal Alien*, while on the 17th in Denver, *Illegal Alien* would again swap places, this time with *Man On*

GENESIS

Tony at the NEC, Birmingham, 26th February 1984

ence's favourite closing piece, underwent a number of important innovations over the course of the tour which would accompany it, in various forms, for a number of years. This all started by chance during the concert in New York on 18 November when Phil, over the guitar riff, started to improvise, throwing in first a bit of *Everybody Needs Somebody* (the song made famous by The Blues Brothers) before adding some of the Rolling Stones' *Satisfaction*. Despite being notoriously averse to improvising on stage, Genesis easily managed to follow the chord changes set by Daryl Stuermer (both he and Mike used to play this song on guitar, using bass pedals for the bass line), while

174

Chester's part remained unchanged from a rhythm point of view but not in the execution (for example, you can hear the continuous beats on the snare drum on *Satisfaction*). For Phil this is obviously great fun and so, over the course of time, the singer would go on to add other '60s hits. In Toronto on the 22nd *All Day And All Of The Night* by The Kinks had been incorporated and by Worcester the musical references had become four (with the addition of *In The Midnight Hour* by Wilson Pickett) and six in Philadelphia on 25 November: *Everybody Needs Somebody / Satisfaction / Gimme Some Lovin'* (Spencer Davis Group) */ The Last Time* (Rolling Stones) */ In The Midnight Hour* and *All Day And All Of The Night*.

But variations were the order of the day: *Gimme Some Lovin'* was dropped in Hartford on 1 December, while in Pittsburgh a week later *All Day And All Of The Night* was replaced by another Kinks' classic, *You Really Got Me*, and in Norman, on 19 January, the sequence was *Everybody Needs Somebody / Satisfaction / All Day And All Of The Night / Pinball Wizard* (by The Who) and *In The Midnight Hour*. To this list, later on in the tour, before and after the Kinks' classic, Phil would add two more songs, The Beatles' hit *Twist & Shout* and *Baby Let Me Take You Home* by The Animals.

The North American tour ended on 20 February 1984 at the Oakland Coliseum, after which the band returned to the UK for the final set of concerts. These were all held, over 5 consecutive nights between 25 and 29 February, at the National Exhibition Centre, Birmingham, with the last two staged in aid of the Prince's Trust (a charity founded by Prince Charles). The shows were rather interesting and heralded a number of variations, apart from the one on 25 February which had the exact same setlist as the last show in America: *Dodo / Abacab / That's All / Mama / Medley: Eleventh Earl Of Mar – The Lamb Lies Down On Broadway – Firth Of Fifth – The Musical Box / Illegal Alien / Home By The Sea / Keep It Dark – It's Gonna Get Better / Follow You Follow Me / In The Cage – The Cinema Show – …In That Quiet Earth – Raven – Afterglow / Drum Duet – Los Endos / Misunderstanding / Turn It On Again*.

From the next day to the last, however, *The Carpet Crawlers* returned to its place between *Home By The Sea* and *Keep It Dark*, replacing *Misunderstanding*, a decision which would again leave the role of sole encore to *Turn It On Again*, by this time of unparalleled length. In fact, for the English shows the medley reached anything up to a dozen or so snippets of other hits. To those already mentioned much more recent ones like Culture Club's *Karma Chameleon* and *Every Breath You Take* by The Police were added. In the last show, the band also threw in a bit of *Sunshine Of Your Love* by Cream. Something for everyone, in other words. Except maybe for many of those fans who would have much preferred hearing one of the old Genesis classics but instead had to put up with this mixed musical bag all the way up to 1990.

Musically speaking however, the band appeared to be in magnificent form. Chester and Daryl were by now two indispensable members of the live band. Rutherford, no longer armed with his Shergold, had switched to a Strata bass and guitar double-neck and was in great shape; unlike on future tours, he always played the solo on *That's All* really well, a song also worthy of note for the vocal harmonies by Mike and Tony during the chorus (but only during the very first gigs of the tour). And while Phil had already proved that he could be a great showman, on this tour he was wittier and more entertaining than ever. For example, at each concert he would begin by exalting the warmth and merits of the host city as if it were the best in the universe, while openly admitting he'd said exactly the same thing in the city before. The introduction to *Home By The Sea* was exhilarating. Informing the crowd that the time had come for 'audience participation time', Phil would go on to explain his idea to experiment with getting in touch with 'the other world'. The singer then invited all the members of the audience to wave their hands in the air and, as the lights came down, he would make ghostly sounds while Tony played sinister chords on the piano. At this point, Phil would ask everyone to put their hands behind their ears and shout out 'masturbation doesn't make me deaf', receiving a thunderous response from the crowd (this particular part would be omitted from the UK shows for fear of censorship).

In terms of lighting effects, one of the most atmospheric moments was created during *It's Gonna Get Better*; blue hues alternated with simple overhead golden spotlights until towards the end of the song when the whole rig gently tilted towards the audience creating a star shape of coloured lights before finally closing with Tony Banks silhouetted against the blue backlighting.

For *Illegal Alien* all the band would wear dark glasses, while Phil, buttoned up in a tight jacket and claiming they were all 'fugitives from justice', would hold a huge radio up to his ear, ostensibly for the purpose of trying to tune into the police radio to see if they were hot on their trail – instead what came out were fragments of hits from the era, like *Jump* by Van Halen, *Owner Of A Lonely Heart* by Yes (greeted by huge applause) and the band's very own *Mama*.

Illegal Alien is linked to a number of funny little episodes. In Toronto, on 23 November 1983, a distracted Chester forgot to put on his dark glasses. Phil stopped talking to stare at him until he sorted

Mike and Phil at the NEC, Birmingham, 26th February 1984

Virgin UK poster advertising the home video *The Mama Tour*, 1984

it out and put them on. While, in Birmingham, some of the band's roadies got up on stage to sing along with the chorus (this was immortalised in the video release, *The Mama Tour*).

As usual, there was the odd setback. For example, a couple of times, the shows were hit by power outages. This happened twice during *Los Endos* in Dallas on 21 January and during *Illegal Alien* in Kansas City on the 29th. In Denver, on 17 January, it was Daryl's guitar that caused problems during the *Firth Of Fifth* solo; after the usual beginning the instrument quite simply went dead. The rest of the band just kept on playing the song until the issue was resolved and the guitarist started playing again.

In Birmingham on 25 February, due to technical hitches, the band had to stop *Eleventh Earl Of Mar* after the first couple of bars and start all over again. Finally, a sore throat meant Phil had to postpone the concert at The Summit in Houston, Texas, scheduled for 22 January 1984, to the following day, the 23rd, when they were supposed to be playing in Austin (also in Texas) which consequently also had to be postponed for 24 hours.

These were all minor setbacks which certainly didn't affect the level of success reached by Genesis, who by this point could comfortably be looked upon as superstars also (and above all) in America. And so the *Mama Tour* came to an end with everyone involved feeling justifiably satisfied. It was followed by a rest period which this time was to prove much longer than usual.

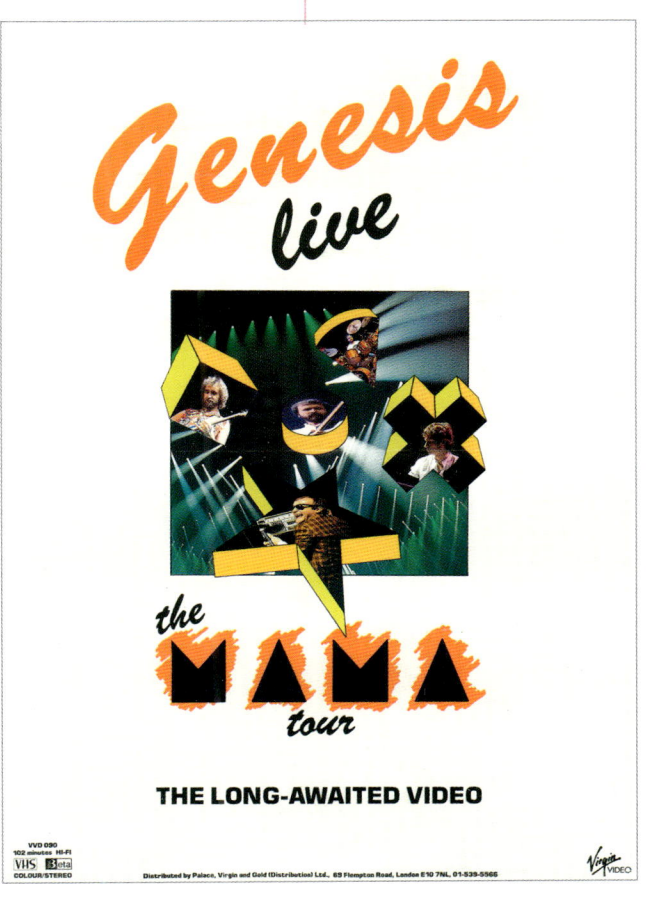

NOTES

(1) Mike Kaufman's Genesis interviews, Chicago / London, October 2007, partially used in the bonus disc accompanying the 2008 remasters

(2) Mario Giammetti's telephone interview with Tony Banks, 26 February 2016

THE MAMA TOUR

1983

NOVEMBER

- 07 **Normal, IL (USA)**, Horton Field House - Illinois State University
- 08 **Ames, IA (USA)**, Hilton Coliseum - Iowa State University
- 10 **Milwaukee, WI (USA)**, Milwaukee Arena
- 11 **Rosemont, IL (USA)**, Rosemont Horizon
- 12 **Rosemont, IL (USA)**, Rosemont Horizon
- 13 **Rosemont, IL (USA)**, Rosemont Horizon
- 14 **Detroit, MI (USA)**, Joe Louis Arena
- 16 **Landover, MD (USA)**, Capital Centre
- 17 **New York, NY (USA)** Madison Square Garden
- 18 **New York, NY (USA)** Madison Square Garden
- 20 **Montréal, QC (CANADA)**, Forum
- 21 **Montréal, QC (CANADA)**, Forum
- 22 **Toronto, ON (CANADA)**, Maple Leaf Gardens
- 23 **Toronto, ON (CANADA)**, Maple Leaf Gardens
- 25 **Philadelphia, PA (USA)**, The Spectrum
- 26 **Philadelphia, PA (USA)**, The Spectrum
- 27 **Philadelphia, PA (USA)**, The Spectrum
- 28 **Worcester, MA (USA)**, Worcester Centrum Centre
- 29 **Worcester, MA (USA)**, Worcester Centrum Centre

DECEMBER

- 01 **Hartford, CT (USA)**, Hartford Civic Center
- 02 **Syracuse, NY (USA)**, Carrier Dome - Syracuse University
- 03 **Buffalo, NY (USA)**, Buffalo Memorial Auditorium
- 04 **Richfield, OH (USA)**, Richfield Coliseum
- 05 **Richfield, OH (USA)**, Richfield Coliseum
- 07 **Pittsburgh, PA (USA)**, Civic Arena
- 08 **Cincinnati, OH (USA)**, Riverfront Coliseum
- 10 **Norfolk, VA (USA)**, Norfolk Scope
- 11 **Greensboro, NC (USA)**, Greensboro Coliseum
- 12 **Nashville, TN (USA)**, Nashville Municipal Coliseum
- 13 **Atlanta, GA (USA)**, The Omni
- 15 **Jacksonville, FL (USA)**, Jacksonville Veterans Memorial Coliseum
- 16 **Lakeland, FL (USA)**, Lakeland Civic Center
- 17 **Hollywood, FL (USA)**, Hollywood Sportatorium

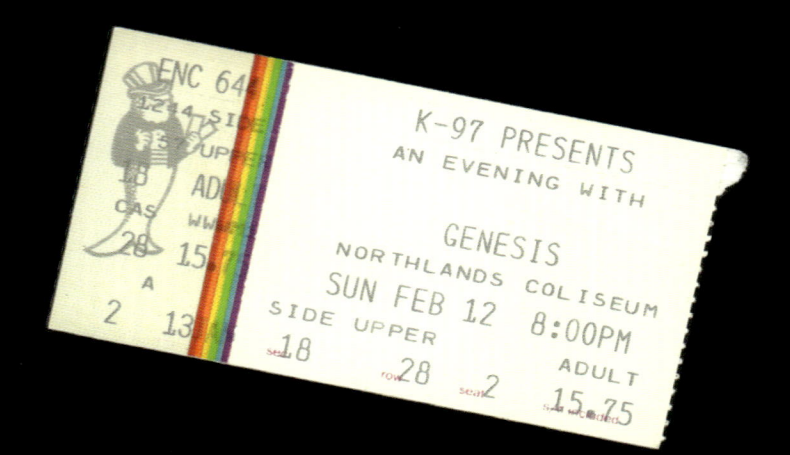

1984

JANUARY

- **09 Vancouver, BC (CANADA)**, Pacific Coliseum
- **10 Tacoma, WA (USA)**, Tacoma Dome
- **12 Inglewood, CA (USA)**, The Forum
- **13 Inglewood, CA (USA)**, The Forum
- **14 Inglewood, CA (USA)**, The Forum
- **15 Tempe, AZ (USA)**, Activity Center - Arizona State University
- **17 Denver, CO (USA)**, McNichols Sports Arena
- **19 Norman, OK (USA)**, Lloyd Noble Center - University of Oklahoma
- **20 Tulsa, OK (USA)**, Assembly Center
- **21 Dallas, TX (USA)**, Reunion Arena
- **23 Houston, TX (USA)**, The Summit
  Rescheduled from January 22 due to Phil being sick
- **24 Austin, TX (USA)**, Frank C. Erwin Jr. Special Events Center - University of Texas at Austin
  Rescheduled from January 23 due to Phil being sick
- **25 New Orleans, LA (USA)**, Lakefront Arena - University of New Orleans (Lakefront Campus)
- **26 Memphis, TN (USA)**, Mid-South Coliseum
- **28 St. Louis, MO (USA)**, The Arena
- **29 Kansas City, MO (USA)**, Kemper Arena
- **31 Lexington, KY (USA)**, Rupp Arena

FEBRUARY

- **01 Indianapolis, IN (USA)**, Market Square Arena
- **03 Omaha, NE (USA)**, Civic Auditorium Arena
- **04 Peoria, IL (USA)**, Peoria Civic Center
- **05 Madison, WI (USA)**, Dane County Memorial Coliseum
- **07 St. Paul, MN (USA)**, St. Paul Civic Center
- **09 Winnipeg, MB (CANADA)**, Winnipeg Arena
- **11 Calgary, AB (CANADA)**, Olympic Saddledome
- **12 Edmonton, AB (CANADA)**, Northlands Coliseum
- **14 Boise, ID (USA)**, Boise State University Pavilion - Boise State University
- **16 Reno, NV (USA)**, Lawlor Events Center - University of Nevada at Reno
- **17 Las Vegas, NV (USA)**, Thomas & Mack Center - University of Nevada at Las Vegas
- **19 Oakland, CA (USA)**, Oakland-Alameda County Coliseum Arena
- **20 Oakland, CA (USA)**, Oakland-Alameda County Coliseum Arena
- **25 Birmingham (ENGLAND)**, Birmingham International Arena - National Exhibition Centre
- **26 Birmingham (ENGLAND)**, Birmingham International Arena - National Exhibition Centre
- **27 Birmingham (ENGLAND)**, Birmingham International Arena - National Exhibition Centre
- **28 Birmingham (ENGLAND)**, Birmingham International Arena - National Exhibition Centre
- **29 Birmingham (ENGLAND)**, Birmingham International Arena - National Exhibition Centre

Invisible Touch

(Charisma / Virgin, 1986)

Invisible Touch / Tonight, Tonight, Tonight / Land Of Confusion / In Too Deep /// Anything She Does / Domino: Part One - In The Glow Of The Night; Part Two - The Last Domino / Throwing It All Away / The Brazilian

- All songs written by Banks/Collins/Rutherford

- Release date: 09 June 1986
- Engineer: Hugh Padgham
- Assistant Engineer: Paul Gomersall
- Recorded and mixed at The Farm, Surrey, 1985/86
- Technical Assistant: Geoff Callingham
- Produced by Genesis and Hugh Padgham
- Sleeve produced at Assorted iMaGes by Baker Dave

- Tony Banks: keyboards, synth bass
- Phil Collins: vocals, drums, percussion
- Mike Rutherford: guitars, bass

THE MAKING OF

With the *Mama* tour over, Tony, Mike and Phil again went off in their different directions with vague plans to get back together at some point in the future, depending on their individual work schedules.

After having written the soundtrack for the 1983 film, *The Wicked Lady*, starring Faye Dunaway, Tony Banks received a fantastic proposition from film director, Peter Hyams, asking him to write the music for *2010: The Year We Make Contact*, the sequel to *2001: A Space Odyssey*. For reasons still unknown, when filming was already underway, the director suddenly changed his mind and commissioned a different composer. Banks went on to write the music for a little-known science fiction film (*Starship* also known as *Lorca And The Outlaws*) before Hollywood was again knocking on his door.

But, although Tony did write the film score for *Quicksilver*, he was again destined to be disappointed when the producers opted to use *Quicksilver Lightning*, written by Giorgio Moroder and performed by Roger Daltrey, as the film's theme song over Tony's *Shortcut To Somewhere* featuring original Marillion frontman, Fish. The *Quicksilver* soundtrack (made up of Banks' score and a selection of pop songs) was released by Atlantic Records in 1986, while, in May that same year, Tony brought out a collection of the music he'd written for *Quicksilver* and *Lorca And The Outlaws* under the title SOUNDTRACKS (with guest appearances from Toyah and Jim Diamond).

In the meantime, Mike Rutherford, always of the opinion that he could offer his best work in collaboration with other musicians, struck up an alliance with Chris Neil (a record producer with a strong tendency towards pop and the promoter responsible for Sheena Easton's success) and Scottish singer-songwriter B.A. Robertson, for a project that he specifically didn't want to release under his own name. Consequently, session musicians and singers were recruited. However, when his album MIKE + THE MECHANICS came out and quite unexpectedly did well in both the UK and US charts (with two hit singles *Silent Running* and *All I Need Is A Miracle*), Rutherford realised that this project deserved to become a band in the real sense of the word, promoting drummer, Peter Van Hooke, keyboard player, Adrian Lee, and singers, Paul Carrack and Paul Young, to full-time members. One song on the MIKE + THE MECHANICS album, *A Call To Arms*, began life as a jam during the recording sessions for the GENESIS album and is credited to Banks / Collins / Rutherford, alongside Neil and Robertson.

Whilst Banks and Rutherford had been productive, the busiest of all was, of course, Phil Collins. As soon as he'd finished touring with Genesis, the workaholic drummer skipped from one project to the next, all of which had one common denominator: massive success. This would result in him being considered one of the most ubiquitous celebrities of the 1980s. His song *Against All Odds*, hastily recorded on 3 January 1984 during a break in the *Mama Tour*, was the highlight of the film of the same name and its soundtrack (which also featured previously unreleased songs by Mike Rutherford and Peter Gabriel) earned Collins an Oscar nomination. He produced CHINESE WALL, the third studio album by Earth, Wind & Fire singer, Philip Bailey, with whom Collins also recorded the duet, *Easy Lover*, which, true to form, was another smash hit in the singles chart. He even managed to top the charts with a song he didn't write, *Separate Lives,* by Stephen Bishop, recorded as a duet with Marilyn Martin for the film *White Nights*. On 13 July

GENESIS

Promotional photo by Atlantic Records, USA 1986

1985, he amazed the world with the incredible feat of taking part in both editions of Live Aid, first singing a duet with Sting at Wembley before flying off to Philadelphia to play with Eric Clapton and Led Zeppelin.

But, perhaps more importantly, Phil Collins recorded his third solo album. Released in March 1985, NO JACKET REQUIRED was yet again another huge hit. It yielded no less than four singles which reached the US Top Ten (*Sussudio* and *One More Night* both made it to No. 1) and went on to win him three Grammy Awards (Album of the Year, Producer of the Year and Best Male Pop Vocal). The album release was followed by a hugely successful world tour which also took him to Japan.

Lost in their own different worlds, it would have come as no surprise had Genesis become a casualty, but their deep friendship proved to be unstoppable.

Rutherford: "We were actually quite surprised that Phil still wanted to do an album. He'd had this huge solo success for quite a while by this point, I mean, you couldn't actually get much bigger. There was quite a long gap between this album and the one before, which was fine. I remember thinking at the time that we'd do another album when the time was right. But there was always a question mark, which was kind of fine too."[1]

The three made plans to get together in October 1985 at The Farm Studios and lay down the foundations of a new album. Happy with the results obtained working together as Genesis, again none of them brought any previously written material into the sessions.

Collins: "There are no other bands really that I've ever come across or heard about that play and write like that. Usually in a band there's one writer or a pair of writers or individual writers who submit material, but our way is a lot like jazz, you know, three guys sitting down in a room just playing until eventually it starts to sound good. It really is a blank sheet of paper. You know, I'll say, 'that sound – what's that?' 'Oh, it's nothing, just me playing with the echo' and I'll go, 'that's good! You play that for a bit and I'll sing on top'. And it just suddenly becomes another song, like the INVISIBLE TOUCH stuff. That's the magic of having chemistry between people. There may be bits that are slightly suspect and bits that aren't as good as others, but there's some great stuff in there that came out of nowhere. That's what's good about the band."[1]

The album had a longer gestation period than

Promotional photo by Virgin Records, UK 1987

usual, with work repeatedly interrupted along the way until it was finally finished in March 1986.

Collins: "It was a long, long process, you know, you could probably say about 3 or 4 months of writing 5 days a week. And the guys were always reluctant to sort of commit and I was there with my list saying, 'well if you put this bit with that bit'… and they'd say, 'no, not yet'. I'm a bit more impetuous than they are, so we ended up with thousands of bits. Some bits, probably great bits, went past us without us noticing; the tapes are all there somewhere. Only the other day (*the interview is from 2007 – author's note*) I found my notes for these albums (I was the keeper of the tapes, you see, and someone had to make notes on all the cassettes). Things like: 'listen to tape 4, about 20 minutes in: there's a great bit'. Then, when they said something like, 'what was that bit we did 4 weeks ago?', it would be my responsibility to come up with it, that was my job." [1]

Banks: "By this point, we'd really kind of broken ground, particularly live. Suddenly we'd started playing big places, you know, universally around the world, and probably we'd finally reached a certain platform in America that we'd never quite made before. We seemed to have an incredible number of ideas. We were just improvising all the time and endless songs kept falling out; there could have been others there as well. We got quite good at developing shorter pieces, it took us by surprise to what extent we could do that. I mean, we ended up using about 5 songs off this album as singles, which was quite strange because we'd never seen ourselves as a singles band at all. It was pure chance that suddenly led us into having a hit single with *Follow You Follow Me*. Suddenly everyone was seeing us as a singles band and saying we'd sold out. But you can't help it; if you put things out there that people like, that's what happens." [1]

So, the group suddenly realised they possessed a commercial vein they had previously failed to tap into.

Banks: "I'm not sure we didn't try to be a commercial group a long, long time before. I don't think we could have done anything conscious about it; we just wrote what came out of us. That's

Phil in Budapest, 18th June 1987

the way it is and for some reason or other on this album a lot of things just got abbreviated. Both *Land Of Confusion* and *Anything She Does* were both destined to be long, heavy pieces as we had other stuff in them. But they just kept becoming more and more concise and ended up being what they are. I don't think you can fight how you're feeling. It was a really enjoyable album to make, we just managed to have the confidence that allows you to write shorter pieces. For someone like me it's much easier to write a quite long piece, full of frills and funny chord changes and everything, you almost don't have to ask yourself if something is really good enough to be there, whereas if you've only got three and a half to four minutes and you want it to be a good song, every bit's got to count, every aspect of it." [1]

Collins: "I think maybe some of these simpler things came about because we had our own studio and we were able to actually hear the material as we were writing it and say, 'hey, this sounds good as it is, why do we need those three extra keyboards on it? Why do we need those four guitar harmonies?'. We were able to create as we went along which bands like Pink Floyd and The Beatles had been able to do, but we had never been in that position before. We'd always written the songs and then gone into the studio to record them exactly how we'd rehearsed them, which is why our early albums were certainly not as good sound-wise, and also why everything was maybe a little too dense." [1]

There is no escaping the fact that the music now being written was much more catchy.

Collins: "In an album we'd always try to show all the kinds of things that the group did. You've also got to remember that this was my golden era as well. *Against All Odds* had just been No. 1, *Easy Lover* with Philip Bailey had been No. 1, NO JACKET REQUIRED was No. 1... I'd had all my hit singles and then this album came out. This was when people started saying, 'hey enough already'. You know, we both fed each other; my success fed the Genesis thing and Genesis fed my thing, so you couldn't really move too much without hearing something from me or Genesis on the radio in lots of places, especially in America." [1]

Banks: "Obviously, Phil had become established more as a singles act and that opened a few doors for us in terms of the radio being more prepared to listen to us. But I think songs like *Invisible Touch* and *Land Of Confusion* would have been hit songs for anybody. We'd never worried about having too many hits or anything. As I've said before, I think if we could have written a couple of hits back in the days of Nursery Cryme, we would have. We did try, we had a song called *Happy The Man* which we tried as a single, it just wasn't as good. You know, when we came into this business back in 1969, when we were with Jonathan King and we did From Genesis To Revelation, we were actually *trying* to write hit singles but no one would record them and we didn't appear to be that good at it. And then other groups of that time, you know, like King Crimson, Family and Fairport Convention, showed us another way of approaching music and that's how we got into progressive rock and found that we were able to do things in that area that no one else was doing, whereas in the pop area we weren't so original. By the time we got to this stage, I think we just felt we'd gone as far as we could in certain directions, you know, into deep progressive music and extended solos and all the rest of it, and the idea of trying to craft songs a little bit more was quite appealing. So that's what ended up on this album." [1]

Rutherford: "We just do a bunch of songs, we're never thinking about what's going to be a hit. I never thought *Land Of Confusion* would be a single. But the album was strong, the energy level was up. The Genesis record before had this strong dark mood whereas Invisible Touch seemed very energetic. Maybe it just had faster songs, by nature of the collection of styles on the album." [1]

As with the music, even writing the lyrics took on a very casual approach.

Collins: "Some songs were triggered by a spontaneous vocal line, like 'she seems to have an invisible touch, yeh'. With other songs, you never knew what the lyrics were going to be until you arrived in the studio. I mean, with *Domino*, Tony just handed them to me and said, 'I've written the lyrics for this; this is how it goes'. The melody was all over the place and the lyrics were something I never would have expected, you know, like the famous 'sheets of double glazing' line." [1]

As well as making changes on a structural level, the band was also happy to work with then-fashionable sounds. The drums in particular left Genesis fans somewhat perplexed and unable to fathom why such a brilliant drummer as Phil Collins would be prepared to sacrifice his feel and technical skills in favour of something so noticeably synthetic.

Collins: "Drums had changed from the wrist-breaking Formica tops to the new breed of Simmons drum kit. There was a fair bit of that on this album, as well as the old, original Formica ones on things like *Domino*. I was using all that electric stuff, you know." [1]

Even recording methods had changed. Collins: "I think by the time we did this album we had rebuilt the control room at the studio, so we were much more high-tech. And we'd got the electrical system sorted out, so we didn't break down every time the wind blew. Obviously technology was changing so much that first of all we would improvise and then we whittled these pieces into song ideas before finally starting to lay down a very skeleton piece of music. Then everybody would move into the control room, you know, because you can take keyboards into the control room now and sit beside the desk as opposed to being on the other side of a glass window, which is what it used to be like. We started to record a little bit more as a group, piece by piece. You'd put down an idea and then you'd replace things and eventually you'd have nothing left of what you first started out with because you just replaced everything, with everybody there, but it wasn't necessarily like a group playing. There was the odd exception, like *Do The Neurotic* (which never made it to the album) that we actually did record playing live as a group. But of the tracks that ended up on the record, I can't remember too many that were done as a live group recording." [1]

THE ALBUM

The commercial results may well tell a different story, but INVISIBLE TOUCH, artistically speaking, is the weakest album in the history of Genesis. There isn't a single song that is exceptional, and the creative aspect seems to be the least of the band's concerns, set as they were on the idea of spontaneity and enjoying themselves, burying everything under mountains of synthesised sounds as they went along.

The harmonic offering is simplified beyond all recognition. Songs like the title track and *Throwing It All Away* have a pop structure which is almost banal. Even the more ambitious tracks, which in any case fail to excel, like *Tonight, Tonight, Tonight*, the mini-suite, *Domino* and the instrumental, *The Brazilian*, tend to emphasise fashionable technology rather than strong composition. The extraordinary song-writing which had, until now, been an almost constant feature of the band's work seemed absent. The sounds, influenced by Hugh Padgham as well as by the new electronic instruments increasingly used by the band, have failed to stand the test of time and are annoying to listen to today. Furthermore, the close to three years which had elapsed between this album and its predecessor had led to a simplification of the harmonies and an emphasis on superficial catchiness.

In the wider musical world, classic hard rock was experiencing a new lease of life thanks to Van Halen's 1984 (MCMLXXXIV) (which, it has to be said, contains a lot of synth) and the reforming, in great style, of Deep Purple Mark II (PERFECT STRANGERS), while another ephemeral supergroup was formed, The Firm with Jimmy Page and Paul Rodgers. In the meantime, new rock stars like Bon Jovi were making their debuts. Solo projects by members of some of the world's most famous bands were springing up like mushrooms (in the spring of 1984, the Pink Floyd family launched David Gilmour's ABOUT FACE and THE PROS AND CONS OF HITCH HIKING by Roger Waters, and, in July, former Japan lead vocalist, David Sylvian, released BRILLIANT TREES). In America, on the other hand, disparate artists like Bruce Springsteen (with his biggest-selling album, BORN IN THE U.S.A), Prince (PURPLE RAIN) and Tom Waits (RAIN DOGS) were consolidating their popularity.

Other new bands appearing in this period worthy of note are the poetic and decadent The Smiths (with their self-titled debut album, followed a year later by MEAT IS MURDER), the combat rock of The Alarm (DECLARATION), the post-punk of Nick Cave and the Bad Seeds (FROM HER TO ETERNITY), the alternative rock of Hüsker Dü (with their second album, ZEN ARCADE) and the funk of the Red Hot Chili Peppers (with their debut album of the same name), while Paul Weller's Style Council (Café Bleu) and Sade (Diamond Life) gave a boost to the new cool, a sub-genre through which other interesting names such as Everything But The Girl, Matt Bianco and later Working Week would make their way from very different starting points.

1985 had kicked off with the huge success of No Jacket Required, and Phil Collins also found time to put his producer's hat back on to work with Eric Clapton on his Behind The Sun. It was to be an even lighter year, musically speaking, in which pop, albeit of quality, would storm the market, with Tears For Fears releasing their second album Songs From The Big Chair, A-Ha bursting onto the scene with their debut album Hunting High And Low, Pre-fab Sprout brought out their great second album, Steve McQueen, and Freddie Mercury and Sting made their first (and in the former case, only) solo albums (respectively Mr. Bad Guy and Dream Of The Blue Turtles).

Following the Band Aid single *Do They Know It's Christmas?*, a host of rock stars based in the US also released a charity single, *We Are The World*, under the name of USA For Africa. Both these initiatives were conceived to raise money for famine relief in Ethiopia and culminated in the previously mentioned Live Aid, one of the biggest events ever staged in musical history. In terms of progressive rock, Marillion reached the No. 1 spot with their third album, Misplaced Childhood.

1986 also saw the return of Joe Cocker, thanks to the soundtrack for *9½ Weeks*. Peter Gabriel finally became a mainstream star with his huge selling album, So, released less than two weeks before Invisible Touch, while GTR, the eponymous debut (and sole) album by the short-lived supergroup founded by guitarist, Steve Howe, and former Genesis member, Steve Hackett, came out one month after.

In his best-selling novel, *American Psycho*, published in 1991, author, Bret Easton Ellis tells the story of a Wall Street yuppie turned ruthless serial killer who also happened to be a massive Genesis fan, so much so that an entire chapter is dedicated to singing the praises of *Invisible Touch*. Ultimately, perhaps this is the only merit (profits aside) of an album which, on an artistic level, is probably best forgotten.

THE SONGS

INVISIBLE TOUCH

Based on a rhythm of electronic drums and synth bass, this song which germinated from a Rutherford guitar riff drags along with a trite melody line and a chorus of almost depressing catchiness.

Rutherford: "On this album a lot of the stuff really just came about starting out with the drum machine, Tony would play some chords, then I'd bash around on the guitar and Phil would start singing. This little loop we started with kind of set the mood for something. I had a guitar riff for this, I think, and off we went."[1]

Collins: "*Invisible Touch* is still one of my favourite songs. I think we all felt that it was a single, you know, the flagship of the record. Mike's riff reminded me of a Sheila E. song, I can't remember the title but I liked it (*The Glamorous Life* – author's note). It's like the idea we got for *Mama* from The

GENESIS

US poster advertising the single Tonight, Tonight, Tonight, 1987

Message; you take an idea but do something different with it." [1]

Rutherford: "Phil later likened this song to a Prince song, in style, I mean. I hadn't seen it that way actually but I can see what he means. It's quite sparse, arrangement-wise. There are no big sustained chords but it's very energetic." [1]

Collins: "I still joke about these lyrics with my son, Simon, you know, when we talk about people I've had relationships with, you know, that had the 'invisible touch'. You're not quite sure what it is, but whatever they do, you can't get them out of your mind. They kind of become what I sing in the live version: 'And though she will fuck up your life, you'll love her just the same'. I like those lyrics because for me it's been part of my life. 'She seems to have an invisible touch, she reaches in and grabs right hold of your heart', you know, she tears it out and you still go back for more, that kind of thing' (*in his autobiography, published in 2016, Not Dead Yet, Collins admits that a large chunk of the lyrics to Invisible Touch were inspired by his first wife, Andrea, Simon's mother, a woman who, in his words was 'ragingly sexy' – author's note*)." [1]

TONIGHT, TONIGHT, TONIGHT

Another drum-machine pattern, a light smattering of keyboards and a swooping guitar riff create the backing track over which electronic drum pads crash. A fine vocal performance from Phil, also author of the lyrics, an attempt to draw attention to the dangers of drug abuse. The instrumental part is pleasant enough, with a nice succession of chords despite the incessant use of synthetic sounds and rhythmic riffs.

Banks: "Phil got together this drum box pattern which was terribly atmospheric and I started playing along on the piano with a kind of marimba beat. It was such a strong atmosphere. You know when you've got something good, something going; it didn't matter what you did with it after that, it was going to be good. I very much liked this idea of these block chords, so it goes up through the keys without any real subtlety. Then I played these serene type chords and Phil just sang these words over the top and it sounded great. And then the middle part: Mike and Phil had got together this kind of jerky thing [3'16"], it was quite odd that duh-da duh-da duh-da. It's a very syncopated part and I thought I'd treat it as a very straight thing and play in 4/4 over the top of it in a classical style. I think it works really well, using all the string sounds, the oboe sounds and building up to the big chords. The bit I'm not all that keen on is the 'Get me out of here' bit, but when it comes back the second time around, with the drums playing along with the drum machine [7'08"] – that's very strong. Phil was always very good at that kind of thing. Obviously he did it with

In The Air Tonight, and when we started using drum machines, he was very good at playing along with them, making the song sound really good when the drums came in." [2]

Rutherford: "I think this song is a prime example of that phase in our writing: Phil would start with this great little sort of loop thing on the drum machine with the echo sound on. And so when the song started, before I or even Tony played a note, you had this atmosphere. It's like setting the stage. That was a very strong song, I think, it's also very unique. Nothing else we've done is quite like it. I was quite proud of the fact that songs like this and *Mama* were hits because they were just so unlike what you would expect of a hit record." [1]

Collins: "It was kind of still one of those journey songs; it went through different changes and was outside the usual format for singles. We were just writing what we felt like at the time, we weren't trying to have hit singles, we weren't trying to be commercial. It just happened to turn out that way on this record." [1]

Banks: "It was more like a traditional Genesis song because it goes through lots of changes. The extended version on the album has quite a long, very ethereal middle part which obviously didn't make it onto the single. It was a particularly big hit in the States, but it was a hit in England too." [1]

UK poster advertising the single *Land Of Confusion* (Virgin 1986)

LAND OF CONFUSION

A relatively powerful rock track, with Tony's synth bass programmed through the sequencer and pounding drums and featuring great lyrics by Mike.

Rutherford: "After all those years, I thought the time was right for a protest song. But done in a fairly subtle way, you know. I remember this was the last lyric to be finished, I was behind schedule and late as usual. We'd sung all the other songs and I hadn't finished it. Phil works at a great tempo, which is great, he pushes it along. I remember I was at home in bed with this horrendous sort of flu; I was nearly delirious. And he came round and he sort of sat in the bedroom. I gave him the lyric without even knowing if it was any good. I wasn't there when he sang it. But it really kind of worked." [1]

Interviewed in 2007, Collins said: "The downside to this was the fact that I was reading the words for the first time when I sang them, you know all afternoon. You kind of want to take it out on the road, sing it, get used to it and then record it, but it didn't happen like that. Because of the Bush administration, this political song means more now to some people, or is as relevant to people now, as when it was written for the Reagan administration. So, in that way, it's kind of timeless, it's good to have one of those songs. We'd never been political; as a band we'd always gone along the fantasy, escapist routes really." [1]

To promote the single, an animated video was made using the puppets from the well-known TV series, Spitting Image, which would go on to win the 1987 Best Concept Music Video Grammy Award.

Collins: "Back then *Spitting Image* was very, very popular. They'd done me on a couple of episodes, you know, taking the mickey out of me, and I was always very flattered by that. Jim Yukich and Paul Flattery thought it would be a good idea to ask *Spitting Image* if they would do the video, which from our point of view was a good idea because we didn't particularly like the idea of being in our own videos. I mean our attention span was pretty short so if we could get away with just mucking about that was OK. So that was given to the *Spitting Image* people and, ironically, the only Grammy Award we ever won was for that video and we weren't even in it." [1]

Rutherford: "It was Jim Yukich's idea. We had a great relationship with Jim, videos were fun to do and he had good ideas. I think we did videos with Jim for two or three of our albums actually. I mean, what a dream video! We didn't have to do anything. We weren't even involved and we even won an award for it. It was a great idea, it really worked and didn't take any of our time. It looked great and told the story nicely." [1]

IN TOO DEEP

A tender ballad guided along by the piano over electronic programming with a bridge driven by ethereal keyboards. The drums and a clear guitar work diligently in the background.

Collins: "The chorus, 'you know I love you but I just can't take this', was something I'd written in Australia for the film, *Playing For Keeps*, but they actually ended up using another one of my songs called *We Said Hello Goodbye*, which is on NO JACKET REQUIRED. And then Bob Hoskins asked me to write a song for his film *Mona Lisa* and *In Too Deep* was used in that." [1]

ANYTHING SHE DOES

Decidedly a lesser track, with a synth horn section and synth bass, while the drums are real as is Mike's upbeat guitar. Banks' prurient lyrics come as a bit of a surprise.

Banks: "In the studio there was always quite a lot of downtime, especially if Mike was doing a guitar part. I'd go out for four hours, come back and he'd still be tuning up. So, in the downtime we used to get 3 or 4 newspapers; we'd have The Times, which I get at home, and The Guardian and then The Sun for a bit of light relief. The Sun is always amazing to me as they write about people I've never heard of, you know, celebrities who just don't impinge on my world at all. And, you know, they always had the page 3 girls with their breasts out. I wrote about those girls because it's weird; you look at them but they don't seem real, they are just objects... You don't think of them as people. They live in this fantasy world in a man's brain and if you take that sort of pornography further, it would be kept in drawers and hidden away so no one else sees them and how you react to them. Even though you're never going to meet them, you still think, 'do I love them?' because they are so beautiful. So *Anything She Does* is a play on words: whatever she does, you won't be a part of it, but also whatever she does, you're quite happy for her to do it. I rather enjoyed the song actually, I thought it worked quite well, I like the fast part and the fast lyrics. And of course, the video was great fun to do. We had Benny Hill, who I think was more Phil's idol than ours. Like the song, the video was totally not politically correct and, of course, he was associated with scantily clad women. It was funny, when he came to do the video he said he was trying to put all that behind him, he didn't want to be just thought of as someone with semi-naked girls running around. But in the end he did it and he was very professional, he'd rehearsed his part and it was fun to work with someone like that." [2]

DOMINO (IN THE GLOW OF THE NIGHT / THE LAST DOMINO)

Here you get a glimpse of the band's past, but again filtered through modern sounds, sometimes successfully (the flute-type sound of the keyboards) and at other times in an overpowering way (Collins' Simmons).

Banks: "To me it's a very important track. In a way it's more me, perhaps than the others. In the lyrics I was trying to get across a political message, you know, about the way politicians don't always think through what it is they've started, about all the unexpected consequences that occur when you start something off. People tend to think in a very blinkered sort of way about things. They think, 'we've got rid of this guy, now we've got to do that' and of course everything else happens; that's what the song was all about really. It was a nice, big, long song which gave us an opportunity to have a bit of fun, both lyrically and musically and the end section was very strong with a great guitar riff." [1]

THROWING IT ALL AWAY

A catchy little song with no great expectations, built on Mike's repetitive guitar riff.

Collins: "It's one of Mike's typical riffs, one of those one-note sambas. He wrote the lyrics for it as well. It turned out to be a great stage tune actually, but it was always a bit of a funny song when you think about it." [1]

Rutherford: "Very often you can tell who has written the lyrics to a song. Phil writes his lyrics like he does. Tony will write it more from scratch. I will often start with a phrase of Phil, the sound of the words. So, in a way, I always enjoyed being more sympathetic towards the sounds and vowels of the words that Phil naturally sang; that was more my sort of role. Quite a lot of the phrasing came from what he was saying." [1]

Banks: "We had never seen it as a single at all. In fact, we were amazed when they suddenly started playing it on the radio in America a lot, so we had to release it as a single." [1]

THE BRAZILIAN

Over a cascade of electronic percussion and syn-drum rolls, Tony draws out a tide of synthesiser riffs, coordinating the frequent percussive inserts. Despite a strong closing section, where Rutherford's guitar comes in with a certain air of magnificence, it is hard not to consider this a minor track. Banks: "In the rehearsal room I'd often just switch on the Emulator and record whatever was happening in the room. Phil was doing something, Mike was just playing along and I recorded it. I slowed it down or something and then combined a couple of different notes to get an effect, because what they played on their own wasn't very interesting, I promise you. I put it together, produced this thing, looped it and thought it sounded really interesting." [1]

Collins: "We just started to fool around with the Simmons, you know, finding out what kind of different odd sounds you could get programmed into one kit. I remember just sort of mucking about and getting a pattern and Tony would start playing. It started off as a bit of a jam and then got moulded into an instrumental song. It's an odd little track, it's like nothing else we've done before or since. A bit like *Who Dunnit?*, this is our punk instrumental." [1]

OTHER SONGS

During the INVISIBLE TOUCH sessions, Genesis recorded another three songs. While *I'd Rather Be You* is completely forgettable, an offshoot of Phil Collins' solo career with '60s-style backing vocals, synth horns and funky bass from Mike, the other two certainly deserved a place on the album.

Opened by a futuristic effect, *Feeding The Fire* is an excellent piece, where Collins does a great job on drums and vocals, while *Do The Neurotic*, despite basically being just a jam, is a splendid instrumental bordering on a jazz-rock sound where, for once, the main role is left to lead guitar with a standout musical performance from Mike Rutherford.

Banks: "We had to decide whether to put *The Brazilian* or *Do The Neurotic* on the album. A lot said they wanted the latter as it was a more interesting song, a more Genesis piece. We liked it as it was a bit off, a bit weird, but this was before the era of CDs, so you had to keep your albums short." [2]

THE ALBUM ARTWORK

A stylised image of a family under a green and yellow mesh pattern is partially covered by a big, shaded orange hand shape.

Banks: "We went through a few ideas really and this idea of the hand came up. It's a nice idea, the invisible touch is all about a girl, but it's also quite a nice way to describe music, so you've got this hand on the front which is coming out to touch you. I don't think the resultant effect was particularly beautiful but it's quite distinctive and you noticed it in the shops, it was instantly recognisable, and it works pretty well in the CD format too. It's a good piece of graphic art without really being particularly beautiful." [1]

Rutherford: "The hand works OK with the title, but looking back it's not a great album cover. It's a prime example of the scenario we used to have. We couldn't do the cover until the album was fin-

Poster advertising the new album, with the hand in the foreground

ished and you knew what songs were on it. Then you had a tour coming up, not too far away, so you had to actually get stuff done quite quickly. There were deadlines. I remember thinking at the time, I think we all did, that it was kind of all right, but a bit dodgy. It was the best we could do in the time available."[1]

Collins: "I like the image of the hand. When you saw it on each side of the stage in the stadiums it was very strong. I must admit I can't remember who did the cover (*the London graphic design studio Assorted Images – author's note*). There were various ideas going around but I think we were just trying to be a bit less pastoral, you know, we were trying to pull people along with what we thought was a slightly different kind of Genesis."[1]

EPILOGUE

Rutherford: "Creatively it was a very exciting time. I felt it just it flowed out very fast, very easily. It's funny, we look back and we try and analyse why things were the way they were. No one really knows. We went in, we were in a good shape and having a good time. The Farm was a nice place to work... so there's no real way to analyse it, it just seemed to work."[1]

Released in June, just as Mike + The Mechanics were setting off for a month of concerts in North America as part of the *Miracle* tour, INVISIBLE TOUCH took the charts by storm the world over. It was the band's fourth consecutive No. 1 studio album in the UK (the live album, THREE SIDES LIVE, only reached No. 2) and it reached No. 3 in America where it remained in the Top Ten for 16 weeks, during which time it sold 6 million copies there.

The singles off the album enjoyed a similar success. A total of 5 were released, and all did reasonably well in the UK (*Invisible Touch* No. 15, *In Too Deep* No. 19, *Land Of Confusion* No. 14, *Tonight, Tonight, Tonight* No. 18, *Throwing It All Away* No. 22) and exceptionally well in America, where they had a resounding success, reaching the following chart positions: *Invisible Touch* No. 1, *Tonight, Tonight, Tonight* and *In Too Deep* No. 3, *Throwing It All Away* and *Land Of Confusion* No. 4.

Collins: "INVISIBLE TOUCH had opened the door to America. I mean, some of these songs were hits in different countries, but in the States they were all Top Five singles. I think the 1986 tour was the first stadium tour and probably our peak in America."[1]

A triumph which in those weeks paid an authentic tribute to the whole extended Genesis family. In fact, the Billboard Hot 100 for the week of 7 June 1986 included *Invisible Touch* at No. 37, *When The*

GENESIS

Heart Rules The Mind by GTR at No. 35, Peter Gabriel's *Sledgehammer* at No. 32, Phil Collins' *Take Me Home* at No. 26 and *All I Need Is A Miracle* by Mike + The Mechanics at No. 5, a trend also reflected in the album charts. In other words, and with all due respect to detractors, Genesis, with a career spanning almost 20 years behind them, were at the height of their popularity.

Banks: "I think that all the changes that occurred in the '70s, you know, punk rock and all the things that came out of that, stirred up the whole thing. I think we were lucky in a way because the opposition, if you like, the more progressive groups, disappeared at that point for whatever reason. And although the critics were not very kind about us, we seemed to become more radio-friendly (however that happened I don't really know) and suddenly we were un-ignorable. Radio was very kind to us, that was our real luck, and, of course, MTV was a big boon to us. Mike and I were reasonably good at doing the videos, although for me, being on film was a very unnatural thing, but fortunately Phil was pretty good at it. So we could sort of dress up in something silly and make these fun little videos and it gave us an incredibly high profile. The easiest videos to do were those where the song could have a little bit of humour in it, like *Invisible Touch* where we were just larking about and playing different instruments; it had a certain atmosphere. The most difficult songs for us to do videos for were always the serious songs, like *In Too Deep* where we just sort of play a piano and sing. It's OK, but it's not classic." [1]

However, the band's older fans were left feeling a bit lost.

Rutherford: "Because MTV was in full swing by now, the public perception of us was that we were having hit singles and the videos were doing well. I think the profile you get with a hit single is so huge it dwarfs everything else, so I think people forget there were long songs on this album, like *Domino*. There's always this thing about us having been a progressive band which did long songs and ended up doing shorter songs, but we never really stopped doing the long songs, they were just overshadowed, perception-wise, by the power of television. Funnily enough, when you see us live that balance is so different. I mean the long songs are probably as big a part of the audience enjoyment as the short ones. The balance is very much half and half. Songs like *Domino* get rather forgotten until we go on stage." [1]

Banks: "I think fans want some long songs as long songs are very much part of what Genesis are. I would say that on this album there are three songs that still very much echo the old Genesis feel: *Domino*, obviously, *Tonight, Tonight, Tonight*, particularly because of the middle section and probably *The Brazilian* because it's got that quirky sort of feel about it. There are a few unusual bits and pieces going on, so it was a good blend, I think. When we finished this album I was pretty excited. I liked it, I thought it was still musically very interesting yet it also had a wider appeal." [1]

Rutherford: "The funny thing is, you know, everyone has their time. The first time you hear a band, the first album you really like, that moment in time is your favourite album. So if you started liking us in the early days, you know, if NURSERY CRYME was the first album you liked, that will always be your favourite album, and vice versa. And that's OK. It is what it is. You can't change that." [1]

THE CONCERTS

Genesis' peak in popularity benefitted from a massive media presence, with the band appearing on the radio, in the press and on television all over the world. For example, on 22 August 1986, Télévision Suisse Romande invited them into the studio to play (or rather mime to) *Anything She Does*, *Invisible Touch* and *Tonight, Tonight, Tonight* as part of the 'Rose d'Or de Montreux' programme.

Inevitably, this led to an even bigger live show operation, now structured on a world tour of gigantic proportions both in terms of dates (over 110 concerts) and venues (almost exclusively in enormous stadiums and arenas).

Rutherford: "We have a big sound, so our big songs definitely work in big venues. Over our career, you know, we've toured an awful lot and our small cult following became this big cult following and suddenly we were playing four days in a row in arenas. Album sales may have influenced things to some extent, but that live scenario with the audience was something we'd been building up for years really. So when we started doing stadiums it was a sort of natural progression." [1]

The live expansion was also geographical, with Genesis now set to return to Japan after nine years and set foot in Australia for the very first time.

After the usual period of rehearsals in Dallas, the first leg of the tour kicked off on 18 September 1986 with three consecutive nights in Detroit at the Joe Louis Arena. With the exception of Toronto (on the 22nd), consecutive dates in the same venue became the norm due to the massive demand for tickets. So that autumn, Genesis played multiple nights in all the American cities to which they took their new show: four nights in Philadelphia, five in New York, six in Chicago (Rosemont Horizon), five in Los Angeles (The Forum, Inglewood) and six in Oakland.

Alas, shortly after the *Invisible Touch* tour began, Mike Rutherford's father passed away. The band was in Chicago but, despite the guitarist's understandable grief, stopping such a complex touring machine involving so many people was quite simply unthinkable. Mike would use his only two days off (11 and 12 October) to fly back to Surrey to be with his family. This sad event would later inspire Rutherford, along with his song-writing partner, B.A. Robertson, to write his biggest success as a solo artist, the beautiful *The Living Years*, from the second album released by Mike + The Mechanics in 1988.

From a stage show point of view, Genesis would excel themselves yet again, taking another leap forward compared to the already amazing set-up taken on the road for the *Mama* tour three years earlier. Back in their traditional positions (from left to right, Daryl, Chester, Mike, Phil and Tony) and with the same lighting system, the band now had two maxi screens on either side of the stage so that even the spectators furthest away could see as well as hear the performance. Before each show the screens were used to show the video for *Anything She Does* starring Benny Hill.

For the first month of the North America tour, the setlist remained unchanged and was as follows: *Mama / Abacab / Land Of Confusion / That's All / Domino / In Too Deep / The Brazilian / Follow You Follow Me / Tonight, Tonight, Tonight / Home By The Sea / Throwing It All Away / In The Cage – ... In That Quiet Earth – Apocalypse In 9/8 – As Sure As Eggs Is Eggs / Invisible Touch / Drum Duet – Los Endos / Turn It On Again.*

GENESIS

Genesis in Milan on 19th May 1987

Rome, 17th May 1987

The show started with the drum machine intro to *Mama* during which the band members would walk out on stage and take up their positions. For *Abacab* they upped the tempo compared to on previous tours which meant Phil always had to make a dash for it to get behind the drum kit in time for the instrumental section.

In terms of the old Genesis repertoire, what really stands out is the unexpected return of a slice of *Supper's Ready* (the closing section made up of *Apocalypse In 9/8* and *As Sure As Eggs Is Eggs*) linked up to the *In The Cage* medley, the central part of which no longer featured *The Cinema Show*, however, but an integral version of ... *In That Quiet Earth* (i.e. including the guitar solo for the first time since Hackett left the band). The setlist closed with a fantastic version of *Los Endos*, now on its eighth consecutive tour, preceded by a *Drum Duet* that was longer and more articulate than ever before.

Rutherford: "Years after, I was talking to Elton John, who'd seen the show, and he said finishing with an instrumental was a great way to end a show; it had never occurred to me, but he was right... what a way to finish, with an instrumental powerhouse!" [3]

The encore was reserved for the *Turn It On Again* medley, now even longer than on the previous tour, with a number of additions, such as *You've Lost That Loving Feeling* by The Righteous Brothers and *Reach Out (I'll Be There)* by the Four Tops. The medley now went like this: *Turn It On Again / Everybody Needs Somebody To Love / (I Can't Get No) Sat-*

isfaction / Twist And Shout / Reach Out (I'll Be There) / You've Lost That Loving Feeling / Pinball Wizard / In The Midnight Hour / Turn It On Again, with the occasional addition of short excerpts of *All I Need Is A Miracle* and *Silent Running*, recent hits by Mike + The Mechanics.

On stage the band were technically an astoundingly tight-knit unit. Even Mike Rutherford (usually, the least reliable on that score, at least when playing guitar instead of bass) was, despite the odd blunder, on the ball. The band's array of technological aids was truly impressive: Phil, and to a lesser extent Chester, had added Simmons electronic pads to their drum kits (the singer also played electronic percussion in centre stage for *Tonight, Tonight, Tonight*), Tony was using massive amounts of Synclavier and Emulator sounds, while Daryl was playing only Steinberger instruments, mainly bass, except for the Hackett era songs and for *Turn It On Again* where both he and Mike played guitar. Mike alternated his Steinberger headless guitar with other models by different makers which contributed to the band's look which, apart from Chester in his red vest, was *very* 1980s: baggy trousers, jackets with rolled up sleeves, and shoulder pads.

The concerts also included some additional touches of showmanship. During Mike's long guitar solo in *That's All*, Phil would go alongside Daryl and start up a crazy little foot dance while all the time playing tambourine. Before *Home By The Sea*, as on the previous tour, the frontman would bring in 'audience participation time' only this time with a story containing more pantomime humour than before. In the introduction to *Domino* Phil would try to illustrate the 'domino principle' by asking the audience to shout out in sections, first to his left, then to his right and then in the middle, using his arms to raise a roar from the crowd. In the final medley, with all the band wearing dark glasses, Phil would imitate the dance moves of the Blues Brothers, Mick Jagger and Motown backing singers.

One episode which added a bit of additional colour to the evening occurred during *Invisible Touch* in New York on 1 October when a woman managed to make it up onto the stage and hug Phil Collins before being dragged away by security.

When the first leg of the worldwide tour was

completed in North America, for the very first time in their career the band flew 'down-under' for the Oceania leg. In fact, the Australian tour was preceded by a single date in New Zealand, something which didn't get off to a great start due to it having to be postponed. Initially scheduled for 22 November in Auckland, it had to be moved to the following day due to it clashing with the arrival of Pope John Paul II in the city. Not wishing to put any unnecessary strain on public security services, the local administration decided it was unable to stage two such big events simultaneously.

In the course of this first concert, Phil was straining to reach the higher notes in *As Sure As Eggs Is Eggs*, so much so that it was dropped from the setlist as of the following day. The medley of old songs, starting with *In The Cage* therefore included *Afterglow* which the band linked up to the end of ... *In That Quiet Earth* with ease.

Their arrival on Australian soil on 25 November 1986 came up against another rather odd requirement: that of having to involve other musicians in the show. This was due to provisions set out in national legislation which imposed the use of local personnel on visiting foreign artists. Genesis came up with a solution to keep everyone happy by recruiting a string quartet, which they baptised The Invisible Strings, and rearranging a couple of songs. And while *In Too Deep*, which was already on the setlist, was altered very little in its new version with the additional string section, the same cannot be said for Rutherford's song, *Your Own Special Way*. Omitted from the setlist for ten years (since the Wind & Wuthering tour), probably due to its not being a great live song, it suddenly became something entirely different in this sparkling new version (which fortunately would become a B-side to a single released a few years later). Guided by Mike's acoustic guitar, it was given a central section reminiscent of chamber music, arguably making it stronger than the studio version.

To make room for the string section, Genesis had to drop *Land Of Confusion* and *Tonight, Tonight, Tonight* while alternating *Follow You Follow Me* and *That's All* into setlist which therefore ran as follows: *Mama / Abacab / Domino / Your Own Special Way / In Too Deep / The Brazilian / That's All* (or *Follow You Follow Me*) */ Home By The Sea / Throwing It All Awsiay / In The Cage – ... In That Quiet Earth – Afterglow / Invisible Touch / Drum Duet – Los Endos / Turn It On Again*.

The Australian tour lasted almost a month, starting and finishing in Sydney with 20 or so dates in between. The tour took the band to a number of major Australian cities, from Brisbane to West Lakes (near Adelaide), from Perth to Melbourne.

After the Christmas holidays, Genesis went back out to North America for the third leg of the tour, a series of indoor shows running between 15 January and 1 March 1987. On average the venues were once again large and again Genesis did more than one date in several cities, playing two consecutive nights in Houston, Dallas, Hampton, Chapel Hill and Atlanta and three nights in both Richfield and Worcester. There were supposed to be two nights in Kansas City too, but unfortunately the second had to be cancelled due to Phil having a cold.

This leg of the tour presented a few minor changes to the setlist. For the first dozen or so concerts, the band kept the song *In Too Deep* (without the string section, obviously) but left out *Follow You Follow Me* (for good) and *Tonight, Tonight,*

Invisible Touch

Press cutting from the newspaper The Palm Beach Post, 27th February 1987

Tonight, a song which was giving Phil some issues. The setlist therefore ran as follows: *Mama / Abacab / Land Of Confusion / Domino / In Too Deep / The Brazilian / That's All / Home By The Sea / Throwing It All Away / In The Cage – ... In That Quiet Earth – Afterglow / Invisible Touch / Drum Duet – Los Endos / Turn It On Again.*

As of 27 January, in Richfield, however, *Tonight, Tonight, Tonight* reappeared while *In Too Deep* was dropped and there were some changes to the running order: *Mama / Abacab / Domino / That's All / The Brazilian / In The Cage – ... In That Quiet Earth – Afterglow / Land Of Confusion / Tonight, Tonight, Tonight / Throwing It All Away / Home By The Sea / Invisible Touch / Drum Duet – Los Endos / Turn It On Again.*

After just short of a fortnight's break, Genesis flew to Japan for the Asian leg of the tour, a week of shows from 13 to 19 March, with a total of six concerts: the first four at the Budokan in Tokyo and two in Castle Hall in Osaka. As was the case in 1978, Genesis didn't play in particularly big venues but Japanese audiences were beginning to show a growing interest in rock music and, of course, Genesis had no intention of missing this particular boat. During the Japanese tour, presumably due to Phil still having problems with his voice, *Tonight, Tonight, Tonight* was omitted three times: on 15 and 16 March in Tokyo and in Osaka on the 19th, the last show in Japan, which, alas, was also the day on which Tony Stratton-Smith, the man who had done so much for the band in its early days, died in London.

At this point, as of 21 March, Genesis should have been playing five concerts in Shanghai, China, which, however, were cancelled. According to The Palm Beach Post (27 February 1987), the cancellations were due to Genesis management refusing to grant permission for the concerts to be filmed. With fees estimated at around $350,000 + expenses, a spokesman for the company in charge of organising the tour stated that it was no longer an economically viable proposition if they were unable to offset some of the expenses with a subsequent video release.

So, after so much rushing around, the band allowed themselves a much-deserved holiday of almost two months before returning to the stage for the last push: the Euro-

---

Genesis China visit canceled

Reuter

LOS ANGELES — A visit by the British pop group Genesis to Shanghai to perform five concerts has been canceled, a spokeswoman for the tour's organizers said.

Tiffany Chu, a spokeswoman for a company called China Amusement and Leisure in Los Angeles, said the tour was called off because the group did not want to tape a video of its visit to China.

Chu said her company had arranged the concerts in cooperation with the Chinese government.

Genesis was to have been paid $350,000 for the concerts, beginning March 21, along with transport, hotel and other costs, she said.

"Without the video film, the tour would not have been profitable for the organizers," Chu said.

"Genesis simply did not want to make a video of its visit," she said. "The group could have gone to Peking, anywhere it wanted to in China to make the video."

China Amusement and Leisure has arranged cultural events in China and other parts of the world, she said.

"Maybe the concerts will be held at a later date, but the present visit is off," Chu said.

199

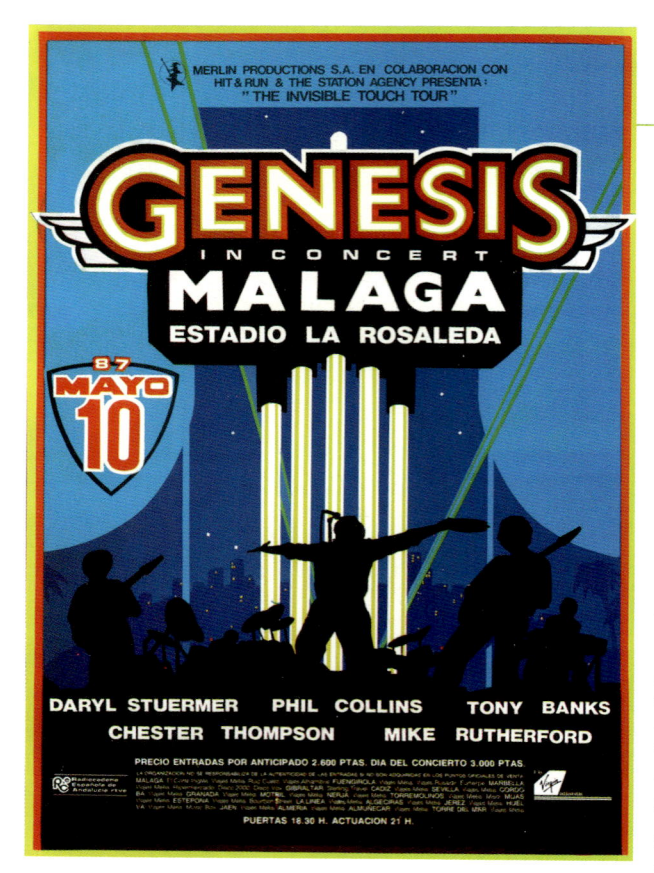

Merlin Productions poster promoting the show in Malaga, Spain, 10th May 1987

pean stadium tour with an exceptional opening act, English singer-songwriter, Paul Young. This leg of the tour started with two dates in Spain (10–13 May) and one in France (Toulouse), where *Tonight, Tonight, Tonight* was again dropped. In other shows Phil would sing the song but alter the melody for the higher parts. The rest of the setlist remained unchanged.

On 16 May, on the other hand, the band made an appearance at the Montreux Casino in Switzerland (a very intimate venue, with a capacity for only 3000 people), where they apparently played a shorter set, part of which was aired on TV. The first leg of the European stadium tour ended triumphantly with two concerts in Italy, the first in the Stadio Flaminio in Rome and the second in San Siro in Milan, respectively on 17 and 19 May. At the Milan concert, hit by pouring rain, Mike broke one of the strings on his guitar during the *Second Home By The Sea* solo and had to change the notes he played before rushing backstage, consequently he didn't play during the end section of the song.

Just three days later, the band were back in America for a quick stadium tour made up of just seven concerts up to 31 May (with two consecutive nights in both Philadelphia and East Rutherford).

The month of June was set aside for more European dates, again with Paul Young as the opening act, starting in Paris, where instead of playing in the stadium they used two different, but still very large locations (2–3 June). The day after the Copenhagen show, on 6th June, Collins and Paul Young appeared in the Prince's Trust Rock Gala, a charity event patronised by the Prince and Princess of Wales, where together they performed *You've Lost That Loving Feeling* and *Reach Out (I'll Be There)*, the two most recent additions to the *Turn It On Again* medley.

After the first three shows in Germany (Hanover, Berlin and Dortmund), the band played in Rotterdam in the Netherlands (where the *Turn It On Again* medley was cut short after a fight broke out in the audience) before moving on to Switzerland, France, Austria and Hungary. The tour then went on to include two more stadium dates in Germany (where in Mannheim, Mike's guitar solo in *That's All* had, shall we say, some issues), and two more dates in France before heading back to the UK for the closing dates.

After a show in Glasgow on 26 June, Genesis played at Roundhay Park in Leeds before bringing

UK poster advertising the concerts at Wembley Stadium in July 1987. The original plan was to perform three nights, but the huge request of tickets made necessary to add the Friday 3rd show

With these four concerts the most successful tour of the band's career up to that moment came to a close. A long adventure blessed by the presence of over one and a half million spectators which put the band, and not just its frontman, Phil Collins, at the top of the world music business.

However, the INVISIBLE TOUCH tour also has two rather surprising appendices. In fact, on 14 May 1988, to celebrate the 40th anniversary of the legendary US label, Atlantic, a huge concert was organised at Madison Square Garden in New York, starring most of the label's artists, each of which had a slot to perform three or four songs. Phil Collins, signed to Atlantic as a solo artist, performed *In The Air Tonight*, while Genesis opted for a rather unusual performance: in fact they decided to play the *Turn It On Again* medley, only this time, instead of paying tribute to other hits, it incorporated their own songs. Around 20 minutes long, the medley, which unfortunately has never been officially released, was structured as follows: *Turn It On Again / Land Of Confusion / Misunderstanding / Throwing It All Away / You Can't Hurry Love / Shortcut To Somewhere / All I Need Is A Miracle / That's All / Tonight, Tonight, Tonight / Invisible Touch / Turn It On Again*. So, alongside the hits written by the three musicians as Genesis, the medley also included a piece from each of their solo careers: *You Can't Hurry Love*, despite being written by Holland-Dozier-Holland, had been a hit for Phil, *Shortcut To Somewhere*, written by Tony Banks, in which Phil appeared to be visibly struggling with the vocals, and lastly *All I Need Is A Miracle*, the hit by Mike + The Mechanics.

the tour to an end in the most spectacular fashion with four consecutive shows (from 1 to 4 July) at Wembley Stadium in front of an overwhelming sea of people, as clearly documented in the VHS video release (later also made available on DVD).

Banks: "When the album came out, it went to No. 1 and everything. Then about a year later we did the four nights at Wembley and the album went back up to No. 2 after already being in the Top Ten for the whole year. It was just extraordinary really. When we did those shows at Wembley Stadium, I just wanted to enjoy that feeling, I remember thinking, 'it will never be bigger than this'. I thought it wouldn't last. It lasted longer than I thought it was going to actually." [1]

The experience, with a double performance by Collins, as a solo artist and then with Genesis, was

Poster from Castle Music Pictures, promoting the official video of the Knebworth performance by various artists. In June 2021, Genesis released a vinyl EP from this show including *Mama* and the *Turn It On Again* medley.

ing '60s hits (in this particular case *Everybody Needs Somebody, Satisfaction, Twist And Shout, Reach Out I'll Be There, You've Lost That Loving Feeling, Pinball Wizard* and *In The Midnight Hour*) but above all because the five members of the Genesis live band were joined on stage by all the other members of Phil Collins' live band: Leland Sklar on bass guitar, Brad Cole on keyboards, Bridgette Bryant, Arnold McCuller and Fred White on backing vocals, Don Myrick on sax, Louis Satterfield on trombone and Rahmlee Michael Davis and Harry Kim on trumpet, for a version lasting almost 13 minutes with a decidedly rhythm'n'blues feel that that laid to rest any illusion of Genesis still being stuck in the 1970s.

repeated on 30 June 1990 at the Knebworth Festival, where the bill included other huge names such as Pink Floyd, Paul McCartney, Robert Plant and Jimmy Page. Genesis played four songs: *Mama / That's All / Throwing It All Away / Turn It On Again*. This performance was released on VHS in 1991 (and on DVD over ten years later), excluding, not surprisingly, *That's All* (again because of Rutherford's mistakes during the guitar solo).

But the most surprising song for the fans was without doubt *Turn It On Again*, not just for the return (for the last time) of the medley incorporat-

NOTES

(1) Mike Kaufman's Genesis interviews, Chicago / London, October 2007, partially used in the bonus disc accompanying the 2008 remasters

(2) Mario Giammetti's interview with Tony Banks, London, Tony Smith Personal Management office, 29 November 2016

(3) Mario Giammetti's telephone interview with Mike Rutherford, 25 February 2016, partially published in the article "Senza Gabriel" in *Classic Rock*, issue n. 44, July 2016

INVISIBLE TOUCH TOUR

1986

SEPTEMBER
- 18 **Detroit, MI (USA)**, Joe Louis Arena
- 19 **Detroit, MI (USA)**, Joe Louis Arena
- 20 **Detroit, MI (USA)**, Joe Louis Arena
- 22 **Toronto, ON (CANADA)**, Exhibition Stadium
- 24 **Philadelphia, PA (USA)**, The Spectrum
- 25 **Philadelphia, PA (USA)**, The Spectrum
- 26 **Philadelphia, PA (USA)**, The Spectrum
- 27 **Philadelphia, PA (USA)**, The Spectrum
- 29 **New York, NY (USA)**, Madison Square Garden
- 30 **New York, NY (USA)**, Madison Square Garden

OCTOBER
- 01 **New York, NY (USA)**, Madison Square Garden
- 02 **New York, NY (USA)**, Madison Square Garden
- 03 **New York, NY (USA)**, Madison Square Garden
- 05 **Rosemont, IL (USA)**, Rosemont Horizon
- 06 **Rosemont, IL (USA)**, Rosemont Horizon
- 07 **Rosemont, IL (USA)**, Rosemont Horizon
- 08 **Rosemont, IL (USA)**, Rosemont Horizon
- 09 **Rosemont, IL (USA)**, Rosemont Horizon
- 10 **Rosemont, IL (USA)**, Rosemont Horizon
- 13 **Inglewood, CA (USA)**, The Forum
- 14 **Inglewood, CA (USA)**, The Forum
- 15 **Inglewood, CA (USA)**, The Forum
- 16 **Inglewood, CA (USA)**, The Forum
- 17 **Inglewood, CA (USA)**, The Forum
- 19 **Oakland, CA (USA)**, Oakland-Alameda County Coliseum Arena
- 20 **Oakland, CA (USA)**, Oakland-Alameda County Coliseum Arena
- 21 **Oakland, CA (USA)**, Oakland-Alameda County Coliseum Arena
- 22 **Oakland, CA (USA)**, Oakland-Alameda County Coliseum Arena
- 23 **Oakland, CA (USA)**, Oakland-Alameda County Coliseum Arena
- 24 **Oakland, CA (USA)**, Oakland-Alameda County Coliseum Arena

NOVEMBER
- 23 **Auckland (NEW ZEALAND)**, Western Springs Stadium
  Originally scheduled for November 22, but moved to November 23 as the Pope was in Auckland at the same time
- 25 **Sydney (AUSTRALIA)**, Sydney Entertainment Centre
  Special guests (for all the Australian dates): The Invisible Strings
- 26 **Sydney (AUSTRALIA)**, Sydney Entertainment Centre
- 27 **Sydney (AUSTRALIA)**, Sydney Entertainment Centre
- 29 **Boondall (AUSTRALIA)**, Brisbane Entertainment Centre
- 30 **Boondall (AUSTRALIA)**, Brisbane Entertainment Centre

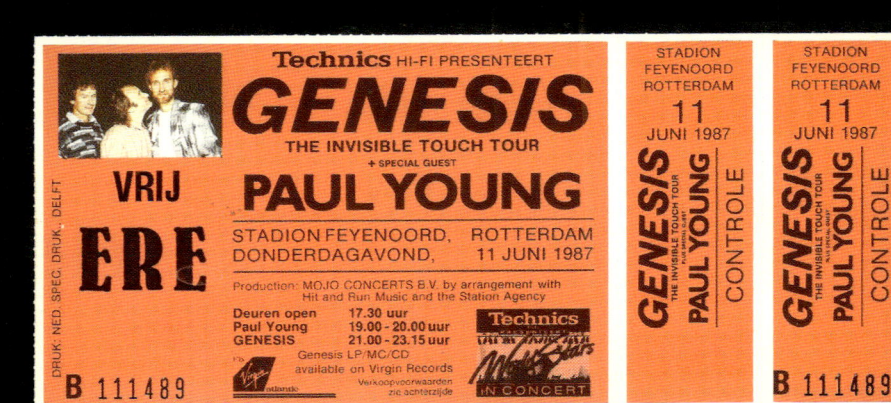

DECEMBER

- **02** **West Lakes (AUSTRALIA)**, Football Park
- **05** **Perth (AUSTRALIA)**, Perth Entertainment Centre
- **06** **Perth (AUSTRALIA)**, Perth Entertainment Centre
- **09** **Melbourne (AUSTRALIA)**, Melbourne Sports & Entertainment Centre
- **10** **Melbourne (AUSTRALIA)**, Melbourne Sports & Entertainment Centre
- **11** **Melbourne (AUSTRALIA)**, Melbourne Sports & Entertainment Centre
- **12** **Melbourne (AUSTRALIA)**, Melbourne Sports & Entertainment Centre
- **13** **Melbourne (AUSTRALIA)**, No. 1 Ground - Melbourne Olympic Park
- **15** **Sydney (AUSTRALIA)**, Sydney Entertainment Centre
- **16** **Sydney (AUSTRALIA)**, Sydney Entertainment Centre
- **17** **Sydney (AUSTRALIA)**, Sydney Entertainment Centre
- **18** **Sydney (AUSTRALIA)**, Sydney Entertainment Centre
- **19** **Sydney (AUSTRALIA)**, Sydney Entertainment Centre

1987

JANUARY

- **15** **Houston, TX (USA)**, The Summit
- **16** **Houston, TX (USA)**, The Summit
- **18** **Dallas, TX (USA)**, Reunion Arena
- **19** **Dallas, TX (USA)**, Reunion Arena
- **21** **Kansas City, MO (USA)**, Kemper Arena
- **24** **Indianapolis, IN (USA)**, Hoosier Dome
- **25** **Richfield, OH (USA)**, Richfield Coliseum
- **26** **Richfield, OH (USA)**, Richfield Coliseum
- **27** **Richfield, OH (USA)**, Richfield Coliseum
- **29** **Landover, MD (USA)**, Capital Centre
- **31** **Chapel Hill, NC (USA)**, Dean E. Smith Center - University of North Carolina at Chapel Hill

FEBRUARY

- **01** **Lexington, KY (USA)**, Rupp Arena
- **15** **Hartford, CT (USA)**, Hartford Civic Center
- **16** **Worcester, MA (USA)**, Worcester Centrum Centre
- **17** **Worcester, MA (USA)**, Worcester Centrum Centre
- **18** **Worcester, MA (USA)**, Worcester Centrum Centre
- **20** **Hampton, VA (USA)**, Hampton Coliseum
- **21** **Hampton, VA (USA)**, Hampton Coliseum
- **22** **Chapel Hill, NC (USA)**, Dean E. Smith Center - University of North Carolina at Chapel Hill
- **23** **Chapel Hill, NC (USA)**, Dean E. Smith Center - University of North Carolina at Chapel Hill

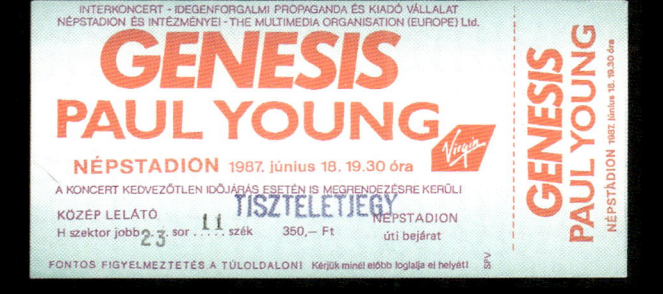

25	**Atlanta, GA (USA)**, The Omni
26	**Atlanta, GA (USA)**, The Omni
28	**Orlando, FL (USA)**, Citrus Bowl

MARCH

01	**Coral Gables, FL (USA)**, Orange Bowl Stadium - University of Miami
13	**Tokyo (JAPAN)**, Nippon Budokan
14	**Tokyo (JAPAN)**, Nippon Budokan
15	**Tokyo (JAPAN)**, Nippon Budokan
16	**Tokyo (JAPAN)**, Nippon Budokan
18	**Osaka (JAPAN)**, Osaka-Jo Hall
19	**Osaka (JAPAN)**, Osaka-Jo Hall

MAY

10	**Málaga (SPAIN)**, Estadio La Rosaleda
13	**Madrid (SPAIN)**, Estadio Vicente Calderon
15	**Toulouse (FRANCE)**, Stade des Sept Deniers
16	**Montreux (SWITZERLAND)**, Casino de Montreux
17	**Rome (ITALY)**, Stadio Flaminio
19	**Milan (ITALY)**, Stadio San Siro
22	**Los Angeles, CA (USA)**, Dodger Stadium
24	**Pittsburgh, PA (USA)**, Three Rivers Stadium
26	**Washington, D.C. (USA)**, Robert F. Kennedy Memorial Stadium
28	**Philadelphia, PA (USA)**, Veterans Stadium
29	**Philadelphia, PA (USA)**, Veterans Stadium
30	**East Rutherford, NJ (USA)**, Giants Stadium
31	**East Rutherford, NJ (USA)**, Giants Stadium

JUNE

02	**Paris (FRANCE)**, Palais Omnisports de Paris-Bercy
03	**Paris (FRANCE)**, Hippodrome de Vincennes
05	**Gentofte (DENMARK)**, Gentofte Stadion
07	**Hannover (WEST GERMANY)**, Niedersachsenstadion
08	**Berlin (WEST GERMANY)**, Platz der Republik
10	**Dortmund (WEST GERMANY)**, Halle 1 - Westfalenhallen
11	**Rotterdam (THE NETHERLANDS)**, Stadion Feyenoord
13	**Basel (SWITZERLAND)**, Fussballstadion St. Jakob
14	**Tomblaine (FRANCE)**, Stade Marcel Picot
16	**Vienna (AUSTRIA)**, Praterstadion
18	**Budapest (HUNGARY)**, Népstadion
20	**Mannheim (WEST GERMANY)**, Maimarktgelände
21	**Munich (WEST GERMANY)**, Olympiastadion
23	**Nantes (FRANCE)**, Stade de la Beaujoire
26	**Glasgow (SCOTLAND)**, Hampden Park
28	**Leeds (ENGLAND)**, Roundhay Park

JULY

01	**London (ENGLAND)**, Wembley Stadium
02	**London (ENGLAND)**, Wembley Stadium
03	**London (ENGLAND)**, Wembley Stadium
04	**London (ENGLAND)**, Wembley Stadium

1988

MAY

14	**New York, NY (USA)**, Madison Square Garden *'Atlantic Records 40th Anniversary Concert'*

1990

JUNE

30	**Stevenage (ENGLAND)**, Knebworth Park *Charity concert for the 'Nordoff-Robbins Music Therapy Centre'. Special guests: Phil Collins' solo band on Turn It On Again*

We Can't Dance

(Virgin 1991)

No Son Of Mine / Jesus He Knows Me / Driving The Last Spike /// I Can't Dance / Never A Time / Dreaming While You Sleep /// Tell Me Why / Living Forever / Hold On My Heart /// Way Of The World / Since I Lost You / Fading Lights

- **All tracks written by Banks/Collins/Rutherford**

- **Release date: 11 November 1991**
- **Engineer: Nick Davis**
- **Assistant Engineer: Mark Robinson**
- **Recorded and mixed at The Farm, Surrey, March-September 1991**
- **Technical assistance: Geoff Callingham and Mike Bowen**
- **Produced by Genesis and Nick Davis**
- **Design and art direction: Icon**
- **Photography: David Scheinmann**
- **Illustrations: Felicity Roma Bowers**

- **Tony Banks: keyboards, vocals**
- **Phil Collins: drums, vocals**
- **Mike Rutherford: basses, guitars, vocals**

THE MAKING OF

After the last concerts of the INVISIBLE TOUCH tour at Wembley in July 1987, the members of Genesis yet again went their separate ways to pursue their solo careers. A couple of get-togethers aside (the previously mentioned Atlantic Records' 40th Anniversary event in 1988 and the performance at Knebworth in 1990), this hiatus would turn out to be even longer than usual. It has to be said, the 1988 version of the *Turn It On Again* medley, featuring a combination of Genesis hits and songs from the trio's solo careers, served as a clear indication that Genesis incorporated individual musicians as opposed to being solely a band entity. Of course, this was primarily due to the popularity of Phil Collins, who was at the peak of his career around this time. November 1988 saw the release of the film *Buster*, in which Phil not only played the leading role but also sang some of the songs in the film's hugely successful soundtrack, in particular the hit singles *Groovy Kind Of Love* and *Two Hearts,* which both reached No. 1 in the Billboard Hot 100 (the latter even won a Grammy Award for Best Song Written Specifically for a Motion Picture or Television).

In the meantime, Rutherford was also enjoying a rise in popularity. The bass player had managed to win himself an audience with his Mike + The Mechanics project which released its second album, LIVING YEARS, at the end of 1988. The second single off the album, *The Living Years*, became a massive hit on both sides of the Atlantic (No. 1 in America and No. 2 in the UK), thus transforming Rutherford and his band into a project which was so successful that in 1989 they had to organise a tour divided into two legs: Europe and North America from the end of February to the end of

April and then another month in the States between the end of July and the end of August.

Seeing Mike's unexpected rise in success, Tony decided to give it another shot, this time recruiting a male singer (Alistair Gordon) and a female singer (Jayney Klimek) for a project he named Bankstatement. BANKSTATEMENT, the album, was also released in 1989 but failed to ignite much interest.

Towards the end of 1989, Phil released his fourth album ...BUT SERIOUSLY, which again was a massive hit: No. 1 in the UK and in the States, where a total of four singles reached the Top Five. The first, *Another Day In Paradise*, topped the charts and won a Grammy Award for Record Of The Year. Collins then set out on a lengthy tour, again with Thompson and Stuermer in tow, scheduled to stop off in four continents between the end of February and the start of October 1990, putting on phenomenally successful shows in Japan, Australia, Europe and North America.

With their bandmate busy, Tony and Mike also continued with their own activities: Tony went back to being a solo artist, albeit featuring a number of guest singers and musicians on his excellent album, STILL, while the Mechanics went on to record their third album. However, delays in the release of WORD OF MOUTH (March 1991) meant that Rutherford had to give up the idea of taking his band out on another tour to promote the album because that would have meant postponing the unpostponable, i.e. meeting up with Banks and Collins, no less than five years after the last Genesis release, to start working on the band's 14th studio album.

Collins: "After the INVISIBLE TOUCH tour I decided to start working on my train set, if I remember rightly. Then I did some film work, *Buster*, and that took up a fair amount of time, you know, preparation, film-

GENESIS

ing, shooting, editing and doing the soundtrack. Then I did my record, ...But Seriously, followed by a whole world tour. So there was every reason for there to be a delay. But in the end we reconvened to write a new album." [1]

Banks: "I was surprised to see that Phil was still there actually. I fully expected him to have disappeared; he'd had so much success, you know, I thought he didn't need us guys anymore. But he was there and he still wanted to do it and obviously still got something out of it. We went into it in just the same way as we had with Invisible Touch; we had nothing written, we just started improvising and seeing what ideas came out of it." [1]

Rutherford: "At this stage we had this thing whereby we were doing a Genesis record and then solo stuff. I was doing Mike + The Mechanics. I think that break, that creative variety you got from working with other people and having learnt things, meant you came back fresh and ready to appreciate what the other two did." [1]

Collins: "This album is probably the best example of the three of us improvising. There'd be a drum machine playing, Mike would be playing something, Tony would be playing and I'd be singing. A lot of the songs, like No Son Of Mine, Hold On My Heart and Driving The Last Spike were totally improvised." [1]

Despite the writing sessions going swimmingly, the band still felt that some changes were in order.

Banks: "We decided to change the producer and engineer, just to give ourselves a bit of a kick in the arse really. I'd worked with Nick Davis when I did my solo album, Still, and Mike had worked with him as well, so we thought it would be fun for Genesis to try someone different." [1]

Collins: "I'd never worked with Nick before, but I think we all thought it was just time for a change, we felt we'd kind of gone as far as we could with Hugh Padgham. I mean, we were only doing an album once every 4 or 5 years, so why not make a change?" [1]

Padgham: "Tony brought in Nick Davis who had done Tony's solo album. So it was a bit like Tony sort of saying, okay, Phil: you've had your day and, and now I'm having mine and he sort of, I felt like, you know, the finger was being stuck up, up at me in a way. I didn't mind at all of course, but, without blowing my own trumpet, my record of working with Genesis was their most successful period, obviously commercially and so-and-so, I'm very

Atlantic Records promotional picture, USA 1991

proud of the three albums that I, that I did with them". [2]

Things came together surprisingly well, especially if you consider the fact that the three musicians hadn't played together for so long. As always, they were enjoying writing what they knew was good material and over a space of two months their collective effort produced a total of 14 tracks. Once all the music had been written, it was time to add the lyrics.

Collins: "What normally happens when we write songs, apart from the odd line which I might spontaneously sing which triggers an idea, the lyrics are written by somebody else. But for some reason, this time round I think I wrote the lyrics to about eight of the songs. I'd never written that many lyrics for a Genesis album." [1]

Musically speaking, catchy songs alternate with very long tracks. Rutherford: "It's part of what we do very easily and, to be honest, I wouldn't be satisfied without doing a long song. We did one album without long songs, ...AND THEN THERE WERE THREE..., and in many ways, apart from *Follow You Follow Me*, it was probably our weakest album. That balance between the long and the short songs is what I think we're about; it creates a good atmosphere." [1]

The result is an album with surprising, sometimes even innovative, sections. Collins: "We've never really discussed it, but I think we've always kind of secretly relished the idea of getting reassessed every time we did an album. I mean you're not playing to anybody in particular, you're just making it for yourself. Of course, you want the people that like you to like it, but you also want people that up until then have dismissed you to say, 'hey, what about this?' you know 'this isn't what we expected from them, is it?'. I mean, frankly, we don't over-think things but it's interesting when you go on a website and you see so many people saying they don't like the album because it's too much for everybody. An 'I-want-something-that's-just-for-me' kind of thing, you know. It's like when everybody judges John Cleese by his *Fawlty Towers*." [1]

THE ALBUM

Over the five years between the release of INVISIBLE TOUCH and its successor, the rock world had been turned inside out and upside down. In 1987 stadium rock was an established phenomenon (Genesis being one of the main players) which consolidated the huge status of acts like U2 (THE JOSHUA TREE), Michael Jackson (BAD) and Pink Floyd, albeit bereft of Waters, (A MOMENTARY LAPSE OF REASON). But the artistic scenario was extremely varied: hair-metal was represented by well-established bands like Whitesnake who released their seventh studio album (imaginatively called WHITESNAKE) and Def Leppard (HYSTERIA), while new artists releasing debut albums included Guns N' Roses (APPETITE FOR DESTRUCTION) in America and Deacon Blue (RAINTOWN) and Sinead O'Connor (THE LION AND THE COBRA) on the other side of the Atlantic. On the other hand, Yes with BIG GENERATOR (falling well short of the success enjoyed by 90125) and Supertramp with FREE AS A BIRD (their second album without Roger Hodgson) were visibly lagging behind.

However, 1988 did see the unexpected return of some of music's finest: Brian Wilson released his self-titled first solo album, Crosby, Stills, Nash &

GENESIS

Virgin Records promotional picture, UK 1991

Young got back together for AMERICAN DREAM, while Bob Dylan, George Harrison, Tom Petty, Roy Orbison and Jeff Lynne joined forces and released THE TRAVELING WILBURYS VOL. 1. The US also saw the release of several debut albums: folk revelation TRACY CHAPMAN and alternative rock bands Soundgarden (ULTRA MEGA OK) and the Pixies (SURFER ROSA), while, over in Europe, Irish singer-songwriter Enya was enjoying the commercial success of her album WATERMARK (containing the hit single Orinoco Flow) and critical acclaim was being showered on British band Talk Talk for their ground-breaking SPIRIT OF EDEN.

1989 also offered a mix of old and new. After a few uninspired years, Lou Reed was back in great form with NEW YORK and Bob Dylan released his critically acclaimed OH MERCY. At the same time, two bands making their debut releases, Nirvana (BLEACH) and the Stone Roses (THE STONE ROSES), were set to be the forerunners (on their respective sides of the Atlantic and with very different fortunes) of two predominant genres: the former became the symbol of grunge, while the latter were one of the leaders (together with the Happy Mondays) of the musical scene known as Madchester which would later spread beyond the confines of Manchester and evolve into Britpop.

Great Britain gave us some other quality albums that year, such as HATS by The Blue Nile and Peter Gabriel's soundtrack album PASSION, released on his newly created Real World Records label. And all the while, progressive rock, both old and new, was trying to reinvent itself. ANDERSON BRUFORD WAKEMAN HOWE marked the return of old-style Yes, even though they were not allowed to use the band name due to opposition from Chris Squire, and Marillion released SEASONS END, the first album with singer, Steve Hogarth, recruited to fill the vacancy left by Fish. Having embarked on a solo career, the latter released his debut album, VIGIL IN A WILDERNESS OF MIRRORS, at the beginning of 1990, a year that would prove to be much less intense, musically speaking albeit with a number of very interesting and vastly diverse bands coming to the fore, including The Beautiful South in England with their WELCOME TO THE BEAUTIFUL SOUTH (released at the end of the previous year) and Alice In Chains (FACELIFT) and Uncle Tupelo (NO DEPRESSION) in the States. Among the veterans, it is impossible not to mention the coming back together of Lou Reed and John Cale (both formerly of the Velvet Underground) who released their song cycle about the late Andy Warhol (SONGS FOR DRELLA), and the return of Paul Simon whose THE RHYTHM OF THE SAINTS continued along the world-music path he had undertaken with GRACELAND.

1991 started off with what would sadly prove to be Queen's last studio album with Freddie Mercury (INNUENDO) and continued with the ill-conceived rehashes put out by Yes, now in its 8-man formation, (UNION) and Procol Harum (THE PRODIGAL STRANGER). But new music also abounded with the debut album by Blur (LEISURE), the simultaneous release of Guns N' Roses' third and fourth studio albums (USE YOUR ILLUSION I and USE YOUR ILLUSION II) and, above all, Nirvana's second album, NEVERMIND.

So, how does WE CAN'T DANCE fit into all of this? Again, like a species unto itself. The Genesis trademark is clearly still present, but where INVISIBLE TOUCH focused on soon-to-become-obsolete electronic sounds and an excessively hooky song formula, the new tracks, also thanks to the additional space made available by the CD format (now prevalent in

genesis

record stores), do not shy away from the opportunity to expand whenever there is room for exploration. Stylistically speaking, on the other hand, new influences appear along with the occasional vague reminiscences of more romantic atmospheres. And all complete with an array of electronic effects which, although still modern, are, if nothing else, free of the Padgham sound.

A contemporary record in other words. Not just in terms of the instrumentation used but also in the way songs are structured and played. However, despite two tracks going beyond the ten-minute mark and another two clocking in at over 7 minutes, there really isn't a lot to remind us of the 1970s. Not a single section evokes the mystery and virtuosity which emanated from the old masterpieces. And perhaps that is how it should be, given the passing of the years, the changing times and the maturing of the band members.

This is also easily perceived in the lyrics, never before so direct (Phil wrote the lyrics to a total of eight tracks with the remaining six divided between Tony and Mike). *No Son Of Mine* tells the tale of a teenage boy who runs away from home to escape his violent father, *Jesus He Knows Me* makes fun out of the phenomenon of US TV evangelists, *Living Forever* is about the obsession of staying fit and healthy, *Driving The Last Spike* is about the dramatic working conditions under which the British railways were built in the 19th century, *Tell Me Why*, written during the Gulf War, is a series of questions for which, obviously, there are no answers, whilst *Way Of The World* is a reflection on mankind's destructive nature.

Virgin Records promotional picture, UK 1991

In terms of execution, the number one rule appears to have been to keep it simple. This change in direction is most noticeable in Tony Banks' keyboards, with his solos increasingly becoming a distant memory: his playing is stripped back, often limiting itself to mere, albeit refined, accompaniment, using very little piano and almost completely abandoning keyboard programming in favour of a greater use of pre-sets.

The percussion section has very little new to offer in terms of execution: electronic rhythms are still very much to the fore and maybe Collins could (and possibly should) have done a bit more on drums, although it has to be said, when he does play, his sound is tight and clean. Beyond the by now typical snare drum riffs, the jazzy tempo of *Living Forever* stands out, while Phil's vocals are technically perfect and more mature.

But the biggest surprise on the album is Mike. Although a brilliant bass player, his lead guitar playing had never been a strong point. However, his guitar work on this album is full of class and invention and, despite limiting solos to a minimum, he deploys a special and particularly crafted sense of rhythm. Musically speaking, the most impressive new aspects are all his: the amazing riff on *I Can't Dance*, the bluesy distortions in the background of *Dreaming While You Sleep*, the psychedelic 12-string arpeggios in *Tell Me Why*, the powerful guitar in *Fading Lights*. Overall, WE CAN'T DANCE takes a stratospheric leap up the scale compared to the compositional mediocrity of INVISIBLE TOUCH, with an artistic disparity (all due consideration being given to the musical variations occurring over the 20-year time period) comparable, in the history of the band, only to that previously seen between FROM GENESIS TO REVELATION and TRESPASS.

THE SONGS

NO SON OF MINE

A ticking metronome and the beat of a kick drum, then an undefinable guttural sound: this is how the seventeenth album by Genesis kicks off.

Banks: "With Genesis songs, as the keyboard player, a lot of the time it's my job to give some distinctive quality to the sound. Here, you know, you hear that very distinctive sort of elephant sound; it's arresting and immediately recognisable, it just sets the mood. Again, this was just me sampling noises in the room. Mike was thrashing around and I just cut out this little bit in the middle and slowed it right down, then I just used the front end of it and stuck it with the E minor chord – the effect was fantastic! I thought, 'this is great, I love this!'. Then Phil started warbling on top of it and we thought we had a song that sounded really good. Sometimes, funnily enough, if you can set up an atmosphere, get a sort of a feel going, what you do after that isn't so important because that initial mood carries you for a long, long time."[1]

Over a base of keyboards, the voice comes in and sings the first verse. Then the bass enters, along with a powerful snare beat. The chords are fantastic, despite falling back on the Banksian cliché of note substitution (E minor becomes C major and D major goes to B minor, while in the second part of the riff the order of the chords changes): a sequence that makes the song intricate and endowed with a beautiful, poignant melody, made all the more so thanks to Phil's excellent vocal work and Mike's finishing touches on guitar.

Collins: "If ever I fancied just listening to a couple of tracks late at night, this would be one of them. I would say that if there is anything I miss about not being in a band, it's writing this kind of stuff, which I don't do on my own. I don't know that many chords, you know. It was just that chemistry; being there at the right time, the right moment." [1]

Banks: "When we actually played the album to the record company, we only played this song to them and said it was the single. We knew that, if we played them the whole album, they would want to release *I Can't Dance* and we didn't really want that one as the first single." [1]

Rutherford: "This is probably one of my favourite recent tracks because once again it was like the start of what we were doing, the next stage. Again, it's got this dark atmosphere with that sound Tony made by looping and messing around with a little guitar thing I played, making it sound like an elephant. And it's a great start to the album, you immediately know it's us. I sometimes feel it's a sort of modern-day version of what we used to do with the earlier stuff. And it has a strong lyric from Phil. I think the Genesis setting is good for Phil to write lyrics. He can be a little tougher, which is something he can do easily but I think he needs the right setting." [1]

Collins: "This is one of those songs where the idea for the lyrics came as we were playing it. I have no idea at all why I started singing the words 'you're no son, you're no son of mine', they just sounded good and sang well. Certain notes have certain words, so you end up improvising. When I sat down to carry on that thought as a lyric, it seemed pretty clear that it was about a father and a son, you know, but it's nothing to do with my childhood or my kids. It's about domestic abuse which is kind of swept under the carpet. There's all this other stuff out there on the street, you know riots, racial stuff, but domestic abuse is something nobody ever talks about. Even the police don't really want to deal with it because it happens inside the house, so there's a kind of, you know, 'you sort it out' attitude. So it's the story of this kid who basically was tired of going home and seeing his parents fighting every time his father came home drunk. He'd just had enough and then eventually he realised that he needed to confront this problem."[1]

JESUS HE KNOWS ME

The most upbeat track on the album is a fusion of styles coming from Phil (the verse) and Tony (the reggae variations); it's musically fun and jaunty also thanks to the praiseworthy vocal performance by Collins whose lyrics are highly original.

Rutherford: "Phil had this idea because at the time there were an awful lot of scandals and stuff concerning American evangelists. So it seemed a nice easy topic to hit."[1]

Collins: "We were all playing, the drum machine was going and I just started to sing 'Jesus he knows me, he knows I'm right'. I hadn't been watching religious television and, when I first started singing it, I don't think Tony and Mike realised I was trying to take it from a funny point of view, you know, they weren't too sure about it! And so I explained it was meant to be a parody, like Monty Python's *Life of Brian*, you know, the 'you are the Messiah, and I should know. I've followed a few' kind of mentality. I mean there was this famous guy, I can't remember exactly if it was Oral Roberts or Jimmy Swaggart, who had actually gone on television saying that he'd had a dream and Christ or God had told him that he had to get 18 million dollars by the weekend. And people were giving him this money. And this was a current story really, and then there was Jim Bakker and his wife Tammy, you know, the horrible, tacky Heritage USA deceit (*the televangelist was convicted of fraud and conspiracy charges in 1989 – author's note*). I mean, these people aren't real, are they? But it was all going on and I couldn't resist the temptation to write about it. When we used to do it live, it got a mixed reaction in some parts of America because basically you're taking the mickey out of the people that are in the audience in some of the southern states, you know, as soon as you say the word Jesus... but I mean, it wasn't meant to be irreverent towards religion or God or Christ, it was actually meant to say 'come on people, wake up, these guys are fleecing you!'."[1]

DRIVING THE LAST SPIKE

A light electronic drum programme, an enveloping keyboard melody and finishing touches on guitar. When Collins' voice enters, the atmosphere is rarefied and soft as he sings a melancholy melody. There is an array of rhythm changes over the song's ten-minute-plus duration with sharp drum beats and the typical toing and froing between the guitar and keyboards before the sudden and very effective ending.

Banks: "This was a slightly interesting thing for us in a way because on previous albums (and certainly on the previous three or four), it was always a case of 'Tony writes the lyrics for the long songs' but, on this one, Phil wanted to have a go. He really enjoyed it because he could stretch out a little bit more and write more of the story and bring in other ideas. Also, the instrumental parts kind of illustrate things; there's the nice sort of mechanical bit in the middle of the song and when you're writing a lyric like that, you listen to the music and little ideas come at you from it, so it has a different character from things like *Domino* and *Home By The Sea* where I tend to get slightly more intense because he's got a slightly different approach." [1]

Rutherford: "When you get all the songs done, you put them out there and ask who wants to write the lyrics and someone will say they're very keen to do a particular song. Certain songs you kind of know it has to be Phil's lyrics because of the way the melody runs and the way he sang to it. For this one, he said he'd read this book and had this idea. Once again a change, but it worked very well actually." [1]

Collins: "I'd been sent this book called *The Railway Navvies*. I read it and it made me think about how many people had been killed building the railways back in the 1800s, when a tunnel collapsed or something, or due to explosions. So I just wrote this song about these people who went off and left their families without knowing if they'd ever come back. I mean, it wasn't a war, this was just to build a railway! Lyrically it was like nothing I'd ever been involved with really. Story songs were never really my thing. I'd written a few, you know, *Like China* (on my second album) was a kind of story type song, but most of the time my lyrics are personal things. For me this was a departure and might have been the beginning of my wanting to write stories and therefore leading to working with Disney later." [1]

I CAN'T DANCE

Collins: "This was like, you know, five minutes' work. It was a classic example of 'let's just record this right now'. I remember Mike was doing a guitar part again and I was on a chair in a corner writing the lyrics. I said, 'I've finished' and we recorded it. It was a very exciting album to make." [1]

Genesis as you never expected to hear them: a rock blues with Phil giving it a great soul voice over a rhythm base characterised by a weird sound from Tony's synth (a pre-set on the Roland JD800) and a characteristic distorted riff from Mike.

Banks: "Mike had this riff that he kept playing and we couldn't quite find a way to do it. We tried doing it heavy, Phil would play big drums and I'd sort of beat calmly but nothing was really sounding very good. Then I got this new Roland keyboard which had a sort of pre-set drum sound on it. I suppose it had a bass drum on it, so I just started this 'boom-ch, boom-boom-ch' going and started playing these silly sounds on top of it. The whole thing suddenly took on this completely different character and we thought we'd do it like that. We didn't do anything to it for the next month and then said, 'where's that song with a guitar riff? let's put it down'. Phil went off and wrote a lyric for it and the next day we had the song. We thought it was great to just keep it really, really simple with lots of humour. And it works. It's a great contrast to other things we've done in our career." [1]

Rutherford: "It wasn't really one of our main sort of songs. A real easy write. I remember it was a day when I think Phil wasn't there for some reason. Tony had this bit which he played on the keyboard and I had this really quite nice riff, very simple but quite unusual in the way it's actually put together. I remember showing it to Daryl; if Daryl can't get something straight away it must be clever... then

Virgin Records poster advertising the single
Tell Me Why, UK 1993

while we were sort of mixing all the other songs, we bunged this version down with the guitar thing. And then we kind of sat in the back of the studio and wrote the lyrics virtually there and then. Kind of how it should have been in the old days, you know: terribly easy to write and record and it's fun." [1]

Collins: "It's a great example of the fact that we see ourselves as being able to do anything, whereas other people seem to think that what we do is very specific. We wrote this after a conversation had come up about some guy that had been in a jeans commercial and then had a Top Ten hit *(Phil is referring to Nick Kamen – author's note)*. I mean, we're talking about someone who's really glamorous and obviously we are three guys who are anything but.... these male models, I'm not saying they're dopey, I'm just saying that the book may not be as good a read as the cover. So the idea was to just give 3 different examples of that and, of course, we then followed that through with the video." [1]

NEVER A TIME

A love song which musically speaking is very similar to Phil Collins' solo work. Although he sings it beautifully, the TV documentary, No Admittance, shows it was anything but easy.

Banks: "We had a camera crew with us all the time while we were doing bits and pieces (although most of the time we didn't let them too near us when we were doing actual real work). But while we were recording this song, the idea was to show Phil while he was actually singing it. Some groups love to have, you know, girlfriends and punters and all sorts of people in the studio, but I think as soon as you do that you're performing. Studio work isn't necessarily about performing, it's about crafting and you don't want to be self-conscious at all, you want to be there, make mistakes, bum notes, anything, until you get a result. Whereas if somebody's there, you don't want to play a bum note, you think, 'oh I can't try that', so you act differently and obviously it's very much the same in front of a camera, suddenly you're performing and it's not the same. Phil didn't sing it well at the time and for some reason or other that particular approach to it all got stuck in his brain and the song just never recovered. In the end it only barely made it onto the album, which was a shame really because again there's a good song buried in there somewhere which didn't quite come out. I always think of it as the song that got away. It's working title was *Big Big Hit* and, of course, the one thing it wasn't was that." [1]

DREAMING WHILE YOU SLEEP

Banks: "Phil's quite good at setting up drum machines that give you a bit of flavour and I particularly liked the one we used on this song. It's got this quite elaborate drum machine riff that goes through the whole thing and adds so much character that you automatically find yourself playing little bluesy things and then a very lush chorus. Funnily enough, this was one of the group's favourite tracks on that album but no one else seems to like it." [1]

And while it may be true that the drum machine does to some extent define the song, what really captures the listener are the particularly intense chorus and the end section with Phil's vocal emphasis. Mike also puts in an excellent performance throughout the song, playing distorted bluesy-style guitar in the background and creating an effective musical backdrop. Mike was also responsible for the rather interesting lyrics which tell the story of a hit and run incident in which a young girl is killed and for the rest of his life the driver is eaten away by remorse.

Rutherford: "Whether it's through an accident or an illness, the idea of being in that state of mind, where you are not in the world but your brain is still there, is a scary concept." [3]

TELL ME WHY

Mike is again at the top of his game with his splendid 12-string Rickenbacker arpeggio played in true Byrds style.

Rutherford: "It was a 12-string electric guitar. It's funny, I have an electric sitar and every album I do I get it out and it never gets used. But the 12-string has always been my favourite instrument really and it worked really well on this song." [3]

Excellent drumming by Phil who is also the author of the lyrics. Banks: "I was never very keen on the lyrics of this song, I thought Phil had done this kind of thing many times before with tracks like *Another Day In Paradise* and I wasn't very keen on that aspect of it. I thought it was a really good pop song with a great melody line and chord sequence, and if it had had a slightly less intense lyric, it might have done well. I think this was the song where Genesis 'went' in the US. We'd had hit singles with the other tracks but when we put this out it didn't do anything at all in the States or in England. In England it was already a time when Radio One had decided they weren't going to play established bands, but I also think that what it was about made them think, 'no, we won't play this song'. After that song, for a while neither we nor Phil released anything; it was at that point that things changed. And obviously we didn't do any more records together, we split up. I don't think it was just the fault of that song, but it was at that point that it happened." [4]

LIVING FOREVER

Introduced by a clever interaction between drums and guitar, the lead voice is often accompanied by numerous vocal counter-melodies. After a typical Banksian interlude the track acquires a genuine Genesis atmosphere with a characteristic instrumental end section, with its melody composed by Tony and with Mike again adding the finishing touches.

Collins: "This song just suddenly came into my head, you know, that kind of offbeat, quirky song. I think we tried to play it live a couple of times but it's all brushes and it's a different kind of Genesis thing." [1]

Banks: "Phil had this kind of hip hop drum riff going. Not knowing anything about hip hop, I just started playing along with it, doing various things. I think chord-wise it was too simple but then there is the solo in the middle which was quite fun. The lyrics are about nutritionists; one day they say this, the next something different. For example, ten years ago you weren't supposed to have too many eggs because they raised your cholesterol. Then they found out that even though eggs are full of cholesterol, they don't raise your levels and that an egg a day is in fact good for you. You have this oldest woman in the world, who might be Italian, she's 117, she has 3 eggs a day and she's still alive... (*Tony is referring to Emma Morano, who was indeed Italian and died at the venerable age of 117 on 15 April 2017, a few months after this interview – author's note*). I just wanted to say that whatever they tell you one day, they tell you the opposite the next. It's a bit like in the film *Sleeper* with Woody Allen. He wakes up (after 200 years in cryopreservation) and as he's a vegan, he wants lentils and beans and they say, 'oh no, that's all gone, it gives you cancer. All we eat is hot fudge.'. (*Tony is paraphrasing: in the film, the character requests wheat germ and organic honey – author's note.*)" [4]

HOLD ON MY HEART

A song that seems to have come directly off a Phil Collins solo album: drum machine, an intimate feel, guitar counterpoint and evocative vocals. And yet...

Collins: "A lot of people thought it was all mine because of the TR-808 drum machines and the love lyric. But I just wrote the lyrics. The track was based on one of Mike's guitar things but it was all Tony's chords, so I had nothing to do with that. It was actually more influenced by John Martyn, that's where I was kind of coming from with 'hold on my heart'. (*Phil Collins had produced John Martyn's GLORIOUS FOOL album in 1981 on which there is a track called Hold On To My Heart – author's note*)" [1]

WAY OF THE WORLD

Another very Collins sounding track, mainly due to the 1960s-style backing vocals and short keyboard solo.

Banks: "There are two or three songs on this record I felt perhaps didn't come out as well as they should have done. This was a missed opportunity. I've always thought there's a better song in there: it's got a great rhythm and the chorus is really good but the verse is not one of our best. There were some better moments in it when we were just improvising and playing along; it's another one of those songs that got away." [1]

The lyrics are full of social comment. Rutherford: "If we were recording it now, I'd do the lyrics again. It was a nice idea but it didn't quite work. The trouble is, when you're writing and there's a tour coming up, you have deadlines so you just steam on. I would have taken the title and rewritten it." [3]

Banks: "Having done it with so much success with *Land Of Confusion*, Mike wrote another lyric that was a bit political. It's a Mike type of song, really: I love the feel, the chords in the chorus are really nice, but we never really got a verse going. It's not a song I like, but I like the solo." [4]

SINCE I LOST YOU

Collins: "We were playing around with this kind of Beach Boys, Phil Spector mood one day. That night, I went home and I heard that Eric's son had died. I came back in the next day and said, 'have you heard?'. We sat round and discussed it, and then we carried on working on the song and that's when I started to improvise these words, and then we decided that that was what it was going to be about. I had this moment when I played it to Eric and he played me *Tears in Heaven*." [1]

Phil is, of course, referring to the tragic death of Conor Clapton, the four-year-old son of Eric Clapton and Italian actress Lory Del Santo, who fell out of an open window of a New York City high-rise on 20 March 1991. That said, however, the melodic structure of the song with its piano backing isn't particularly memorable, despite the excellent work from Mike on guitar, both in a short solo and with his beautiful counterpoint at the end.

Banks: "I wouldn't have put it on the album. I thought it was a nice idea but it didn't really come off. Unfortunately, this meant leaving off what I thought was probably the second or third best track we'd written for the album which was called *On the Shoreline*. For some reason or other Mike and Phil both ganged up against me and said, 'no, we don't want that one'." [1]

FADING LIGHTS

The song features a beautiful keyboard chord sequence over a drum machine backing with guitar adding the finishing touches. The vocal melody is steeped in melancholy. Later in the song, a lengthy synth solo is underlined by a heavy guitar riff and excellent drumming.

Banks: "It was another one of those drum riffs that Phil used to come up with, just a drum loop, and I started playing these very wistful chords. We all decided to get away from the idea of the intense young boys we'd once been. But we'd always had humour even in those days, you know things like, 'me, I'm just a lawnmower, you can tell me by the way I walk', or songs about a restaurant owner who serves up his toes for tea (*Harold The Barrel* – author's note). There were always jokes in there and we always tried to keep some of the lyrics quite lightweight for that reason, just to sort of steer away from being too serious. But then we wanted intense moments that were strong and serious as well, that was always part of us." [1]

GENESIS

The cover and back cover of the Italian Genesis magazine Dusk, *Issue No, 18, May 1996*

Reading between the lines of Tony's lyrics, we see a message to fans that the Genesis story is drawing to a close.

Banks: "I'd felt it after the previous two albums that Phil would probably leave the band. I already felt it on ABACAB, actually, but I really felt that this time he was going to go, so I wrote this as a kind of goodbye song really, you know, that's it, that's how it was... A nostalgic look back really, how you see things in the past and how you see them now. I think it's quite a moving song, particularly the lyrics and I know that Tony Smith finds it a moving song. You know, 'Another time it might have been so different'. Sometimes you want to relive your life and do things differently. Phil always said the lyrics were a bit like Anthony Newley. He was a singer in the 1960s who used to do these big ballads and was quite a big influence on David Bowie. It was almost like an old show song, like a musical and it's one of my favourite lyrics that I wrote for the group. The solo was quite funny but the strong moment is when it's coming out of the solo and back into the verse; that's when it really works." [4]

OTHER SONGS

During the album sessions, Genesis recorded another two songs which were then released as B-sides. While *Hearts On Fire* is inconsequential with its annoyingly synthetic sounds produced by the synth bass and drum machine and a banal melody, *On The Shoreline* is a pleasant pop-rock song which, in the opening section full of electronic effects, reuses the 'elephant noise' of *No Son Of Mine* before developing with a keyboard riff and rhythmic guitar patterns.

Banks: "It was just that sort of obstinate thing, you know, 'Tony wants it, so we don't', because I'd written the lyrics, I suppose. Anyway, Phil and Mike said no, so *On The Shoreline* isn't on the album. At the time, Mike played the album to his son who said it was the best track on the album. Anyhow later on, of course, they said, 'yeah, we should have put that on'." [1]

THE ALBUM ARTWORK

After three really poor sleeve designs, the artwork on this album is far stronger. Icon were responsible for creating the cover based on an idea Phil had while looking at a photo in a book. The illustration by Felicity Roma Bowers is beautiful and shows that a cover can be captivating without relinquishing simplicity.

Rutherford: "The little men on the moon. It reminded me of the book *The Little Prince* by Antoine de Saint-Exupéry; it had the same look. I think it works quite well, it's slightly animated." [1]

Banks: "I thought it was the best album cover

We Can't Dance

Poster advertising the album and the first single, 1991

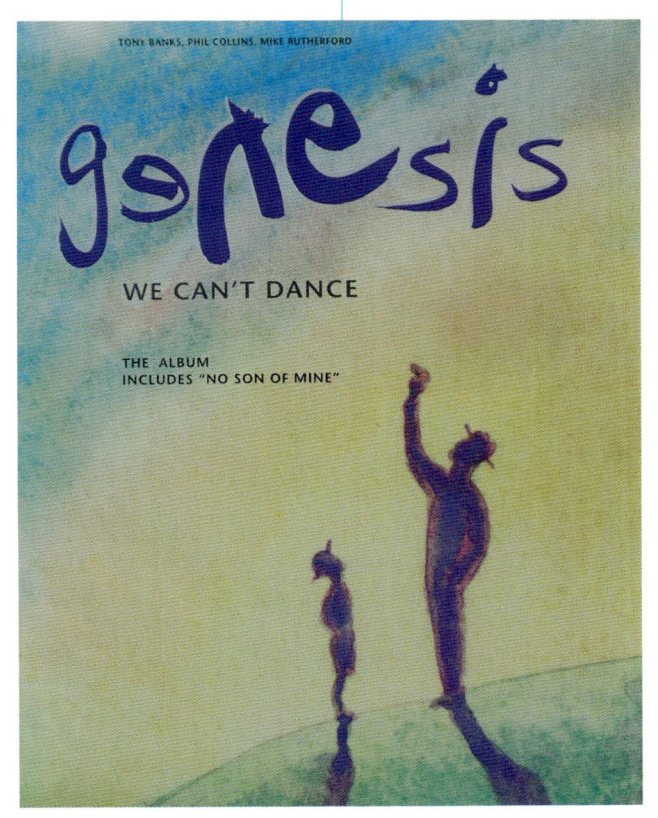

thing."[1]

The artwork on the inside of the album includes a couple of photos of the band which appear to have been decisive in choosing the title of the album.

Rutherford: "You start by looking for an album title among the song titles. It seemed to work and then there are the pictures inside of us sitting in that club in Chiddingfold, near the studio, with that after-party look with the hats on, like three wallflowers; it seemed to fit quite nicely."[1]

EPILOGUE

Despite the topics touched upon in the lyrics and a sound which was much less commercial, WE CAN'T DANCE was a huge success, selling somewhere in the region of 20 million copies worldwide. In the UK it went straight into the album chart at No. 1 and reached No. 4 in the States. In fact, it was a major success the world over, particularly in Germany where it sold 3 million copies, keeping it in the charts for around 24 weeks.

In Great Britain it would become the fifth highest-selling album of the 1990s and it also did magnificently well in terms of singles: *No Son Of Mine* and *I Can't Dance* made it into the Top Ten (No. 6 and No. 7 respectively), while *Hold On My Heart* only managed to climb to No. 16 and *Jesus He Knows Me* reached No. 20. In the States, the most popular single was *I Can't Dance*, which reached

we'd had, certainly since DUKE. It's kind of similar to DUKE in a way; there's a very simple cartoon type picture but with a strong atmosphere and a feel about it that suggested that the album had a little more romance in it than the previous one. And there was a great logo too which we've ended up using ever since. The N and the E are the wrong way round and, you know, it just still seems to fit."[1]

Rutherford: "It's a nice logo. I mean, we've had a few over the years. The fact that we chose this one to sort of stay with us (*for the subsequent archive releases – author's note*) I think probably says some-

No. 7, followed by *No Son Of Mine* and *Hold On My Heart* (No. 12) and *Jesus He Knows Me* (No. 23). *Never A Time* was also released as a single in America (No. 21), while in the UK a live version of *Invisible Touch* (off the live album The Way We Walk, Volume 1: The Shorts) got to No. 7 and the last single, *Tell Me Why*, released well into 1993 reached No. 40.

As with its predecessor, the album was given a promotional boost by the numerous videos created to accompany the single releases.

Banks: "The video for *No Son Of Mine* just suggested enough of what the lyrics were about without going over the top. It was about child abuse and everything but it was done in quite a light way and the idea of the son going back and being turned away all the time I just found very moving actually."[1]

Collins: "A great video. We were like three flies on the wall watching everything happen. I thought it was a good visual interpretation of what the song was about."[1]

Rutherford: "I always loved dressing up on the videos. I like to think it was a way we could sort of be humorous without being embarrassing. The lyrics to *Jesus He Knows Me* are very tongue in cheek, and because the lyrics are about quite a strong subject, it made any kind of fooling around by us OK, I think."[1]

Collins: "There's this evangelist guy called Ernest Angley who became my hero. Any time I saw him on TV, I had to watch him, I mean, I even collected videos of him. I was just obsessed with this guy because I couldn't believe how awful he was, his awful suits and his awful wig (and no matter how old he got, the wig stayed the same). We made the video, which is basically me taking the mickey out of him, in Dallas. Later, I think it was someone in Jim Yukich's entourage (*the director – author's note*), who'd appeared in the video, said he'd heard that Ernest Angley had seen the video and thought it was quite flattering that somebody had taken the trouble to do something in his honour. So it kind of went right over his wig."[1]

Rutherford: "The dance in the *I Can't Dance* video was Phil's idea really. We were in the studio doing a three-day shoot in Los Angeles and he suddenly just started doing it. It took an hour and a half to record it and now I'll always be forever known as the guy who did that dance. But better than Tony, I hope. Forty years of making music and that sticks!"[1]

Collins: "I remember reading a Roger Waters interview in *Rolling Stone* where he said, 'and as for Genesis, you know, doing a stupid walk with that awful song'. Now I've met Roger a few times and I know that he's basically a miserable bastard. He knows love his music but he's got no sense of humour at all, or rather he has a very dark, cynical sense of humour. He didn't see the fun in it at all. I think he felt that this was our statement, so I wrote to him to tell him, but he just replied that what he'd said was meant to be off the record, which didn't exactly make it any better. I still think it's a good example of Genesis: you could put that next to *Supper's Ready* and say this is pretty much the same band, the same heads are at work here. The same people that brought you *Apocalypse In 9/8* are bringing you We Can't Dance, you know. For me, and not because it's the most recent album with Genesis, it's actually the one with the most happy memories. Which is kind of ironic because I left afterwards."[1]

THE CONCERTS

The band's return to live performing came five years after their previous tour. Despite this long absence, interest in the band had anything but waned. As it happens, the success achieved by WE CAN'T DANCE fuelled massive interest in the live shows as soon as rumours of a tour began to circulate. So much so, it soon became evident that the only solution was another stadium tour: the band was simply too big an attraction to be able to contemplate indoor venues. Consequently, a long tour of open-air concerts was scheduled covering North America and Europe with over fifty dates between May and the beginning of August 1992.

After final rehearsals held, as always, in Dallas, the tried and tested line-up with Thompson (now with his head completely shaven) and Stuermer played a couple of warm-up gigs on 8 and 9 May in Irving, Houston. Here the absolutely incredible stage show set-up was perfected. The lights were once again Vari-Lite Series 200, but this time visuals were taken care of by lighting designer, Marc Brickman, (of Pink Floyd and Paul McCartney live show fame) who immediately set about positioning the sound towers 46 metres apart as opposed to the standard 26 metres, thus improving the stereophonic effect. The set also included three massive Sony Jumbotron screens measuring 7x5m, used both separately and together, onto which live images and ad hoc footage were displayed. Videos and lights were tightly interlinked in order to give the audience a show that was truly unforgettable for the time, also thanks to a computer system that controlled the hundreds of lights suspended on steel cables which could be moved backwards and forwards.

Finally, the massive stage (which cost Genesis a staggering $3 million) was 48 metres high, 75 metres across and 30 metres wide. It gave the impression of being totally out in the open but was in fact completely covered by a Plexiglas canopy to protect the band and gear in the event of rain.

The following setlist was played at Irving: *Land Of Confusion / No Son Of Mine / Driving The Last Spike / Old Medley (Dance On A Volcano – The Lamb Lies Down On Broadway – The Musical Box – Firth Of Fifth – I Know What I Like) / Dreaming While You Sleep / Fading Lights / Jesus He Knows Me / Home By The Sea / Hold On My Heart / Mama / Domino / Drum Duet / I Can't Dance* with *Tonight, Tonight, Tonight – Invisible Touch* and *Turn It On Again* as encores. As of the following day in Houston, another song was added to the encores, *Throwing It All Away* (before *Turn It On Again*).

In other words, the band continued with the trend of focusing primarily on their more recent repertoire. And so, the show kicked off with a song from the INVISIBLE TOUCH album, four more tracks of which were included in the show (although *Tonight, Tonight, Tonight* was played without the long instrumental interlude and ran straight into the album's title track). Most of the show, however, revolved around WE CAN'T DANCE, with seven tracks in the setlist and as many as nine planned if any of the recordings of the rehearsals are anything to go by, as these also feature *Way Of The World* and an excerpt of *Living Forever* (neither of which were ever actually played live on the tour). GENESIS was represented by two songs and the finale was reserved, as always, to *Turn It On Again* only now, thank goodness, back in its original form without the medley of classic rock songs.

Fans of the progressive rock era had to be con-

Atlantic promotional picture, USA 1992

tent with a twenty-minute 'summary' of the band's early history. Despite generating mixed impressions, the so-called *Old Medley*, still managed to stir the emotions the second Phil handed over to 'Mr. Rutherford' who began playing the opening notes of *Dance On A Volcano* on his Rickenbacker, as images of flames filled the screens which then turned lava red. Mike would switch over to bass during the half intro into *The Lamb Lies Down On Broadway* through which the screens showed images of New York skyscrapers. The transitions between songs weren't always particularly smooth, but before Stuermer's glorious *Firth Of Fifth* solo, *The Musical Box* was absolutely magnificent with a stunning interpretation and performance from Phil which, also thanks to a special lighting effect (a yellow beam which distorted his features), momentarily catapulted the audience back to the Gabriel era. The musical part wasn't quite so exquisite due to Mike playing bass and not 12-string guitar, which meant the intro arpeggios were left solely to Daryl on electric guitar and with standard tuning (so not quite the right notes). Phil's crazy little dance to *I Know What I Like* was great fun and this part of the medley also incorporated brief excerpts from other Genesis songs (*That's All, Illegal Alien, Follow You Follow Me* and *Stagnation*, with the occasional tiniest hint of *Your Own Special Way* or alternatively *Misunderstanding*).

On the other hand, both *In The Cage*, which for the past five tours had been the strongest link with the band's past, and, surprisingly, *Los Endos*, were dropped from the set. This meant that the drum duet was now an entirely separate entity, being neither the beginning nor the ending of any other song.

One of the most memorable parts of the show was without doubt *Fading Lights*, performed solely by the three members of Genesis, i.e. without Daryl and Chester (in order to give Phil time to leave centre stage and take up his place behind the drum kit, Tony added the synth phase which would then close the song). *No Son Of Mine* with an extended guitar solo from Rutherford featured a very moving performance from Phil sitting on the edge of the stage.

Banks: "When we play it on stage, it sends shivers down my spine. If you can do that with just a few chords and a simple rhythm, then I think there's nothing to be said against that. You know, you've got some things which have got more notes in three seconds than we have in the whole song. That doesn't make it a better song, just different." [1]

The delivery of *Driving The Last Spike* was also interesting. After the first few shows, it was lowered a tone so as not to strain Phil's voice and Daryl

Poster advertising the concert in Sacramento, California, 19th June 1992

brought in some variations on bass.

Stuermer: "As I stayed in the band longer, I got to play more bass. On the We Can't Dance tour I was playing 70% bass. I would have loved to play more guitar and, yes, it was maybe a little bit frustrating." (5)

As the band played *Driving The Last Spike*, the videos on the screens showed images of Victorian railway construction workers, while for *Home By The Sea* there was no shortage of special effects, including a haunted house on the screen which kept changing colour, although often pausing on a bright red, and at times the faces of three ghosts appeared, desperately trying to materialise through the wall, but every time they were about to break through they were dragged back inside.

Other characteristic tracks were *Domino*, during the second part of which Phil would sing standing on a platform raised high above the stage in the centre of the three screens now joined together, *Jesus He Knows Me*, for which Phil gave a fantastic portrayal of a TV evangelist, included a new guitar solo from Daryl, and *Hold On My Heart*, again with Phil seated, was performed in an extended version even more similar to Collins' solo work.

Phil once again confirmed his position of consummate showman. For *I Can't Dance*, as well as the dance from the video (with the help of Daryl

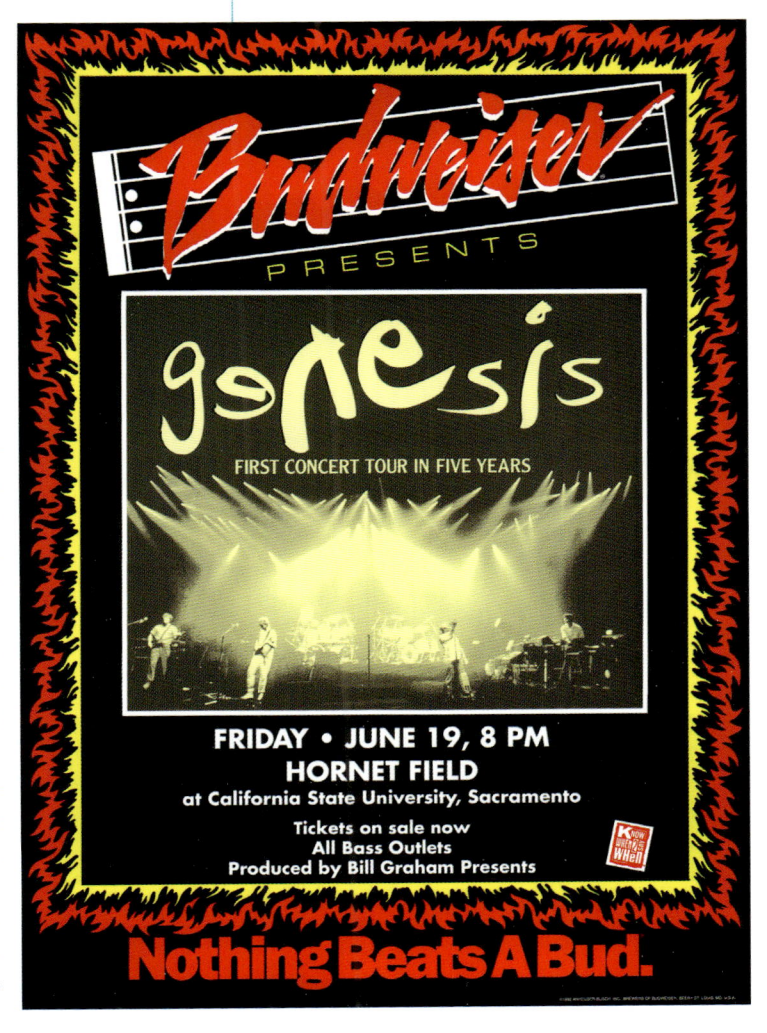

GENESIS

Tony in Hanover, 13th July 1992

and Mike), Collins clowned around with great expertise, imitating the sound of a harmonica with his mouth, grabbing his crotch and taking the mickey out of himself when doing 'the perfect face'.

However, after the first few dates problems began to arise, starting with the Tampa concert on 17 May. After just two songs (*Land Of Confusion* and *No Son Of Mine*) Phil was forced to announce, much to the consternation of the audience, that due to issues with his voice the concert would have to end there.

As of the next show, in Washington on the 19th, *Mama* (the most difficult song of all to sing) was dropped from the setlist and would only return on one occasion. In fact, the track was performed for the last time, albeit in a different position in the setlist (between *Jesus He Knows Me* and *Home By The Sea*) at Foxborough on 28 May, a date which also saw a change regarding *Throwing It All Away*: added, as already mentioned, as the second to last encore very early on in the tour, it was brought a lot higher up in the running order, now being performed directly after *Old Medley*, a position it would retain for the rest of the tour.

The other setlist variation seen in the North American tour concerns *Dreaming While You Sleep*: in the Cleveland concert on 25 May it was moved

Poster promoted by Volkswagen, the sponsor of the European tour. The famous motor car company even manufactured a new model called Genesis

Devinez comment s'appelle le nouveau modèle hors-série du Coupé Polo?

genesis

two places down the running order to be performed straight after *Jesus He Knows Me*, but was then dropped completely for seven shows, returning only on 5 June in Syracuse and only for five more shows. From Edmonton (12 June) onwards, the song was definitively dropped, apparently as a sign of respect towards an American fan who was killed by a hit and run driver just like the girl in Mike's lyrics.

The last curious fact concerns the Philadelphia concert on 31 May, where, probably due to Phil having problems with his voice, the band didn't do the *Turn It On Again* encore.

The North American tour was economically big business, with massive takings at each date and with stops in most of the American states: from Indiana to Ohio, Michigan to Massachusetts, Pennsylvania to New Jersey, Wisconsin to Minnesota, California to Illinois and a handful of dates in neighbouring Canada. In some cities, such as Philadelphia, East Rutherford and Tinley Park in Illinois, one stadium date wasn't enough and two nights were scheduled.

With the North American leg of the tour over, the band had just two days off before starting out on the European leg (sponsored by Volkswagen). The first show was in Belgium on 28 June at the Rock Werchter festival, where a minor incident occurred: Phil was booed after he began to tell the story of the American preacher in French, something which didn't go down quite as well as expected due to most of the audience being Flemish. Upset by the crowd's reaction, he stopped his introduction, threw away his notes and simply said that the next track was *Jesus He Knows Me*.

The setlist for the European tour was by this time definitive and no variations were recorded. *Land Of Confusion / No Son Of Mine / Driving The Last Spike / Old Medley (Dance On A Volcano – The Lamb Lies Down On Broadway – The Musical Box – Firth Of Fifth – I Know What I Like) / Throwing It All Away / Fading Lights / Jesus He Knows Me / Home By The Sea / Hold On My Heart / Domino / Drum Duet / I Can't Dance* with *Tonight, Tonight, Tonight – Invisible Touch* and *Turn It On Again* as encores.

Twenty-two concerts were scheduled for the old world, but these were not without their trials and tribulations. After the first concert in Belgium, the tour was due to move on to France for two shows followed by three in Germany. However, at this time French lorry drivers had decided to strike and proceeded to blockade the borders with their trucks, wreaking imaginable consequences on the tour. The Paris show, originally planned for 1 July, had to be moved to the following day, while the Munich show, originally on the 5th, had to be postponed with knock-on effects for the rest of the

GENESIS

Nice, 19th July 1992

itinerary. The official schedule has 7 July down as Gothenburg, Sweden, but this too was moved to the day after, which was the date originally planned for the show at the Gentofte Stadion in Copenhagen (which ended up being cancelled altogether).

The tour then went on for more dates in Germany from 10 to 17 July with a quick detour into Austria (16 July, Vienna). Three shows were held in Hanover (oddly enough with a show in Berlin in between on the 12th), whereas the 17th was reserved for the Munich show which had been postponed due to the protests staged by the truckers in France (66,000 tickets had already been sold). This in turn led to the only concert on Italian soil, scheduled for the 18th at the Stadio delle Alpi in Turin, being cancelled. The official version gave logistics as a reason, stating that it wasn't possible

Genesis on the cover of the British television and radio listings magazine *Radio Times*, the issue covered broadcasts from 1st-7th August 1992

to get the gear from Munich to Turin in time. However, especially when you consider the fact that in 1992 Genesis managed to insert shows in different cities in the middle of a string of concerts in the same location (as was the case with Syracuse and Hanover), it seems highly unlikely that the well-oiled touring machine was unable to cope with a distance of just 600 kilometres. The real reason behind the cancellation was in fact due to poor ticket sales; the just over 10,000 seats sold in advance definitely did not justify such an enormous financial risk. Undeniable proof of this lies in the fact that the tour convoy actually pulled up in Nice, France, which paradoxically, due to the greater distance and heavier traffic, is a couple of hours further away from Munich than Turin.

The concert in Nice on 19 July, for which tickets to the cancelled Turin show were also valid (which explains why droves of Italians descended on the Côte d'Azur), was followed by the second French show in Montpellier on the 20th, a particularly sad day for the band due to the death of stage engineer, Dixie Swanson, who suffered a fatal heart attack.

On 22 July Genesis played at the Estádio José Alvalade in Lisbon, the band's first show in Portugal since the days of THE LAMB tour, while the concert scheduled for the 24th in Madrid was cancelled.

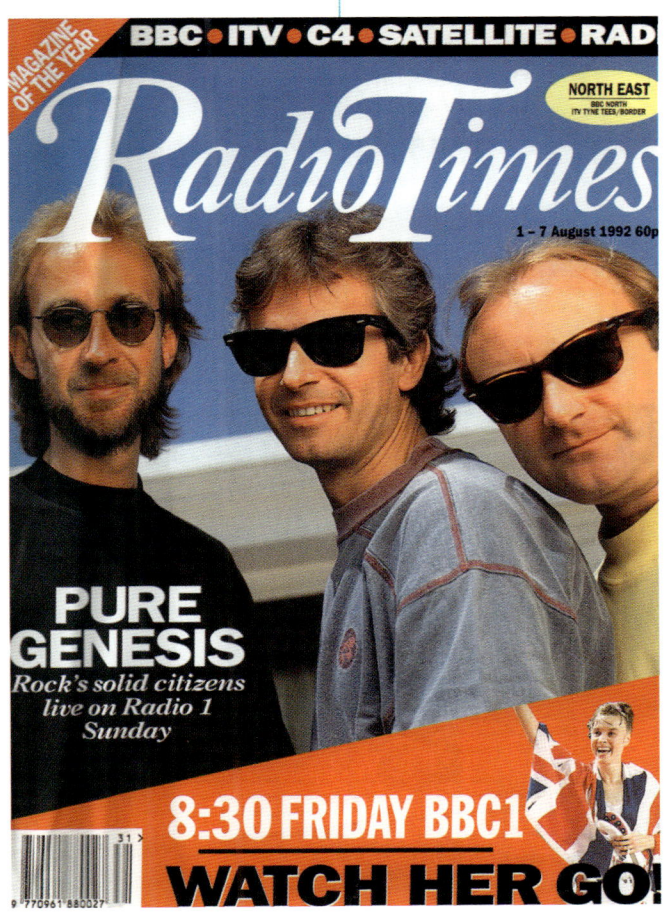

The last week of the European tour was spent crossing Switzerland (Basel), Germany (again – Cologne and Kiel) and the Netherlands (Rotterdam) before finally returning to home soil. On 31 July the band played at Roundhay Park in Leeds, which should have been followed by two concerts at Knebworth on the first two days of August. The first of the two, however, was cancelled, which meant a concentration of 100,000 ecstatic fans were present at the final show of the tour on 2 August. This show was aired on both radio and TV.

Then, when it seemed like the tour was done

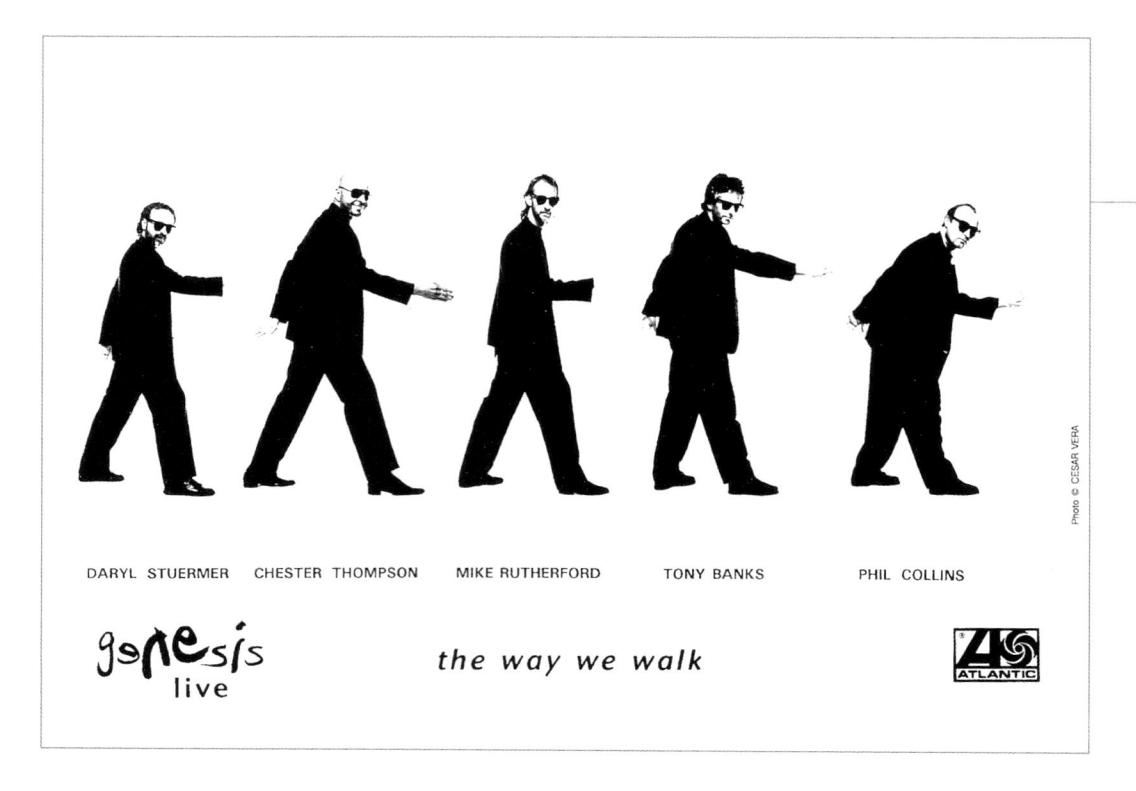

DARYL STUERMER   CHESTER THOMPSON   MIKE RUTHERFORD   TONY BANKS   PHIL COLLINS

genesis live — the way we walk

and dusted, Genesis unexpectedly announced a theatre tour of the UK. Quite a risky decision from a certain point of view: at this time the band was one of the most prestigious acts in the world and just back from a triumphant stadium tour attended by millions of fans: how were they planning to do shows in theatres with a very limited audience capacity? But the lure of having closer contact with the audience for the first time in 12 years (since the DUKE tour) was stronger than any concerns the band may have had and, in the blink of an eye, fifteen or so dates were organised. At the same time, THE WAY WE WALK, VOLUME 1: THE SHORTS, the album recorded in July in Hanover containing live versions of the band's biggest hits was released.

The theatre tour started out at the Mayflower Theatre in Southampton, where the audience was given a real treat: the only performance in the whole tour of *The Carpet Crawlers* halfway through the setlist (between *Jesus He Knows Me* and *Home By The Sea*). The Southampton show also marked the last performance of *Throwing It All Away*, already shelved as of Newcastle on 28 October (because the concerts in Newport and Wolverhampton, scheduled for the 25th and 26th, were postponed to later in the year, again due to Phil having some issues with his voice).

As well as *Throwing It All Away*, in Newcastle Genesis also dropped another song, *Driving The Last Spike*, albeit not definitively (it would occasionally reappear), taking the *Old Medley* to third place in the running order. It was replaced by the return of *Dreaming While You Sleep* (played between *Jesus He Knows Me* and *Home By The Sea*).

The highlight of the tour was the six concerts at Earls Court from 2 to 8 November (with the 5th being a day off). Despite a moment of panic caused by a bomb scare on the 6th (resulting in a slight delay to the start of the show), the marathon of shows in the famous London venue was a veritable triumph: all the concerts (which were recorded and filmed for a video) were sold out way ahead of the dates with an incredible 90,000 tickets sold.

The band were back in London shortly after-

Atlantic press photo advertising the live albums THE WAY WE WALK, USA 1993

wards, on 16 November, for a prestigious event linked to the Prince's Trust. The concert at the Royal Albert Hall was supposed to be the glorious ending to a magnificent tour, but in the end that particular honour went to the city of Wolverhampton on the 17th due to the rescheduling of the concert originally planned for 26 October (the postponed Newport show in Wales had been rescheduled for 11 November).

With the incredibly successful WE CAN'T DANCE tour over, Genesis once again bade each other farewell so everyone, especially Phil, could pursue their solo projects. In the meantime, fans were able to console themselves with memories of the recently finished tour thanks to a second live album (THE WAY WE WALK, VOLUME 2: THE LONGS, featuring, as the title suggests, the long tracks) and THE WAY WE WALK - LIVE IN CONCERT VHS, featuring a whole concert as filmed at one of the Earls Court shows.

Both these releases came out in 1993, a year which would unexpectedly prove to be a crucial one in the band's career. The turning point arrived on 18 September, when Genesis were involved in an all-star charity show to raise funds for the King Edward VII's Hospital, organised by a committee of which Mike Rutherford was a member. The show, for which tickets were sold at exorbitant prices (to help raise funds to re-equip the hospital's X-ray department), was held in the ruins of Cowdray Castle. The impressive star-studded line-up also included Pink Floyd, Eric Clapton and Roger Taylor and John Deacon of Queen. The musicians played on stage in different combinations in the joyous spirit of improvisation (for example, Mike played bass for Pink Floyd's performance and came back on stage for an all-star band final jam together with Tony and Phil for *Gimme Some Lovin'* performed as a duet with Paul Young of Mike + The Mechanics). Genesis played five songs (*Turn It On Again, Hold On My Heart, I Can't Dance, Tonight, Tonight, Tonight* and *Invisible Touch*) with the help of Queen's Roger Taylor and Gary Wallis of Pink Floyd on drums, Tim Renwick (then part of the Pink Floyd live line-up) on bass and backing vocals, Aitch Andrew, Margo Buchanan and Chyna Gordon (for *Turn It On Again*). For Phil, forced to interrupt the recording sessions of his new album, BOTH SIDES, in order to take part in the event, this unexpected recall to the ranks would have devastating consequences.

NOTES

(1) Mike Kaufman's Genesis interviews, Chicago / London, October 2007, partially used in the bonus disc accompanying the 2008 remasters

(2) Mario Giammetti's Skype interview with Hugh Padgham, 5 February 2021, partially published in the article "Il sound degli Eighties" in Dusk, issue n. 97, May 2021

(3) Mario Giammetti's telephone interview with Mike Rutherford, 25 February 2016, partially published in the article "Senza Gabriel" in *Classic Rock*, issue n. 44, July 2016

(4) Mario Giammetti's interview with Tony Banks, London, Tony Smith Personal Management office, 29 November 2016

(5) Mario Giammetti's interview with Daryl Stuermer, Milan, Filaforum, 9 October 1997, partially published in the article "Daryl Stuermer special – intervista esclusiva", Dusk, Issue n. 24, January 1998

We Can't Dance Tour

1992

MAY
- 08 **Irving, TX (USA)**, Texas Stadium
- 09 **Houston, TX (USA)**, Astrodome
- 16 **Miami, FL (USA)**, Joe Robbie Stadium
- 17 **Tampa, FL (USA)**, Tampa Stadium
  Cancelled after two songs as Phil was sick
- 19 **Washington, D.C. (USA)**, Robert F. Kennedy Memorial Stadium
- 21 **Indianapolis, IN (USA)**, Hoosier Dome
- 22 **Columbus, OH (USA)**, Ohio Stadium - Ohio State University
- 24 **Pontiac, MI (USA)**, Pontiac Silverdome
- 25 **Cleveland, OH (USA)**, Cleveland Stadium
- 26 **Pittsburgh, PA (USA)**, Three Rivers Stadium
- 28 **Foxboro, MA (USA)**, Foxboro Stadium
- 29 **Montréal, QC (CANADA)**, Stade du Parc Olympique
- 31 **Philadelphia, PA (USA)**, Veterans Stadium

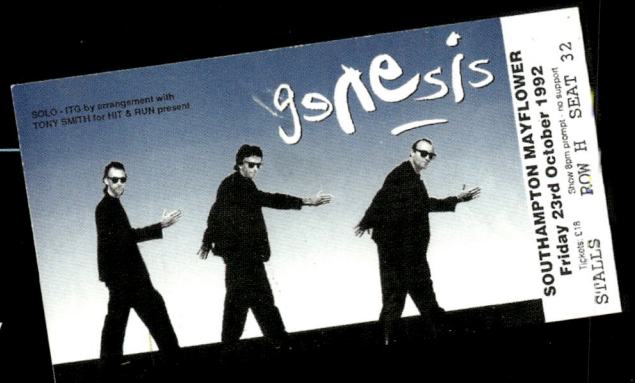

JUNE
- 01 **Philadelphia, PA (USA)**, Veterans Stadium
- 02 **East Rutherford, NJ (USA)**, Giants Stadium
- 03 **East Rutherford, NJ (USA)**, Giants Stadium
- 05 **Syracuse, NY (USA)**, Carrier Dome - Syracuse University
- 06 **Toronto, ON (CANADA)**, Skydome
- 07 **Syracuse, NY (USA)**, Carrier Dome - Syracuse University
- 09 **Madison, WI (USA)**, Camp Randall Stadium - University of Wisconsin
- 10 **Minneapolis, MN (USA)**, Hubert H. Humphrey Metrodome
- 12 **Edmonton, AB (CANADA)**, Commonwealth Stadium
- 14 **Vancouver, BC (CANADA)**, B.C. Place Stadium
- 15 **Tacoma, WA (USA)**, Tacoma Dome
- 18 **Los Angeles, CA (USA)**, Dodger Stadium
- 19 **Sacramento, CA (USA)**, Hornet Field - California State University at Sacramento
- 20 **Oakland (USA)**, Oakland-Alameda County Coliseum Arena
- 23 **Ames, IA (USA)**, Cyclone Stadium - Iowa State University
- 24 **Tinley Park, IL (USA)**, World Music Theatre
- 25 **Tinley Park, IL (USA)**, World Music Theatre
- 28 **Werchter (BELGIUM)**, Festivalpark
- 30 **Lyon (FRANCE)**, Stade Municipal de Gerland

JULY
- 02 **Paris (FRANCE)**, Hippodrome de Vincennes
  Originally scheduled for July 1, but postponed due to a truckers' strike
- 03 **Gelsenkirchen (GERMANY)**, Parkstadion
- 04 **Hockenheim (GERMANY)**, Hockenheim Ring
- 08 **Gothenburg (SWEDEN)**, Ullevi
  Originally scheduled for July 7, but postponed due to a truckers' strike
- 10 **Hannover (GERMANY)**, Niedersachsenstadion
- 11 **Hannover (GERMANY)**, Niedersachsenstadion
- 12 **Berlin (GERMANY)**, Maifeld
- 13 **Hannover (GERMANY)**, Niedersachsenstadion

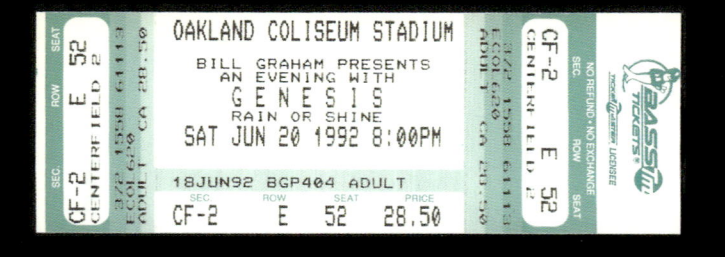

NOVEMBER

- **02** **London (ENGLAND),** Earls Court
- **03** **London (ENGLAND),** Earls Court
- **04** **London (ENGLAND),** Earls Court
- **06** **London (ENGLAND),** Earls Court
- **07** **London (ENGLAND),** Earls Court
- **08** **London (ENGLAND),** Earls Court
- **10** **Paignton (ENGLAND),** Torbay Leisure Centre
- **11** **Newport (WALES),** Newport Centre
  Originally scheduled for October 25
- **13** **Nottingham (ENGLAND),** Royal Concert Hall
- **14** **Brighton (ENGLAND),** Brighton Centre
- **16** **London (ENGLAND),** Royal Albert Hall
- **17** **Wolverhampton (ENGLAND),** Wolverhampton Civic Hall
  Originally scheduled for October 26

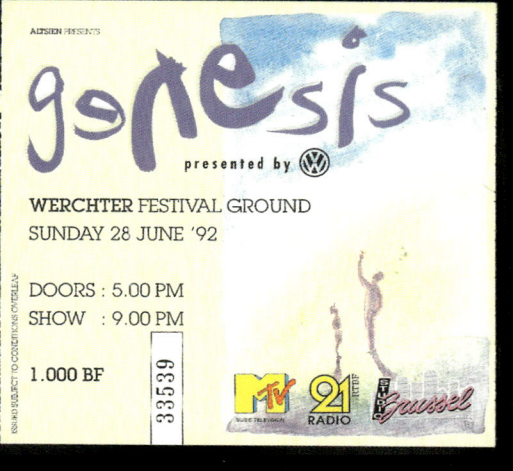

- **15** **Mannheim (GERMANY),** Maimarktgelände
- **16** **Vienna (AUSTRIA),** Praterstadion
- **17** **Munich (GERMANY),** Olympiastadion
  Originally scheduled for July 5, but postponed due to a truckers' strike
- **19** **Nice (FRANCE),** Stade de l'Ouest
- **20** **Montpellier (FRANCE),** Espace de Grammont
- **22** **Lisbon (PORTUGAL),** Estádio José Alvalade
- **26** **Basel (SWITZERLAND),** Fussballstadion St. Jakob
- **27** **Cologne (GERMANY),** Müngersdorfer Stadion
- **28** **Rotterdam (THE NETHERLANDS),** Stadion Feyenoord
- **29** **Kiel (GERMANY),** Nordmarksportfeld
- **31** **Leeds (ENGLAND),** Roundhay Park

AUGUST

- **02** **Stevenage (ENGLAND),** Knebworth Park

OCTOBER

- **23** **Southampton (ENGLAND),** Mayflower Theatre
- **28** **Newcastle (ENGLAND),** City Hall
- **29** **Edinburgh (SCOTLAND),** Edinburgh Playhouse
- **30** **Manchester (ENGLAND),** Manchester Apollo

1993

SEPTEMBER

- **18** **Midhurst (ENGLAND),** Cowdray Castle Ruins
  Charity concert for the King Edward VII Hospital. Line-up for this show was Collins, Banks, Rutherford, Roger Taylor and Gary Wallis on drums, Tim Renwick on bass. Also featuring Aitch Andrew, Margo Buchanan & Chyna Gordon on backing vocals on Turn It On Again

Calling All Stations
(Virgin 1997)

Calling All Stations (Banks/Rutherford) / Congo (Banks/Rutherford) / Shipwrecked (Banks/Rutherford) / Alien Afternoon (Banks/Rutherford) / Not About Us (Banks/Rutherford/Wilson) / If That's What You Need (Banks/Rutherford) / The Dividing Line (Banks/Rutherford) / Uncertain Weather (Banks/Rutherford) / Small Talk (Banks/Rutherford/Wilson) / There Must Be Some Other Way (Banks/Rutherford/Wilson) / One Man's Fool (Banks/Rutherford)

- Release date: 01 September 1997
- Engineer: Nick Davis
- Assistant Engineer: Ian Huffam
- Recorded at The Farm, Surrey, January to June 1997
- Technical assistance: Geoff Callingham and Mike Bowen
- General assistance: Dale Newman
- Production: Nick Davis, Tony Banks and Mike Rutherford
- Sleeve design: Wherefore ART?

- Tony Banks: keyboards
- Mike Rutherford: guitars
- Ray Wilson: vocals

- Nir Zidkyahu: drums
- Nick D'Virgilio: drums on Alien Afternoon (first half), If That's What You Need, Uncertain Weather, Small Talk

THE MAKING OF

Collins: "Prior to the We Can't Dance tour, my marriage was going slightly rocky. Because of that I guess, during the tour I let the blinkers down for a minute and I coincidently bumped, quite literally, into an old school friend of mine; she was my first girlfriend, my first real true love. We'd had plans, you know, but then that all fell apart. My marriage really was never the same after that, so my life changed completely. During all that time I was writing Both Sides, Genesis was getting bigger and broader and yet I'd done this thing that was really so personal and so inside. It was my thing and I was really totally proud of it. I didn't want anybody to play on it, I didn't want anybody else to sing on it, you know, because nobody else would understand quite what I was trying to do. So that was the reason, I finished the album and I couldn't really see myself going back. I'd tasted the forbidden fruit, if you like, and I wanted to do more." [1]

Things came to a head at the charity event in the ruins of Cowdray Castle in September 1993, where Collins found himself back in the role of Genesis' lead singer a year after the last tour had ended, and realised it wasn't really something he wanted to be doing anymore. Although he had well and truly made up his mind to leave the band, for the time being he opted not to let anyone in on his decision. The release in November 1993 of Collins' fifth album, Both Sides, was followed by a gruelling world tour which, with just a few breaks along the way, lasted from April 1994 to May 1995, taking in places like South Africa, South America, Australia and the Far East. A tour which emotionally took its toll on the singer as it was also during this time that Phil asked his second wife, Jill, for a divorce ('dumped', according to the tabloid press at the time, 'by fax').

Collins: "While on tour, in Switzerland, I met this lady who would later become my wife (*the very young Orianne Cevey – author's note*). So, you know, I moved countries. Some people put it down to being a mid-life crisis; it wasn't. I'd been in the same band for 24 years and I just wanted to do other things but couldn't because I only have 24 hours in a day." [1]

In the meantime, the other two were far from idle. In the spring of 1995, Mike + The Mechanics released their fourth album, BEGGAR ON A BEACH OF GOLD, and on the back of their hit single *Over My Shoulder*, this record (quite possibly the band's best output) was another success which the group then took out on the road in June. Starting in South Africa, the tour of over 30 dates continued well into July. Tony, on the other hand, launched yet another project, with Jack Hues, lead vocalist of Wang Chung (a band which had a hit single in the 1980s called *Dance Hall Days*), but, again, STRICTLY INC. was all but ignored by public and critics alike. To date it remains the last rock album released by the keyboard player.

Shortly afterwards, Tony and Mike were officially informed of Phil's decision to leave.

GENESIS

The handwritten fax that Phil Collins sent to the author of this book on 1st April 1996

Rutherford: "In August 1995, we sat down for lunch, Phil, Tony and I, although by the time we discussed it, we already knew he wanted to leave. We have the same manager, who'd told us Phil wanted to move on, which I think is perfectly understandable given that his career was so busy. Tony and I had a conversation about carrying on. We said, 'let's not worry about it. Let's go and do what we always do and write some new music and see if that inspires us'. So we waited until January '96 to go into the studio and the first week was great." [2]

Banks: "When Phil left, my inclination was to call it a day or wait, you know, to see if in ten years' time Phil wouldn't want to have another go. But Mike, particularly, was quite keen to just go into the studio to see what happened." [1]

With the world still oblivious to what was going on, in January 1996, Tony and Mike met up at The Farm. Banks: "So, of course, we went into the studio and started improvising and I thought it sounded really good, even though it was just the two of us." [1]

Rutherford: "When we composed the last three of four albums, Phil wanted to sing most of the time, he didn't drum until quite late on. So we tended to have Tony on keyboards, me on guitar and Phil programming a drum machine and singing. What we lost in the rehearsals wasn't the drumming, but the vocals." [2]

Nevertheless, with some encouraging results, the pair found the courage they needed to finally inform the world of the latest development. They proceeded to release a press statement, which reached newsrooms around the globe on 28 March 1996, with an unequivocal and yet cryptic headline: 'Genesis end twenty-year experiment, decide to replace Peter Gabriel as vocalist'.

Three days later, on 1 April 1996, the author of this book was surprised to receive a hand-written fax from Phil Collins in which the artist, realistically and generously said: "I realise that to many fans, my leaving will sound like the end, but I assure you it is Tony and Mike's intention to carry on and I can also assure you that the spirit of Genesis is completely safe with them, as you will see. When a group is together for such a long time, it's hard to be the one to make a change, but we still are the best of friends and that is important after so long."

So the disappointment felt by fans was at least in some way mitigated by reassurances that the band would continue to exist. That said, who could possibly replace Phil Collins who had been keeping Genesis on the crest of a wave for over fifteen years? Without knowing who would sing or who would play the drums, at the end of spring 1996, Tony and Mike began recording the backing tracks for twenty or so songs, while the management began listening to hundreds of audition tapes as part of the initial selection process to find new band members.

The battle for the job of lead vocalist was eventually whittled down to two main contenders: David Longdon and Ray Wilson.

The latter, born in Scotland in September 1968, was already active in the music business. He had been the lead singer of Scottish rock band Stiltskin (famous for the 1994 No. 1 hit *Inside* used in a Levi's TV commercial) and was by this time busy trying to establish his own band, Cut, with his brother Steve.

Wilson: "I took the Cut demos to the head of Virgin Germany (he was the person who had signed

> Dear Mario,
> thank you for your letter which I had the office fax on to me, regarding my decision to leave Genesis. I have actually been thinking of it for some time, but left the news til now. I realise that to many fans, my leaving will sound like the end, but I assure you it is Tony & Mike's intention to carry on, and I can also assure you that the spirit of Genesis is completely safe with them, as you will see. When a group is together for such a long time it is hard to be the one to make a change, but we still are the best of friends and that is important after so long.
> Anyway, my love to our fans, and to my fans and I have a record coming out at the end of the year which should please someone !!!   Luv Phil

Stiltskin). He agreed to sign us, but after a few days I received a phone call from Tony Smith asking me to audition for Genesis. I thought it was a joke, really. You don't expect that kind of phone call. I thought about it and it was difficult. I'd been writing for a year and a half and all of a sudden got a record deal, and then I was being asked to give it all up to sing for another band who had a 30-year history and who had achieved more than I ever will in my entire life. My first reaction was 'I can't do this. I have my brother and my best friend in a band'. I called my brother and he said to go for it. He said I should at least meet Mike and Tony and see if it was right for me."[3]

Longdon: "At the time I was working with another songwriter, Gary Bromham. Gary was in a band called The Big Blue who were signed to EMI and were recording their album with Nick Davis at

237

David Longdon performing with his band, The Gifthorse, Nottingham Playhouse, 1995

The Farm. Gary had played a song of mine called *Hieroglyphics Of Love* to Nick who'd liked it enough to pass it on to Tony Banks. Tony played it to Mike Rutherford and they thought it was worth a shot. I received a call from Tony Smith inviting me to come down to The Farm to audition." [4]

Obviously, getting to be the lead singer of one of the biggest rock bands in history was a tempting proposition for many. David Longdon: "I know Fish was mentioned but I don't recall him actually being auditioned. Paul Carrack wanted to do it but I'm not sure how comfortably that sat with Tony Banks. Sadly Kevin Gilbert (*an American music producer and musician who had already collaborated with Madonna, Michael Jackson and most notably with Sheryl Crow – author's note*) passed away before having the chance to audition. Francis Dunnery (It Bites) and Nick Van Eede (Cutting Crew) auditioned but it came down to being between Ray and me pretty quickly." [4]

Nick Van Eede has vivid memories of the audition process: "Out of the blue I got the call from Hit & Run Music in the early months of 1996 asking me if I wanted to audition for the job. The next day a courier arrived with a package of two audio cassette tapes and lyrics to about 10 songs. I arrived at their studio complex in Chiddingfold, Surrey, and was ushered into the control room at the studio. Tony Smith offered tea and sandwiches and of course Mike Rutherford and Tony Banks were there. One of the assurances I'd been given from their management company was that if any of the songs were in the wrong key I needn't worry: "just learn the melodies and words and the band will adjust the keys accordingly". The slightest hint of my first panic was when I looked around and it was quite obvious there was no fucking band! I'd already decided that a few of the songs were a little too high for me so I guess this could be an even more challenging day than I had expected. In fact, when I got to sing *Tonight, Tonight, Tonight* which really is at the high end of my range, I said to the engineer: 'I was hoping we could drop it down a tone...' and he wittily said 'I can put my finger on the reel to reel and slow it down a bit... is that okay?' I learned a bunch of their hits, including *Turn It On Again, Mama, I Can't Dance, No Son Of Mine* and I think *Follow You Follow Me*. My most special memory was sitting down afterwards with a guitar I found in the studio and calling Mike over and I played an edited acoustic version of *Dancing With The Moonlit Knight* craftily joined to *Carpet Crawlers*; it was a really sweet moment as he sat right next to me and sang along a little and even corrected a few of my wrong chords as well". [5]

For Francis Dunnery, the chance to sing with Genesis, even if only at an audition, was too much to resist: "Nick Davis the Genesis engineer called

Promotional picture, Virgin Records, UK 1997

me up and asked me to go down and audition. I knew in the back of my mind that I could never sing Phil's songs because he screams a lot at a very high range and my voice can't do that, but I couldn't turn down something like that so I went along because singing with Genesis is something I always wanted to do. I arrived at The Farm and I already knew from my past dealings that Mike and Tony were quite uptight so I wasn't very comfortable. They definitely don't try to make you comfortable. They are very stoic and emotionally distant which is completely different from the way I was raised and the way I am in the world. Not because they are mean, it's because that's how they were brought up. Every person you meet is wonderful at heart but we've all had things to deal with growing up that makes us fearful and defensive. Genesis are no different. The old English public schools were called 'privileged abandonment'. The parents would drop their children off at the boarding schools and not see them for months at a time. The kids were too young to be alone. They were all terrified. You had to be extremely tough in those early English public school systems. If you showed weakness you would be trampled. I think Mike and Tony had long since shut down their emotions. They learned not to open up. That's why you never hear personal songs from Genesis. They would never take the risk to expose themselves emotionally. They learned not to. It's never 'I' or 'me'. It's always someone else they sing about. So, Mike, Tony and Nick Davis the engineer was there and Nick is a nice guy. I was happy to see him. But standing in a studio with Mike Rutherford and Tony Banks staring at you is like being on trial with Stalin and Chairman Mao". [6]

Back to the two main contenders, Longdon and Wilson. At one point, the band considered the idea of hiring them both. Wilson: "The other guy sounded more like Phil Collins than I do. So, because they thought I had a Gabriel quality, they were thinking of having us both and doing what Mike + The Mechanics had done successfully with

Nick D'Virgilio's contract for the album recording sessions

Paul Carrack and Paul Young."[1]

The final decision arrived at the end of November 1996, with Ray Wilson being chosen as the replacement for Phil Collins. David Longdon, however, would be back in the limelight many years later reaping his just rewards as lead singer and multi-instrumentalist in Big Big Train, one of the best progressive rock bands of recent times.

Longdon: "At that time I had less professional experience than Ray and, because of his success with Stiltskin, he was used to being interviewed by the press."[4]

Nick Davis: "Unfortunately, Dave Longdon had never really been in a band before. So it was a hell of a leap of faith to say he could be the singer, whereas Ray he was in Stiltskin and also, he had a really nice voice. So, you know, it was down to the two of them obviously, Ray had the experience of working in a professional band, whereas Dave didn't. But you know, having heard stuff that Dave has done since I don't know, he also could have been really good."[7]

Banks: "Both had merits, obviously, but we thought Ray definitely had the better voice; it's dark and it's got a real sort of power to it when he wants to use it. It recalled Peter Gabriel's voice slightly, which was quite nice for us, and we'd consciously made the decision that this album would be a little bit heavier than the previous two records. He came on board a little bit later and some of the songs we'd already written as we normally had in the past, you know, for a voice more like Phil's. Ray's voice is different and it didn't necessarily lend itself to some of the songs we had, so a few things didn't work so well. But the tone quality of his voice was great on *There Must Be Some Other Way* and on *Not About Us*."[1]

Rutherford: "The slow, powerful moments suit Ray's voice really well. What he wasn't very good at (and he would agree) was letting rip to get fast staccato, aggressive singing. That's his nature really."[1]

Finding a replacement drummer was an equally laborious task. Rutherford: "We had a big list of drummers which included some of the top American session drummers but we wanted someone with less history."[2]

Not even, their old friend, Chester Thompson's volunteering for the job succeeded in arousing much enthusiasm. Rutherford: "When you have a change, it's rather nice to change completely; it brings new energy into the group. Chester never played on the albums and, to be honest, he's a fantastic drummer but I don't think he's the right drummer on an album; we need someone a bit heavier."[2]

To play the drum parts, initially set on the drum machine by Tony and Mike, two musicians were called in from two completely different worlds, both geographically and musically: Israeli, Nir Zidkyahu and Nick D'Virgilio, then a member of upcoming American progressive rock band, Spock's Beard.

D'Virgilio: "Kevin Gilbert called me in London because he heard Phil had quit and said I should try and get an audition. I found out where the Hit & Run offices were located in London (*the publishing house which managed Genesis – author's note*) and went there with a Spock's Beard CD, THE LIGHT (the only one we had out at the time and the only thing I had recorded in my career at that point). I was on the road with Tears For Fears so I invited everyone

27 NOV '96 15:55 HIT & RUN MUSIC 0171 584 5774   P.1

TELEFAX TRANSMISSION

27 November, 1996

To: Nick D'Virgillio
        001818 795 1430
        001415 546 9411

From: Carol Willis Impey

Re: GENESIS RECORDING

hit&run music

Dear Nick,

Thank you for your fax of yesterday confirming your availability for the later recording dates. I have now booked your flight as follows:-

Friday 6th December	BA282	Departing LAX	17.15
Saturday 7th December		Arriving LHR	11.30 Terminal 4
Saturday 14th December	BA283	Departing LHR	12 Noon Terminal 4
		Arriving LAX	15.00

LOCATOR NUMBER T6QISL

As discussed with James Wyllie, you fees will be £1,000 per day commencing on Monday 8th December to Saturday 14 December inclusive. Please address your invoice to Gelring Limited reference Genesis Recording. You will be paid a per diem of £30.00 per day commencing Friday 6 December to Saturday 14 December inclusive. The recording fees will be wire transferred direct into your account; please supply account name, account number, bank sort code, address etc. The per diem will be paid in cash by Dale Newman at Fisherlane Farm.

You will stay at Fisherlane Farm, Fisher Lane, Chiddingfold, Surrey.
   Tel 0142868 4475. Fax -0142868 4947

Should you have any queries please do not hesitate to contact me.

Regards,

Carol
c.c.   James Wyllee 0181 742 7789
        Fisher Lane Farm 0142868 4947

in the office to the show. I didn't see anybody at the show, but I did end up getting a phone call from Nick Davis about six months later asking for some other things I had recorded. I sent them whatever I could find and they called back to say they wanted me to come and audition. They flew me to the UK and I went to The Farm and jammed with Tony and Mike. I was on cloud nine!"[8]

Zidkyahu: "I had a band in New York and we signed a publishing deal with Hit & Run Music. Tony Smith came to see us play live and he really liked the band. A year and a half later I got a phone call saying Genesis were looking for a new drummer and they would like to audition me. To be quite honest, I really thought it was a joke. I was really confused because the band I was playing in was a young, alternative rock band. I knew their music but, with all due respect, I was never a fanatic fan; I didn't have all their records, although they were a part of my musical education, my musical experience, and, of course, I knew Phil Collins; he was one of the most original, unique drummers I'd ever heard."[1]

The Israeli drummer, who ended up recording most of the songs on the album, has quite an aggressive style. Zidkyahu: "I think that's really the only reason they called me. I was never one of those progressive drummers, you know. I've never had one of those huge drum kits and I didn't really want to play complex music, you know, even though I can and I could, that wasn't my goal. And I think probably my energy and my approach to rhythm and supporting a song made Tony Smith go, 'okay, I think it can work'."[1]

The change in drummer also imposed a few changes to the way the band worked.

Rutherford: "In the past when the drums were being recorded, I kind of made tea, you know. I didn't have to worry about that part. And now here we were, Tony and myself, being asked by Nir how we wanted it, what kind of beat we wanted... And that was a little hard actually because it's not really our area; I mean, we had our opinions but we always knew Phil would get it right."[1]

Wilson: "I thought Nir brought a great energy to the band. He would almost stand up to hit a cymbal, just so he could hit it that bit harder. I loved that rock drumming, you know, and I know Mike and Tony loved it because that's what Phil has. Nir's Israeli, he's quite a hot-blooded character, a bit like me, you know, being Scottish."[1]

Wilson also appears in the writing credits, albeit marginally because he arrived after most of the work had already been done.

Banks: "Writing as a two-piece was quite difficult. Obviously I write on my own all the time, as does Mike, but when there are two of you, one has got to hold down the riff while the other guy does everything else."[1]

Rutherford: "Phil has a real natural ability to get musical phrases that work very well over shorter songs and that's not something Tony and I do. Nor Ray. So you have to just deal with what you have and see where it takes you."[1]

New musicians aside, the album reveals a very different Genesis. Musically speaking, contrary to what many expected, Phil Collins' departure did not lead to an expansion in the band's instrumental spectrum. If anything, compared to WE CAN'T DANCE, there is a significant drop in solos.

Rutherford: "We both wanted to do a lot more instrumentally but the main problem on this album was to write the songs and to make Ray's voice work on them. That was the thing to get right. In doing that we forgot the instrumental pieces; we actually had one or two songs we didn't finish… we just ran out of energy. The funny thing is, we'd set out to do the same thing when Peter left; initially we were going to do a mainly instrumental album but ended up with an album of songs." [2]

The changes also impacted the lyrics.

Rutherford: "The thread is communication and isolation. I feel that communication is improving so much at the moment. You can receive all this information in your home as it happens, which is wonderful, but no one is teaching us how to deal with it all. So it actually becomes *more* difficult to communicate." [2]

THE ALBUM

Five years between INVISIBLE TOUCH and WE CAN'T DANCE, six and a half, no less, between the latter and CALLING ALL STATIONS. A period of time during which the rock world had yet again undergone a sea-change.

In 1992, the veterans were still dominating the scene. Bruce Springsteen brought out two albums simultaneously (HUMAN TOUCH and LUCKY TOWN) and Eric Clapton released UNPLUGGED, which would become the best-selling live album of all time, while, in September, Roger Waters and Peter Gabriel were back respectively with AMUSED TO DEATH and US. The year also saw the release of DRY, the debut album of the English rock singer-songwriter, PJ Harvey, while Dream Theater released IMAGES AND WORDS, their first album with new lead vocalist, James LaBrie, confirming their position as champions of prog metal.

1993 showed signs of unrest. Radiohead brought out their debut album, PABLO HONEY, and (former Sugarcubes lead singer) Bjork released her first solo album, DEBUT, The Smashing Pumpkins took off with their second album, SIAMESE DREAM, but, above all, it was the year of the third and final studio album by Nirvana, IN UTERO. This would come to represent the touchstone of grunge, a style that had been dominating the music scene since the beginning of the 1990s, also thanks to other bands such as Pearl Jam, Soundgarden, Alice In Chains, to name just a few. An era which symbolically ended in April 1994 when Kurt Cobain committed suicide.

1994 was also the year in which Green Day released DOOKIE, launching a new wave of punk rock, Oasis made their debut with the hugely successful DEFINITELY MAYBE and Jeff Buckley, son of the legendary Tim, released GRACE, which would become an even more poignant testament when, like his father, he died tragically young (he accidentally drowned in a river in 1997). And while English journalist, Simon Reynolds, coined the term 'post-rock' to label bands such as Tortoise, Mogwai and Don Caballero, the old supergroups were left trailing. Yes (in the Trevor Rabin formation) released TALK, while both Emerson, Lake & Palmer (IN THE HOT SEAT) and Pink Floyd (THE DIVISION BELL) brought out what would be their last studio albums.

Historic bands were still trying to stay afloat in 1995, with the passable ROOTS TO BRANCHES by Jethro Tull and yet another last-ditch effort from King Crimson, now a cacophonous double trio who, with their album THRAK, seemed to be leaning more towards Tool than towards progressive rock.

The phenomenon of 1996, on the other hand, has to go to the lo-fi style of Beck with his album Odelay in a year which also saw the release of Phil Collins' first album as a full-time solo artist since leaving Genesis (Dance Into The Light) and Porcupine Tree's Signify (possibly the best effort by the band headed by the new prog idol, Steven Wilson), not to mention the growing assertion in the States of the new rap/hip hop scene with the debut albums of Eminem (Infinite) and Lil' Kim (Hard Core).

Preceded a few months earlier by albums that were ground-breaking for different reasons, such as OK Computer by Radiohead and The Fat Of The Land by the electronic dance band, The Prodigy, Calling All Stations sought desperately to carry Genesis into the new millennium. In this it was only partially successful. The innovative sound elements consist mainly of decidedly harder and darker atmospheres. Rutherford's electric guitars (often filtered through the keyboards) have never been so heavy, while Banks adds the odd layer of strings, in some way reminiscent of the old days, as is the use, albeit limited, of the acoustic guitar. But these are mere palliatives which failed to please those fans (of which there were many) who, for some unexplainable reason, were expecting things to go back to being more progressive following Phil's departure.

Of course, Ray Wilson's amazing voice manages to steer towards a less poppy area, as clearly seen in the exceptional title track and *Uncertain Weather*, but the substance of certain tracks (*Congo, Small Talk, If That's What You Need*) is clearly lacking, whereas at other times (above all in *There Must Be Some Other Way* and *One Man's Fool*) all the good intentions seem to fall by the wayside with compositions which somehow fail to hit the mark.

The lyrics on the other hand, which talk about difficulties in relationships and communication, are beyond reproach. The sense of disorientation expressed in the title track, the feeling out of place in *Shipwrecked*, the idea of demarcation in *The Dividing Line*, the communication breakdown in *If That's What You Need* and *There Must Be Some Other Way* make it an outstanding album in terms of lyrics.

Clearly an album of transition, stylistically unique in the Genesis catalogue, Calling All Stations should really have been followed up by another album if the new line-up were to have had any chance of becoming a closer-knit unit and realising its true potential.

THE SONGS

CALLING ALL STATIONS

An ultra-distorted guitar riff, almost hard rock, tears open the atmosphere over dry drum strokes and a supporting keyboard. The chord change to the major key introduces Ray's voice. A track that echoes the atmospheres of *No Son Of Mine*, both on the rhythmic level and for the cyclical repetitions of bass and electric guitar, it is enriched by Tony's sumptuous chord changes, a strange insert with electronic percussion and a short but intense solo from Rutherford on guitar.

Banks: "A dramatic, kind of traditional Genesis song, I suppose, in terms of the chords and the rhythm and vocals that slightly echoed more earlier Genesis. Towards the end of the song, it really lifts and gets a fantastic sound about it." [1]

Calling All Stations

Shooting the video for *Congo* in Malta, 2nd July 1997

Rutherford: "The opening track was meant to be something that showed our darker side and that kind of melody really suits Ray's voice." [1]

Wilson: "I fought hard for this to become the opening track because I think they wanted to open it with *Congo*, because it was the first single, or *Shipwrecked*. I said that *Calling All Stations* just sounded like an authentic Genesis song to me and it's a bit heavier than the other two. It's always stood out for me; it just had an energy about it and I sang it well. For me it was like the *Mama* track of the album, it had that same drama about it. Mike came up with the melody and lyrics. It's quite a long song and it just seems to get higher and higher and higher. When I go into the studio… I'm not one of those artists that takes five hours to get the vocal right; if I haven't got it in two or three takes then, quite frankly, I'm not gonna get it. I remember with these songs, I'd sing them two or three times and then Nick Davis would kind of comp together the best from each take. The last take I did of *Calling All Stations* was the one that just took everything I had. You know, I was singing from the pits of my stomach. Singing that song live was a real challenge, a bit like *Mama* was for Phil." [1]

CONGO

To introduce the general public to the new Genesis, a rather insipid, poppy song was chosen as the first single, very similar in style to much of

Tony's solo work with an opening full of percussion and vocals which sound like they should be part of an African ritual of some kind.

Rutherford: "It was a sample thing Tony had. It's slowed down and he fiddled with it a lot and made it sound very different. I play a synthesised 12-string guitar sound on this." [2]

The uninspired keyboard solo adds absolutely nothing to the track.

Banks: "We edited it down for the single. The end bit, I don't know, I don't like it very much. I don't know that there were any other singles on the album really. I always thought the chorus worked well with Ray's voice but we didn't get any radio play. It's hard to know if it was a good choice or not; it never got played, so you can't tell." [9]

SHIPWRECKED

Rutherford: "This is one of my favourite songs on the album, although looking back, we could have recorded the backing track a lot better. Nick Davis is mainly an engineer but also a producer. Had we had a real producer who was more capable, in terms of trying to get ideas and develop songs, we probably could have done a better version. But it's a very nice mood and *Shipwrecked* is a nice title." [1]

Wilson: "Mike wasn't sure about the title, because, for him, *Shipwrecked* is such an ugly word to sing. He said it just didn't sound right, although he liked the message it delivered. So he said, 'Could you sing it so I can hear what the word sounds like with a singer singing it?'; he wasn't quite sure if the most important word of the song would actually sound right." [1]

The song starts with a guitar riff and drums which sound like they are coming through a radio speaker.

Banks: "Mike played this little riff which sounded really good, I sampled it and screwed it up to make this sort of very thin sound. Then we sort of wrote the song around this riff." [1]

Zidkyahu: "It was a combination of drum machine and live drums. If I'm not mistaken I did the overdubs on this, meaning there was a drum machine playing and I played the hi-hat, cymbals and drum fills over the top of it, so that was a typical Genesis production. Collins has done that many times: there is a drum machine playing and then there are live drums playing along with it. I'm not sure if it was Tony or Mike who came up with the drum pattern but, you know, they liked it and it really worked for the song, it has this kind of train groove." [1]

The song has a deeply melancholy mood which transmits the state of mind of people feeling distressed and out of place, an aspect which is illustrated magnificently in the accompanying video.

Banks: "I always felt there was a better song in there somewhere. Mike wrote the lyric to that and I didn't feel it quite hit the mark." [9]

ALIEN AFTERNOON

A song which is decidedly the combination of two separate parts: the first features a quirky riff and an irregular rhythm dictated by the drumming of Nick D'Virgilio, who brings the last beat on the snare forward by a half-beat at the end of every bar, while the second part (with Nir on drums) has a more symphonic sound, with an effective guitar solo from Mike in the background.

Zidkyahu: "Tony said that he would love to get back to the old Genesis approach, and if you listen to the instrumental section in this song, it really takes you back to the Genesis progressive music of the '70s which made them what they are." [1]

Banks: "For me this track didn't really work. I liked the sound of the opening part and the second half is good; the bit where the introduction is repeated but with the vocal on it is very good. But I don't really like the first half; I wrote the lyrics and I think they're pretty bad. Since coming into this business I'd always wanted to start a song with the words 'I woke up this morning', you know, that standard start to a song that all the old blues guys used to use, so I thought it would be great to use it here, but it didn't really work. I love the end, but had it been Phil singing, he would have done much more with the improvised vocals. I wrote all the so-called improvised vocals on that for Ray and he sang it which is fine. But I'm not a singer and I thought he or someone else would have done more with it. The same thing happened on the last track, *One Man's Fool*; again on the end of that I needed someone to run with it more than Ray did." [9]

NOT ABOUT US

A ballad driven by a six-string acoustic guitar which is then bolstered by the keyboards and Ray's husky voice. Soft, light drumming enters from the second verse and, after a synth lead variation, Mike adds another guitar but this time an arpeggio on electric.

Wilson: "It sounds like a basic singer-songwriter song. Actually, it's got a bit of Mike + The Mechanics about it, in a way. The interesting thing about it is that the chords in the chorus take on such a strange order; you never know what the next chord is, which is something very typical of Genesis: just when you think you know where you're going next, it doesn't go there, it's something slightly different, another inversion or the bass note changes. It sounds such a simple song, but try playing it and remembering it; that's a whole different kettle of fish." [1]

Rutherford: "Ray was involved in writing the lyrics and, together with *Small Talk*, it's lyrically one of his best moments on the album. You could see what he was starting to do and could have done." [1]

Wilson: "I remember Mike jamming his part and I had this 'little piece of something falling gently down, down, down' part which we used without really knowing what the hell we were singing about. To this day we still don't know what we were writing about but lyrically it was a combination of Mike's and my words." [1]

IF THAT'S WHAT YOU NEED

A keyboard arrangement featuring romantic strings over a guitar riff: a song which is clearly Mike's using the classic Rutherford song-writing technique already tried and tested with The Mechanics. The words are also Mike's, a letter to his wife, Angie, apologising for all their communication difficulties.

Wilson: "*If That's What You Need* always sounded to me like it should be on a Mike and the Mechanics album. I like the song, but I always hear Paul Carrack singing it, in my head. I always felt the bridge in the song could have been a bit different, but apart from that, it works very well". [10]

THE DIVIDING LINE

Banks: "Mike had this drum thing going and I started playing this Bo Diddley type of thing. It sounded really strong so we used that as a basis. Then there was a second bit where I started doing this fuzzy keyboard stuff that sounded quite good too. It was mostly an instrumental track and then we put the vocals on it. Mike wrote a lyric on it that was kind of OK."[9]

The track opens with a synth bass which is quickly supported by flashy drumming on top of which Mike's heavy-handed guitar playing does a couple of rounds before the glorious entry of Tony on a keyboard string sound and with a second synth to provide an element of rhythm. Despite the song containing swathes of instrumental sections, it is basically without any solos as Tony and Mike limit themselves to playing rhythmic riffs, although there is a section dominated by the drums.

Zidkyahu: "It was like being a kid in a candy store. It doesn't happen very often that people tell you, 'OK, you can hit whatever drum you want on this song', you know, usually less is more. I think that was one of the tracks that got me the gig really, because I played it when I did the audition and, if I'm not mistaken, I had to study my own part from the audition because I'd just improvised but they liked many of those parts, so when we officially recorded the album, I had to listen to my audition and it was like, 'OK, what the hell did I play there?'. I put my own signature on this track, you know, because this is me, this is something I just came up with. I didn't think about it, I didn't plan it, I didn't write down any part; before the first downbeat of the song I didn't know really what I was going to play. That's the beauty of music, you know, it does happen; there are producers out there who will let you do that."[1]

UNCERTAIN WEATHER

Banks: "This is a classic sort of Genesis piece and I think it would stand up on any other Genesis album. Big chorus and build-up, you know, and just a lovely sort of feel and good drumming."[1]

The song developed from a drum pattern set up by Mike.

Banks: "He wrote a lot of stuff on that, which was a slight weakness, but this was a nice part and I started just playing along with it and wrote the whole song, the melody and lyrics on top of that."[9]

The strongest moment in the track is the chorus; Wilson's voice is really moving, while Tony's powerful keyboards supply a succession of beautiful chords and a touch of class is provided by Mike's 12-string arpeggios, something that had been largely absent since the time of DUKE. And Nick D'Virgilio gives an impressive performance on drums.

Banks: "When we auditioned for drummers initially Nick played along to this song and it sounded great. We always wanted to use him on this track whatever else we did with the other things. The sad thing is, Nick never really told us he could sing. Having listened to the versions he did of THE LAMB LIES DOWN ON BROADWAY (*on REWIRING GENESIS – A TRIBUTE TO THE LAMB LIES DOWN ON BROADWAY, a double album featuring various artists released in 2009 – author's note*) I can say he's got a great voice, an incredible

Nick D'Virgilio at Real World with Peter Gabriel, October 14th 1997

range, and though we might have still had Ray, the combination of the two of them would have been great. I think he could have done some things better, he could have run with the end of the songs, his voice is higher. I've met him a few times since then and each time I've said, 'why didn't you tell us you could sing?'. 'I was hired as a drummer', he says. But his drumming is really strong on that track and makes it a great piece of music." [9]

Whilst Nick's time with Genesis was over, there was a short second act in October 1997 when he was recruited for a session with Peter Gabriel at Real World studios. D'Virgilio: "The big difference from recording with Peter to recording with Mike and Tony is that Peter played along and jammed with me. He played electric piano and sang and then and the end of the track we just jammed. What an experience!" [8]

The lyrics to *Uncertain Weather* (by Tony) are also interesting. Banks: "I've always liked this photograph idea, you know, you find an old photograph and you have no idea who the person is and you start building a life for them, what might he or she have been, what did they do. It has a wistful quality about it, nostalgic… how life might have been…" [9]

SMALL TALK

A disappointing track, although it is a bit more upbeat than usual, with a pulsating bass and the typical later Genesis brass sounds of Tony's keyboards.

Banks: "This was not a song that I particularly remembered after the album was recorded. I didn't really think about it very much, but when we were doing the remixes and the 5.1 version of it I thought, 'this is a really good song'. I really enjoyed it almost more than all the others. Which just shows really, sometimes songs come out the woodwork and you think it was worth it, this was good." [1]

Ray not only sings it really well, but he is also the sole author of the lyrics.

Wilson: "It always had that *Solsbury Hill* feel about it (*a Peter Gabriel song – author's note*). I love that song. I remember listening to the backing track and thinking it had quite an unusual sound to it and I came up with a couple of ideas for it. It's quite a quirky song, certainly not one of my favourites I have to say. I think *Run Out Of Time* would have been a better song on the album than *Small Talk*; I would have swapped them." [1]

THERE MUST BE SOME OTHER WAY

The introduction is steeped in a markedly percussive atmosphere with synth strings and a bass that is slightly more to the fore. Ray's voice is very intense in the quieter moments and then becomes really hard in the chorus, reminiscent of his past with Stiltskin, and the distorted guitar certainly plays its part. After the second verse, there is a long instrumental section with powerful drumming which also contains Tony's only real solo on the whole album.

Banks: "The chords have this very sort of yearning quality. It's about how something might have been, how it was and all the rest of it. The instrumental break in the middle of the song is quite interesting and probably the nicest instrumental part of the album really. It's a jerky kind of thing which is slightly different to what we'd done in the past." [1]

Wilson: "I wrote this with Tony Banks. I had the chorus, he had the verse. It was more my type of song; a little darker, more menacing and a bit more sinister. I sang 'there must be some other way' repeatedly during the second audition I did. Tony took that idea and then wrote lyrics based on divorce. I don't know why he was writing about that, maybe a friend of his had just been through it or whatever, I don't know." [1]

Banks: "That particular line was something Ray improvised when we were writing the songs. Being as everyone around me seemed to be going through a divorce I had the idea of writing about it, you know, all the stuff people go through, all the pettiness that creeps in. And I just thought there must be some other way. The verses relate to different aspects of divorce. Depressing really, isn't it?" [1]

An approach which is light years away from the old Genesis lyrics. Banks: "On this album all the lyrics I wrote had a more adult look at life, I wasn't trying to write like a teenager. I haven't been divorced myself but so many people around us had been through it and it always seemed so difficult. It always seemed to end up with discussions about who owned what, the 'this is mine' – 'no it's not', kind of thing. The triteness of it and yet you are going through such an awful thing." [9]

ONE MAN'S FOOL

The album ends on its longest track (almost 9 minutes), but even this, at the end of the day, leaves the listener somewhat perplexed in terms of the overall result. Mike does a good job over the programmed percussion, both on arpeggioed electric guitar and on bass, then when the drums make a hefty entrance Tony launches into a synth brass riff which characterises the whole piece. The second part features a more relaxed repeated section which leads up to the conclusion with a constant guitar riff.

Banks: "Compositionally it's the song that I was most excited about. I thought it was going to be the standout track on the album. I think the first half of the song works really well, the second half, in a musical sense, doesn't quite get there. I know it could have been a fantastic classic Genesis piece but the vocal wasn't quite right and perhaps the drums... it needed what Phil would have given to it, I think. It's a curious lyric, a weird one really, because it's about terrorism and religious fanaticism. The first half of the song could have been a direct description of what occurred on 9/11, but of course written 4 years before. A lot of people have mentioned it actually. It's kind of slightly uncanny." [1]

OTHER SONGS

Rutherford: "We wrote over two hours of music. Eleven songs went on the album then there were four more finished songs which sounded pretty good and four more which really weren't finished. You couldn't have too much on an album, it becomes too long." [2]

Wilson: "I remember songs called *Sign Your Life Away, Anything Now, Run Out Of Time*, all good songs, but there was a bit of pressure not to turn it into a double album. When I joined up there were around 26 songs so we had to discipline ourselves a bit." [3]

Banks: "There are a few moments on the album that I wasn't really keen on and again, the tracks we didn't use were some of the strongest tracks. Mike and I did argue about this really. " [9]

Seven of the songs recorded during the CALLING ALL STATIONS sessions were edited onto three singles released alongside the album.

The two tracks which ended up as the 'B-side' of *Congo* are hardly memorable. *Papa He Said* has an American feel with nice guitar work from Mike and a reasonable bass, while Tony merely soft-pedals his way through it. Mike also drives *Banjo Man* playing guitar to sound a bit like a banjo which never ceases to jangle away under Ray's vocals. Ray also wrote the lyrics which talk about the busker's life. Wilson: "I heard Mike's guitar which sounded like a banjo and thought of someone busking. A busker who writes his own music and loves his own music, but people only want to hear the hits. It's just one man's frustration about not being able to get his music across to the people." [3]

The two tracks which appeared on the single *Shipwrecked* are two instrumentals, basically electronic, without doubt never really completed; in fact, they have what must surely be working titles. The title *Phret* probably comes from the riff which dominates the song and is vaguely reminiscent of a fretless bass only played on the keyboard. In fact, Tony is the main instrumentalist with his initial synth; reminiscent of Muzak it almost has a new age feel. *7/8* on the other hand is an instrumental where Nir Zidkyahu's irregular time signature is the most striking feature, along with the usual winning riffs from Tony.

When the idea, initially a serious consideration, to release an EP in February 1998 with the remaining out-takes was abandoned, Genesis left one of their songs in limbo. Never officially released to this day, *Nowhere Else To Run* has a melancholy feel to Ray's vocals, with a driving keyboard riff, Mike + The Mechanics style guitar and a catchy chorus.

The last three songs which didn't make the album were included in the single release *Not About Us*, for a total of over 18 minutes of music.

Anything Now is clearly a Banksian track, with a moderately fast rhythm and Mike's rhythmic guitar, leaving the job of guiding the song to the keyboards, where at long last there is a fine piano section played with split chords with an acid jazz feel, not to mention a short synth solo. Banks: "I don't think it suited Ray's voice but I thought it was a great song: he didn't sing the verses well and that's why we didn't put it on the album. If Phil had been around it would have been a really good song. But again, the guitar riff is great, and I wrote the lyric and I was quite pleased with that." [9]

Sign Your Life Away is a pretty anonymous track, most likely a predominantly Rutherford track, with touches of rock in the distorted guitar of the main riffs and the arpeggios in the verses. Ray seems particularly at ease in this track.

The best of the three is in any case *Run Out Of*

Time, which certainly wouldn't have brought the level of the album down (in fact, it was still on the track-list up until just a few weeks before the album was released), especially had a few appropriate adjustments been made, for example using a real saxophonist in the long intro instead of the sample which also appears later on in the track. The melancholy sequence of the chords created by Tony show a touch of his old genius, and Ray gives an excellent vocal performance, with a few phrases sung in a lovely falsetto. The additional instrumentation provided by Mike on a slightly muted lead guitar and the keyboard crescendo before the synth-sax returns manage to transport the listener to eras past. Banks: "I really liked *Run Out Of Time*. I thought it was really strong and I thought Ray sang it great, his voice suited that kind of world-weary drunk. It had some great chords." [9]

THE ALBUM ARTWORK

Rutherford: "It's funny, you can be quite tough looking back at the covers This is one of those that's a bit weak. Sometimes when you do an album cover, like WE CAN'T DANCE, you go, 'yep, that's it; it's great'. For other covers you've got a list of five things and it's like the menu where you can't find a damn thing you want to eat. That's how this cover felt. It was OK but it didn't feel especially strong." [1]

Wilson: "Isolation was a topic that kept cropping up on the album. I remember Mike Rutherford talking about one of the songs and saying that the more ability we have to communicate with each other, the less we actually do. And I always found that really quite an interesting statement because it was so, so right. People text each other now because it saves actually bothering to talk. The cover, with the man standing isolated in the middle of nowhere, you know, in this ever-increasing circle, worked for the vibe of the album. I remember they used it on the Jumbotron monitors on tour as well; this guy walking in the cold and snow coming down. It kind of captured the atmosphere of a lot of the songs that were on that record." [1]

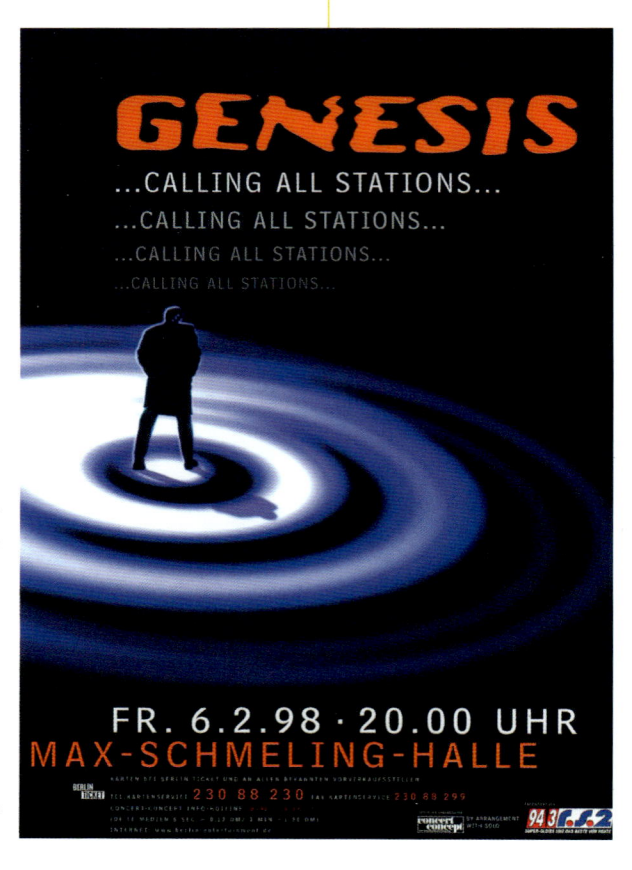

EPILOGUE

Collins: "I was given CALLING ALL STATIONS way ahead of its release and, as is always the case with albums by people that I really like, I kind of wait, I

Poster advertising the concert in Berlin on February 6th 1998. The show was actually moved from the original venue, Max-Schmellling Halle, to the Radsporthalle Velodrom

put them on the table and wait for the right time because I want to listen, I don't want to sort of just have it on, and of course I never really have time. One night I put it on and I could imagine how it was made, I could hear the sound, I could picture the studio, I could hear the riffs: 'that's one of Tony's, that one's Mike's' sort of thing. A lot of it washed over me, it didn't get inside very easily, which is typical of Tony's and Mike's material. This is where the three of us kind of had the best of all worlds because I'm kind of pretty immediate, with Tony, you may not know it but you'll be singing it to yourself in a couple of weeks' time and Mike is somewhere in the middle. When you've got the three of us writing, it makes things deeper. There wasn't much of that immediacy there which means people had to invest their time in listening to it and I don't think they wanted to. Either didn't want to or unfortunately the timing was such that we were entering the sound-bite stage of our lives, you know where everything is reduced to the shortest possible time, and if people don't like something, they immediately skip onto the next track." [1]

Longdon: "I like the album on the whole. Tony's keyboards are up in the mix throughout the whole of the album and I think Ray does a good job with the vocals. It's a Genesis album without Phil and of course he's missed. It is a different interpretation of what the band is and at least Genesis had the courage to do something that went in a different direction. For this reason, artistically I think they chose the right singer. Over the years, people have told me that when they heard the new Genesis material on the radio, they weren't too sure if it actually was Genesis, because the sound of Phil's voice and drums in the context of the band was an instantly recognisable signature sound. Altering that signature sound to a vocalist with a much lower and huskier range, obviously had a significant impact." [4]

Although the very first copies arrived in Italy on 25 August, in the UK the official release date for the new Genesis album was set for 1 September 1997. At that particular moment in history, the whole country was reeling from the shock of Princess Diana's death (the car crash in the Pont de l'Alma tunnel in Paris had occurred the previous day). With the media talking of little else amid the grief weighing on the entire nation, it is understandable that most people had other things on their minds than the latest Genesis album, and one without Phil Collins to boot. In fact, the album did quite well on home turf, entering the charts at No. 2, behind BE HERE NOW by Oasis which had been released just over a week earlier, but it was falling down the charts within just a few weeks.

This trend was replicated more or less throughout Europe, even in Germany, where 600,000 albums were bought. Overall, the album sold over 2 million copies worldwide, hardly numbers to be sniffed at, but clearly no comparison with the dizzying figures achieved in the Collins era. Perhaps, this was only to be expected.

But the real crash came in the American market. In the States the new Genesis album sold just 110,000 copies, never climbing beyond No. 54 in the charts.

Even the three singles struggled, despite being promoted by excellent videos. *Congo* reached No. 29 in the UK, *Shipwrecked* No. 54 and *Not About Us* No. 66.

253

THE CONCERTS

With CALLING ALL STATIONS sent off to press, it was time to get a band together to take it out on the road. Having turned down Chester Thompson's offer to appear on the record, it seemed only logical to forgo his presence on the stage too.

Zidkyahu: "After doing the recording, I went back to New York and about two weeks later I got a phone call from Tony Smith saying, 'we want you to go on the road with us, we would like you to be a member in the band'. And I was like, 'wow, okay'. 'So we'd love to get some pictures', you know... Everything happened so fast, I went and got a haircut, got some nice pictures done and sent them over. But then things changed and all of a sudden it was 'no, actually we want you to play with us, but the members of the band are only Tony, Mike and Ray'. It was clear that they wanted me to play the tour, but my position in the band was not really clear." [1]

The task confronting the Israeli drummer was far from simple: having to replace not one but two people considered real idols by Genesis fans would have had anyone shaking in their boots. Zidkyahu: "I've got to say, Tony and Mike said to me very clearly when we did the live shows, 'don't put yourself under any pressure to play every note that Phil or Chester played, you know, you can bring your own thing'. I really appreciated that, it gave me some headroom. But at the same time, there's only so much you can change because the drumming on most of the songs is such a signature sound in their music, and I didn't want to mess with 15,000 fans expecting to hear that particular drum feel. I had to find a balance." [1]

Banks: "As a drummer Nir was great, he made the drums sound loud which is something Phil does very well but not every drummer can do it. He was incredibly tight and had wrists that really sort of smacked. We'd kind of got used to hearing Phil and Chester up there and sometimes Nir was doing stuff on his own which they'd done together. He was really good." [1]

Genesis also had to manage without their other long-standing session man, Daryl Stuermer, who'd been working with them for twenty years. Rutherford: "If he hadn't been out with Phil (*for the* DANCE INTO THE LIGHT *tour which was around the same time – author's note*), we'd have liked him with us, but, obviously, that wasn't possible." [2]

For the guitar parts, the band considered a number of musicians. Steven Wilson, one of the most high-profile progressive rock artists of recent years remembers being contacted in connection with the role: "I was one of many people I am sure who were invited to audition for that band. It happened through my publisher of that time, who was at Hit & Run Music, which was related to Tony Smith. And so Tony asked me if I was interested in auditioning for that, but I'm sure they asked hundreds of people... Anyway I didn't do it, because I was involved in my own projects. Taking that job would have meant pretty much to giving up everything else. But it was nice to be asked" [11] Eventually, the band chose Irish musician Anthony Drennan (Clannad, The Corrs, Paul Brady). Drennan: "The Corrs and Genesis had the same agent, John Giddings. I was in Australia when he said, 'do you want to do an audition for Genesis?'. I went, 'yeah, maybe'. I thought they had people who were more connected, so I didn't want to go to England to do an audition if someone else was guaranteed to get it. Then they phoned up and asked me to send them

Nir in Berlin on
26th August 1997

a tape. I found a bit of a Paul Brady concert with me playing and sent it to them. Mike Rutherford likes Paul Brady so he said, 'get him over'. So I went over, played *Firth Of Fifth* and that was it." [12]

In the meantime, a team of designers was on a mission to create a spectacular stage show. Use of the Jumbotron maxi screens was confirmed for showing even more video content and there was also talk of special visual effects, including one that was supposed to make it look like the screens were exploding and shattering into tiny pieces.

As part of the album release promo, Genesis did a couple of showcase performances, one in Europe (at the Berlin Television Tower near the Alexanderplatz in Berlin) and one in the States (at the Apollo/Saturn V Center - Kennedy Space Center in Cape Canaveral), with a new four-man line-up: Tony Banks (keyboards and acoustic guitar), Mike Rutherford (acoustic guitars), Ray Wilson (vocals and acoustic guitar), Nir Zidkyahu (percussion). In Berlin, on 26 August, the four-piece performed semi-acoustic versions of *Not About Us*, *No Son Of Mine*, *Lovers' Leap* and *Turn It On Again* (with Banks playing guitar on the first and third songs). The same setlist was repeated at Cape Canaveral but with the first two songs swapped round.

A 26-date North American tour was planned, running from 11 November to 21 December with concerts scheduled for the states of New York, Pennsylvania, Ohio, Michigan, Wisconsin, Missouri, Illinois and Florida, along with three shows in Canada. All of these shows were to take place in quite big arenas with audience capacities of between 15,000 and 20,000, similar to the venues booked for the Collins era, including the Civic Arena in Pittsburgh, the Rosemont Horizon, the Maple Leaf Gardens in Toronto, Madison Square Garden in New York and the Miami Arena. But it soon became apparent that Genesis without Phil Collins was something that did not appeal to the American fans at all. Contingency plans were immediately rolled out and the whole tour was re-dimensioned. The number of shows was reduced to 22 and the venues went from being arenas to smaller theatres with capacities of around 3,000, some of which had witnessed the commercial growth of the band in the early years, like the Beacon Theater in New York, the Orpheum Theater in Boston, the Civic Centre in Ottawa, the Tower Theater in Philadelphia and the Cleveland Music Hall.

But even the revised schedule failed to arouse adequate interest. And while the band would probably have had no problems in filling the venues in the larger cities, the lack of interest in other states would have resulted in the need to cancel some of the shows, making the whole tour financially unviable. Genesis were left with no other choice than to cancel the North American tour. A massive blow to both band and management, who initially justified the cancellation as being down to 'technical problems', suggesting that the tour would be postponed to a later date, something

GENESIS

Anthony Drennan with Genesis, Berlin, 6th February 1998

Berlin, 26th August 1997

album as possible and a mixture of old songs. We have a four and a half hour setlist to reduce to two and a half. Some songs we won't do, like *Jesus He Knows Me* and the humorous ones, because they're too much Phil's, but *No Son Of Mine* and *Mama* sound great." [2]

Even before setting off on tour, the new singer wasn't entirely sure about some of the choices. Wilson: "I'd always expected some songs to work and other not to work. *Invisible Touch*, for example, I didn't expect to work, it's very difficult for me to sing, too poppy. We're trying to approach the medleys from a different angle and do something different. Because Phil isn't there, even songs that people have heard before in the last couple of tours sound different. From that point of view it's been exciting. *Mama*, for example, is much more rock now. Some of the songs have become better, some aren't as good as they were with Phil but it's early days." [3]

With time on their hands, Genesis allowed themselves the luxury of playing a couple of concerts exclusively for radio in front of small audiences. The first was on 15 November 1997 at the Richmond Hotel in Copenhagen, Denmark. With Anthony Drennan in the ranks for the very first time, Genesis played *No Son Of Mine / Congo / Land Of Confusion / Calling All Stations / Turn It On Again / Alien Afternoon / Invisible Touch* and *Shipwrecked* in a short show featuring four songs

which never happened.

With the live shows now kicking off directly in Europe, Genesis, who had already started rehearsals in October at the Bray Film Studios, in Windsor, England, suddenly found themselves with a lot of extra time in which to get ready. The first leaks concerning the setlist seemed interesting.

Rutherford: "We'll play as much of the new

256

from the new album and four from the previous two albums with Collins.

The setlist played in Paris on 13 December of the same year was much more interesting. Although it was again in a radio show format (this time for RTL), this performance was structured more like a concert and included *No Son Of Mine / Congo / Land Of Confusion / Small Talk / Mama / Not About Us – Dancing With The Moonlit Knight – Follow You Follow Me – Lovers' Leap / Calling All Stations / Invisible Touch / Shipwrecked / Alien Afternoon / Turn It On Again*.

Apart from the sole performance of *Small Talk* (dropped from the setlist immediately afterwards), what really stood out were the four central songs (from *Not About Us* through to *Lovers' Leap*) played by Banks, Rutherford and Drennan on acoustic guitars (with Ray on vocals only), a kind of trial run for what would become the central moment of the actual tour.

23 January 1998 was the date chosen by Genesis to present the new tour to the European press with an invitation-only dress rehearsal concert held in the Bray Film Studios near Windsor. The setlist performed was: *No Son Of Mine / Land Of Confusion / The Lamb Lies Down On Broadway / Calling All Stations / Hold On My Heart / That's All / There Must Be Some Other Way / Domino / The Carpet Crawlers / Firth Of Fifth (Instrumental Section) / Congo / Home By The Sea / Acoustic set: Dancing With The Moonlit Knight – Follow You Follow Me – Lovers' Leap / Mama / The Dividing Line / Invisible Touch / Turn It On Again / Throwing It All Away / I Can't Dance*.

A good balance between the old and new: the *Old Medley* was gone with the band opting instead to include two complete songs from Gabriel era (*The Lamb Lies Down On Broadway*, which hadn't been on the setlist since 1982, and *The Carpet*

Crawlers, last played live in 1984) and the instrumental section of *Firth Of Fifth* (the synth and guitar solos introduced by a quick drum fill). Furthermore, two-thirds of the acoustic set, the initial parts of *Dancing With The Moonlit Knight* and *Supper's Ready*, two touching performances thanks to Ray's voice, combined well with what was perhaps the biggest surprise of all: an excellent country version of *Follow You Follow Me*.

The rest of the set (opened as per tradition with a song from the previous album, in this case *No Son Of Mine*) included three songs from WE CAN'T DANCE, four from INVISIBLE TOUCH and three from GENESIS (soon to become two as *That's All* would only be performed on this one occasion) and just four tracks from CALLING ALL STATIONS: the title track, the single *Congo* (with an extended interlude of sampled tribal singing and rhythms which, let's be honest, didn't quite work), *The Dividing Line* and *There Must Be Some Other Way* (*Not About Us* had already disappeared from the acoustic set).

If some of the songs from the old repertoire sounded convincing enough, the end section of the concert came across as being somewhat forced, especially *Invisible Touch* and *Throwing It All Away* which just didn't seem to suit Ray's voice at all. On top of this, Drennan's style was different to both Steve Hackett's and Daryl Stuermer's. Drennan: "The starting point is to stick to the original. During *Firth Of Fifth* I start playing the way Steve used to do it, also because I like it a lot, but then I carry on in my own way." [12]

Banks: "Anthony Drennan is a really good guitarist but very different to all the ones I'd worked with before. Mike is not a natural lead guitarist but he's good at working at it and he worked out some good stuff, whereas Anthony is like Daryl or Steve, a lead guitarist who could do all sorts of stuff, a slightly more bluesy guitarist. I loved his solos on *Firth Of Fifth*; he never played the same thing twice, obviously he played the melody line but in the second bit he would do whatever he felt like and in

Ray live in Leipzig on 5th February 1998

the show I'd always listen to what he played as it was always good. Steve and Daryl, on the other hand, always used to play the same thing. Maybe Anthony didn't play the same thing because half the time he couldn't remember how it went, whatever the reason, I thought the interplay between him and Mike on that song live was great." [9]

Of course, for some songs, Drennan was given the role of bass player. Drennan: "It's physically demanding. When you're rehearsing, you don't really notice, because you stop, even if it's just for a minute, and then start playing again. But live, and one, and two, and three, it hurts! In some songs there's no bass at all, on *Turn It On Again*, for example, I play the guitar and also bass pedals. Mike did the same on *The Dividing Line*." [12] This song was presented in an interesting way, preceded by a long intro for lead guitar played by Rutherford and Drennan.

But clearly, Ray was the one really under pressure. Wilson: "I felt I had to sound a bit like Phil Collins when I was singing his songs and a bit like Peter Gabriel when I was singing his. When I was singing a song that I'd help to write I felt I had to sound like me, so I was trying to combine these three singers. I managed to make *No Son Of Mine* my own, but then there were other songs like *Invisible Touch* that I should never have sung, I was just terrible. I always compare Phil's voice to a trumpet, he's very good at that staccato type singing. Peter Gabriel is kind of round and warm, a bit like a saxophone, and that type of singing is more the way I sing. So what Peter did was easier for me to grasp than what Phil did; there were one or two exceptions but predominantly that was the case. Doing all this, while all the time trying to be true to who you are, is really quite a challenge. Most of the songs we chose to do live were the ones that I did more convincingly. And if I did change them a bit it was in such a way that actually sounded quite cool and quite modern. When performing there was also the challenge of having to take on a little bit of Phil's character. You know, he's obviously a great entertainer and he's got that acting quality as well. Given the humorous side of Phil's character, I thought I had to bring in some of my own humour, but my humour is very dry." [1]

The singer did have some weight when choosing songs for the setlist. Wilson: "There were two things I wanted to get across really to Mike and Tony. One was, you know, start the album with something that's truly Genesis (*Calling All Stations*) and not something that's going to be the first single. The other thing I wanted them to do was introduce an acoustic element to the show. So we put a little acoustic section in the middle of the show which was very popular. I always remember Tony Banks being especially against the idea." [1]

That the setlist was still in its experimental phases was plain to see from the very first concert: as already mentioned, *That's All*, after just one appearance in the setlist, was dropped never to return again, while the same fate awaited *Hold On My Heart* after the two shows in Budapest, on 28 January (a trial gig in front of just a handful of people) and on the 29th (the official starting date of the tour), where, by way of compensation, *There Must Be Some Other Way* was preceded by another song from the new album, *Alien Afternoon*, with Drennan on bass for the first part of the song and on guitar (including the solo) for the second part. Immediately afterwards *Shipwrecked* was added

Nir in Rome on 18th February 1998

which took the number of songs from CALLING All STATIONS up to five, a number certainly more suitable for a new album.

On 31 January, Genesis were greeted by delirious fans in Katowice where their whole concert was broadcast by TVP (Poland's public TV broadcaster) and the country began to show clear signs of affection for the young lead singer (who would set up home there a few years later). The setlist at this point in the tour was as follows: *No Son Of Mine / Land Of Confusion / The Lamb Lies Down On Broadway / Calling All Stations / Alien Afternoon / The Carpet Crawlers / There Must Be Some Other Way / Domino / Shipwrecked / Firth Of Fifth / Congo / Home By The Sea / Acoustic Set: Dancing With The Moonlit Knight – Follow You Follow Me – Lovers' Leap / Mama / The Dividing Line / Invisible Touch / Turn It On Again / Throwing It All Away / I Can't Dance.*

Eastern Europe, previously ignored by Genesis, gave the band a very warm reception, and part of the concert in Prague on 2 February was also broadcast on national TV. In fact, to make space for this new and interesting market the tour had been rescheduled, the four shows in the UK originally planned for 27–30 January (Cardiff, Manchester, Glasgow and Newcastle) being postponed until the following March to become part of a larger British leg of the tour.

At the start of February the tour moved into Germany for five concerts (interrupted by a quick

Acoustic set in Milan
19th February 1998

excursion into France for a show in Amnéville) where the concert in Berlin, on the 6th, was moved from the original venue, the Max-Schmeling-Halle, to the Velodrom. The band then travelled down into Switzerland (where *Mama* was dropped from the setlist in Zurich on 13 February) before heading off to Vienna, Austria.

Halfway through the month, the band arrived in Italy. The initial schedule included a show in Bologna on 17 February and one in Milan on the 18th, the latter, however, was moved to the 19th so organisers could slot in a third Italian show in Rome. Genesis' return to Italy was a huge disappointment; the country that had loved the band more than any other in the world back in the 1970s gave the new incarnation of the band a glacial reception. The chosen venues, all rather large, were anything but full, with an embarrassingly large number of empty spaces in the Bologna Palasport. The negative atmosphere severely affected performances and every evening saw another song cut from the setlist: in Bologna *Alien Afternoon* was dropped, in Rome *There Must Be Some Other Way* also vanished and by Milan the setlist was three songs shorter when *Throwing It All Away* failed to materialise (making the Milan show the shortest of the whole tour). Banks: "They were very small crowds and to be honest the crowds that came weren't that enthusiastic. I don't know how much they liked Ray, really, I couldn't tell. The shows were not great and in some ways they were the most depressing part of the tour because Italy used to be so great back in the early days." [13]

When the crew moved on to France for two concerts, the setlist was still somewhat diminished, but not to the extent it had been in Italy: missing from the shows were *Alien Afternoon* and *Shipwrecked* (the latter definitively) but at least *There Must Be Some Other Way* and *Throwing It All Away* had been reinstated.

At the end of February, when the band played the NEC in Birmingham, the acoustic set was lengthened by the addition of a fourth piece, an abridged version of *Not About Us* (which hadn't been played live since the radio show in Paris), while on 5 March, in Cardiff, after a long absence *Alien Afternoon* was back, only this time to replace *There Must Be Some Other Way* (from this moment onwards up to the end of the tour, these two tracks would basically be alternated in and out of the setlist). In total there were nine concerts in the UK, all of which were reasonably well received by the audiences.

Afterwards, the band went on to play in Belgium and the Netherlands before the tour went back to France for half a dozen dates divided into two lots to make room for a couple of shows in Spain. In Bordeaux, on 16 March, *Mama* was again omitted, while the show in Clermont-Ferrand, scheduled for the 23rd, was cancelled.

At the end of the month, the tour once again stopped off in Germany where on the 27th, Tony celebrated his birthday in Munich with Nir walking out on stage with a cardboard cake during the acoustic set.

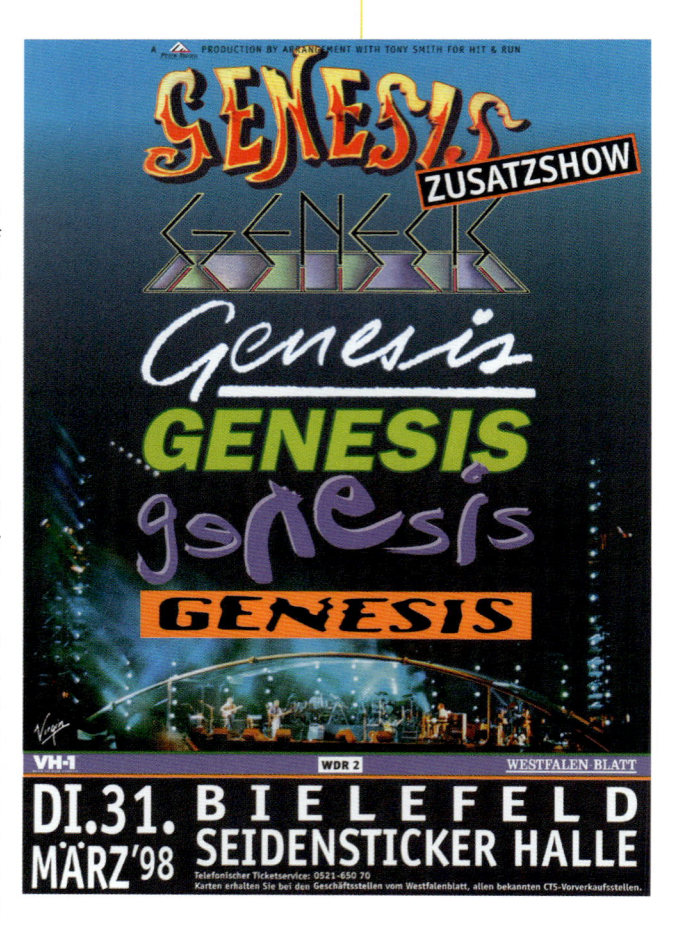

The end of the tour saw another two concerts cancelled, the one in Seidensticker Halle in Bielefeld, Germany, on 31 March, and the one at the Forum in Copenhagen on 1 April, while the show in Stockholm on the 3rd, originally planned for the Globen, was moved to another location, the Annexet. In these final stages of the tour, the setlist always included *Alien Afternoon* (to the detriment of *There Must Be Some Other Way*), only now placed after *The Carpet Crawlers* (as opposed to before as

Poster advertising the concert in Bielefeld, Germany, on March 31st, 1998, which was eventually cancelled. As with UK promoters, the promoter for this show, Peter Rieger, tried to attract a bigger audience by using all the past logos of the band

had been the case in previous concerts).

The tour came to a close in Helsinki, Finland, on 5 April. Taken as a whole it met with various degrees of success. Italy aside, the response from audiences was decidedly variable, with full houses in Germany and good crowds in England and France, but interest in the tour as a whole was a mere fraction of what it had been for the previous WE CAN'T DANCE tour.

In terms of setlist (which never included certain songs that had definitely been rehearsed, such as *In The Cage* and *If That's What You Need*), the band's performance was professional, albeit not exactly captivating. Vocally, Ray Wilson was flawless, but he clearly had a lot to learn as a frontman. Genesis, who in Phil had had a showman capable of effortlessly winning over an entire stadium, suddenly found themselves with an inexperienced frontman and this vacuum certainly couldn't be filled by either Tony or Mike, notoriously static and inconspicuous on stage. Even the two new session men, despite their obvious qualities as musicians, were never totally convincing. They came across as lacking motivation and stage presence, although, to be fair, the attitude of audiences, who would much rather have seen Thompson and Stuermer in their place, can't possibly have helped.

From a stage show point of view, the downsizing compared to the previous tour was all too apparent. Not only was there no trace of the shattering screen effect, but the Jumbotrons themselves also failed to materialise at the majority of dates (including the three in Italy) due to the venues being too small to install them (or possibly for financial reasons). This meant that most of the shows didn't even benefit from the use of any video footage (mostly inherited from the previous tour, with some new additions, like the desperate man of *Calling All Stations*). In the end, the stage was rather sad looking, with a minimal light show and some towers in the middle which could be lowered hydraulically; these would become props to one of Ray's funnier moments when, before *Home By The Sea*, he would introduce the hydraulic towers on stage as his bandmates' fiancées. Another light-hearted moment which Ray brought into the show came during *I Can't Dance* when, following the example set by U2 and Springsteen, he would call up a girl from the audience to dance with him. Wilson: "I'd just look into the audience or sometimes someone in the crew like Geoff Banks, who could see through the Plexiglas stage, would be telling me which girl they wanted me to choose from the audience and that was a good laugh. I just used to choose whoever looked like they would be fun and generally it was very, very good. The only time it didn't work was in Oslo when I chose a female security guard, and she just did not want to be there. In the end she ended up just pushing me off my feet and walking off the stage. That was embarrassing. I thought, 'if I'm going to have to incorporate a bit of entertainment, I'm going to have to think about how I can do that in my own style, so people know that I'm not acting a part'. I really feel I would have been much happier if I'd left that out. I didn't want to do that. I just wanted to go there and be a proper rock band and not be a show band like it was when Phil used to do medleys of other people's music. If you went to watch a Pink Floyd concert, you never saw Roger Waters or David Gilmour telling jokes between songs. They would go up there and probably say

Rome, 18th February 1998

one word throughout the entire concert. But it wasn't about that, it was about the music and the atmosphere of the music. And, personally, that's what I wanted it to be." [14]

Clearly Genesis also had to deal with the obvious difficulties which came with a line-up that was 3/5 new.

Banks: "For Mike and me it was fantastic; we had these three younger guys out with us. We felt like Dave Brubeck; we're the old guys, you know, sort of hammering along and we had these great guys playing with us." [1]

Wilson: "I think mine and Nir's involvement in Genesis Mark III was very important, we did bring an energy to it. Mike and Tony are quite laid back and even Anthony Drennan, the guitarist who worked with us, was very musical, very talented but also very laid back. Me and Nir were right in there and I think it was good for the balance of the band to have these different characters. If everybody had been laid back, you know, it's possible the audience might have fallen asleep." [1]

After a couple of weeks' break, the tour had a brief but gratifying appendix when Genesis were called up to headline two prestigious festivals in Germany on 30 and 31 May, and, incredible as it may seem, the support act was Bob Dylan.

At the first of the two, the Rock Am Ring Festival held at the Nürburgring race track, Genesis played a shorter setlist which completely turned around the original running order and now had the title track of the new album as the opening song: *Calling All Stations / Land Of Confusion / No Son Of Mine / Domino / Congo / Home By The Sea / Acoustic Set: Dancing With The Moonlit Knight – Follow You Follow Me – Not About Us / Mama / The Dividing Line /* *Invisible Touch / Turn It On Again / Throwing It All Away / I Can't Dance.*

The setlist on the following day for their performance at Rock Im Park held at the Frankenstadion, Nuremberg, was different again. *Land Of Confusion* became the opening song, followed by *Calling All Stations*, while in the acoustic set *Lovers' Leap* replaced *Not About Us* and *Throwing It All Away* disappeared from the encores.

Wilson: "Funnily enough, the very last show we ever did was when it became apparent that we actually felt like a band. At Rock Im Park we did encores, it was raining and people were jumping up and down. It was all very festival-like, a very, very cool environment to be in. I remember walking off the stage, looking at Tony Smith, the manager, and saying, 'is that it?', you know, meaning 'is that the last song we can play?' because there was a curfew, and Tony Smith saying 'yes'. And at that moment, I just felt it in my soul that that *was* it. It was May, about the same month I started, only now it was 1998, so it lasted two years, I guess. I remember that moment. I actually have it on my little digital video camera as well, me saying 'is that it?' and Tony Smith saying, 'yes'. So he knew something I didn't." [1]

NOTES

(1)   Mike Kaufman's Genesis interviews, Chicago / London / Edinburgh / New York, 2007, partially used in the bonus disc accompanying the 2008 remasters

(2)   Mario Giammetti's telephone interview with Mike Rutherford, 5 September 1997, partially published in the article "Intervista esclusiva a Mike Rutherford" in *Dusk*, Issue n. 23, October 1997

(3) Mario Giammetti's telephone interview with Ray Wilson, 28 October 1997, partially published in the article "Intervista esclusiva a Ray Wilson" in *Dusk*, Issue n. 24, January 1998

(4) Mario Giammetti's e-mail interview with David Longdon, November 2010, partially published in the article "Calling another station" in *Dusk*, Issue no. 66, December 2010

(5) Mario Giammetti's e-mail interview with Nick Van Eede, 26 January 2021, partially published in the article "Calling more stations – Nick Van Eede" in *Dusk*, Issue n. 97, May 2021

(6) Mario Giammetti's e-mail interview with Francis Dunnery 26 February 2021, partially published in the article "Calling more stations – Francis Dunnery" in *Dusk*, Issue n. 97, May 2021

(7) Mario Giammetti's Skype interview with Nick Davis, 10 March 2021

(8) Mario Giammetti's e-mail interview with Nick D'Virgilio, 13 April 2011, partially published in the article "Come Talk To Me" in *Dusk*, Issue no. 68, September 2011

(9) Mario Giammetti's interview with Tony Banks, London, Tony Smith Personal Management office, 29 November 2016

(10) Personal e-mail sent to Mario Giammetti by Ray Wilson, dated 22 December 2020

(11) Mario Giammetti's telephone interview with Steven Wilson 21 July 2011, partially published in the article "Come Talk To Me" in *Dusk*, Issue no. 68, September 2011

(12) Mario Giammetti's interview with Anthony Drennan, Windsor, Bray Film Studios, 23 January 1998, partially published in the article "Interviste esclusive Windsor 23.1.98" in *Dusk*, Issue n. 25, April 1998

(13) Mario Giammetti's telephone interview with Tony Banks, 6 March 2001, partially published in the article "Calling All Genesis - Interviste esclusive a Ray Wilson, Mike Rutherford & Tony Banks" in *Dusk*, Issue n. 35, April 2001

(14) Mario Giammetti's telephone interview with Ray Wilson, 18 January 2001, partially published in the article "Calling All Genesis - Interviste esclusive a Ray Wilson, Mike Rutherford & Tony Banks" in *Dusk*, Issue n. 35, April 2001

265

CALLING ALL STATIONS TOUR

1997

AUGUST
- 26 **Berlin (GERMANY)**, Berliner Fernsehturm
  Acoustic showcase. Line-up for this set was Banks (keyboard and acoustic guitar), Rutherford (acoustic guitar), Wilson (vocals and acoustic guitar) and Zidkyahu (percussion)
- 28 **Cape Canaveral, FL (USA)**, Apollo/Saturn V Center - Kennedy Space Center
  Acoustic showcase. Same line-up.

NOVEMBER
- 15 **Copenhagen (DENMARK)**, Hotel Richmond
  Radio live show. First gig with the complete line-up, including Anthony Drennan on guitar and bass

DECEMBER
- 13 **Paris (FRANCE)**, RTL Grand Studio
  Radio live show

1998

JANUARY
- 23 **Windsor (ENGLAND)**, Bray Film Studios
  Rehearsal concert
- 28 **Budapest (HUNGARY)**, Budapest Sportcsarnok
  Rehearsal concert
- 29 **Budapest (HUNGARY)**, Budapest Sportcsarnok
- 31 **Katowice (POLAND)**, Spodek

FEBRUARY
- 02 **Prague (CZECH REPUBLIC)**, Sportovní Hala
- 04 **Mannheim (GERMANY)**, Maimarkthalle
- 05 **Leipzig (GERMANY)**, Messehalle 7
- 06 **Berlin (GERMANY)**, Radsporthalle Velodrom
  Originally scheduled at Max-Schmeling-Halle
- 08 **Amnéville (FRANCE)**, Galaxie
- 10 **Dortmund (GERMANY)**, Halle 1 - Westfalenhallen
- 12 **Stuttgart (GERMANY)**, Hanns-Martin-Schleyer-Halle
- 13 **Zürich (SWITZERLAND)**, Hallenstadion
- 15 **Vienna (AUSTRIA)**, Halle D - Wiener Stadthalle

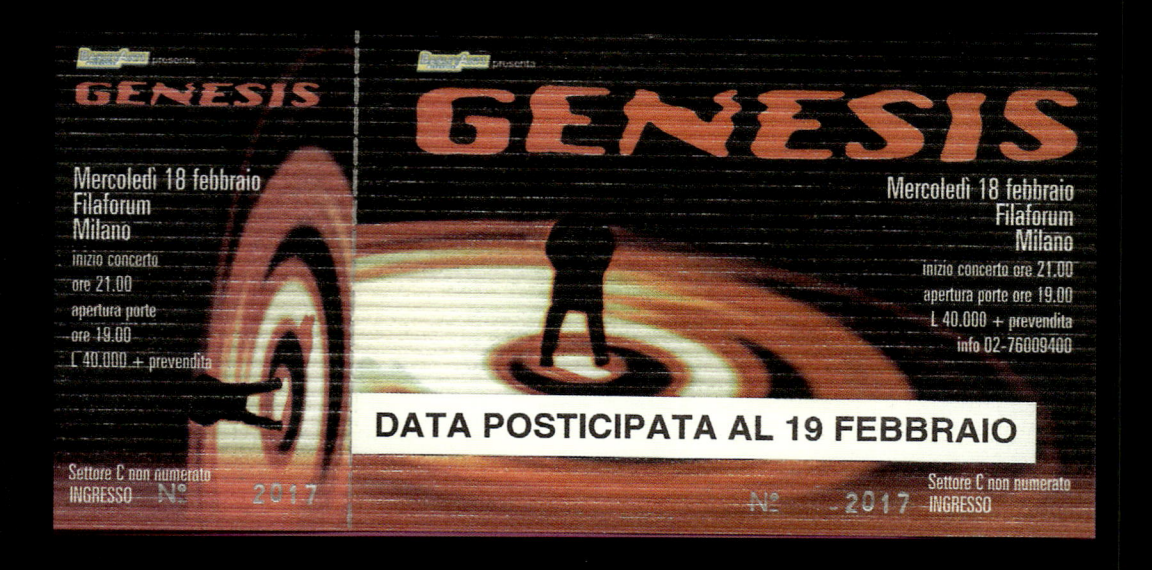

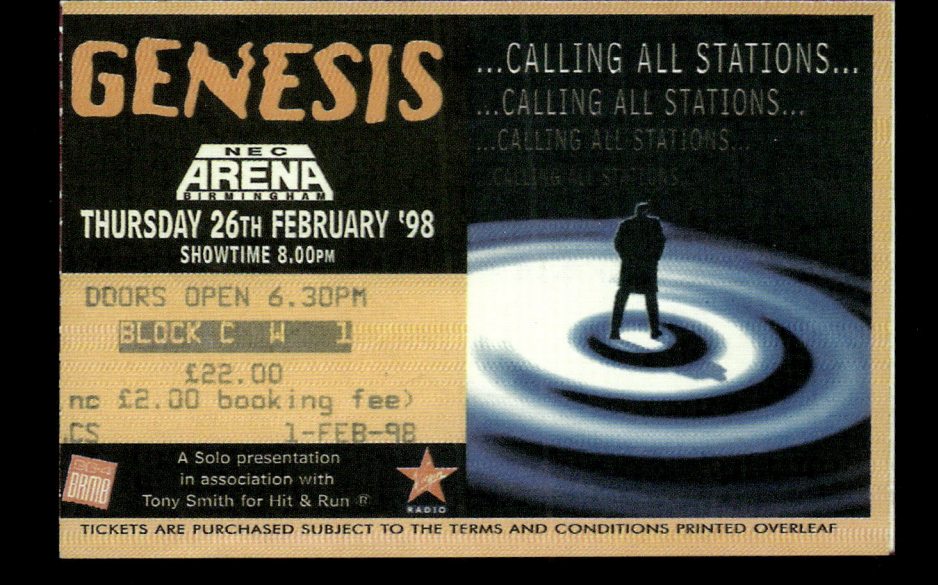

17	Casalecchio di Reno, Bologna (ITALY), Palasport
18	Rome (ITALY), PalaEUR
19	Assago, Milan (ITALY), Filaforum
	Originally scheduled for February 18
20	Lyon (FRANCE), Halle Tony Garnier
23	Paris (FRANCE), Palais Omnisports de Paris-Bercy
25	Birmingham (ENGLAND), NEC Arena - National Exhibition Centre
26	Birmingham (ENGLAND), NEC Arena - National Exhibition Centre
27	London (ENGLAND), Earls Court

MARCH

01	Glasgow (SCOTLAND), Scottish Exhibition + Conference Centre
	Originally scheduled for January 29
02	Newcastle (ENGLAND), Telewest Arena
	Originally scheduled for January 30
04	Cardiff (WALES), Cardiff International Arena
	Originally scheduled for January 27
05	Cardiff (WALES), Cardiff International Arena
06	Manchester (ENGLAND), NYNEX Arena
	Originally scheduled for January 28
08	Dublin (IRELAND), The Point Theatre
10	Forest (BELGIUM), Forest National
11	Rotterdam (THE NETHERLANDS), Ahoy Sportpaleis
14	Lille (FRANCE), Le Zénith
15	Saint-Sylvain-d'Anjou (FRANCE), Amphitea 4000
16	Bordeaux (FRANCE), Patinoire
18	Pau (FRANCE), Zénith-Pau
19	Madrid (SPAIN), Palacio de Deportes Comunidad de Madrid
21	Barcelona (SPAIN), Palau Sant Jordi
22	Marseille (FRANCE), Le Dome
24	Caen (FRANCE), Le Zénith
26	Strasbourg (FRANCE), Hall Rhénus
27	Munich (GERMANY), Olympiahalle
28	Erfurt (GERMANY), Messehalle
30	Hamburg (GERMANY), Sporthalle Hamburg

APRIL

02	Oslo (NORWAY), Oslo Spektrum
03	Stockholm (SWEDEN), Annexet
	Originally scheduled at Globen
05	Helsinki (FINLAND), Hartwall Areena

MAY

30	Nürburg (GERMANY), Nürburgring *'Rock Am Ring' festival*
31	Nuremberg (GERMANY), Frankenstadion *'Rock Im Park' festival*

Turn It On Again
Reunion Tour

As had often been the case during the Collins era, Genesis decided to take a break after the Calling All Stations tour so members could concentrate on their solo projects.

Wilson: "I remember a conversation we had on the tour bus during quite a long journey between Italy and Switzerland, after the Milan show. Tony Banks wanted to go back into the studio straight away and do another album. I didn't want to do that because obviously I'd written the Cut album, the band were waiting to do it and I'd organised the record deal. And Mike also wanted to do a Mike + The Mechanics album first." [1]

The first to bring out a new album, in March 1999, was Ray Wilson, with Millionairhead by Cut, the band he had formed with his brother Steve and which, despite being signed to Virgin Germany, had been put on a back burner while Ray dedicated his time to Genesis. This was followed at the end of May by the Mike + The Mechanics release, M6.

In an interview given at the time, the young singer expressed how he couldn't wait to give his contribution to the band as a writer. Wilson: "I wasn't involved much last time and it'll be interesting to hear the difference I'll make to their music. I think Mike and Tony are happy to have a singer to write and share the lyrics with as well. And I look forward to touring again. I had a wonderful time with Genesis on tour." [2]

However, in October Turn It On Again: The Hits came out, the band's first ever greatest hits album made up almost exclusively of songs from the Collins era plus one with Peter Gabriel and one with Wilson. What's more, the record also contained a brand new version of *The Carpet Crawlers* which originally should have preceded the release of the Genesis Archive 1967–75 box set which came out the year before. Recorded over a couple of years in various studios by the most famous 5-man line-up (Banks-Collins-Gabriel-Hackett-Rutherford), for the first time since 1971, production of a Genesis track was handed over to an outsider. This job fell to Trevor Horn, former member of Buggles and Yes but best-known as a producer. Bringing in a number of programmers, Horn added sound effects and artificial percussion, burying Banks' keyboards in the process.

Banks: "Mike and I went down to Real World Studios and did our parts together. To be honest, an awful lot of what I played didn't get used at all. The reason we got Trevor Horn on board was because we thought we would all argue with each other. So we said, 'do what you want with it' really. I thought what he did was pretty good really. I wasn't too sure about the little drum loop he used all the way through, but I thought the way Phil's voice took over from Pete's was just an amazing moment. Their voices have always had a certain similarity in intensity, but Phil has a slightly higher pitch that seemed to give such excitement to that third verse when he came in." [3]

But the original plan was to have all three Genesis singers on the track. Wilson: "I got a phone call to say that I was going to be singing on *The Carpet Crawlers*. I was going to do a verse, Peter Gabriel was doing a verse and Phil Collins was doing a verse. And then I got a call telling me that I wasn't singing on the song anymore. They never told me why." [1]

Obviously, the disappointment of the CALLING ALL STATIONS tour resurfaces. Without doubt, going from stadiums to smaller venues, not to mention the cancellation of the whole North American tour, can't have been easy for Tony and Mike. Wilson: "They were obviously used to stadiums and huge success and then all of a sudden it changed. For them, it must have been a bit like being asked to drive a Mini or a Fiat 126 after driving around in a Rolls Royce for years. But it was still pretty successful, I mean, we were still playing in arenas and things with big audiences. Obviously, it wasn't as successful as it had been with Phil, but I don't think anybody ever really expected that. Before we released our album Phil Collins had released DANCE INTO THE LIGHT and the tour he did to promote that album in America wasn't really all that successful by his standards. I think, in many respects, we suffered a little bit because of that as well because a lot of people in America still thought that Phil Collins was the singer with Genesis." [1] Collins, however, was able to console himself in March 2000, when he took home an Oscar for Best Original Song for his *You'll Be In My Heart*, from the Disney film *Tarzan*.

On 15 July, Paul Young of Mike + The Mechanics died of a heart attack and a few weeks later the publishing house, Hit & Run, run by Genesis manager, Tony Smith, announced that Ray Wilson's contract had expired and there would therefore be no follow-up.

Rutherford: "I came to realise that musically, Tony and myself are much further apart than I'd really thought. Phil was that person in the middle who kind of drew from both of us and made us work, I think." [4]

But the problem also lay in the changes sweeping through the music business.

Collins: "The commitment that people had to listening to music, when they first started buying our records, simply isn't there anymore for most people. That's mirrored in things like reality TV, sound bites, celebrity… it's a different way of living. I could see that CALLING ALL STATIONS wasn't going to be an immediate success and not because the songs weren't good but because they weren't immediate and people didn't give them enough time, didn't invest that patience. The band couldn't sustain it and I think Tony and Mike just lost the will to keep going against the tide." [4]

For Ray, the end of his contract with Genesis opened up a sort of abyss. Wilson: "I think I was on the point of giving everything up and not just because of this. When I got the news from management, I'd just broken up with the girlfriend I'd been with for about ten years. Straight after that, Virgin didn't renew our contract for Cut and I lost my home. It was a difficult time. But I took some comfort from the internet, from all the other people who, like me, were angry about the end of Genesis. They felt I'd never been given a proper chance." [5]

GENESIS

Rutherford: "For the world to get to know Ray, Genesis would have had to do an album and a tour every year for the next five years, like we did at the beginning. I don't think I could do that again. I've been in Genesis for thirty years, I built up Genesis and the Mechanics and I don't think it's time to go back and work like that again. The success Genesis had was great. We felt there was still something good there, but the musical climate was different and it was difficult to start something new. That's the problem, you see, you don't get played on the radio like you used to, so you have to work harder." [6]

Banks: "I would have liked to carry straight on and make another record right away while everything was going, but Mike wanted to do a Mechanics album. After a few months apart it became very apparent to me and Mike that, if we put out another record, we just wouldn't get a chance. We'd get no radio play, be faced with a very hostile press and a diminishing audience. We felt that even the people who had bought CALLING ALL STATIONS might not have liked what they heard. It was a feeling that we'd lose some more audience without gaining any, seeing as no one would hear it. It just seemed like a depressing way to carry on." [7]

Wilson: "I think they were afraid to release a Genesis album that maybe no one would buy. As much as I don't agree with that, I can understand their feelings. There may also have been pressure from management and the record companies, and I think, with Phil talking so openly about possibly getting back together with the guys to do some music, then the last thing they would have wanted was to release a Genesis album with me singing; if it turned out to be a complete disaster commercially, then there would have been less chance of Phil coming back. And, in all honesty, because Mike, Tony and Phil have obviously been friends for many, many years, I think that they wanted to preserve the good name of Genesis, and the success that they'd achieved over the years and keep the name intact." [1]

Banks: "We were very much past our prime when we did CALLING ALL STATIONS, both the record and the tour, everywhere really, apart from possibly Germany, but even there it wasn't like it was. We had no encouragement, really. Certainly there are fans out there who would have liked to have heard more, we know that. We can make music in other ways. We don't have to do it with Genesis and take Genesis right to the bottom. If, in the future, if we decided to do any kind of reunion tour, it would have some meaning, which it wouldn't have if we'd driven the thing into the ground, which is how it seemed to be going." [7]

Wilson: "It was great while it lasted and not so great when it didn't. I learnt a lot from it and have a lot of respect for everybody involved, you know, the management, the musicians, the crew and everything. To see a big machine like that working was quite interesting, you know, taking a tour that size on the road and seeing how it all worked. It's quite difficult coming down from that actually. As an artist I now play in clubs and stuff, so I've had to kind of go back to the beginning. From being able to work at that level, where everyone around you is the best at what they do, to facing a situation where nobody around you is the best at what they do, well, it's quite a contrast. You start to doubt that you're the best at what you do as well." [4]

Banks: "I'd have liked to have worked with Ray in a studio from the word go. It would have been interesting to try to write for that voice, it would have been a different approach. And we could have done something with Nir and Anthony Drennan, a great guitarist who I really liked. Using them a bit on an album as well, rather than sticking with just the three of us, would have been quite an interesting thing to do. But there came a point when the writing seemed to be on the wall and we just sort of read it and felt it was probably time to give it a bit of a break." [4]

Zidkyahu: "At the end of the tour, at the end of this journey, I thought this new generation Genesis really sounded like a band. Many people, myself included, thought that was the time to continue, to get back in the studio and really work together seeing as we had passed the first stage, the tough stage. Ray and I wanted to continue, we wanted to prove that we could take it to the next level and show people that we could take the band forward, even if it might have been a different Genesis and not the same as before. But it didn't happen. We were disappointed, big time." [4]

So in 2000, although no official statement was ever made, Genesis went into the creative hiatus which continues to this day.

Rumours of a reunion with their old bandmates had never ceased to circulate, however, and these were occasionally fuelled by things like the triple box set release GENESIS ARCHIVE 2: 1976–1992 or Tony Smith winning the Manager Of The Year award. The award ceremony was held on 21 September 2000 in the presence of Banks, Rutherford, Collins and even Peter Gabriel. Although the latter limited himself to having the moment immortalised in a photo, Phil surprisingly joined Tony, Mike and Daryl Stuermer on stage for a short semi-acoustic set, playing *Invisible Touch / Follow You Follow Me / Tonight, Tonight, Tonight / I Can't Dance*.

And that's not all, after fans had been hungering for archive material for so long, Genesis realised there was a demand for celebratory releases and in 2001 brought out the first two DVDs of their career: THE GENESIS SONGBOOK, features interviews with members of the band, past and present, including Ray Wilson and drummer, John Silver. But again the lion's share was dedicated to the three-man line-up which even went as far as performing *I Can't Dance* and a moving version of *Afterglow* (featuring Phil and Tony only) in the studio. This was followed by THE WAY WE WALK - LIVE IN CONCERT, a re-release of the concert filmed during their last tour with Phil (originally released on VHS).

It was clear that Phil had never truly left the Genesis family and, in fact, he joined Tony and Mike in the promo interviews. But this didn't mean that solo careers stopped here. In 2002 Phil released what to date is his last solo album of his own music, TESTIFY, meanwhile Mike and Tony entered a phase of reflection. Mike had to decide whether or not to carry on with the Mechanics following the premature death of Paul Young, and Tony was wondering to what extent it was worth persevering with a solo career given the unlikely chance of success. Both would come out of their respective reveries in 2004: Banks with his first classical album, SEVEN: A SUITE FOR ORCHESTRA, and Mike + The Mechanics, with the ranks now reduced to just Rutherford and Carrack, released REWIRED. Collins, on the other hand, was busy with what he jokingly described as *The First Final Farewell Tour*, but which

Genesis tour announcement, 7th November 2006

does in fact reveal the first indications of his need to slow down after ten years of hyperactivity on stages around the world. In the meantime, Ray Wilson also managed to get himself together and, as a follow-up to his first solo release, CHANGE (2003), he released THE NEXT BEST THING.

2004 also saw the release of more anthologies: the PLATINUM COLLECTION, a triple CD containing no previously unreleased material but featuring a selection of songs chosen to throw a spotlight on the band's entire career, where once again the consideration given to the Ray Wilson period is noticeable by its almost total absence (just one song out of the 40 included in the collection), and the DVD THE VIDEO SHOW, a collection of all the videos created by the band over the years. Phil once more appeared alongside Tony and Mike to promote both releases, making the possibility of a reunion increasingly more credible.

However, at the end of 2005, a project with a much broader ambition looked to be on the cards: a reunion of the most famous five-man line-up, with Gabriel and Hackett, for the purpose of staging a complete performance of THE LAMB LIES DOWN ON BROADWAY. All five, accompanied by their respective managers, met in Glasgow on 19 November, before one of the concerts in Phil's *Farewell* tour. Alas, the meeting did not conclude as expected due to the uncertainties displayed by Peter Gabriel.

Banks: "When we went there, our understanding, I think for all of us (apart from Peter), was that we were just going to say 'when' we were going to do it, not 'if'. But Peter was still saying we were just talking about 'if'." [9]

And yet it was Banks himself who rejected the idea of creating a musical with the music from THE LAMB.

However, as soon as Gabriel and Hackett left the room, the idea of implementing a plan B took root in Tony, Mike and Phil: a reunion of the three-man line-up with the usual help from Stuermer and Thompson. Before making any kind of official announcement, both the band and management decided it would be best to first test the waters: it had been fifteen years since their last concert together, so it was essential to assess how much rust had built up on a technical level and, above all, to see if the chemistry was still there. So the 3 + 2 agreed to meet up in New York in October 2006.

Stuermer: "You never know; after that many years of not being together, it may not have had the magic anymore. But as soon as we started playing it felt like Genesis again. We played for a couple of hours and then I saw the guys, Mike, Tony and Phil, walk over to the manager and start talking about a tour. It felt great, we all got along so well. It didn't feel like we hadn't been together for fourteen years, it felt like fourteen months." [8]

Still, it goes without saying that after such a long period of inactivity, they were indeed all a bit rusty.

Stuermer: "When Phil started playing drums he felt very stiff, and his bones were aching after he played, like a runner that hasn't been running for quite a while. Then all of a sudden there he was playing the drums again! Mike and Tony were a little bit rough in the beginning too, but as the rehearsals went on everybody seemed to get better. And no matter how practised you are or how experienced you are, it's still brand new music when you have to go back to something that you haven't played for fourteen years, so I wasn't perfect either." [8]

And so it was that, on 7 November 2006, Genesis held a press conference in London to announce the *Turn It On Again* tour, scheduled for the following summer. There were to be around 20 European dates and an absolutely fantastic venue for the final show: the Imperial Fora in Rome, with the Colosseum in the background. During this meeting with the world press the three seemed very relaxed and at ease, although Phil was clearly manifesting the after-effects of the breakdown of his marriage to his third wife, Orianne, with whom he had two children. This may be why the drummer insisted on rejecting the term 'tour' in favour of a more comfortable definition 'a selection of shows': for Collins, the idea of having to be away from his kids, after a lifetime of running around to the four corners of the globe, was unthinkable; consequently, under no circumstances would it be a long tour. During another press conference (New York, 7 March 2007) however, the first American dates for that summer were announced. At the same time, 10 years after Calling All Stations, Ray Wilson's offer to be the tour's support act was rejected. Wilson: "Tony Smith said he'd talked to the guys about it but they thought it would be a bit strange. I don't really understand why it would have been strange; it would have been nice for me and good for my career and it would have been good for the concert because people would have seen something before the big Genesis show. I wouldn't have been any competition for them because I would have been doing something acoustic and I wasn't going to be better than Genesis. I would have just done a few of the songs, good versions and then leave. But it's politics, money and bullshit. It's the music business." [10]

On 17 April 2007, at the Lincoln Center, New York, a huge concert was organised to pay tribute to Ahmet Ertegun, the founder of Atlantic Records, who had passed away a few months earlier. Sharing the stage with other superstars (including Mick Jagger, Eric Clapton, Stevie Nicks and Crosby, Stills, Nash & Young) Collins appeared as both a solo artist (performing *In The Air Tonight* with piano accompaniment) and with Genesis, accompanied by Tony, Mike and Daryl, all on acoustic guitars for an unplugged version of *Follow You Follow Me*.

After many years in which Genesis had always rehearsed for their tours in America, this time the two and a half weeks needed to get the machine ready to roll were carried out in a different location, in Cossonay, near Lausanne, Switzerland, so that Phil could stay near his sons, Nicholas and Matthew.

In April the Genesis 1976-1982 box set was released containing all the albums of that period remixed in

GENESIS

Paris, 30th June 2007

5.1 by Nick Davis together with additional bonus audio and video material, representing the first chapter in a significant operation to re-release works including both studio recordings (1983-1998 and 1970-1975) and live albums and DVDs.

At the end of rehearsals in Switzerland, the band moved to Brussels to perfect the stage set-up.

On 24 May 2007, Genesis made their first public non-acoustic appearance with Phil Collins since the Cowdray Concert in September 1993. The event was in Las Vegas for the VH-1 Rock Honors ceremony, where the TV network celebrated artists who had influenced rock music. Awards in 2007 went to ZZ Top, Ozzy Osbourne, Heart and Genesis. Introduced on stage by actor and comedian, Robin Williams, and preceded by a cover of *That's All* performed by British trio Keane, Genesis performed *Turn It On Again, No Son Of Mine* (shortened due to TV timing restrictions) and *Los Endos*.

But the real baptism of fire came on 4 June at the Belgium Expo, Brussels, for a pre-tour production rehearsal performed in front of just 250 guests. The setlist was the following: *Behind The Lines – Duke's End – Turn It On Again / No Son Of Mine / Land Of Confusion / In The Cage – The Cinema Show – Duke's Travels – Afterglow / Hold On My Heart / Home By The Sea – Second Home By The Sea / Follow You Follow Me / Firth Of Fifth – I Know What I Like / Mama / Ripples / Throwing It All Away / Domino / Drum Duet – Los Endos / Tonight, Tonight, Tonight – Invisible Touch / I Can't Dance / The Carpet Crawlers*.

The band seemed rather stilted and some of the instrumental parts were simplified or slowed down. That said, the opening section was very interesting thanks to the return of the instrumental section of *Behind The Lines* which this time also incorporated a small section of *Duke's End* before flowing effortlessly into *Turn It On Again* (where Phil left the drum kit to take centre stage). The return of *In The Cage* was a surprise, and instead of going directly into *Afterglow* the band first touched upon *The Cinema Show* as well as fragments of *Duke's Travels*. On the other hand, the first half of *Tonight, Tonight, Tonight* was back in the setlist and was linked up to *Invisible Touch* as had been the case on the 1987 tour.

For *Follow You Follow Me*, Collins sang while simultaneously playing drums, the first time this had ever been done for a whole song (in the past he had only done this for brief sections of *One For The Vine* and *Duke's Travels*), while Chester played a shekere, bringing back the song's original rhythmic feel. The instrumental version of *Firth Of Fifth* (starting from Tony's synth solo where Chester would leave the honour of playing the first part to Phil) merged into *I Know What I Like*.

The most magical moment of the concert was *Ripples*, despite a few questionable choices (the drumbeat in the entire instrumental section, the cutting short of Stuermer's electric guitar solo) while the two encores slots were given to *I Can't Dance* and, surprisingly enough, *The Carpet Crawlers*, quite an unsuitable choice really, if you consider the moment of collective joy which the final song usually represents.

Incredible as it may seem, this setlist remained exactly the same for the whole tour, especially when you consider that other songs had definitely been rehearsed (such as *Jesus He Knows Me, In Too Deep, That's All* and *Abacab*) but never found their way into the performance. To justify this choice, Genesis underlined the complexity of the stage show. It has to be said, the stage set-up was one of the most futuristic ever seen in the history of rock, registering staggering figures: a W-shaped structure, 64 metres across, 28 metres wide and 28.2 metres high, anchored down with enormous water-filled blocks.

On either side stood two oval hi-res mega-screens, while the enormous backwall incorporated 90 million LEDs creating a screen 54 metres across and 28 metres high on which various images were projected. And finally, towering 10 metres above the ground, seven metal 'ribs' each held 6 massive spotlights. According to Entertainment Technology Press, Genesis' new stage set-up was record-breaking: in fact, XL Video UK supplied 15,098 Barco 510 O-Lite panels with 270 control boxes plus 102 panels of Mitsubishi 16:8 high-resolution screen. For everything to function, 6 power generators were needed to provide 5,200 amperes distributed along seven and a half kilometres of wiring. The staff was capable of building four complete stages, installed in the various cities by seven different teams and transported in 45 trucks, while production needed 18 articulated lorries and 22 vans. The tour convoy therefore totalled 85 vehicles plus the 11 tour buses needed to carry the 235 members of the *Turn It On Again* tour crew.

Just reading these figures gives you some idea as to the size of the stage show Genesis put on for their fans with the help of architect Mark Fisher (already famous for the stages he'd built for U2, Pink Floyd, The Rolling Stones and the 'Millennium Show' with music by Peter Gabriel) and lighting wizard Patrick Woodroffe (Cirque de Soleil, Bob Dylan, Elton John).

Some parts of the show were quite simply stunning. At the beginning of the concert, when the pre-recorded music stopped and the lights all went down, a giant television appeared on the backwall showing excerpts of Genesis' history before being joined by hundreds of increasingly smaller televisions whirling round like a vortex before turning into a swarm which arranged itself into a world map before being washed out in white lights as the first notes of *Behind The Lines* blasted out. During *Follow You Follow Me* a stylised line cartoon of a figure was seen walking until he reached a small boy where he raised his arm, recreating the image from the WE CAN'T DANCE album cover, and seemingly turned on one of the spotlights before disappearing. Other figures who have featured in Genesis artwork over the years then appeared, including Cynthia with her croquet mallet (NURSERY CRYME) Albert (from DUKE), the fantasy characters from A TRICK OF THE TAIL and the man on the bench from SELLING ENGLAND BY THE POUND, before turning back into the initial father and son pair. As the song drew to a close the father figure reached up once more, this time to turn the spotlight off. *I Know What I Like* was steeped in pure nostalgia,

with images scrolling by on the screen covering the band's career, whereas *Invisible Touch* ended with a spectacular firework display.

The complexity of the stage show, however, doesn't really justify the decision to keep the same setlist throughout the entire tour; the lack of variation merely confirms a far too easy-going musical performance which characterised the tour from the word go: zero surprises, zero complications. The aim was merely to play splendid music and make sure the audience had a great time. The band, it seems, were not prepared to take a single risk. Better to play safe.

The setlist deliberately skipped any reference to the CALLING ALL STATIONS experience, almost as if it were just a bad memory best forgotten (as would appear to be confirmed by the rather irate reaction the author of this book received from Rutherford to a question posed during an otherwise soporific press conference the previous November), and was back in the far more comfortable territory of the 1992 tour with Phil, to which the show was very similar in its structure, albeit with due distinction. In fact, all the hits from the three-man era remained intact, except for the omission of *Jesus He Knows Me*, replaced by *Follow You Follow Me*, back on the setlist after sitting out a few tours.

The same goes for the *In The Cage / Afterglow* medley (with the addition of a small section of *Duke's Travels*), which had been left out of the tour with Wilson, and *Los Endos* which hadn't been played since the INVISIBLE TOUCH tour; songs to please the older fans along with *Firth Of Fifth / I Know What I Like* and *The Carpet Crawlers*.

It was great, however, to see the return of *Mama* (left out of the WE CAN'T DANCE tour after just a few

Conversation With Two Stools, Lyon 12th July, 2007

shows because Phil was having problems with his voice), but the band showed it was distinctly lacking in initiative by sticking to songs which were anything but essential, such as *Hold On My Heart* and *Throwing It All Away*. And even when it came to the long songs, yet again the band played both *Home By The Sea* and *Domino*, undeniably good songs and well-performed, but maybe it would have been more exciting to have swapped in some other pieces from their more recent past.

And finally, the usual drum solo: no longer stand-alone as in the last tour with Collins, but again used as an introduction to *Los Endos*. The duet began with the two drummers playing on the seats of two stools (which is why it was renamed *Conversation With Two Stools*) to then continue on their respective drum kits.

The tour, in the real sense of the word, kicked off in Helsinki on 11 June 2007 (preceded by a rehearsal show in the same location on the previous day) and then moved on to Herning in Denmark. Nine non-consecutive concerts in all were performed in Germany over the whole tour. The first, in Hamburg on the 15th, was followed by a concert in Switzerland (Bern) after which a few problems with the itinerary occurred. The concert at the Linz Gugl Stadion in Austria, initially scheduled for the 18th, was moved to the following day, while the show on the 20th was particularly troublesome: initially planned for the Ferenc Puskás Stadium in Budapest, Hungary, it was moved to Prague in the Czech Republic, first to the Stadion Evžena Rošického and then to the Sazka Arena. After a show in Poland (Chorzów on 21 June) the tour was back to Germany for the concert in Hanover on 23 June, attended by Ray Wilson.

Wilson: "They invited me because I told them that I didn't want to be involved in anything ever again. I wrote to them and said, 'look, leave me out of everything: your book, your re-releases, your DVDs' (*all things Genesis would have been working on in those months – author's note*). I said to Tony Smith, 'just leave me out, please, I wish you all the best, but just go away!', because for me it was just bad memories. Not the time with them, but after. They treated me really badly and disrespectfully. Tony Banks phoned me and tried to sort of apologise and said, 'I know we didn't do things well'. He didn't go as far as saying sorry and nor did I ask him to. After that Nick Davis called me saying the guys would like me to go to one of the shows. I said, 'with all due respect, Nick, if they want me to come to a show why are they not calling me?'. He said, 'Mike asked me to call, you know he's busy'. And I said, 'yes, you can give me all the bullshit you want, but I've been in Genesis, I understand what's going on, I know the politics!'. So the next thing, Mike calls me just to arrange the room, 'how are you?' and all that stuff. The truth of the matter is they were just papering over the cracks. My feelings towards them are the same. I still think they're nice people, good people, but from a business point of view they were bastards. That's how I feel! They were horrible bastards to me, and it caused me a lot of stress, a lot of pain. And if they think bringing me to a gig and giving me a hotel room and a glass of wine changes that, it doesn't." [10]

After returning to Brussels on 24 June, it was time to do another three shows in Germany, including a double date in Düsseldorf (26th and 27th). The second show was broadcast live in HD and Dolby 5.1 Surround (mixed by Nick Davis) to 30 cinemas in the UK and cities in Spain and Sweden, two countries not included on the tour itinerary.

The show in Stuttgart on 28 June (a day earlier than originally planned) was followed by dates in France and the Netherlands before returning yet again to Germany (Berlin, Leipzig and Frankfurt).

On 7 July, Genesis were finally playing on home turf, not without an element of confusion. In fact,

Phil in Lyon, 12th July 2007

originally they were booked to play at Twickenham Stadium in London on the 7th and at Old Trafford in Manchester on the 8th, but then these two shows were switched around, not without difficulty for the band, because they were expected to be a part of Live Earth on the 7th, an event organised by eight countries simultaneously to raise awareness on climate change. The show most anticipated was the one at Wembley thanks to the stellar line-up which included, among others, Madonna, Metallica and Red Hot Chili Peppers. Genesis opened the London event at 1.30 pm when the stadium was far from full. They played *Behind The Lines / Duke's End / Turn It On Again*, *Land Of Confusion* and *Invisible Touch* (on this one occasion not preceded by *Tonight, Tonight, Tonight*) for a slot lasting a little over 20 minutes. The concert was broadcast live by the BBC, with the presenter, Jonathan Ross, then having to apologise to viewers for Phil's bad language (as was his way with the live version, he sang 'and though she will fuck up your life' during *Invisible Touch*). With their brief appearance over, Genesis dashed up to Manchester for their evening show before coming back down to London for the Twickenham date the following day.

The European tour was coming to a close. Following their last show in Germany (Munich, 10 July), which started an hour later than it should have due to heavy rains, and the show scheduled for the 12th at the Stade Louis II in Monaco being cancelled and rescheduled in Lyon, Genesis were ready for the final show, the only date in Italy. The event was sponsored by telecommunication giant, Telecom Italia, which in previous years had organised performances in the Italian capital by other top artists, including Paul McCartney and Simon & Garfunkel. Initially the show was supposed to have been held at the Imperial Fora, but it was then moved to the Circus Maximus, an enormous open-air space which, according to estimates, was filled by half a million people. Although these figures may need to be taken with a pinch of salt, it was still without doubt the biggest audience the band had ever performed to in their entire career. On a boiling hot 14 July, hordes of fans came to show their love and support for the band, although many members of the audience were simply curious onlookers drawn by the attraction of a free live event, something further underlined by the fact that without the sponsorship of Telecom, Genesis probably wouldn't have played in Italy at all. But play they did, a performance which was captured on the official DVD release WHEN IN ROME which came out in 2008 (Phil completely lost his way on the drums during a section of *Firth Of Fifth* but the DVD was carefully edited to spare his blushes). Being as Peter Gabriel had been touring in Italy in the days leading up to the event, when Phil stepped up to the mic before the last encore, paper in hand, many fans were desperately hoping he was about to introduce his old friend; instead, with words of affection Phil introduced bandmates, Chester and Daryl, before he, and not Gabriel, sang *The Carpet Crawlers*. At the end of the show, first all five musicians bowed to the crowd's applause, then the session men very humbly stepped to one side leaving just Tony, Phil and Mike to bask in the ovation.

Banks: "In Europe we originally planned to play places that would be indoor arenas. We thought we'd do one show in each country or something.

GENESIS

Mike and Tony, Paris 30th June 2007

But when we started talking about it, promotion and everything, they felt very confident we could do stadiums in order to accommodate all the people who wanted to see us, so we were very surprised really. In some countries, particularly in England, we definitely didn't play nearly enough. In Rome we covered a lot of people. That was a very memorable night for us, playing to, I don't know how many people were there, but we recorded half a million. A staggering moment." (9)

After over one and a half months' break, Genesis set off for Canada. On 5 September, the Air Canada Centre in Toronto witnessed a second production rehearsal, followed, two days later, by the first concert of the North American leg, again in Toronto, but in a different venue (the BMO Field). After four days spent between New York, Pennsylvania and Massachusetts, Genesis returned to Canada (Québec and Ontario) before returning to the States. Worthy of note are the three consecutive nights in two cities which have always been particularly fond of Genesis (Philadelphia from 17 to 29 September and Chicago from 2 to 4 October) but the tour also went to numerous other states such as Connecticut, Ohio, Michigan and Colorado. The tour ended up in California, with two concerts at San Jose and Sacramento and the final two shows at the Hollywood Bowl on 12–13 October. The first evening at the Mecca of cinema was hit by pouring rain, resulting in problems with the amplifier system to a point that the band had to give up on the idea of playing the two encores, making this the only variation of the whole tour.

Banks: "The nature of the Genesis shows, particularly with all the lighting effects, screens and the things we're using, means we look at it more like a theatrical performance really. So you don't swap things around. If you're doing a Shakespeare play, you don't suddenly do away with one-fourth of an act or do a different act instead. You know, we make it so that we feel it has a nice flow to it. It's a good balance between old and new. The reason we thought it might change in America was because we weren't quite sure how things like *Ripples* would go down, because obviously at the time of A Trick Of The Tail the group was nothing like as big in America as it was in England or in Europe in general in fact, but, as it's turned out, I think it went down just as well as it did in Europe, which is good. In all honesty, the only reason why people sort of noticed it is because of the internet. I mean, in the old days you'd come to a town and no one knew what songs you were going to play. I think it's a pity in some ways because half the fun was doing things like *Duke's Travels* or *Ripples* or *Los Endos* or whatever when people weren't expecting them. It would be much more exciting, I think, if they didn't know what songs we were going to play. But that's the way it is now. Even if we changed the songs, everyone would know by the next show." (9)

Although the commercial success of the *Turn It On Again* tour was of course exceptional, the same cannot be said of the tour as a whole. Years of inactivity had their effect on the performance which wasn't at the level of earlier tours. However, Rutherford (now with a new double-neck guitar which he had specially made with a 4-string Yamaha bass at the bottom and Gibson EDS 12-string on the top) managed relatively well, although the audience was often left guessing on some solos, especially when he changed notes every night (he often seemed unsure of himself on

Home By The Sea). Tony Banks meanwhile was as flawless as ever when playing chords but was a little off the pace on some of the more difficult solo sections. Thompson and Stuermer, of course, were still playing well. Daryl played guitar (with Mike on bass) for *Behind The Lines, In The Cage / Afterglow, Firth Of Fifth / I Know What I Like, Ripples* and *Los Endos*, while for *Turn It On Again* and *The Carpet Crawlers* both used guitar and bass pedals.

And while Phil certainly hadn't forgotten how to play drums, a number of parts had been slightly simplified. When it came to the vocals, many songs had been lowered a tone (*Tonight, Tonight, Tonight* by a tone and a half!) so Phil could sing them more easily. An unavoidable solution, but one which resulted in a certain loss of depth in some songs like *No Son Of Mine*.

Banks: "I sometimes have a problem where there is a particular inversion of the chord, when you're playing it too low and it doesn't sound right, so you've got to move the inversion up and that can change the quality of it a little bit. The most important thing was to get it so that Phil felt comfortable singing. We were very conscious of being a little bit older, and if you're forcing your voice too much every night then there's a risk of having to start cancelling shows, so, rather than risk that, we just brought the keys down. On most of the songs I don't think it really makes that much difference. I actually think *Mama* seems better than ever, it has an even darker quality than it originally had." [9]

When it came to connecting with the audience, Phil was the usual showman: fun, charismatic, engaging and still energetic on stage despite his years. However, behind the mask, something was brewing in the musician's morale.

Thompson: "Already during his *First Final Farewell* tour (2004-2005) he was starting to be a little bit depressed but we didn't find out till the end of that tour that he and his wife were breaking up (they divorced very soon after that). When we did the Genesis tour in 2007, he was a little bit depressed but he enjoyed it, but when we got together he started to feel sad again. He said, 'it's finished, I don't want to do this anymore'." [11]

Daryl Stuermer has subsequently confirmed that more dates were discussed: "I remember somebody mentioning that they were talking about doing South America and Australia, but then all of a sudden it was taken off. I mean, it was never actually put down on paper, but it was talked about, and I think Phil didn't want to do it and I think he was kind of done. I was a little disappointed. I would have loved to have done that, but it didn't happen. And you know, it's like one of these things: I thought that was it. I thought 2007 was the end of Genesis". [12]

NOTES

(1) Mario Giammetti's telephone interview with Ray Wilson, 18 January 2001, partially published in the article "Calling All Genesis - Interviste esclusive a Ray Wilson, Mike Rutherford & Tony Banks", *Dusk*, Issue n. 35, April 2001

(2) Mario Giammetti's telephone interview with Ray Wilson, 17 February 1999, partially published in the article "Intervista esclusiva a Ray Wilson", *Dusk*, Issue n. 28, April 1999

(3) Mario Giammetti's telephone interview with Tony Banks, 8 May 2013, partially published in the article "Il mistero di Lady Barbara", *Dusk*, Issue n. 74, July 2013

(4) Mike Kaufman's Genesis interviews, Chicago / London 2007, partially used in the bonus disc accompanying the 2008 remasters

(5) Mario Giammetti's interview with Ray Wilson, Ancona, Barfly, 19 January 2002, partially published in the article "Ray Wilson Special", *Dusk*, Issue n. 38, February 2002

(6) Mario Giammetti's telephone interview with Mike Rutherford, 3 March 2001, partially published in the article "Calling All Genesis - Interviste esclusive a Ray Wilson, Mike Rutherford & Tony Banks", *Dusk*, Issue n. 35, April 2001

(7) Mario Giammetti's telephone interview with Tony Banks, 6 March 2001, partially published in the article "Calling All Genesis - Interviste esclusive a Ray Wilson, Mike Rutherford & Tony Banks", *Dusk*, Issue n. 35, April 2001

(8) Mario Giammetti's telephone interview with Daryl Stuermer, 8 March 2007, partially published in the article "Daryl Stuermer Special - Go, Daryl go!", *Dusk*, Issue n. 55, April 2007

(9) Mario Giammetti's telephone interview with Tony Banks, 19 September 2007, partially published in the article "There Must Be Some Other Way – interviste esclusive a Tony Banks e Ray Wilson", *Dusk*, Issue n. 57, December 2007

(10) Mario Giammetti's interview with Ray Wilson, Orvieto, Sala dei Quattrocento, 22 September 2007, partially published in the article "There Must Be Some Other Way – interviste esclusive a Tony Banks e Ray Wilson", *Dusk*, Issue n. 57, December 2007

(11) Mario Giammetti's telephone interview with Chester Thompson, 16 May 2013, partially published in the article "Nashville Samba Jazz - Chester Thompson intervista esclusiva", *Dusk*, Issue n. 74, July 2013

(12) Mario Giammetti's telephone interview with Daryl Stuermer, 17 March 2021, partially published in the article "Sulla strada verso il paradiso" in *Dusk*, issue n. 97, May 2021

Turn It On Again Tour

2000

SEPTEMBER
21 **London (ENGLAND)**, Hilton Hotel
'Music Managers Forum's'. Short acoustic set with a 4-piece band: Banks, Rutherford, Collins, Stuermer

2007

APRIL
17 **New York, NY (USA)**, Lincoln Center
'Ahmet Ertegun: A Celebration Concert'

MAY
12 **Las Vegas, NV (USA)**, Mandalay Bay Events Center - Mandalay Bay Resort and Casino
'VH1 Rock Honors'

JUNE
04 **Brussels (BELGIUM)**, Hall 5 - Brussels Expo
Production rehearsals
10 **Helsinki (FINLAND)**, Olympiastadion
Rehearsal concert
11 **Helsinki (FINLAND)**, Olympiastadion
14 **Herning (DENMARK)**, Concert Arena - Messecenter
15 **Hamburg (GERMANY)**, AOL Arena
17 **Bern (SWITZERLAND)**, Stade de Suisse
19 **Linz (AUSTRIA)**, Linz Gugl Stadion
Originally scheduled for June 18
20 **Prague (CZECH REPUBLIC)**, Sazka Arena *(parking lot) Originally scheduled at Puskás Ferenc Stadion - Budapest, Hungary, then moved to Prague but at a different venue (Stadion Evžena Rošického)*
21 **Chorzów (POLAND)**, Stadion Śląski
23 **Hannover (GERMANY)**, AWD Arena
24 **Brussels (BELGIUM)**, Stade Roi Baudouin
26 **Düsseldorf (GERMANY)**, LTU Arena
27 **Düsseldorf (GERMANY)**, LTU Arena
28 **Stuttgart (GERMANY)**, Gottlieb-Daimler-Stadion
Originally scheduled for June 29
30 **Paris (FRANCE)**, Parc des Princes

JULY
01 **Amsterdam (THE NETHERLANDS)**, Amsterdam Arena
03 **Berlin (GERMANY)**, Olympiastadion
04 **Leipzig (GERMANY)**, Zentralstadion
05 **Frankfurt (GERMANY)**, Commerzbank Arena
07 **London (ENGLAND)**, Wembley Stadium
'Live Earth Show'. Afternoon concert
07 **Manchester (ENGLAND)**, Old Trafford
Originally scheduled for July 8
08 **London (ENGLAND)**, Twickenham Stadium
Originally scheduled for July 7
10 **Munich (GERMANY)**, Olympiastadion
12 **Lyon (FRANCE)**, Stade Municipal de Gerland
14 **Rome (ITALY)**, Circo Massimo
'Telecomcerto'

SEPTEMBER
05 **Toronto, ON (CANADA)**, Air Canada Centre
Production rehearsals
07 **Toronto, ON (CANADA)**, BMO Field
08 **Buffalo, NY (USA)**, HSBC Arena
09 **Pittsburgh, PA (USA)**, Mellon Arena
11 **Boston, MA (USA)**, TD Banknorth Garden
12 **Albany, NY (USA)**, Times Union Center
14 **Montréal, QC (CANADA)**, Stade du Parc Olympique
15 **Kanata, ON (CANADA)**, Scotiabank Place
16 **Hartford, CT (USA)**, Hartford Civic Center
18 **Philadelphia, PA (USA)**, Wachovia Center
19 **Philadelphia, PA (USA)**, Wachovia Center
20 **Philadelphia, PA (USA)**, Wachovia Center
22 **Columbus, OH (USA)**, Nationwide Arena
23 **Washington, D.C. (USA)**, Verizon Center
25 **New York, NY (USA)**, Madison Square Garden
27 **East Rutherford, NJ (USA)**, Giants Stadium
29 **Cleveland, OH (USA)**, Quicken Loans Arena
30 **Auburn Hills, MI (USA)**, The Palace of Auburn Hills

OCTOBER
02 **Chicago, IL (USA)**, United Center
03 **Chicago, IL (USA)**, United Center
04 **Chicago, IL (USA)**, United Center
06 **Denver, CO (USA)**, Pepsi Center
09 **San Jose, CA (USA)**, HP Pavilion at San Jose
10 **Sacramento, CA (USA)**, ARCO Arena
12 **Hollywood, CA (USA)**, Hollywood Bowl
13 **Hollywood, CA (USA)**, Hollywood Bowl

Afterglow

In November 2008, the release of the splendid Genesis 1970 - 1975 box set once again turned the spotlight on the band's progressive era. As well as newly mixed versions of five albums from the Peter Gabriel period, the release also contained video footage and 20 minutes of previously unreleased music: the 1970 soundtrack written for the never completed documentary on painter, Michael Jackson, recorded by the Banks-Rutherford-Gabriel-Phillips-Mayhew line-up. John Mayhew had only recently returned to England after having lived in Australia for over thirty years, during which time he had been totally oblivious to the considerable sums of money he had accrued in royalties. He was, however, denied the chance of fully enjoying the benefits of this unexpected windfall as he died of a heart condition in Scotland on 26 March 2009.

This passing away of a former Genesis band member coincided with an apparently irreversible trend of falling back on archive material. In fact, a total of five box sets would be released in the three years between 2007 and 2009 covering almost the entire catalogue of Genesis records and videos.

In 2010, Genesis were finally inducted into the Rock & Roll Hall Of Fame at a ceremony held in New York attended by Banks, Rutherford, Collins and Hackett. Gabriel was unable to attend as he was in the middle of rehearsals for the tour to promote his album Scratch My Back containing covers of songs by various artists arranged for voice and orchestra. Following in his predecessor's footsteps, Phil Collins also opted against recording new material in favour of a selection of covers paying tribute to his love of Motown in his album Going Back (to date his last release).

In the meantime, Tony and Mike were also picking up the reins of their solo careers. Following the disastrous album featuring just Paul Carrack on vocals, Rutherford reformed the Mechanics, recruiting two new singers, Andrew Roachford and Tim Howar, releasing The Road in 2011, followed by Let Me Fly in 2017 and Out Of The Blue in 2019 (an album mostly featuring re-recordings of old Mechanics songs, with just three new tracks). Tony Banks, on the other hand, decided to pursue classical music, releasing Six Pieces For Orchestra in 2012 and Five in 2018.

Other former members were also keeping busy. Ray Wilson, now with a solid studio and fruitful live career on his hands, was often playing more than a hundred gigs a year mainly in Germany and Poland (with a generous portion of the setlist dedicated to Genesis songs).

2012 turned out to be a particularly interesting year: Anthony Phillips, in collaboration with Andrew Skeet, released the ambitious double album Seventh Heaven, while Steve Hackett brought out A Life Within A Day under the name Squackett (his project with Yes bass player, Chris Squire) and Genesis Revisited II, another album paying tribute to the guitarist's former band. The major difference between this release and Genesis Revisited (1996) lies in Hackett's decision to promote it with a tour. Playing exclusively Genesis material for the first time ever, he successfully filled theatres all over the world and has continued to do so in recent years.

2012 was also the year in which Genesis won a Lifetime Achievement award at the annual 'Prog Awards' ceremony hosted by Prog Magazine. The award was picked up by Banks and Rutherford, while Hackett, also present (on the winners' list along with Chris Squire for their *A Life Within A Day* which took home the 'Anthem of The Year' award) was not included in the official photos; something which seems even more paradoxical if one considers the fact that the award was for the band's progressive rock period and not the later pop era. This raises the question as to what exactly does that first, fantastic period of the band's history mean to its members.

Banks: "I did sort of go through our whole career; to be honest, we wouldn't be here if it hadn't been for what came later. If we had only gone up to The Lamb Lies Down On Broadway, we wouldn't be very well remembered, we would just be an appendage of Peter's history. It's because of what we did later that the name became as well-known as it is. When talking to people I see that a lot of them consider the whole period, some people stop after Pete left, others after Steve left, but I don't feel that the music changed very much between Trespass and Duke. We changed a bit from Abacab on, but even then there was always a lot hanging in both areas."[1]

In 2013 *The Living Years* by Mike Rutherford was published, the first autobiography by a member of Genesis. In 2014 a triple CD and a DVD/Blu-Ray were released offering parallel perspectives which highlighted the greatness of Genesis as a whole. In fact, for the first time ever, the R'Kive compilation brought together Genesis' music and three songs from each of the five band members' solo careers, thus finally honouring one of the characteristics which makes Genesis truly unique: their strength as individual composers and musicians.

Banks: "Mike, who was the instigator of all this, originally wanted to put all the hits of Genesis on it and those from our individual solo works, but it didn't quite happen like that. I would have particularly loved to have had *Sledgehammer* on it, but Peter and Phil wanted to take tracks from their albums which hadn't done so well in order to give them publicity, which is fair enough, I understand the reason for doing that. But it is an interesting compilation nonetheless and I think the chronological aspect works rather well because you see where the solo tracks fitted into the Genesis history. I think it's quite nice to know where everybody was at in a certain period of time. And I quite like the fact that I was able to have the last track on the record being as it was the most recent recording made."[2]

The DVD Genesis: Sum Of The Parts, on the other hand, is the extended version of the documentary *Genesis: Together And Apart* created by the BBC which premiered at the Empire Cinema, Haymarket, London, on 2 October 2014, with all five members of the classic era in attendance. Yet another look back over the history of Genesis, as well as videos, including previously unseen film footage shot at the Roundhouse in 1970 (the only material in existence which captures Genesis with Phillips and Mayhew in the line-up), the documentary revolves around a series of individual chats with band members and a group interview with Banks, Rutherford, Collins, Hackett and Gabriel, all together in the same room for the first time in decades, with this latter aspect, alas, not being exploited as much as perhaps it should have been. Not only that, the end result is heavily biased in that Steve Hackett's solo career is completely ignored in favour of the clearly inferior output (in terms of both quantity, quality and success) of Tony Banks. Hackett, for once abandoning his usual sense of diplomacy, would later openly air his grievances. The album featuring Ray Wilson, on the other hand, wasn't deemed worthy of even so much as a mention.

Wilson: "I'm not surprised. These guys have been behaving like that since they invited me to sing on the re-recording of *The Carpet Crawlers* and then never called me again. And that was in 1999! Since then, they've almost tried to hide that part of their career, which I think is kind of stupid because CALLING ALL STATIONS has a lot of good songs on it, especially the title track which, for me, is one of the best songs they did. It's a magnificent song. The real fans, the followers, they all know what the history of the band is: some of them like the Gabriel era the most, some like Phil. Some like my period and many don't. But why try to cover it up or avoid it? Fans get unhappy about it and I don't care if they behave like a bunch of fucking children, I think they need to grow up, but when I saw Steve's message, he was really upset and I really felt for him, because Steve is obviously a much bigger part of Genesis than I was – five albums (*six actually – author's note*) of what most consider the best – so for him to be treated that way is unacceptable and wrong." [3]

After this reunion, albeit for promo purposes only, the members of Genesis went back to their individual projects. Paradoxically, the member who remained in the shadows during this period was the one who had previously been an absolute workaholic: Phil Collins, plagued by a series of physical health issues since 2002.

Banks: "I think that playing drums on *Behind The Lines* in the reunion tour is what really screwed poor old Phil up. When we came to the rehearsal room, I'd done all my pre-rehearsal stuff and I was OK, just about able to play some of this stuff as it's quite hard and we hadn't played some of it for 20 years or so. Phil hadn't done any practice, we sat down to play this thing and Phil was nowhere, he couldn't play it at all. So I said, 'let's forget it, let's

Afterglow

Promotional shot by Virgin Records. Left to right: Tony Banks, Steve Hackett, Peter Gabriel, Anthony Phillips, Mike Rutherford, John Silver and Phil Collins. This photo was taken at Heathrow Airport on 11th May 1998 to promote the first Genesis box set

play something else', but Phil was very keen on the idea, he wanted to do it and so he worked on it until he got it right. It is very hard to play, very fast with all sorts of stuff going on and I'm sure that playing that piece is what did his hands and back in. I don't know if he feels it was worth it, but it was a very exciting piece to play, it was a peak moment of the show on that tour." [4]

In 2016, following a very dark period in which he underwent several surgical procedures, suffered from depression and had a drinking problem, Collins, also thanks to the (temporary) reconciliation with his third wife, Orianne, set about getting his life back on track. He took a look back at his past and not only did he reissue remastered versions of his entire solo discography but also published his autobiography, *Not Dead Yet*, a title he also gave to his massive comeback tour in 2017. No longer able to play and forced to remain seated to sing, Phil Collins was back to filling big arenas supported by a magnificent band featuring his 16-year-old son, Nic, on drums. His world tour would include six legs and only come to an end in the autumn of 2019.

Peter Gabriel, on the other hand, following his tour with Sting in 2016, released his album RATED PG in 2019, a compilation of songs, some previously unreleased, written for film soundtracks, while Anthony Phillips proceeded with a luscious reissue of almost his entire substantial catalogue on Cherry Red Records. A new album, STRINGS OF LIGHT, would also be released on the same label in 2019. And finally, in 2020, Steve Hackett published his oddly-titled autobiography, *A Genesis In My Bed*, whilst still continuing to release both live and brand new studio albums on a regular basis, most recently the acoustic UNDER A MEDITERRANEAN SKY (2021) and the electric SURRENDER OF SILENCE (scheduled for release in September 2021).

When it comes to Genesis as a band, however, the *Turn It On Again* tour appeared to be the band's final farewell.

Collins: "When I left, they carried on with Ray Wilson and that was great. I was very pleased for them and I wished it had worked. I wished the fans had given them a bit more time to sort themselves out, you know, it was a big change. But Genesis never really finished and the idea was that we would go out and say goodbye properly, which is kind of what we did in 2007." [5]

Banks: "Mike and I see each other and we'd be quite happy to do something, really, but Phil certainly can't play like he used to and so I don't think we could tour or anything. I know Steve would probably be up for stuff, he's still out there playing lots of Genesis stuff anyhow. As for Peter, well he's the most difficult person in the world to tie down." [2]

A deep friendship exists between the band members, and especially between Tony, Mike and Phil, where there is a special degree of complicity.

Rutherford: "I think half the fun is that you can joke with everyone, make fun of them because we're all comfortable in what we've done with each other. Having worked outside Genesis, with the Mechanics and different musicians and different people, it made me appreciate the chemistry we had, not just between us three but with Daryl and Chester too. I mean, if I were to read or see something Phil or Tony had said, nothing would ever upset me because it's just chat, but I remember the first round of interviews I did with the Mechanics; some people involved were a bit miffed about something I'd said. I suddenly realised that a lot of outfits outside Genesis have ego problems; people are touchy whereas we just take the piss." (6)

Collins: "What we did in the three-man line-up was something to enjoy. The way we wrote was unlike anything else that I have ever been involved in. When you write a song on your own you're improvising until something happens. But to do it with three people or more, I mean that's what we did even when Peter and Steve were in the band, we were mainly writing things from thin air. When there were just the three of us, we got improvising as a band down to a fine art and that's something special, it doesn't happen all the time." (5)

But why has there never been a reunion of the historical Genesis line-up?

Hackett: "We came close to a reunion in 2005 but Pete wanted to do THE LAMB LIES DOWN ON BROADWAY as a musical and Tony was adamant that that shouldn't happen. So there's no common ground for everyone coming together; they need to put aside their differences, I'm not part of that fight. I'd be quite happy with a THE LAMB musical or an INVISIBLE TOUCH musical, I don't care if that's what it takes to heal any rift. But I think we may have left it too late, as no one else is doing as many gigs as I am at this point in time." (7)

The guitarist is without doubt the one left feeling most upset.

Hackett: "When I was young I had a terrible inferiority complex that I was the ugly duckling with the glasses and beard sitting on the stool not saying a word in interviews. It was a bit like the George Harrison effect: by the time of the WHITE ALBUM he had flowered and to my mind was plainly writing the best songs, as I don't think Lennon and McCartney were getting the best out of themselves. Eventually, something happens, you start to grow and I'm not just referring to me. Look at Phil: he had something, the Midas touch, he was able to turn everything into gold and outpaced the band in many ways being as his albums outsold Genesis'. Now, when people buy old Genesis albums (although it's all 'old' now) it's still the ones with Pete from '71 to '75 and Phil from '76 to '77 that sell the most. That's the period all the tribute bands go for as that was the time of most idealism and the most change and doing stuff that other bands weren't doing. It's always difficult for me to talk about Genesis because I don't want to blame any-

Press shot taken at New York's Waldorf Astoria Hotel on 15th March 2010 when Genesis was inducted into the Rock & Roll Hall Of Fame. Left to right: Phil Collins, Tony Banks, Steve Hackett and Mike Rutherford. Peter Gabriel did not attend the event because he was rehearsing with the orchestra for his *New Blood* tour.

one. In terms of positives, it was a great big, beautiful band with a great deal of talent and maybe one day they will all come to the realisation that there should have been a reunion, to celebrate that level of commitment to that level of music, and I'm talking about everyone's careers, both solo and group work." [7]

Before turning the last page in the book of Genesis, on 4 March 2020, breaking news came from the BBC Studios when Banks, Rutherford and Collins announced *The Last Domino?* tour, a dozen or so dates planned for the UK in the month of November with a five-man line-up including the ever-loyal Stuermer on guitar and the still very young Nic Collins on drums. The name of the tour, with its enigmatic question mark at the end, seems to imply that if all goes well, other concerts might follow, quite possibly even in other countries.

Alas, however, no sooner had the announcement been made when the whole world found itself in the grip of the Covid-19 pandemic. Unsurprisingly, in September the tour was officially postponed. Now totalling 40 shows, after more dates (and a North American leg) were added, the tour was re-scheduled to the autumn and winter months of 2021. A short but spectacular piece of footage from rehearsals was released in January showing an extraordinary production and the presence of two male backing vocalists, Patrick Smyth and Daniel Pearce.

Will Genesis really manage to bring their live music back to British arenas and why not to audiences in other countries too? Only time and Phil's precarious state of health will tell.

What we do know for sure is that the band's legend is far from fading. Banks, Collins, Gabriel, Hackett, Phillips and Rutherford, six of the very best, listed, as can only be the case, in alphabetical order (and without forgetting Wilson and all the other fantastic musicians that have joined them on stage or in the studio over the years), have given immense pleasure to generations of fans and will continue to do so thanks to their musical masterpieces which have become part of rock history.

NOTES

(1) Mario Giammetti's telephone interview with Tony Banks, 8 May 2013, partially published in the article "Il mistero di Lady Barbara", *Dusk*, Issue n. 74, July 2013

(2) Mario Giammetti's telephone interview with Tony Banks, 24 July 2015, partially published in the article "Somebody Else's Mantra", *Dusk*, Issue n. 81, December 2015

(3) Mario Giammetti's interview with Ray Wilson, Erding, Stadthalle, 6 February 2015, partially published in the article "Arcobaleno in Baviera", *Dusk*, Issue n. 79, April 2015

(4) Mario Giammetti's interview with Tony Banks, London, Tony Smith Personal Management office, 29 November 2016

(5) Mario Giammetti's telephone interview with Phil Collins, 1 December 2016, partially published in the article "You Know What I Mean", *Dusk*, Issue n. 85, March 2017

(6) Mike Kaufman's Genesis interviews, Chicago / London 2007, partially used in the bonus disc accompanying the 2008 remasters

(7) Mario Giammetti listening to '*Wind & Wuthering*' with Steve Hackett, Naples, Chiaja Hotel De Charme, 12 September 2016